ABIDING WORDS

Society of Biblical Literature

Resources for Biblical Study

Tom Thatcher, New Testament Editor

Number 81

ABIDING WORDS

THE USE OF SCRIPTURE
IN THE GOSPEL OF JOHN

Edited by

Alicia D. Myers and Bruce G. Schuchard

SBL Press
Atlanta

Copyright © 2015 by SBL Press

All rights reserved. No part of this work may be reproduced or transmitted in any form or by any means, electronic or mechanical, including photocopying and recording, or by means of any information storage or retrieval system, except as may be expressly permitted by the 1976 Copyright Act or in writing from the publisher. Requests for permission should be addressed in writing to the Rights and Permissions Office, SBL Press, 825 Houston Mill Road, Atlanta, GA 30329 USA.

Library of Congress Cataloging-in-Publication Data

Abiding words : the use of scripture in the Gospel of John / edited by Alicia D. Myers and Bruce G. Schuchard.
    p. cm. — (Resources for biblical study ; number 81)
  Includes bibliographical references and index.
  ISBN 978-1-62837-094-2 (hardcover binding : acid-free paper) — ISBN 978-1-62837-093-5 (paper binding : acid-free paper) — ISBN 978-1-62837-095-9 (electronic format)
  1. Bible. John—Criticism, interpretation, etc. 2. Bible. Old Testament—Quotations in the New Testament. 3. Bible. John—Relation to the Old Testament. I. Myers, Alicia D., editor. II. Schuchard, Bruce G. (Bruce Gordon), editor.
  BS2615.52.A25 2015
  226.5'06—dc23
                                                                                             2015004297

Printed on acid-free, recycled paper conforming to
ANSI/NISO Z39.48-1992 (R1997) and ISO 9706:1994
standards for paper permanence.

Contents

Acknowledgments vii
Abbreviations xi

Abiding Words: An Introduction to Perspectives on John's Use
　of Scripture
　Alicia D. Myers 1

Part 1: The Form of John's Citations

Form versus Function: Citation Technique and Authorial Intention
　in the Gospel of John
　Bruce G. Schuchard 23

Quotations of Zechariah in the Fourth Gospel
　William Randolph Bynum 47

Quotations with "Remembrance" Formulae in the Fourth Gospel
　Michael A. Daise 75

Part 2: Social and Rhetorical Perspectives

Scripture Cannot Be Broken: The Social Function of the Use of
　Scripture in the Fourth Gospel
　Jaime Clark-Soles 95

A Voice in the Wilderness: Classical Rhetoric and the Testimony of
　John (the Baptist) in John 1:19–34
　Alicia D. Myers 119

Whose Zeal Is It Anyway? The Citation of Psalm 69:9 in John 2:17 as a Double Entendre
    Benjamin J. Lappenga 141

The Testimony of Two Witnesses: John 8:17
    Ruth Sheridan 161

Part 3: Memory and Scripture in John

Patriarchs and Prophets Remembered: Framing Israel's Past in the Gospel of John
    Catrin H. Williams 187

Sympathetic Resonance: John as Intertextual Memory Artisan
    Jeffrey E. Brickle 213

Conclusion
    Bruce G. Schuchard 237

Bibliography 247
Contributors 273

Subject Index 275
Modern Authors Index 281

Acknowledgments

The beginnings of this book stretch back to a meeting of the Johannine Literature Steering Committee during the Society of Biblical Literature annual meeting in San Francisco in 2011 with the suggestion of then member Mary Coloe. Mary had been recently impressed with the doctoral work of fellow Australian Johannine scholar Ruth Sheridan, and upon hearing that Alicia Myers's doctoral research focused on this topic from a different angle, she thought it was high time to get an update in the field. Mary's insight prompted a well-attended and stimulating session, "John and Scripture," at the 2012 SBL annual meeting in Chicago, which featured the work of Jaime Clark-Soles and Bruce G. Schuchard, as well as that of Ruth and Alicia. The positive response we received, as well as the knowledge of additional recent monographs published on our topic, soon prompted us to work toward a collection of essays with the four presentations from Chicago as our starting point. In addition to these four papers, we solicited contributions from other scholars—both those whose work in this area has been well-established and those just entering the field with recently published doctoral work. The present collection, therefore, represents a well-rounded glimpse at current scholarship in the area of the Fourth Gospel's employment of Scripture, offering work from diverse perspectives that aims both to introduce new readers and update seasoned ones to past and current approaches, as well as fuel continued conversations on the subject.

With so many moving parts in this collection, there are plenty of thanks to be shared. First and foremost, we would like to thank Mary Coloe and the rest of the Johannine Literature Steering Committee for sponsoring the session in 2012 that formed the foundation of this project. Thank you to all those who participated and attended, offering thought-provoking work and comments for continued refinement and energy for the ideas presented. A special thank-you to Tom Thatcher, who not only helped to organize the 2012 session but also encouraged us to pursue publication of this collection and invited us to consider the SBL Resources for Biblical Study series. We found in this series a perfect fit for the aims of our project as well as an able and accessible editor whose helpful advice and counsel guided this volume to completion. Bob Buller and Leigh Andersen at SBL Press have also provided quick responses and dealt deftly with potential problems, providing solutions and handling the behind-the-scenes mechanics to make this book a success. In addition to SBL Press, E. J. Brill graciously granted permission for the reprinting of portions of Jaime Clark-Soles's *Scripture Cannot Be Broken: The Social Function of the Use of Scripture in the Fourth Gospel* (Leiden: Brill, 2003) so that her valuable work on the sociological aspects of scriptural appeals could be included. No collection can be compiled, however, without the willingness of talented participants who offer their time and skills to create insightful essays. Thank you all for participating in this volume, for contributing your thoughts and allowing us the great privilege of bringing all of our work together.

I (Alicia) would also like to thank Bruce Schuchard for his partnership in this endeavor. It was a delight to work with Bruce, whose energy for the project as well as attention to detail and patience, first with a sudden illness in my family, and second with my move to a new institution in the midst of this project, kept things on track. Thank you, also, to my colleagues at United Theological Seminary in Dayton, Ohio, for providing support for the beginnings of this project and to those at Campbell University Divinity School in Buies Creek, North Carolina, for assistance as it comes to print. Finally, thank you to my family—especially to my husband, Scott, and our son, Keaton—for your encouragement of my work even in the midst of much more challenging, and significant, events. And thank you, Jesus, that we can all be here to hold the finished product together.

I (Bruce) am also thankful for the opportunity to have worked with Alicia. More hands—better yet, more eyes—made both the load lighter and the work much more enjoyable and efficient, as each of us supported and spot-checked the efforts of the other in bringing this project to fruition. I have enjoyed very much the opportunity to become acquainted and to work with Alicia, whose own recent contributions to the study of the employment of Scripture in John I have admired greatly. To be sure, it has been a great pleasure to work and to become acquainted with all of the contributors to this project. I have found the engagement to be most stimulating. Thanks are due to my graduate assistant Kevin Armbrust for his help with the construction of this book's bibliography, its author and subject index, and its list of abbreviations, and to family, colleagues, and others here at Concordia Seminary in St. Louis, Missouri, without whose support my work on this project would not have been possible. It is the hope of this book's editors that its collection of essays will be of benefit to researchers both old at and new to the ongoing study of the use of the Old in the New.

Abbreviations

א	Codex Sinaiticus (ca. fourth century CE)
Γ	Codex Tischendorfianus IV, Uncial 036 (ca. tenth century CE)
Θ	Codex Coridethianus, Uncial 038 (ca. ninth–tenth century CE)
Ψ	Codex Ψ, Uncial 044 (ca. ninth–tenth century CE)
AB	Anchor Bible
ABR	*Australian Biblical Review*
ACCS	Ancient Christian Commentary on Scripture
Adv. Jud.	John Chrysostom *Adversus Judaeos* homilies
AGJU	Arbeiten zur Geschichte des antiken Judentums und des Urchristentums
AIL	Ancient Israel and Its Literature
AJS	*American Journal of Sociology*
Anab.	Arrian, *Anabasis of Alexander*
AnBib	Analecta biblica
ANS	Ancient Narrative Supplements
Ant.	Josephus, *Jewish Antiquities*
Apoc. Ab.	Apocalypse of Abraham
ARS	*Annual Review of Sociology*
As. Mos.	Assumption of Moses
ASLL	Anglo-Saxon Language and Literature
ASMAR	Arizona Studies in the Middle Ages and the Renaissance
ASR	*American Sociological Review*
B	Codex Vaticanus (ca. fourth century CE)
b. Sanh.	Babylonian Talmud, tractate Sanhedrin
2 Bar.	2 Baruch (Syriac Apocalypse)
BBR	*Bulletin for Biblical Research*
BCAW	Blackwell Companion to the Ancient World

BECNT	Baker Exegetical Commentary on the New Testament
Bell. Cat.	Sallust, *Bellum catalinae*
BETL	Bibliotheca ephemeridum theologicarum lovaniensium
BDB	Brown, Francis, S. R. Driver, and Charles A. Briggs. *A Hebrew and English Lexicon of the Old Testament*
Bib	*Biblica*
BibInt	*Biblical Interpretation*
BIS	Biblical Interpretation Series
BIMW	The Bible in the Modern World
BNTC	Black's New Testament Commentaries
BO	Berit Olam
BTB	*Biblical Theology Bulletin*
BTNT	Biblical Theology of the New Testament
BU	Biblische Untersuchungen
BZNW	Beihefte zur Zeitschrift für die neutestamentliche
CBET	Contributions to Biblical Exegesis and Theology
CBQ	*Catholic Biblical Quarterly*
CBQMS	Catholic Biblical Quarterly Monograph Series
CCS	Classical Culture and Society
CD	*Damascus Document* (Dead Sea Scroll)
CE	Cultural Exegesis
1 Clem.	*1 Clement*
CNT	Commentaire du Nouveau Testament
Comm. Jo.	Origen, *Commentary on the Gospel of John*
ConC	Concordia Commentary
CSMC	*Critical Studies in Mass Communication*
CSML	Cambridge Studies in Medieval Literature
De or.	Cicero, *De oratore*
DRev	*Downside Review*
EBib	Études bibliques
ECIL	Early Christianity and Its Literature
Enc	*Encounter*
Epist.	Jerome, *Epistles*
EvangR	Evangelical Ressourcement
ESCO	European Studies on Christian Origins
ESEC	Emory Studies in Early Christianity
EUS	European University Studies
FG	Fourth Gospel

FGrHist	*Fragments of Greek History*
HB	Hebrew Bible
HBT	*Horizons in Biblical Theology*
Hom. Jo.	John Chrysostom, *Homilies on John*
HUCA	*Hebrew Union College Annual*
IBC	Interpretation: A Bible Commentary for Teaching and Preaching
IECOT	International Exegetical Commentary on the Old Testament
Il.	Homer, *Iliad*
Inst.	Quintillian, *Institutes of Oratory*
Int	*Interpretation*
JBL	*Journal of Biblical Literature*
JBT	*Jahrbuch für biblische Theologie*
JETS	*Journal of the Evangelical Theological Society*
JPSTC	Jewish Publication Society Torah Commentary
JSJ	*Journal for the Study of Judaism in the Persian, Hellenistic, and Roman Periods*
JSNT	*Journal for the Study of the New Testament*
JSNTSup	Journal for the Study of the New Testament Supplement
Jub.	Book of Jubilees
J.W.	Josephus, *Jewish War*
KEK	Kritisch-exegetischer Kommentar über das Neue Testament (Meyer-Kommentar)
KNNE	Kontext und Normen neutestamentlicher Ethik
KTAH	Key Themes in Ancient History
L	Codex Regius (ca. eighth century CE)
LASBF	*Liber annuus Studii biblici franciscani*
LBS	Linguistic Bible Studies
LCL	Loeb Classical Library
Leg.	Plato, *Laws*
Legat.	Philo, *Legatio ad Gaius* (*On the Embassy to Gaius*)
Liv. Pro.	Lives of the Prophets
LNTS	Library of New Testament Studies
LSJ	Liddell, Scott, Jones Lexicon
LXX	Septuagint
m. Naz.	Mishnah, tractate Nazir
m. Šabb.	Mishnah, tractate Shabbat

Mart. Ascen. Isa.	Martyrdom and Ascension of Isaiah
Matrix	Matrix: The Bible in Mediterranean Context
MatT	Material Texts
MNS	Mnemosyne Supplements
Mos.	Philo, *Life of Moses*
MT	Masoretic Text
NCB	New Century Bible
NCBC	New Collegeville Bible Commentary
NCI	New Critical Idiom
NETS	New English Translation of the Septuagint
NGC	*New German Critique*
Nic. eth.	Aristotle, *Nicomachean Ethics*
NICNT	New International Commentary on the New Testament
NovT	*Novum Testamentum*
NovTSup	Novum Testamentum Supplements
NRSV	New Revised Standard Version
NSBT	New Studies in Biblical Theology
NT	New Testament
NTC	New Testament Commentary
NTL	New Testament Library
NTOA	Novum Testamentum et Orbis Antiquus
NTR	New Testament Readings
NTS	*New Testament Studies*
NTSI	The New Testament and the Scriptures of Israel
NTTSD	New Testament Tools, Studies and Documents
NVBS	New Voices in Biblical Studies
OBT	Overtures to Biblical Theology
OG	Old Greek
OT	*Oral Tradition*
OT	Old Testament
OTL	Old Testament Library
OTS	Old Testament Studies
P^{66}	*Papyrus* 66, Papyrus Bodmer II (ca. 200 CE)
P^{75}	*Papyrus* 75, Papyrus Bodmer XV (ca. 175–225 CE)
PBM	Paternoster Biblical Monographs
PCNT	Paideia Commentaries on the New Testament
PNTC	Pillar New Testament Commentary
Poet.	Aristotle, *Poetics*

Prob.	Aristotle, *Problems*
Prog.	*Progymnasmata*
Pss. Sol.	Psalms of Solomon
Q	Codex Guelferbytanus B, Uncial 026 (ca. fifth century CE)
1QH	*Hymns of Thanksgiving* (Dead Sea Scroll)
1QS	*Community Rule* (Dead Sea Scroll)
RB	*Revue biblique*
Rep.	Plato, *Republic*
Rhet.	Aristotle, *Rhetoric*
Rhet. Alex.	Pseudo-Aristotle, *Rhetoric to Alexander*
Rhet. Her.	Pseudo-Cicero, *Rhetorica ad Herennium*
SAGN	Studies in Ancient Greek Narrative
SBAB	Stuttgarter biblischer Aufsatzbände
SBL	Society of Biblical Literature
SBLDS	Society of Biblical Literature Dissertation Series
SBLRBS	Society of Biblical Literature Resources for Biblical Study
SBLSP	Society of Biblical Literature Seminar Papers
SBLSymS	Society of Biblical Literature Symposium Series
SemeiaSt	Semeia Studies
SHS	Scripture and Hermeneutics Series
SI	*Sociological Inquiry*
Sir	Sirach, Ben Sira, Ecclesiasticus
SJ	Studia Judaica
SNTI	Studies in New Testament Interpretation
SNTSMS	Society for New Testament Studies Monograph Series
Soph.	Plato, *Sophist*
SP	Sacra Pagina
Spec.	Philo, *De specialibus legibus* (*On the Special Laws*)
SPCK	Society for Promoting Christian Knowledge
SR	Studies in Religion
SRR	Studies in Rhetoric and Religion
SSEJC	Studies in Scripture in Early Judaism and Christianity
STI	Studies in Theological Interpretation
T. Ab.	Testament of Abraham
T. Isa.	Testament of Isaiah
T. Levi	Testament of Levi
T. Mos.	Testament of Moses

TDNT	Theological Dictionary of the New Testament
Tg. Frg.	Fragmentary Targum
Tg. Onq.	Targum Onquelos
Tg. Ps.-J.	Targum Pseudo-Jonathan
Theat.	Plato, *Theatetus*
Tim.	Plato, *Timeaus*
Top.	Cicero, *Topica*
TS	Texts and Studies
W	Washington Codex (ca. fifth–seventh century CE)
WBC	Word Biblical Commentary
WGRW	Writings of the Greco-Roman World
WUNT	Wissenschaftliche Untersuchungen zum Neuen Testament
y. Ta'an.	Jerusalem Talmud, tractate Ta'anit
ZNW	*Zeitschrift für die neutestamentliche Wissenschaft und die Kunde der älteren Kirche*

Abiding Words: An Introduction to Perspectives on John's Use of Scripture

Alicia D. Myers

As with numerous other New Testament writings, Israel's Scriptures form the foundation on which the narrative of the Gospel of John is written. Ushered in with the opening verses of the prologue, Scripture appears throughout the Gospel and is even identified as one of the "witnesses" for Jesus's defense (5:31–47), showing up in explicit quotations along with a number of varyingly transparent allusions and references. Indeed, so crucial is Scripture to the Gospel's plot that the narrator winds the sequence of events tightly to the Jewish festival calendar whose own roots stretch into Israel's scriptural past.[1] Yet it is also the Fourth Gospel that is frequently accused of anti-Jewish language, if not explicit sentiment, in its presentation of "the Jews." With this mixed relationship with Israel's history—the incorporation of Scripture as a pillar of support for its presentation of Jesus alongside a sustained conflict with the religious leaders of that very scriptural tradition—John's use of Scripture has drawn the attention of a number of scholars.[2] Such persistent attention, however, makes entering into the conversation and deciphering the various voices a challenge. In an attempt to clarify the dialogue and offer possible avenues forward, the

---

1. See Michael A. Daise, *Feasts in John: Jewish Festivals and Jesus' "Hour" in the Fourth Gospel*, WUNT 2/229 (Tübingen: Mohr Siebeck, 2007); Dorit Felsch, *Die Feste im Johannesevangelium: Jüdische Tradition und christologische Deutung*, WUNT 2/308 (Tübingen: Mohr Siebeck, 2011).

2. Due to continued attention to this area of research, the Johannine Literature section of the SBL sponsored a session on this topic, hosted at the annual meeting in Chicago in 2012. This session provides the impetus for the present collection, which also incorporates additional papers from the annual SBL meeting in Baltimore from 2013 as well as independently solicited contributions.

present volume provides an overview of past research before featuring a collection of essays that showcase some current approaches to studying the use of Scripture in the Gospel of John.

1. Israel's Scriptures in John's Gospel: An Overview of Past Scholarship

When approaching the Fourth Gospel's use of Scripture, scholars are in agreement that, like other New Testament writings, the Gospel demonstrates a Christocentric hermeneutic. Scripture quotations, allusions, and echoes provide support for the Gospel's presentation of Jesus as the Christ, the Son of God (20:30–31).[3] According to J. Louis Martyn, however, the reverse of this statement is also true: namely, that belief in Jesus supports interpretation of Scripture in the manner that the Fourth Gospel epitomizes.[4] Martyn's statement highlights the tension in which the Gospel's employment of Scripture exists. Scripture testifies to Jesus's identity as understood by the Gospel, thereby adding an authoritative voice to its presentation; nevertheless, the persuasiveness of this testimony depends largely on one's predisposition to the Gospel's perspective. Indeed, that the same Scripture passages, images, and figures could be interpreted to oppose the Gospel's views is highlighted in the debates that flair up when Jesus's interpretations of Scripture come into conflict with those of religious leaders and crowds during his ministry (e.g., 7:14–53; 8:12–59).

This tension is also reflected in a number of earlier studies on the use of Scripture in the New Testament in general. C. H. Dodd and Barnabas

---

3. The debate over the purpose of the Gospel of John is well worn. The crux of the debate centers on the text-critical issue in 20:31 concerning the tense of πιστεύω. Is this a present subjunctive, encouraging continuing faith for a believing community, or an aorist subjunctive, suggesting the Gospel means to initiate belief among nonbelievers? For representative viewpoints, see Gordon D. Fee, "On the Text and Meaning of John 20.30–31," in *The Four Gospels 1992*, ed. F. Van Segbroeck et al., BETL 100 (Leuven: Leuven University Press, 1992), 3:2193–205; D. A. Carson, "Syntactical and Text-Critical Observations on John 20.30–31: One More Round on the Purpose of the Fourth Gospel," *JBL* 124 (2005): 693–714.

4. J. Louis Martyn, "Listening to John and Paul on the Subject of Gospel and Scripture," *WW* 12 (1992): 73. In this way, then, Scripture does not function as a "proof" in a strict sense because it does not convince anyone to have faith, but only to reinforce the faith they already possess. Such a reading necessarily endorses a particular purpose for the Gospel: it is meant to encourage those who already believe.

Lindars understood the Christocentric hermeneutic of the New Testament as indicative of the foundational role of scriptural interpretation for early believers. For Dodd, small collections of texts acted as the "substructure" for New Testament theology, undergirding the canonical authors' communication of the kerygma.[5] Building on Dodd's work, Lindars focuses on the apologetic function of this substructure, which showcased how Jesus fulfilled messianic expectations.[6] Thus Richard Longenecker argued that the earliest believers interpreted Scripture in such a way that Jesus exemplified the Jewish belief that the meaning of the Torah would be made plain through the Messiah.[7]

Yet not all scholars are convinced that this exercise was as seamless as a cursory reading of Dodd, Lindars, and others might suggest. While agreeing with the Christocentric nature of New Testament hermeneutics, Donald Juel emphasizes the catechetical role of scriptural interpretation alongside any external apologetic functions it served. Juel writes: "Christian interpretation of the Scriptures arose from the recognition that Jesus was the expected Messiah *and* that he did not fit the picture."[8] In other words, "messianic exegesis" had to explain the scandal of the cross and the reality of the resurrection as events entirely unanticipated by Israel's scriptural narratives. Thus expectations during the New Testament era may have been that the Messiah should make the Torah plain, but early believers were faced with the reality that Jesus's life, death, and resurrection were not easily explained by contemporaneous understandings of Scripture. Hence, New Testament authors had to explain *how* Scripture related to Jesus as Messiah. Moreover, the Christocentric readings of Scripture helped early believers to "clarify the implications of faith in Jesus for one's relationship with Israel's God and with the world."[9] Juel's comments rightly

---

5. C. H. Dodd, *According to the Scriptures: The Sub-structure of New Testament Theology* (New York: Scribner's Sons, 1953), 110.

6. Barnabas Lindars, *New Testament Apologetic: The Doctrinal Significance of the Old Testament Quotations* (London: SCM, 1961), 18.

7. Richard N. Longenecker, *Biblical Exegesis in the Apostolic Period*, 2nd ed. (Grand Rapids: Eerdmans, 1999), 79 (see further 77–79). In addition to a Christocentric hermeneutic, Longenecker highlights the pneumatological interpretation of Scripture by New Testament authors (p. xxxi). The role of the Holy Spirit in remembrance is particularly significant for interpreting the Fourth Gospel's use of Scripture.

8. Donald H. Juel, *Messianic Exegesis: Christological Interpretation of the Old Testament in Early Christianity* (Philadelphia: Fortress, 1988), 26 (emphasis original).

9. Ibid., 2.

highlight the fact that the "apologetic" function of scriptural interpretation among early believers is two-sided, helping to support the claims of believers both for outsiders and, *or even primarily*, for believers themselves.

Agreeing on the Christocentric nature of scriptural interpretation in the New Testament, then, does not result in a "disappointingly commonplace" discussion.[10] Rather, this consensus only forms the foundation on which scholars build. Debates surface concerning which Scripture texts are referenced, how such references are incorporated into their surrounding context, and especially on the possible implications of their incorporation. Studies on the Fourth Gospel's use of Scripture reflect these areas of concern as well. In what follows, I will offer an overview of past scholarship on the use of Scripture in John's Gospel by dividing past research into three main areas of study, those that focus on (1) the sources of John's references to Scripture; (2) the method of John's incorporation of these references; and (3) the sociological, theological, and rhetorical functions of the references. While such categories inevitably run the risk of oversimplification, they will aid in our understanding of the major contributions on John's use of Scripture in the past, setting the stage for the present collection of essays, which showcases current and continuing methods of analyzing John's employment of these sacred traditions.

1.1. The Sources of John's Scripture References

As mentioned above, studies on Scripture in the Fourth Gospel have mirrored approaches prevalent among those studying the use of Scripture in the New Testament as a whole. Initially such study primarily reflected historical concerns; that is, what does John's use of Scripture reveal about the Gospel's historicity or its own historical location? The works of Dodd and Lindars fit into this category insofar as both scholars sought to explain the historical use of scriptural interpretation in the early church. Indeed, both Dodd and Lindars agree that the characteristically Christocentric hermeneutics of early believers began with Jesus himself before it was developed by later New Testament authors, of whom Paul, John, and the author of Hebrews are considered the most creative.[11] Other scholars continued Dodd and Lindars's work by examining the form of the quotations. Such

---

10. Ibid., 1.
11. Dodd, *According to the Scriptures*, 110; Lindars, *New Testament Apologetic*, 88.

studies, like other source, form, and redaction-critical studies, sought to identify the sources used by New Testament authors as well as any changes made to them. By identifying these elements, interpreters hoped to hone in on the specific theological positions made by various New Testament authors, including John. When the quotations disagreed sharply with any known source material, scholars were left to explain such discrepancies. For J. R. Harris and Dodd, the differences were the result of New Testament authors using early *testimonia*, which were lists of ready-made scriptural prooftexts for the nascent Christian movement.[12] Those less convinced of the existence of such collections suggested faulty memories or intentional crafting of traditions to fit the theological perspectives of various authors and their communities.[13]

Among Johannine interpreters, the work of Alexander Faure, Edwin Freed, Günter Reim, and Maarten J. J. Menken typify these historical-critical approaches.[14] Focusing largely on the most explicit quotations in the Fourth Gospel, these scholars seek to demonstrate the evangelist's employment of one or more sources in the construction of his own quotations. The most often agreed-on quotations and references include John 1:23; 2:17; 6:31, 45; 10:34; 12:13, 15, 38, 40; 13:18; 15:25; 19:24, 28, 36, 37. In addition to studying these quotations, Reim explores a number of scriptural allusions in his attempt to construct the general Old Testament

---

12. J. Rendel Harris, *Testimonies*, 2 vols. (Cambridge: Cambridge University Press, 1916–20); Dodd, *According to the Scriptures*, 23–60. See also the recent histories of Harris's *testimonia* proposal in Martin C. Abl, *"And Scripture Cannot Be Broken": The Form and Function of the Early Christian* Testimonia *Collections*, NovTSup 96 (Leiden: Brill, 1999), 7–69; and Alessandro Falcetta, "The Testimony Research of James Rendel Harris," *NovT* 45 (2003): 280–99.

13. Charles Goodwin, "How Did John Treat His Sources?" *JBL* 73 (1954): 61–75, for example, argues that John must have had a faulty memory since his quotations vary so much from known written traditions. Such an interpretation, however, assumes the priority of written sources in the construction of the Gospel rather than oral communication.

14. Alexander Faure, "Die alttestamentlichen Zitate im 4. Evanglium und die Quellenscheidungshypothese," *ZNW* 21 (1922): 99–121; Edwin D. Freed, *Old Testament Quotations in the Gospel of John*, NovTSup 6 (Leiden: Brill, 1965); Günter Reim, *Studien zum alttestamentlichen Hintergrund des Johannesevageliums*, SNTSMS 22 (Cambridge: Cambridge University Press, 1974); Maarten J. J. Menken, *Old Testament Quotations in the Fourth Gospel: Studies in Textual Form*, CBET 15 (Kampen: Kok Pharos, 1996).

background for the Gospel.[15] Faure, Freed, and Menken also tackle the often-debated "quotation" in John 7:38, which, while introduced with a quotation formula, nevertheless does not conform to any known scriptural passage.[16] Faure includes this reference as a result of his particular interest in the introduction of scriptural quotations that will be mentioned below. Menken leaves John 7:37–38 for the end of his collection of essays because his reconstruction of the form of this quotation relies on conclusions drawn from other analyses. Menken also excludes quotations that are identical to the LXX in form or are what he considers "theological" or "juridical" propositions rather than legitimate quotations (cf. 7:42; 8:17; 12:34).[17] Freed explores the standard quotations along with most of the texts that Menken omits as well as 17:12, another highly debated quotation, which Freed suggests is an adaptation of Prov 24:22a LXX.[18]

For Faure, the analysis of John's explicit citations has the potential to uncover pre-Gospel sources employed by the Fourth Gospel, thereby contributing to theories of its composition. Highlighting the switch to fulfillment language in the passion narrative, Faure suggests that the Gospel includes at least two layers of source material redacted by a later editor: the first, in which Scripture is incorporated as unintroduced "prooftexts"; and the second, in which Scripture is actualized in the person and words of Jesus.[19] Although Faure's thesis concerning John's sources has not convinced many, his attention to the switch in introductory formulae in the later chapters of John's narrative is regularly noted.

Instead of focusing on the introductory formulae of the explicit citations, Freed, Reim, and Menken center their attention on deciphering the sources behind the individual citations themselves. The sources suggested by these authors vary greatly depending on the quotation considered. Freed finds room for influence from the LXX, extant portions of the Masoretic Text (MT), several targumic traditions, and corresponding excerpts

---

15. Reim, *Studien*, 1–188.
16. Freed, *Old Testament Quotations*, 21–38; Menken, *Old Testament Quotations*, 187–203 (cf. 18).
17. Menken, *Old Testament Quotations*, 14–15.
18. Freed, *Old Testament Quotations*, 96–98.
19. Faure, "Die alttestamentlichen Zitate," 101–2. According to Faure, such "actualization" is reflected most clearly in John 18:32 but also surfaces in John 17:12; 8:28; and 3:14.

from the Dead Sea Scrolls.[20] Reim is more restricted in his interpretation, arguing instead that John's use of Scripture was dependent largely on Deutero-Isaiah and other early Christian traditions.[21] Menken repeats the source- and redaction-critical approaches of Freed and Reim, but insists predominantly on the use of the LXX by John, although he leaves room for infrequent influence from Hebrew sources.[22] Menken's investigation centers on uncovering the reasons for John's apparent editorial activity with his sources. For Menken, the differences between the citations and textual traditions expose not a faulty memory on the part of the evangelist, but intentional changes made to highlight unique aspects of Johannine theology, especially its Christology. While concerned with historical elements, these scholars, especially Menken, demonstrate a concerted interest in the theological motivations for John's employment and reshaping of Israel's scriptural traditions mirroring the practices of contemporaneous redaction critical approaches.

Continuing in this vein of study is the past work of two contributors to the present volume: Bruce Schuchard and William Randolph Bynum.[23] Schuchard's 1992 monograph establishes him as a contemporary of Menken, whom he acknowledges as a key influence on his methodology and his interest in the editorial activity of the evangelist.[24] Nevertheless, Schuchard's methodological alignment with Menken does not always result in the same interpretation of John's source material or the theological motivations for John's intentional changes to that material.[25]

---

20. Freed, *Old Testament Quotations*, 127–30.
21. Reim, *Studien*, 188–90 (cf. 241–46).
22. Menken, *Old Testament Quotations*, 205–6.
23. Bruce G. Schuchard, *Scripture within Scripture: The Interrelationship of Form and Function in the Explicit Old Testament Citations in the Gospel of John*, SBLDS 133 (Atlanta: Scholars Press, 1992); Wm. Randolph Bynum, *The Fourth Gospel and the Scriptures: Illuminating the Form and Meaning of Scriptural Citation in John 19:37*, NovTSup 144 (Leiden: Brill, 2012).
24. Schuchard, *Scripture within Scripture*, xv.
25. For example, both Menken and Schuchard suggest that the author has purposefully altered the quotation of Isa 40:3 in John 1:23 by suppressing ἑτοιμάσατε and substituting εὐθύνατε rather than εὐθείας ποιεῖτε. Menken suggests that the author has done this because of his disagreement with the Synoptic tradition that John's ministry must end before Jesus can initiate his own (*Old Testament Quotations*, 30–31). In contrast, Schuchard argues that none of the gospels would present such an argument since "Jesus will come whether the way is prepared or not" (*Scripture within Scripture*,

Unlike Menken, Schuchard understands John's primary source material to be what he calls the "Old Greek" (OG) as a more precise designation for the Greek textual traditions available in the first century. Moreover, unlike Menken, Schuchard leaves greater room for the possibility of John citing material from memory in light of the oral culture in which he existed.[26] Yet, like Menken, Schuchard displays confidence in the ability to identify specific changes to citations made by the author of the Gospel and, therefore, in his ability to posit theological emphases that result from such changes. Bynum repeats such optimism in his recent monograph, which focuses in particular on the use of Zechariah in John 19:37. Although specifically concerned with John 19:37, Bynum's research has far-reaching implications concerning the relationship between John and the Dead Sea Scrolls and even leads him to the provocative suggestion that John's consistently careful citation style can be used to support increased confidence in the Gospel's historicity.[27] With Bynum, then, the concern for historicity inherent in the work of Dodd and Lindars is again palpably felt, reflective of an increased integration of John's Gospel in dialogues on reconstructing the "historical" Jesus in recent years.[28]

---

10). Instead, εὐθύνατε is used as a result of the influence of wisdom traditions, which frequently employ (κατ)ευθύνω with ὁδός (p. 11).

26. Schuchard dialogues with the work of Paul J. Achtemeier ("*Omne verbum sonat*: The New Testament and the Oral Environment of Late Western Antiquity," *JBL* 109 [1990]: 3–27) concerning the importance of oral transmission of traditions over written documents. While acknowledging the importance of Achtemeier's observations, Schuchard is not convinced by his blunt conclusion that searching for the form of citations is "an exercise in futility." Instead, Schuchard maintains that "even if John cited from memory, his citations do, in fact, represent precise and therefore perceptible recollections of a specific textual tradition" (*Scripture within Scripture*, xvi–xvii).

27. Bynum, *Fourth Gospel*, 173.

28. See the publications of the SBL section "John, Jesus, and History" in particular: *Critical Appraisals of Critical Views*, vol. 1 of *John, Jesus, and History*, ed. Paul N. Anderson, Felix Just, and Tom Thatcher, SBLSymS 44 (Atlanta: Society of Biblical Literature, 2007); and *Aspects of Historicity in the Fourth Gospel*, vol. 2 of *John, Jesus, and History*, ed. Paul N. Anderson, Felix Just, and Tom Thatcher, ECIL 2 (Atlanta: Society of Biblical Literature, 2009).

1.2. The Method of John's Scripture References

In addition to examining citation forms, other studies have focused more on the method of John's scriptural citations: that is, how the evangelist incorporates Scripture into the sequence of the narrative. Such exploration has connections to studies interested in John's citation form and sources since those studies are also often interested in how John incorporates his material, although they are necessarily more focused on individual references.[29] Moreover, scholars studying the method of John's Scripture referencing often utilize the conclusions of those studying citation forms in order to strengthen their claims.[30] Debates center on questions such as, (1) Does the Gospel simply "prooftext" for the sake of its argument, and thus disregard the original context of the quotations, or does it somehow incorporate the larger context from which the quotations come? (2) Does it matter whether or not the Gospel writer intended such quotations and allusions to incorporate the larger context of its scriptural material, if these connections were or can be made by ancient as well as contemporary audiences? And, (3) does the Gospel reflect interpretation practices current in Second Temple Jewish circles or even the larger Greco-Roman milieu and, if so, what does this reveal about the Gospel's origins or rhetorical goals? Studies on deciphering John's hermeneutical method, then, have largely settled into two main areas: first, those interested in discovering the intersection between John and ancient interpretive techniques, both Jewish and Greco-Roman; and, second, those exploring John's use of Scripture under the broad heading of "intertextuality," which can privilege either the original audiences of the Gospel or create fertile fields for contemporary reader-response and ideological readings.

---

29. The interest in individual quotations does not prevent many of these scholars from suggesting aspects of John's hermeneutics; indeed, some studies explore individual quotations as a means to identify John's interpretive tools. For example, from his studies, Dodd concludes that John is not interested in the original context of his quotations, but uses Christian *testimonia* as sources for his prooftexting.

30. For example, Catrin H. Williams ("The Testimony of Isaiah and Johannine Christology," in *"As Those Who Are Taught": The Interpretation of Isaiah from the LXX to the SBL*, ed. Claire Matthews McGinnis and Patricia K. Tull, SBLSymS 27 [Atlanta: Society of Biblical Literature, 2006], 109–12) notes Menken's findings in her own analysis of the use of Isaiah in the Gospel of John even though her main interest lies in John's shaping of Isaian material, especially the servant material, for his own christological ends.

Turning first to connections between John's use of Scripture and ancient interpretive practices, most attention has been given to discovering John's reflection of Jewish exegetical practices of the first centuries. Thus, beginning with the work of Lindars, those studying John's use of Scripture have often noted a pesher quality to John's quotations, although few go far in fleshing out this characterization.[31] Generally, such a definition is used to explain John's references as prooftexts, but with the addition of finding a precedent for such a practice in a Jewish context. Daniel Patte develops Lindars's observation in more detail and suggests that New Testament use of Scripture is pesher-like with its eschatological focus on fulfillment through the person and work of Jesus as the Messiah. For Patte, pesher becomes a way to understand what he sees as a typological perspective of Second Temple Judaism. Nevertheless, Steven Witmer has recently questioned the association between pesharim and scriptural references in John in particular. In addition to lacking the characteristic line-by-line interpretation of pesharim, Witmer suggests that John's "radically Christocentric hermeneutic" sets it apart from the exegetical technique of Qumran.[32]

Rather than suggesting the specific practice of pesher, many scholars prefer the more general expression of midrash to explain John's scriptural interpretations. Peder Borgen's 1965 study represents the first fully developed attempt to trace the connections between John's use of Scripture in John 6:31–58 and midrashic practices from Second Temple Judaism, especially as demonstrated in the work of Philo of Alexandria.[33] In addition

---

31. Lindars, *New Testament Apologetic*, 265–70. A few examples include Juel, *Messianic Exegesis*, 49–57; Longenecker, *Biblical Exegesis*, 80–87; Martin Hengel, "The Old Testament in the Fourth Gospel," in *The Gospels and the Scriptures of Israel*, ed. Craig A. Evans and W. Richard Stegner, JSNTSup 104, SSEJC 3 (Sheffield: Sheffield Academic, 1994), 380–95; J. Harold Ellens, "A Christian Pesher: John 1:51," *Proceedings: Eastern Great Lakes Biblical Society* 25 (2005): 143–55.

32. Stephen E. Witmer, "Approaches to Scripture in the Fourth Gospel and the Qumran *Pesharim*," *NovT* 48 (2006): 313–28 (esp. 327–28).

33. Peder Borgen, *Bread from Heaven: An Exegetical Study of the Concept of Manna in the Gospel of John and the Writings of Philo*, NovTSup10 (Leiden, Brill: 1965); Borgen, "John 6: Tradition, Interpretation, and Composition," in *Critical Readings of John 6*, ed. R. Alan Culpepper, BIS 22 (Leiden: Brill, 1997), 95–114; Borgen, "The Scriptures and the Words and Works of Jesus," in *What We Have Heard from the Beginning: The Past, Present, and Future of Johannine Studies*, ed. Tom Thatcher (Waco: Baylor University Press, 2007), 39–58.

to showcasing remarkable similarities, Borgen's analysis supports a Jewish milieu for the Fourth Gospel in contrast to studies arguing for Hellenistic roots, which presented the Gospel of John as a response to gnostic and protognostic groups. Borgen's study has paved the way for later scholars to dig more deeply into Jewish interpretive practices, including exploration of Hillel's middot, as a means to understand the specific techniques behind the Gospel's scriptural appeals.

Most scholars, however, have accepted Jewish exegetical practices as the backdrop for John's scriptural interpretations without precisely defining the techniques used through either discussions of pesher or middot. Aside from brief references, the majority of scholars studying the use of Scripture in the Fourth Gospel do not delve deeply into Jewish techniques.[34] This result is in large part because while there is agreement that rabbinic texts offer some information concerning first-century interpretive practices, it is unclear how much they reveal since rabbinic texts were not codified until centuries later. Michael Fishbane attempts to deal with this issue in his work, which traces inner-biblical interpretations across a variety of genres. He notes how established traditions (*traditum*) are transformed into what he calls *traditio* by various authors as a means to contemporize religious practices and reaffirm allegiance to Israel's heritage.[35] Without the confidence to tie down specific techniques, Fishbane instead notes general tendencies meant to "authorize" later "innovations" made by various Jewish groups influenced by their own historical locations and ideologies.[36] No doubt the same impulses are present among the Jewish writers of the New Testament, who seek both to legitimatize and explain their beliefs concerning Jesus of Nazareth by illustrating his relationship with Israel's sacred *traditum*. But without the identification of specific techniques, most scholars are limited to discussing John's midrashic practices as a way of noting his indebtedness to Jewish exegetical traditions. As a result, then, the term *midrash* itself runs the risk of becoming a loose description, providing little more than an assertion of John's Jewish milieu rather than a substantial statement concerning John's interpretive practices.

---

34. An exception to this trend is found in Frédéric Manns, "Exégèse Rabbanique et Exégèse Johannique," *RB* 92 (1985): 525–38.

35. Michael A. Fishbane, *Biblical Interpretation in Ancient Israel* (Oxford: Clarendon, 1985), 409–10.

36. Ibid., 528 (see further 528–42).

A few other scholars have suggested looking to the more developed canon of classical Greco-Roman rhetoric for categories to understand the use of Scripture in New Testament writings.[37] This exploration expands on the broader trend of utilizing ancient rhetorical categories to analyze New Testament writings, particularly discourses and letters, pioneered by George Kennedy.[38] Such studies are particularly popular among interpreters of John's Gospel, with its frequent and lengthy discourses.[39] The blending of Hellenistic and Jewish modes of thought and argumentation necessarily present in the Greco-Roman world indicates the potential for classical rhetoric to provide some language and insight into the ways in which Israel's Scriptures are incorporated into the New Testament. In particular, the close association between several middot—especially *gezera shewa* and *qalwalhomer*—and classical rhetorical techniques has been well established.[40] Since ancient education was rooted in the imitation of past masters (mimesis), it is no surprise that rhetorical manuals and works provide numerous examples of how literature could be integrated into a variety of speeches and writings. Although scholars have noticed that there is little explicit instruction on how to "quote" material, classical handbooks and *progymnasmata*

---

37. The most thorough development of this approach is in my own recent publication: Alicia D. Myers, *Characterizing Jesus: A Rhetorical Analysis of the Fourth Gospel's Use of Scripture in Its Presentation of Jesus*, LNTS 458 (London: T&T Clark, 2012). However, previous studies have indicated the potential of such an approach. See Dennis L. Stamps, "Use of the Old Testament in the New Testament as a Rhetorical Device: A Methodological Proposal," in *Hearing the Old Testament in the New Testament*, ed. Stanley E. Porter (Grand Rapids: Eerdmans, 2006), 26–33; Jerome H. Neyrey, *The Gospel of John in Cultural and Historical Perspective* (Grand Rapids: Eerdmans, 2009).

38. George A. Kennedy, *New Testament Interpretation through Rhetorical Criticism*, SR (Chapel Hill: University of North Carolina Press, 1984).

39. See, for example, Harold W. Attridge, "Argumentation in John 5," in *Rhetorical Argumentation in Biblical Texts: Essays from the Lund 2000 Conference*, ed. Anders Eriksson, Thomas H. Olbricht, and Walter Übelacker, ESEC 8 (Harrisburg, PA: Trinity Press International, 2002), 188–99; George L. Parsenios, *Rhetoric and Drama in the Johannine Lawsuit Motif*, WUNT 258 (Tübingen: Mohr Siebeck, 2010); Jo-Ann A. Brant, *John*, PCNT (Grand Rapids: Baker Academic, 2011).

40. David Daube, "Rabbinic Methods of Interpretation and Hellenistic Rhetoric," *HUCA* 22 (1949): 251–59; Saul Liebermann, *Hellenism in Jewish Palestine: Studies in the Literary Transition, Beliefs and Manners of Palestine in the I Century B.C.E–IV Century C.E.*, TS 18 (New York: Jewish Theological Seminary of America, 1962), 59–61; Juel, *Messianic Exegesis*, 35–41.

provide a number of examples of quoting and alluding to existing material in ways meant to increase the persuasiveness of one's work.

A far more popular approach to deal with the lack of solid categories from Jewish interpretive practices in the first century, however, is the theory of intertextuality. Aiming to respond in part to the problem of imprecise language and methods from those discussing midrash and typologies, Richard B. Hays turns to contemporary literary theory as a means to add more substance to intertestament exegesis.[41] From its roots in the poststructuralist movement, intertextuality maintains that texts are written in relationship to other texts and, as such, necessarily reverberate with both intended and unintended echoes from other materials. Acknowledging the existence of intertextuality has pushed scholars to explore the relationship between the citations found in John's Gospel and the larger contexts from which they come in Israel's Scriptures. Rather than seeing John's employment of Scripture as prooftexting similar to pesher models, these scholars find support for John's awareness of the larger context from which his quotations and allusions come, adding depth to John's incorporation of Israel's sacred story.[42]

---

41. Richard B. Hays, *Echoes of Scripture in the Letters of Paul* (New Haven: Yale University Press, 1989), 11–14. See also Stefan Alkier, "Intertextuality and the Semiotics of Biblical Texts," in *Reading the Bible Intertextually*, ed. Richard B. Hays, Stefan Alkier, and Leroy A. Huizenga (Waco: Baylor University Press, 2008), 3–22; Julia Kristeva, "Word, Dialogue, and Novel," in *The Kristeva Reader*, ed. Toril Moi (New York: Columbia University Press, 1986), 34–61. In his most recent contribution, Hays presents John's intertextual awareness as part of a larger hermeneutic that "reads the entirety of the OT as a web of symbols" pointing toward Jesus's life and the life he offers to believers (*Reading Backwards: Figural Christology and the Fourfold Gospel Witness* [Waco, TX: Baylor University Press, 2014], esp. 92).

42. Examples of this type of study include a number full-length monographs, a few of which include Margaret Daly-Denton, *David in the Fourth Gospel: The Johannine Reception of the Psalms*, AGJU 47 (Leiden: Brill, 2000); Andrew C. Brunson, *Psalm 118 in the Gospel of John*, WUNT 2/158 (Tübingen: Mohr Siebeck, 2003); Gary T. Manning, *Echoes of a Prophet: The Use of Ezekiel in the Gospel of John and in the Literature of the Second Temple Period*, JSNTSup 270 (London: T&T Clark, 2004); Susan Hylen, *Allusion and Meaning in John 6*, BZNW 137 (Berlin: de Gruyter, 2005); as well as a number of articles, including Robert L. Brawley, "An Absent Complement and Intertextuality in John 19:28-29," *JBL* 112 (1993): 427–43; Diana M. Swancutt, "Hungers Assuaged by the Bread of Heaven: 'Eating Jesus' as Isaian Call to Belief: The Confluence of Isaiah 55 and Psalm 78(77) in John 6.22-71," in *Early Christian Interpretation of the Scriptures of Israel*, ed. Craig A. Evans and James A. Sanders, JSNTSup 148, SSEJC 5 (Sheffield: Sheffield Academic, 1997), 218–51.

Catrin Williams's investigations into the Fourth Gospel's use of Isaianic traditions reflect intertextual methods.[43] Focused in particular on tracing how John's use of Isaiah resonates with Jewish interpretive traditions surrounding the prophet, Williams argues that the Gospel does much more than simply use Isaiah quotations to prooftext its narrative. Instead, Williams underscores the significant weight Isaiah traditions place on Johannine Christology by examining the explicit references to "Isaiah" in John 1:23 and 12:38–41, which bracket Jesus's public ministry. Reviewing ancient Jewish beliefs surrounding Isaiah, Williams suggests that Isaiah was particularly open to interpretations that combined its images of a future, returning, triumphal Lord *and* a Suffering Servant. Noting the confluence of vocabulary in Isa 6, 40–42, and 52–53, Williams concludes that the reception history of Isaiah paved the way for John's shaping of the material around his presentation of Jesus as the Christ.[44] John's Gospel, therefore, reflects awareness of this broader intertextual environment and uses it to support its Christology.

The results from intertextual studies, however, can vary widely in their findings, depending on the perspective from which the study is conducted. Many repeat the practices of earlier redaction and source-critical models to note variations in the form of a citation before offering theological rationales for such changes based on the larger context from which the original citation comes. Others use the reader-oriented method of intertextuality to prioritize contemporary perspectives over ancient ones, finding fodder for more ideological interpretations. Intertextuality, then, has opened a number of avenues for continued reflection on John's employment of Scripture, encouraging interpretive possibilities that have remained previously unexplored and taking seriously the variety of implications emerging from John's incorporation of Scripture. Yet it can be difficult to place methodological parameters on intertextual readings. This is both a strength that allows for a variety of interpretations and voices otherwise muted by tradi-

---

43. Williams, "Testimony of Isaiah," 107–24; Williams, "'He Saw His Glory and Spoke of Him': The Testimony of Isaiah and Johannine Christology," in *Honouring the Past and Shaping the Future: Religious and Biblical Studies in Wales. Essays in Honour of Gareth Lloyd Jones*, ed. Robert Pope (Leominster: Gracewing, 2003), 53–80; Williams, "Isaiah in John's Gospel," in *Isaiah in the New Testament*, ed. Steve Moyise and Maarten J. J. Menken (London: T&T Clark, 2007), 101–16.

44. Williams, "Testimony of Isaiah," 121–22.

tional approaches and a potential weakness, particularly for those seeking to discover how texts were heard and understood by ancient audiences.[45]

1.3. The Functions of John's Scripture References

All studies on John's use of Scripture generally hope to touch on at least some of the theological implications of his incorporation of Israel's traditions, even if these theological aspects are limited to individual passages or citations. Thus the studies described above often aim to uncover unique aspects of Johannine theology, especially Christology, by means of their analyses. For the most part these studies underscore the Christocentric hermeneutic of the Gospel and its interest in presenting Scripture as somehow made complete by Jesus's ministry and death.[46] A few studies, however, have devoted extended attention to the various functions the use of Scripture has in John's Gospel.

In her 2003 monograph, Jaime Clark-Soles lays out a sociological model for analyzing the Gospel's use of Scripture. Influenced by the work of Wayne Meeks, Clark-Soles likewise turns to sociology in order to explore how John's use of Scripture sheds light on the Johannine community's historical situation.[47] For Clark-Soles, John's incorporation of

---

45. See Thomas R. Hatina's criticism of the use of "intertextuality" by historical-critical biblical scholars in "Intertextuality and Historical Criticism in New Testament Studies: Is There a Relationship?" *BibInt* 7 (1999): 28–42; cf. Stanley E. Porter, "The Use of the Old Testament in the New Testament: A Brief Comment on Method and Terminology," in *Early Christian Interpretation of the Scriptures of Israel*, ed. Craig A. Evans and James A. Sanders, JSNTSup 148, SSEJC 5 (Sheffield: Sheffield Academic, 1997), 80–88. Other scholars have responded to these criticisms by suggesting even more precise terms for the different types of intertextuality that are often explored. Stefan Alkier, for example, suggests using three categories: production-oriented, reception-oriented, and experimental perspectives ("Intertextuality," 9–11). See also Steve Moyise, "Intertextuality and the Study of the Old Testament in the New Testament," in *The Old Testament in the New Testament: Essays in Honor of J. L. Noth*, ed. Steve Moyise, JSNTSup 189 (Sheffield: Sheffield Academic, 2000), 14–41.

46. See especially Francis J. Moloney, "The Gospel of John as Scripture," *CBQ* 67 (2005): 454–68. Moloney's own argument interfaces on many fronts with that of Andreas Obermann, which is discussed below.

47. Jaime Clark-Soles, *Scripture Cannot Be Broken: The Social Function of the Use of Scripture in the Fourth Gospel* (Leiden: Brill, 2003), 7–8. The influence of J. Louis Martyn's historical and compositional reconstruction of the Johannine community is also present: "To be sure, the reader will easily detect my debt to Martyn's scholarship

Scripture reflects a sectarian community, much like the Qumran community in the ancient world and even similar to the modern-day example of the Branch Davidians. Scripture is used to justify and, indeed, exalt the members of the sect as ones who have truly understood in contrast to those who remain a part of the "parent" tradition.[48] Clark-Soles contends that the Johannine leaders used Scripture as an authoritative voice to reinforce their community's elect, sectarian status in the midst of their conflict with mainstream Jewish thought. In this way, John's use of Scripture reflects the Gospel's social reality and constructs an identity of "elect" insiders versus those who are outside the believing group.

Andreas Obermann and Saeed Hamid-Khani are more interested in the theological implications of John's use of Scripture, though similarities to Clark-Soles's conclusions also emerge. Both Obermann and Hamid-Khani note the role of Scripture in addressing John's opponents, "the Jews." In these contexts, Scripture acts as a witness, testifying in favor of Jesus's identity and points toward his coming passion. For Obermann, Scripture specifically supports various presentations of Jesus, including as temple (2:17), living bread (6:31), and the king (12:15), among others.[49] Because of Scripture's christological and testifying role, Hamid-Khani suggests that it can act as part of a polemic against those who deny Jesus as the Christ since "true" scriptural understanding only occurs as a result of belief.[50] John's conviction that Jesus fulfills Scripture, and indeed somehow makes Scripture manifest as the *Logos* (Word) incarnate, guides the Gospel's use of Scripture. Obermann argues that such a hermeneutical position enables the Gospel to function as a new Scripture for Johannine believers.[51] For Hamid-Khani, Jesus's fulfillment and completion of Scripture renders Israel's institutions "obsolete" except for the ways in which they can help one understand the Christ event more clearly.[52]

---

as my presuppositions about the traumatic, antagonistic social situation in which the Fourth Gospel was forged become evident" (p. 5).

48. Clark-Soles, *Scripture Cannot Be Broken*, 317.

49. Andreas Obermann, *Die christologische Erfüllung der Schrift im Johannesevangelium: Eine Untersuchung zur johanneseichen Hermeneutik anhand der Schriftzitate*, WUNT 2/83 (Tübingen: Mohr Siebeck, 1996), 91–203.

50. Saeed Hamid-Khani, *Revelation and Concealment of Christ: A Theological Inquiry into the Elusive Language of the Fourth Gospel*, WUNT 2/120 (Tübingen: Mohr Siebeck, 2000), 251–52.

51. Obermann, *Die christologische Erfüllung der Schrift*, 418–22.

52. Hamid-Khani, *Revelation and Concealment*, 258–59.

The recent work of Ruth Sheridan and myself also centers on the function of John's incorporation of Scripture; however, we are more interested in the characterizations that result from the Gospel's scriptural appeals. Sheridan focuses on the presentation of "the Jews" in John's Gospel. Analyzing the explicit citations of Scripture in John 1:19–12:15, Sheridan uses contemporary rhetorical theory to examine how "the Jews" are constructed as characters by the ideal reader. For Sheridan, studying the rhetorical function, instead of potential historical situations, of this characterization puts the examination of John's "anti-Judaism" in sharper focus and exposes "the Jews'" role in drawing the ideal reader to faith in Jesus even as "the Jews" themselves are presented as increasingly "obdurate."[53] My own approach differs from that of Sheridan in my use of classical Greco-Roman rhetorical categories as well as my attention to the characterization of Jesus rather than "the Jews."[54] Nevertheless, we agree that Scripture acts as a witness for Jesus's identity and simultaneously draws in the ideal audience while, or even by means of, alienating other characters within the narrative itself. Moreover, both studies call attention to the need to understand the rhetorical functions of scripture in John's Gospel in addition to primarily historically oriented studies.

The preceding overview of these three approaches—by form, method, and function—demonstrates the lasting interest in studying the Fourth Gospel's use of Scripture. Overall, such studies have some basic areas of consensus. Scholars generally emphasize the Gospel's use of Greek source material and cite Jewish interpretive practices as predecessors for John's incorporation of Scripture as well as intertextual echoes to explain John's incorporation of larger scriptural contexts into the narrative. Building on these conclusions, interpreters seek to understand unique aspects of John's theology, especially his christological emphases, as well as the wider implications of this theology. Nevertheless, just as the consensus

---

53. Ruth Sheridan, *Retelling Scripture: "The Jews" and the Scriptural Citations in John 1:19–12:15*, BIS 110 (Leiden: Brill, 2012), 235. This conclusion does not signify that Sheridan understands "the Jews" to be undeveloped characters in John's Gospel. Instead, she writes that "'hope' is held out to 'the Jews' in the Gospel narrative" but that since they "do not avail themselves of this hope (cf. 12:39–42), ... they remain on the underside of the Gospel's dualism despite the relative character development and occasional understanding and belief" (236).

54. Myers, *Characterizing Jesus*, 39–77. Sheridan suggests that John's scripture citations "should be generically categorized as *midrash/pesher*" instead (*Retelling Scripture*, 46).

concerning John's Christocentric hermeneutic has not dampened studies on our topic, these areas of agreement have not quelled debates. Continued research in these areas along with emerging approaches are pushing the understanding of John's use of Scripture in new directions, sometimes down avenues quite divergent from the accepted conclusions. It is to these more current projects and approaches that we now turn.

2. Continuing the Conversations: The Present Contribution

The present volume continues the conversation on John's use of Scripture, offering both studies that highlight and perpetuate several of the approaches discussed above as well as others that initiate new methodological possibilities. The following essays are divided into three parts, intended to highlight the various approaches utilized in each section.

The first section contains the work of Bruce Schuchard, William Randolph Bynum, and Michael Daise, who are interested in what the form of John's explicit quotations can reveal about their functions in the Gospel. Schuchard traces the "explicit" citations in John, analyzing them to demonstrate that the evangelist's citations consistently rely on a Greek source. The differences that do exist between extant versions of the Greek Bible and forms of John's quotations are the result of John's intentional shaping and, indeed, his ability as a storyteller to cast these Scriptures into the new literary and theological contexts of the Gospel. The resulting quotations, therefore, serve to elucidate the person and work of Jesus, especially his crucifixion, with the goal of convincing the hearer to believe and "have life in his name." Bynum limits his own study to the references to Zech 9:9 and 12:10 in John 12:15 and 19:37. He argues that John uses citation techniques reflected in his own milieu and creates a Zecharian *inclusio* around the passion narrative. Such a move effectively evokes the postexilic context of Zechariah 9–14 throughout the passion sequence to underscore the Johannine irony of Jesus's exalted death. Like Schuchard, Bynum suggests that such use of Israel's Scriptures ultimately encourages the faith of the Gospel audience. Rounding out the first part of this collection is the work of Daise, which centers on the "remembrance" quotations found in John 2:17, 12:13, and 12:15. Daise maintains that these quotations should be read in light of each other since they all mention the role of "remembering" on the part of the disciples. Suggesting that these three quotations were originally located together in an earlier form of the tradition, Daise contends that in their present form they create an *inclusio* in the Book of Signs that has profound pneumatological implications.

In the second portion of the book, the essays of Jaime Clark-Soles, Ruth Sheridan, Benjamin Lappenga, and me provide examples of sociological and rhetorical methodologies in the study of John's use of Scripture. Clark-Soles's chapter begins this section by outlining her sociological method described in the previous section. She describes the impact of John's incorporation of Scripture on the construction of various social identities, especially those "inside" and those "outside" the Johannine community. My essay explores the insight classical rhetoric can provide on understanding how the Gospel of John uses Scripture. After providing an overview of the relevance of classical rhetoric for the interpretation of the use of Scripture in the New Testament, I explore John 1:19–34 and suggest that the use of Isaiah as *exemplum* results in the blending of his voice with that of John (the Baptist) to offer a confession, and indeed a "divine testimony," consistent with that of the Johannine believers. Building on his research of ζῆλος in other New Testament works, Lappenga here turns his attention to the quotation of Ps 69:9 in John 2:17. Rather than "zeal for your house" simply acting as a description of Jesus's devotion to the Father, Lappenga uses literary-compositional arguments to conclude that this zeal is *also* a reference to the zeal of "the Jews," which ultimately, but not inevitably, leads them to pursue Jesus's death (i.e., their zeal "consumes" Jesus). This portrayal of the "misguided zeal" of "the Jews" leads *not* to a "portrait of hatred" but instead to an emphasis on the importance of accepting Jesus's identity claims. Sheridan's essay also centers on the presentation of "the Jews" in John's Gospel. Mixing contemporary rhetorical theory with ancient Jewish practices of biblical interpretation, Sheridan centers her attention on John 8:17. Her work explores neglected resonance between John 7–8, the accusations, and the three scriptural texts that express the stipulation of the testimony of two or more witnesses (Deut 17:6; 19:15; Num 35:30) in order to assess how they are rhetorically reconfigured in John 8:17. In this mutually hostile exchange, Jesus and his opponents mete out accusations of deception and apostasy (Deut 13; 17:2–7; 29:18, 25–28), homicide, the punishment for "false witnesses" and perjury (Deut 19:16). As a result, the two groups persist in speaking past each other through their scriptural applications, "the Jews" identifying Jesus as an apostate, while he condemns them of perjury. Overall, John 7–8 reinforce that it is not necessarily the use of Scripture on its own that makes the Gospel's identification of Jesus persuasive to an audience, but rather the Gospel's rhetoric, which uses Scripture to elevate its perspective over that of other characters in the text and those outside the Gospel community.

The third part of this collection includes essays in the growing area of memory and performance theory, which pays particular attention to the oral preservation and transmission of New Testament traditions. Catrin Williams's contribution opens this section by examining the presentation of various figures from Israel's past into the Gospel of John. Using insights from social memory and social identity theories, Williams focuses on how these figures are reconfigured in the Johannine narrative in order to explore how John's christological beliefs, and encounters with other group(s), shape his presentation of scriptural figures as witnesses to Jesus and, in the case of Abraham and Isaiah, as prototypes of the Johannine community's group identity. As part of a larger project exploring memory theory in John's Gospel, Jeffrey Brickle draws on insights from a number of subdisciplines in addition to memory theorists in order to explore how John shapes his Gospel in light of septuagintal subtexts and personal participation. Examining first the farewell discourse, passion narrative, and epilogue, Brickle then turns to the prologue to demonstrate how John uses the Jewish Scriptures as the primary locus upon which he builds his memory images for his audience. Recognizing the significance of orality, aurality, and memory in antiquity, these essays remind contemporary readers how ancients built on traditions to cue the memories of their audiences in the formation of group beliefs.

This collection of essays offers a snapshot of some current approaches to the lasting questions surrounding John's use of Scripture. Although a gospel often highlighted for anti-Jewish tendencies, it is nevertheless a gospel that uses Israel's Scripture as the backdrop for its presentation of Jesus as the Christ. Acknowledging the crucial role that Scripture plays in the Gospel of John, the essays in this volume consistently argue for the intentional shaping of John's citations in light of the late first century CE. Moreover, they show appreciation for the larger context from which these scriptural references come, exploring the possible influences these contexts have on John's theology and rhetoric. This collection also gives voice to a diversity of perspectives, providing space for those examining the form of John's quotations, the sociological ramifications and rhetorical techniques, and the role of memory in John's scriptural interlacing. In this way, we hope that this volume enables readers to catch a glimpse at how Scripture informs the world constructed by the Gospel, both for those in the ancient Mediterranean and for contemporary readers.

Part 1
The Form of John's Citations

Form versus Function: Citation Technique and Authorial Intention in the Gospel of John

Bruce G. Schuchard

In 1985, Maarten Menken's essay "The Quotation from Isa 40,3 in John 1,23"[1] signaled an important development in the direction of the work being done at the time to characterize the form of the explicit Old Testament citations in the Gospel of John.[2] Over a roughly ten-year time span, Menken continued to publish one after another article devoted to a focused treatment of each of the Gospel's citations[3] until, in 1996, his book *Old Testament Quotations in the Fourth Gospel: Studies in Textual Form* republished the revised sum of his previous work, adding to it an introduction, a conclusion, and a fresh treatment of the citation appearing in 15:25.[4]

---

* An initial form of this essay including its illustrations was first shared at a themed session titled "The Use of Scripture in the Johannine Literature" for the Johannine Literature section of the Society of Biblical Literature at its 2012 gathering (November 17–20) in Chicago.

1. See Maarten J. J. Menken, "The Quotation from Isa 40,3 in John 1,23," *Bib* 66 (1985): 190–205.

2. See the useful surveys of the history of research in both Ruth Sheridan, *Retelling Scripture: "The Jews" and the Scriptural Citations in John 1:19–12:15*, BIS 110 (Leiden: Brill, 2012); and Alicia D. Myers, *Characterizing Jesus: A Rhetorical Analysis on the Fourth Gospel's Use of Scripture in Its Presentation of Jesus*, LNTS 458 (London: T&T Clark, 2012).

3. Seven of these appeared in English, two in German, and one in Dutch.

4. See Maarten J. J. Menken, *Old Testament Quotations in the Fourth Gospel: Studies in Textual Form*, CBET 15 (Kampen: Kok Pharos, 1996). It is to be noted, however, that Menken's 1996 publication purposefully omits from extended consideration the explicit citations of the Old Testament appearing in 10:34; 12:38; and 19:24.

Though other dimensions of the Fourth Gospel's use of the Old Testament were then and continue even now to be equally deserving of serious study, the deliberate focus of Menken's work was then the yet to be resolved problem of the textual form of the Gospel's citations. Scholars had long since noted that the majority of the citations do not agree exactly with any version of the Old Testament that is known to us (in Hebrew, in Greek, or in any other language). At times, it is also less than clear which Old Testament passage the evangelist is intending to recall. This state of affairs leaves the expositor of the Gospel with a number of fairly critical questions. Which Old Testament texts in which Old Testament versions are the citations recalling? Does the evangelist alter at all the biblical texts he cites? Does he add to, or subtract from, or otherwise modify them? Are such modifications deliberate? If indeed he modifies his citations in adapting them to their eventual place and purpose in the narrative of his Gospel, what exactly is either his method or his motivation for doing so? How measurable are either his method or his motivation? And, as regards his method, is it possible to situate his technique for incorporating his Old Testament citations into the narrative of his Gospel within the extant procedures of his day?

When Menken first pursued his own study of the citations in John, the principal interest of the scholarly research that was being done at the time was on the question of sources. But the conclusions to which so many were coming were typically various and frequently in conflict with each other. At times, significantly unverifiable contributing factors such as the authorial freedom of the evangelist not to follow his source or his failing memory were posited. Does the evangelist then freely or consciously paraphrase?[5] At times, wholly hypothetical and otherwise

---

5. One, of course, must take into serious consideration the evident preference of the period for orality, accounting therefore also for the very real possibility that the evangelist consciously and perhaps also quite freely (in lieu of troubling himself with painstaking physical examination of actual texts) cites from memory, not troubling himself with the need for word-for-word precision with his recitation of texts. See, e.g., the importance of orality in Jeffrey E. Brickle, *Aural Design and Coherence in the Prologue of First John*, LNTS 426 (London: T&T Clark, 2012). What follows, however, will attempt to show that a significant sort of precision does, in fact, attend the evangelist's manner of citing texts, suggesting that the citing-from-memory versus citing-by-painstaking-examination question should be handled less as an either/or and more as a both/and. The evangelist has spent a long and distinguished lifetime both preferring orality and delighting in the physical examination of actual texts. Therefore, at the

unknown versions of the Old Testament were said to have served as John's source. Only rarely did the evangelist's role as a discerning redactor of texts, and only rarely did the persuasive character of his storytelling art, receive any kind of serious consideration in the work that was done.

Therefore, at the time, the principal contribution of Menken's manner of approaching the problem of the citations came with his manner of *combining* the questions of source and redaction. The search for sources, posited Menken, can lead to credible and informing results only if one takes into serious consideration the role of the evangelist as a skillful redactor of texts.[6]

Still, some have lamented the abiding uncertainties and the enduring lack of consensus that continue to dog some of the more discrete aspects and findings of such close study. Some have gone so far as to suggest that the efforts of Menken and others like him constitute an exercise in futility.[7] I, however, would argue that, even when the close study of the shape and form of the citations and their possible sources still involves tough questions and leads still to occasionally inconclusive results, such work,

---

end of his career (the time of the composition of the Gospel), he likely does not need to "look it up again." He cites from memory. But when he does so, the precision with which he operates distinguishes the evangelist as a first-century biblical scholar of the highest rank.

6. Menken, *Old Testament Quotations*, 13, writes, "Due attention to the Johannine redaction and meaning of the quotations should go hand in hand with the quest for their origin. Of course, it is necessary to start with determining the sources as precisely as possible, but often this does not lead to conclusive results. In such cases one should not resort to hypothetical versions of the OT text which are otherwise unknown or to 'free quotations' and the like. Rather one should investigate whether an adequate explanation of the form of the quotation can be reached by taking into account Johannine redaction of the OT passage, in a textual form which is known or which can be reasonably argued. It seems to me that although it is very probable that several versions of the OT were in circulation in the environment of the fourth evangelist, a theoretical recourse to this multiplicity of versions is unnecessary if John's text … can be explained quite well by his redaction. Results of research in the field of early Jewish and early Christian exegetical techniques and devices should also be taken into account here: many deviations in scriptural quotations and in the transmission of the biblical text are the result not of a defective memory, but of conscious application of exegetical techniques in his rendering of OT passages. The combination of source criticism and redaction criticism may even throw some new light on a thorny question such as the source of the OT quotation in John 7:38."

7. See Sheridan, *Retelling Scripture*, 22–25.

Menken's work, and the work of those like myself who have followed Menken's lead,[8] can be and is instructive,[9] especially if one is careful to construct the parameters of such study around the most measurable and meaningful goals.

For this reason—recognizing that the Fourth Gospel's references to the Old Testament can be to discrete texts, or not,[10] and may reproduce somehow some or all of the words of a conscious source text (or combination of texts), or not[11]—my own previous study of the Gospel's citations sought a close and careful analysis of each of the Gospel's citations where (1) explicit reference to a discrete Old Testament text (or combination of texts) is marked by the evangelist with the offering of an introductory formula and (2) the actual words of the Gospel's source text (or combination of texts) are reproduced somehow with the offering of the citation. Such an admittedly select definition of what constitutes an "explicit citation" may to some seem an unnecessarily narrow starting point. And yet, as just that, as a starting point, the parameters of such a study as defined provide the expositor of the Gospel with an opportunity to focus first with the best possible precision on the most measurable work of the evangelist not only as redactor but also as rhetorician,[12] as an eyewitness to Jesus[13] who

---

8. See Bruce G. Schuchard, *Scripture within Scripture: The Interrelationship of Form and Function in the Explicit Old Testament Citations in the Gospel of John*, SBLDS 133 (Atlanta: Scholars Press, 1992).

9. Even when uncertainty remains, the hermeneutical value of such study is considerable. We benefit greatly from the opportunity to see in concrete terms how the evangelist read texts and as redactor/rhetorician put texts to work in the persuasive construction of his story of the life, the times, and the accomplishment of the Son of God.

10. See, e.g., John 1:45.

11. Thus in John 17:12 and 19:28, observes Menken, *Old Testament Quotations*, 12n3, "we meet quotation formulae without a specific quotation." In John 7:42; 8:17; and 12:34 as well, adds Menken (18), "not the wording but the content of each [OT text] was relevant to the evangelist." To these I would add John 7:37-38 (see further below). See further Andreas J. Köstenberger, "John," in *Commentary on the New Testament Use of the Old Testament*, ed. G. K. Beale and D. A. Carson (Grand Rapids: Baker Academic, 2007), 415–507 (including the excellent bibliography on 507–12).

12. See Myers, *Characterizing Jesus*; and Sheridan, *Retelling Scripture*. See also Wm. Randolph Bynum, *The Fourth Gospel and the Scriptures: Illuminating the Form and Meaning of Scriptural Citation in John 19:37*, NovTSup 144 (Leiden: Brill, 2012).

13. See Richard Bauckham, *Jesus and the Eyewitnesses: The Gospels as Eyewitness Testimony* (Grand Rapids: Eerdmans, 2006).

consciously composed his Gospel with the intention to persuade, with the expectation that the result of his work would be Scripture.[14]

With such constraints mustered, conscious too of the influence of such presuppositions, my own study argued for the evangelist's incorporation of thirteen explicit citations of the Old Testament into the narrative of the Gospel (see illustration 1).[15] It argued further that the evangelist's consistent source for these was not a Hebrew text form, but was instead a Greek Bible whose form, again with considerable consistency, coincides with what Septuagint scholarship has identified as the most likely form of the earliest Jewish translation of the Hebrew Bible into Greek.[16]

Space constraints prevent the defense of such a conclusion from going here into especially great detail. Perhaps in short the following will make such a finding at least possible—if not plausible.

---

14. See Francis J. Moloney, "The Gospel of John as Scripture," *CBQ* 67 (2005): 454–68.

15. While some have argued that our inability to define in the first century what was and was not held by all to be "Scripture" so complicates the study of the shape of the Gospel's citations that little confidently can be known, this study will argue that what was and was not regarded in the first century *on the fringes* as "Scripture" matters little to the study of the Gospel's citations. How far one casts the net of one's consideration in the search for sources is an important question, but the evangelist only cites those texts that both the synagogue and the earliest church of his day would have readily recognized as Scripture. He also, we shall see, consistently cites a Greek Bible, whose translated form is invariably close to the Hebrew. In fact, "in the various forms in which John cites the Scriptures," observes Bynum, "nowhere does he blatantly contradict the essence of known Hebrew textual traditions" (*Fourth Gospel*, 116).

16. "It was both the bible of primitive Christianity," observes Martin Hengel, *The Septuagint as Christian Scripture: Its Prehistory and the Problem of Its Canon*, with the assistance of Roland Deines, intro. Robert Hanhart, trans. Mark E. Biddle (Grand Rapids: Baker Academic, 2002), xi, "and the early church well into the second century." See further Karen H. Jobes and Moisés Silva, *Invitation to the Septuagint* (Grand Rapids: Baker Academic, 2000); and Natalio Fernández Marcos, *The Septuagint in Context: Introduction to the Greek Versions of the Bible*, trans. Wilfred G. E. Watson (Leiden: Brill, 2001). While some have questioned the likelihood that a solitary (proto MT) textual tradition of the Hebrew Bible first gave rise over time to an essentially singular first Greek form of Moses and the Prophets (the Old Greek) that was held in high regard in the first century by both the synagogue and the earliest church, this study will argue that recourse to the possibility of alternative first-century textual traditions of the Hebrew Bible (or their Greek equivalents) does little to inform what likely contributed to the shape of the evangelist's citations.

First, three of the Gospel's thirteen citations correspond in their form word for word with the form of the earliest Jewish translation of the Hebrew Bible into Greek.[17] While some have argued that, because John's Greek agrees also with what one finds in the Hebrew "no conclusion can be drawn"[18] as regards their source, still what follows suggests strongly that the evangelist cites not the Hebrew but the Greek.[19] In the citation appearing in 10:34 ("I said, you are gods"), the vocable εἶπα ("I said," bearing a weak aorist alpha) appears only here in the Gospel. Elsewhere, the evangelist always and quite frequently uses the more regular εἶπον (bearing a strong aorist omicron) for the aorist first person singular of λέγω.[20] The evangelist's sole use of εἶπα comes from the Greek of Ps 81:6.[21] In 12:38 ("Lord, who has believed our report, and to whom has the arm of the Lord been revealed?"), the evangelist's citation and the Greek of Isa 53:1 agree "against" the Hebrew in prefixing the vocative "Lord."[22] Also, for the citation's reference to "revealing," a form of ἀποκαλύπτω again appears only here, whereas the evangelist exhibits elsewhere a consistent preference for φανερόω.[23] His source is again the Greek. And finally, in 19:24 ("They divided my garments among them, and for my clothing they cast lots"), *had* the evangelist translated Ps 22:18 from the Hebrew, he just as easily could have used either a form of μερίζω or διαίρω,[24] or perhaps even διαδίδωμι, to translate the Hebrew's reference to "dividing."[25] He also could have considered translating the Hebrew's imperfects with something other

---

17. See Bynum, *Fourth Gospel*, 112–15.

18. Charles K. Barrett, *The Gospel according to St. John: An Introduction with Commentary and Notes on the Greek Text*, 2nd ed (Philadelphia: Westminster, 1978), 28.

19. Similarly, see Menken, *Old Testament Quotations*, 15.

20. The first person singular εἶπον appears in the Gospel a total of twenty-four times. Third person plural forms of the same vocable appear sixteen times. The weak aorist third person plural εἶπαν appears twenty-six times.

21. While the reading εἶπον exists for John 10:34, observes Menken, *Old Testament Quotations*, 15n13, it may well "have been influenced by the context" (see 10:36). While it is possible that εἶπα is "an assimilation to the LXX," its peculiarity in John is best seen as "a strong point in favour of its being original."

22. See Menken, *Old Testament Quotations*, 15. "Against," however, only means here that the Hebrew's implicit addressee is made explicit in the Greek, not that the Greek disagrees with the Hebrew.

23. See ibid. The verb appears a total of nine times in the Gospel, nine times in 1 John, and twice in Revelation. Cf. ἀποκάλυψις in Rev 1:1.

24. See ibid.

25. See Schuchard, *Scripture within Scripture*, 127. Cf. John 6:11.

than Greek aorists.²⁶ Or he could have used as an alternative for either ἱμάτιον²⁷ or for its synonym ἱματισμός²⁸ the noun στολή,²⁹ or just as easily could have reversed the ordering of the nouns.³⁰ Here too, then, that the evangelist's citation exhibits word-for-word agreement with the Greek of Ps 21:19 suggests strongly that the evangelist is citing the Greek. Now, if he did so thus far with these three, what prevents him from having done so elsewhere?

While three of the Gospel's thirteen citations are verbatim citations of the Greek, seven differ only slightly from the Greek. Not only is it a relatively straightforward matter to demonstrate that the differences are slight, but it is also a relatively straightforward matter to show that the differences are quite likely due to the very conscious work of the evangelist as redactor, who rather naturally, but also quite deliberately, shortens and/or reorders or refocuses the texts that he cites in the necessary service of their adapted and critical purpose in the narrative of the Gospel. Therefore, if one is open to (1) the regular and quite natural first-century phenomenon of a significantly abbreviated Old Testament reference, or to (2) the occasional substitution of an available synonymous expression, or to (3) adjustments derived from context, or from a so-called model's model,³¹ or from some other analogous context, or to (4) adjustments in the syntax of phrases, clauses, and sentences for the purpose of adapting the Gospel's citations to their place and purpose in the narrative of the Gospel, what one finds in the form of the citations is traceable evidence of the evangelist's work as redactor. What one sees is the hand of an adept and persuasive storyteller. What one encounters is more evidence for the evangelist's use of the Greek.

- In 1:23 ("I am the voice of one crying in the wilderness, 'Make straight the way of the Lord'"), the evangelist's *shortened* citation otherwise differs from the Greek of Isa 40:3 only where

---

26. See Ibid.
27. The noun appears a total of six times in the Gospel and seven times in Revelation.
28. The noun appears only here in all of John's works.
29. The noun appears a total of five times in Revelation.
30. See Menken, *Old Testament Quotations*, 15.
31. Cf. the OT's own later use of earlier OT texts.

a synonym indicative of the evangelist's sapiential interest is substituted for εὐθείας ποιεῖτε.[32]

- In 2:17 ("The zeal of your house will consume me"[33]), the evangelist's citation differs from the Greek of Ps 68:10 only where the future καταφάγεται appears rather than the aorist κατέφαγεν for the purpose of underscoring the predictive force of the psalm.[34]
- In 6:31 ("He gave them bread from heaven to eat"), the evangelist's *shortened* citation, whose word order is also different,[35] otherwise differs from the Greek of Ps 77:24 only where the citation recalls the Greek of an earlier text, Exod 16:4, that the later itself recalls.[36]
- In 6:45 ("And they will all be taught by God"), the evangelist's *shortened* citation otherwise differs from the Greek of

---

32. See Köstenberger, "John," 427. See also Bynum, *Fourth Gospel*, 120–21, who observes further that εὐθύνατε "may been taken from another context, such as the famous passage found in Josh 24:23, the only other passage in the LXX where the verb is used in this exact form." In John's citation, the *hapax* βοῶντος in particular strongly suggests that the evangelist, who otherwise exhibits a preference for either κράζω or κραυγάζω when referring to a "crying" or a "crying out," here cites the Greek.

33. Steven M. Bryan, "Consumed by Zeal: John's Use of Psalm 69:9 and the Action in the Temple," *BBR* 21 (2011): 479–94, argues rightly that with his citation of Ps 69:9 the evangelist intends for his hearers "to conclude that the zeal that consumes Jesus is that of his enemies" (479; see also Benjamin Lappenga's contribution in this volume). Bryan neglects, however, to observe further that, accordingly, the evangelist likely also takes τοῦ οἴκου σου ("of your house") to be a subjective genitive referring to the psalmist's kinsmen (cf. LXX Ps 68:9; see also vv. 5 [cf. John 15:25], 8, 10b [in synonymous parallelism with 10a], 11–13, 15, and 19–29 [cf. v. 22 and John 19:28–30; and v. 24 and John 12:37–40]).

34. See Marianne Meye Thompson, "'They Bear Witness to Me': The Psalms in the Passion Narrative of the Gospel of John," in *The Word Leaps the Gap: Essays on Scripture and Theology in Honor of Richard B. Hays*, ed. J. Ross Wagner, C. Kavin Rowe, and Katherine Grieb (Grand Rapids: Eerdmans, 2008), 275–76.

35. See in John's citation the relocated concluding position and function of φαγεῖν from the first of the psalm verse's two parallel clauses. Cf. here the collapsing of two parallel clauses with the citation in John 1:23.

36. See further Margaret Daly-Denton, *David in the Fourth Gospel: The Johannine Reception of the Psalms*, AGJU 47 (Leiden: Brill, 2000), 131–44 (esp. 133). The psalm's ἄρτον is also the only occasion in the Greek of the OT where ἄρτος renders לֶחֶם, suggesting again that the evangelist here cites the Greek. Cf. Ps 77:26: ἀπῆρεν νότον ἐξ οὐρανοῦ.

Isa 54:13 only where the citation transforms into an equative clause what appears in Isaiah as a phrase.[37]
- In 15:25 ("They hated me without cause"), the evangelist's citation differs from the Greek of Ps 68:5[38] only where the citation again transforms into a clause what appears in the psalm as a phrase.
- In 19:36 ("Not a bone of it/him will be broken"), the evangelist's citation differs from the Greek of Exod 12:10[39] only where it agrees with the Greek of a later text, Ps 33:21, that itself recalls the earlier one.[40]
- In 19:37 ("They will look upon him whom they have pierced"), the evangelist's *shortened* citation differs from the Greek of Zech 12:10 where many—even those who have argued for the evangelist's direct use of the Hebrew elsewhere—take it rightly here to be recalling an extant "corrected" form of the Greek[41] that was "current in early Christian circles in the textual form given in Jn 19,37,"[42] and where a synonymous verb

---

37. The *hapax* διδακτοί is a *hapax* in the Greek OT as well.
38. See also Ps 34:19.
39. See also Exod 12:46.
40. See Köstenberger, "John," 503. "The fact that his bones were not broken," observes Thompson, "They Bear Witness to Me," 279, "would have demonstrated that he was the Righteous One, chosen and vindicated by God—over against all other authorities, Jewish or Roman, who opposed him."
41. For the need for such a correction, see Bynum, *Fourth Gospel*. In 19:37 especially, observes Bynum (131), "one is struck immediately by the fact that there is not a single word of agreement between John's form of citation and the LXX text." And yet, while John's citation shows "definite affinities with the consonantal MT," adds Bynum (141), "it does not appear to be a precise translation of that text."
42. Maarten J. J. Menken, "The Minor Prophets in John's Gospel," in *The Minor Prophets in the New Testament*, ed. Maarten J. J. Menken and Steve Moyise, LNTS 377, NTSI (London: T&T Clark, 2009), 86. The form of the Greek text that the evangelist recalls may not have existed as anything other than a marginal reading entered into what otherwise was a first-century Christian copy of the earliest Jewish translation of Zechariah into Greek. No attempt on the part of the earliest church to produce its own comprehensive recension of the Greek and/or independent translation of the Hebrew is in evidence until much later. Therefore, while it may seem that the most serious threat to the case for the evangelist's thoroughgoing use of the first Jewish translation of the Hebrew Bible into Greek is the last of his citations in 19:37 (the only citation which *seems* to agree with the Hebrew against the Greek), Menken (87)

of seeing more suitable to the Gospel's thoroughgoing interest in the relationship of seeing and believing is substituted for the Greek's ἐπιβλέψονται.[43]

Again, space constraints prevent the offering of a more detailed defense of the suggestion that as many as ten of the Gospel's thirteen citations are not as difficult to describe as at first they might seem to be. Three remain, however, that are admittedly more challenging, are more highly redacted citations, and so are less given to the kind of straightforward analysis that might lead to conclusions for which a high level of confidence regarding the plausibility of the result attends the analysis. But if one again consciously proceeds from—dare one suggest it—the relatively straightforward, from (1) the Gospel's three verbatim citations of the Greek, to the less so, to (2) the Gospel's seven citations exhibiting close but not exact agreement with the Greek, for which a credible case can still be made for the evangelist's continued use of the Greek, to (3) the Gospel's most challenging citations of all, the three remaining citations whose significantly redacted shape and form do not exhibit close agreement with the Greek—as one then moves from that which is relatively forthcoming and foundationally informing to those citations where the insights of the foundational fundamentally inform what one considers as possible as one proceeds—what one finds is that a rather plausible case can, in fact, be made for the evangelist's thoroughgoing use of a Greek source in the construction of all of his citations.[44]

- In 12:15 ("Fear not, daughter Zion; behold, your king is coming, sitting on the foal of an ass"), the evangelist's *short-*

---

rightly observes that the last of the evangelist's citations in all likelihood cites not the Hebrew but a form of the Greek that the church itself created. Contrast the suggestion of Bynum, *Fourth Gospel*, that 19:37 recalls either the Greek Minor Prophets Scroll known as 8HevXIIgr (or R, which in fact lacks a reading for Zech 12:10) or "a similar manuscript" (6; see before Bynum Hengel, *Septuagint*, 7), which then "places John's form in harmony with the LXX correction movement represented by R."

43. See Bynum, *Fourth Gospel*, 5–6, 142, 176–79. R is not a hypothetical version, but the reading that Bynum proposes for it (for Zech 12:10) is.

44. It is sometimes suggested that, in the largely oral environment of the late first century, the longer a citation is the greater is the likelihood that a citation by John would depart from its *Vorlage*. In point of fact, only one of John's three most redacted citations is all that lengthy.

ened citation[45] otherwise differs from the Greek of Zech 9:9 where the spelling of a word has been adjusted,[46] and where amplifying analogous material from the Greek of Isa 44:2, 1 Kgs (3 Kgdms) 1, and Gen 49:10–11 has been substituted.[47]

- In 12:40 ("It has blinded their eyes and hardened their heart, lest they see with the eyes and understand with the heart and turn, and I would heal them"), the evangelist's *shortened* citation otherwise differs from the Greek of Isa 6:10 where stylistically preferable synonymous expressions are utilized,[48] and where amplifying analogous material from the Greek of Isa 42:18–20, Job 17:7, and Isa 44:18 has been substituted.[49]
- In 13:18 ("The one who ate my bread has lifted his heel against me"), the evangelist's citation differs from the Greek of Ps 40:10 where a stylistically preferable synonymous expression

---

45. "It is ... evident," observes Menken, "Minor Prophets," 82, "that the quotation in John has been abbreviated, both to adapt it to its present context (only the arrival of Jesus as king and his sitting on a donkey have been retained) and to eliminate the parallelisms at the beginning and end [of the cited text]. Comparable abbreviations, especially the suppression of parallelism, occur in nearly all other Old Testament quotations in John."

46. Cf. θύγατερ in Zech 9:9 with θυγάτηρ in John 12:15.

47. Because "John normally makes use of the LXX," observes Menken, "Minor Prophets," 82, "he will probably have done so here as well." "Fear not" in the Greek of Isa 44:2 is substituted for "rejoice greatly" in Zech 9:9. See Schuchard, *Scripture within Scripture*, 74–80. "Sitting" appears rather than "mounting," recalling Solomon, whose act of sitting on the king's mule in 1 Kgs (3 Kgdms) 1 (see vv. 33, 38, 44) singled him out as one designated to sit on the throne (see vv. 13, 17, 20, 24, 27, 30, 35; cf. 46, 48). See ibid., 80–82. And, again, "to emphasize Jesus' regal dignity," adds Köstenberger ("John," 473, citing Freed, Schuchard, and Menken), "new foal" is replaced by "foal of an ass" from Gen 49:11.

48. Cf. μήποτε ... ἐπιστρέψωσιν in Isa 6:10 with ἵνα μὴ ... στραφῶσιν in John 12:15. The marker of negated purpose μήποτε appears in John only in John 7:26; ἐπιστρέφω appears only in John 21:20.

49. Thus "blinded" in the Greek of Isa 42:19 is substituted for "closed" in Isa 6:10, "hardened" in Job 17:7 is substituted for "made dull," and "their heart" and "understand" in Isa 44:18 are substituted for "the heart of this people" and "comprehend." See Schuchard, *Scripture within Scripture*, 102–6. John "streamlines" his citation, observes Köstenberger, "John," 481, "in order to establish a direct correlation between seeing and believing" that denounces "the Jewish nation for turning a deaf ear to God's message of judgment and salvation."

is used,⁵⁰ and where amplifying analogous material from the Greek of Ps 77:24 (cf. John 6:31), 2 Sam (2 Kgdms) 20:21 (see also 18:28), and Gen 3:15 has been substituted.⁵¹

The evangelist's Old Testament Bible was a Greek Bible. His (at least) frequent use of the Greek is now widely acknowledged as a given.⁵² What is disputed is where, if ever, the evangelist cites and so also translates from the Hebrew or from any other source other than the Greek. A degree of uncertainty likely will always attend the best efforts of those who do this kind of work. And yet the careful study of the Gospel's citations together with the best evidence that we have for what first defined the form of the earliest translation of the Hebrew Bible into the lingua franca of the Greco-Roman world⁵³ strongly suggests that the same Greek Old Testa-

---

50. Cf. ὁ ἐσθίων in Ps 40:10 with ὁ τρώγων in John 13:18 (see also the latter in John 6:54, 56, 57, 58).

51. Thus "my bread" (singular) in the Greek of Ps 77:24 is substituted for "my bread(s)" (plural) in Ps 40:10 (cf. John 6:11, 31). "Lifted" in 2 Sam (2 Kgdms) 20:21 (see also 18:28) is substituted for "made great." And "his heel" in Gen 3:15 is substituted for "heel" (πτερνισμόν). See Schuchard, *Scripture within Scripture*, 112–17. Indeed, the Gospel's three most redacted citations (12:15, 40; 13:18) appear at a juncture in the Gospel's narrative that itself may have incited the evangelist to provide his three most greatly textured invitations to intertextual associations.

52. "The presence and influence of the LXX is quite evident," observes Bynum, *Fourth Gospel*, 113, "and its role as a primary source is clear." See further 113–15. See also Menken, *Old Testament Quotations*, 205. It should not surprise, adds Menken (206), "that the fourth evangelist, who writes in Greek for people who understand Greek, derives his OT quotations from the current Greek version of the OT." Neither should it surprise if for any reason it appears that "he has a command not only of Greek but also of Hebrew (and Aramaic). We might compare the evangelist in this respect with a modern preacher who normally employs the Bible translation that is common in his church, but who on occasion, when this translation is, in his view, inadequate or erroneous, quotes from another translation or makes his own one," exhibiting both a willingness and a commendable capacity to shape and to form his citations to their skillfully adapted and intended purpose in the narrative of his Gospel.

53. Not the Hebrew Bible, but the Septuagint, observe Jobes and Silva, *Invitation to the Septuagint*, 23, "was the primary theological and literary context within which the writers of the New Testament and most early Christians worked. This does not mean that the New Testament writers were ignorant of the Hebrew Bible or that they did not use it. But since the New Testament authors were writing in Greek, they would naturally quote, allude to, and otherwise use the Greek version of the Hebrew Bible. This process is no different from that of a modern author writing, for example,

ment that the earliest church claimed as its own served also in natural terms and for natural reasons as the evangelist's preferred source not for some, but for all of his citations.

Here, then, is chiefly where I part company with Maarten Menken and others. Simply put, I do not find at all convincing the evidence that has been adduced or the arguments that others have given for the evangelist's direct use of the Hebrew Bible.[54] While the evangelist's use of the Greek in no way excludes the theoretical possibility of "occasional recourse to the Hebrew,"[55] and while I am entirely sympathetic to the suggestion that the evangelist was a Palestinian Jew whose first language was Aramaic and who would have had little difficulty either hearing or reading Hebrew with understanding,[56] the burden of proof still lies with those who continue to suggest that evidence for the evangelist's direct use of the Hebrew Bible is at all to be found in the Gospel of John. I, for one, am not convinced.

Nor do I find that the evangelist's citations are as inexplicably arranged in the balance of the Gospel's narrative as some have surmised.[57] But my defense of this latest suggestion now begins with an understanding of the Gospel's Christoconcentric literary structure that finds its *midpoint* not, as many do, at the end of chapter 12 of the Gospel but at the end of chapter 10. Responding to Mathias Rissi, Jeffrey Staley, and others,[58] my own

---

in Spanish, and quoting a widely used Spanish translation of the Bible." See further 23–26.

54. Again, John 19:37 is no exception. Instead, the words "They will look upon him whom they have pierced" come directly not from the Hebrew, but from an early, extant, corrected Christian copy of the Greek. In other words, the phrasing of 19:37 strongly suggests that as early as the latter days of the first century, the church's Old Testament text is already in *some* places (i.e., in *some* passages in *some* OT books) a "corrected text." John is a Jew, has the ability to work with the Hebrew, and is acquainted with the Hebrew Bible, yet for the sake of his hearers and for posterity's sake (and for other reasons too?) prefers the Greek.

55. Menken, *Old Testament Quotations*, 205.

56. See Bynum, *Fourth Gospel*, 171–72.

57. See, e.g., Menken, *Old Testament Quotations*, 12. Alternatively, see Edwin Freed, *Old Testament Quotations in the Gospel of John*, NovTSup 11 (Leiden: Brill, 1965), 129, who argues that with "no other writer are the O.T. quotations so carefully woven into the context and the whole plan of composition as in Jn."

58. See Mathias Rissi, "Der Aufbau des vierten Evangeliums," NTS 29 (1983): 48–54; Jeffrey L. Staley, "The Structure of John's Prologue: Its Implications for the Gospel's Narrative Structure," CBQ 48 (1986): 241–64, whose published dissertation *The Print's First Kiss: A Rhetorical Investigation of the Implied Reader in the Fourth Gospel*,

manner of accounting for the location of the Gospel's thirteen citations in its narrative begins with an understanding of the Gospel's organization and structure (see illustration 2) that finds design and salutary unity in a first half of the Gospel that begins and ends with Jesus and his disciples beyond the Jordan.[59] There the significance of the testimony of the Baptist is twice prominently advanced in the Gospel. There the Baptist first is in chapter 1, and then is again and finally the focus of the crowd that goes there at the conclusion of chapter 10.[60] Design and unity are thus also to be found in a second half of the Gospel that (1) begins in John 11 and ends

---

SBLDS 82 (Atlanta: Scholars Press, 1988), 50–71, notes also Jesus' "ministry tours," the third of these ending at 10:42. See also the related observations of Fernando F. Segovia, "The Journeys(s) of the Word God: A Reading of the Plot of the Fourth Gospel," *Semeia* 53 (1991): 23–54.

59. See Bruce G. Schuchard, "The Wedding Feast at Cana and the Christological Monomania of St. John," in *All Theology Is Christology*, ed. Dean O. Wenthe et al. (Fort Wayne, IN: Concordia Theological Seminary Press, 2000), 101–16, where both agreement with and points where I diverge from that which has been argued by Rissi, Staley, Segovia, and others is indicated. See also D. A. Carson and Douglas J. Moo, *An Introduction to the New Testament*, 2nd ed. (Grand Rapids: Zondervan, 2005), 227, who refer to 1:19–10:42 as a "first large unit" of text. See further Andreas Köstenberger, *A Theology of John's Gospel and Letters: The Word, the Christ, the Son of God*, BTNT (Grand Rapids: Zondervan, 2009), 169, who similarly finds that "the *inclusio* between 1:19–34 and 10:40–42 marks off 1:19–10:42 as a unit."

60. Segovia, "The Journey(s)," 39, observes that the Gospel's references to the Baptist (1:19–34; 3:22–26; 10:40–42; see also 5:33–36) not only mark the beginning and the end of narrative units of text but also progressively decrease in length. "In other words, by their very length these three narrative sections show how, as the ministry of Jesus begins to unfold, the ministry of John comes to an end." This same waxing of Jesus and waning of John (3:30) transpires first in the four days of 1:19–51. For the suggestion that 10:22–29 is the "structural summit" of the Gospel, which details its hero's "change of fate," around which the rest of John's story is arranged, see Egil A. Wyller, "In Solomon's Porch: A Henological Analysis of the Architectonic of the Fourth Gospel," *ST* 42 (1988): 151–67 (esp. 153). For the related suggestion that 11:1–20:29 constitutes in John's Gospel the Book of Jesus's Hour, see George Mlakuzhyil, *The Christoconcentric Literary Structure of the Fourth Gospel*, AnBib 117 (Rome: Editrice Pontificio Istituto Biblico, 1987). For the complementary suggestion that the Gospel's two books or halves are the Book of the Testimony (1:19–10:42) and the Book of Jesus's Hour (11:1–21:24), see Gunnar Østenstad, "The Structure of the Fourth Gospel: Can It Be Defined Objectively?" *ST* 45 (1991): 33–55.

in John 20 with a dead man rising[61] and with a troubled Thomas[62] and that (2) features in John 12 and in John 13–19 the first and last days of a final six-day-long week of days[63] that begins in John 12 and ends in John 13–19 with an evening meal (see only in 12:2 and 13:2), with foot service (see 12:3 and 13:4–17; cf. 1:27), with an anointing of Jesus for burial (see esp. the framing references to an anointing of Jesus only in 12:3, 7, and 19:38–42),[64] with Judas the betrayer (see 12:4–6 and 13:2, 21–30; 18:1–5),[65] and with the arrival and the consummation of Jesus's "hour" (see 12:23,

---

61. The Gospel's second half therefore also begins and ends with the beginning and end of the last of the Gospel's four narrated occasions in which its pilgrim Messiah, Jesus, purposefully makes his way to the environs of the Holy City, Jerusalem, where finally he goes to suffer, to die, and to rise again. The last of Jesus's seven forward-looking signs sees its fulfillment (the summing fulfillment of all of the signs) in John 19–20. See Mathias Rissi, "Die Hochzeit in Kana Joh 2,1–11," in *Oikonomia: Heilsgeschichte als Thema der Theologie. Oscar Cullmann zum 65. Geburtstag gewidmet*, ed. Felix Christ (Hamburg: Reick, 1967); and Craig R. Koester, "Jesus' Resurrection, the Signs, and the Dynamics of Faith in the Gospel of John," in *The Resurrection of Jesus in the Gospel of John*, ed. Craig Koester and Reimund Bieringer, WUNT 222 (Tübingen: Mohr Siebeck, 2008), 47–74. Cf. the sign of Moses in John 3:14.

62. The result is an *a b b a* frame for the second half of the Gospel. Thus the resurrection of Lazarus, observes Köstenberger, "John," 477, "anticipates Jesus' own resurrection." See also Thomas in John 14:5 and in 21:2. Therefore, as do the repeated references to the figure of the Baptist in the prologue and the first half of the Gospel, so too do the repeated references to the figure of Thomas mark both the Gospel's second half and the epilogue.

63. The temporal marker πρὸ ἓξ ἡμερῶν τοῦ πάσχα in John 12:1 therefore locates the evening meal that follows it in John 12:2–8 on the Saturday evening that preceded Jesus' suffering and death on the cross and followed the Sabbath that would have begun at sundown Friday night and ended at sundown Saturday evening. The Saturday night that included an evening meal followed by the Sunday morning and Sunday afternoon narrated by John in the remainder of John 12 is thus reckoned by him as a single twenty-four hour day, the tenth of Nisan (see the selection of the lamb in Exod 12:3; cf. the selection of Jesus in John 12:7). Later that week, Thursday evening followed by Friday morning and Friday afternoon is therefore similarly reckoned by John as a single twenty-four hour sixth day. Thus the evangelist devotes fully a third of the Gospel's narrative (John 13–19) to a detailed description of a final twenty-four-hour period of time.

64. See also Jesus and his disciples "reclining" at table only in 12:2 and 13:23, 28 (cf. 6:11); and the suggestive references to a "house" in the Gospel's second half only in 12:3 and 14:2.

65. See also Judas's role as the keeper of the "moneybag" only in 12:6 and 13:29; and the plight of the "poor" only in 12:5, 6, 8; and 13:29.

27 and 17:1),⁶⁶ a week-long "hour," which is the week of the Gospel's third and final Passover.⁶⁷

If one is willing to consider at least the most basic aspects of this alternative proposal for seeing in the Gospel's design a midpoint for its structure, then one is in a position also to note the (perhaps surprising) degree to which certain aspects of the citation technique of the evangelist contribute impressively to an overall balance and shaping rhythm to the offering of the Gospel's citations from the first half of the Gospel's narrative to its second and climactic half. As one attends to *who* in the narrative cites each text, to *where* in the Old Testament each citation comes from, and to *what*

---

66. See also Jesus as "king" in 12:13, 15, and esp. in 18:33–19:22 (cf. 1:49; 6:15); Philip in 12:21 and 14:8–9 (cf. 1:43–48; 6:5–7); Jesus's glorification in 12:23, 28 and 13:31–32; 14:13 (cf. 15:8); 16:14; 17:1, 4–5, 10 (cf. 7:39; 8:54; 21:19); the bearing of "fruit" in 12:24 and 15:2, 4–5, 8, 16 (cf. 4:30); "losing" and "keeping" in 12:25, 47, and 17:12; 18:9; Jesus "troubled" in 12:27 and 13:21 (cf. 11:33 and 14:1, 27); Jesus prays to the Father in 12:28 and 17:1–26; "the judgment of this world" and of its "ruler" only in 12:31 and 14:30; 16:8, 11; Jesus's death "signified" by his words only in 12:32–33 and 18:32 (cf. 21:19); the human "heart" only in 12:40 and 13:2; 14:1, 27; 16:6, 22; and "put out of the synagogue" in 12:42 and 16:2 (cf. 9:22).

67. The Gospel's first reference to its third and final Passover appears in John 11:55 (cf. 2:13, 23; 6:4; 12:1; 13:1; 18:28, 39; 19:14). Cf. the six-day-long week of days in 1:19–2:11 (noted also by Köstenberger, *Theology of John's Gospel and Letters*, 169); and the six-day-long first creation whose life-creating labor accomplished by the same creator (1:3) likewise achieved its nuptial telos on day six (thus there is a day one in Genesis, a day one in John 1:19–23, and a day one in John 12). The Gospel's first week, which ends with its own nuptial (John 2:1–11; cf. 3:29), is followed by its own first Passover (John 2:13). The Gospel's final week *is* its final Passover. Cf. the sixth hour (19:14) of the sixth day of the week (Friday) of the sixth day of the final Passover (cf. 12:1), the last of the Gospel's six festivals (see 2:13; 5:1; 6:4; 7:2; 10:22; 11:55). Cf. the Gospel's six references to fulfillment, all in the second half of the Gospel, in John 12:38; 13:18; 15:25; 17:12; 19:24, 36. Like Adam before him, Jesus sleeps on day six (cf. Gen 2:21) and rests on day seven (cf. Gen 2:2). See also in John 1 Jesus and his disciples are six in number (see 1:35–37, 40–42, 43, 45), six messianic designations describe Jesus (see 1:29, 34, 38, 41, 49, 51), and in John 2 the six waterpots of stone (2:6). See further the six anticipatory citations of the OT in John 1:19–12:15 and the six anticipatory signs of Jesus in John 1–10. As with the six days of creation, observes Martin Hengel, "The Old Testament in the Fourth Gospel," in *The Gospels and the Scriptures of Israel*, ed. Craig A. Evans and W. Richard Stegner, JSNTSup 104, SSEJC 3 (Sheffield: Sheffield Academic, 1994), 393, "Jesus dies in the evening of the sixth day of the week and thereby finishes God's work" (19:30).

formula is made to introduce each of the citations, the following emerges (see illustration 3).

(1) The Gospel's thirteen citations are provided in the course of the telling of the Gospel's story by five instrumental "testifiers" (three reliable, two less so).[68] The Gospel's first three citations are offered first by the Baptist (1:23), then by Jesus's disciples (2:17), and then by the crowd in John 6 (6:31). Then two are offered by Jesus (6:45; 10:34),[69] three by the narrator (12:15, 38, 40), two again by Jesus (13:18; 15:25), and three again by the narrator (19:24, 36, 37). Thus there is balance and there is rhythm to the identity of those who sequentially cite the Old Testament. See in this regard especially the narrator, whose six citations, three at the beginning and three at the end of the Gospel's narrative of its concluding and climactic week, help impressively at each position to frame the week, on day one, then, and day six of its six-day week.[70] Noteworthy also, helping further to frame, are the first and the last of the narrator's six citations, which alone come from Zechariah.[71]

(2) There are additionally three explicit references to a "saying" of "Isaiah the prophet":[72] one at the beginning of the Gospel (1:23); and two more, closely paired, again in John 12 at the beginning of the final week

---

68. Five instrumental testifiers testify to the testimony of Moses and the Prophets (i.e., the first testament; see John 1:45) in strikingly balanced terms from the beginning to the end of the Gospel, beginning with the Baptist.

69. See also 7:37–38; 8:14–17.

70. Cf. Brian J. Tabb, "Johannine Fulfillment of Scripture: Continuity and Escalation," *BBR* 21 (2011): 495, for whom "the appeal to the OT witness becomes more pronounced as Jesus moves deliberately toward the cross."

71. Strengthening the likelihood that John means for his use of Zechariah to frame in this way is the related observation that "when John cites explicitly from the Twelve," adds Bynum, *Fourth Gospel*, 136, "he does so only from Zechariah." This is not to say that there are no *implicit* references to Zechariah. See Menken, "Minor Prophets," 89–96; and Adam Kubiś, *The Book of Zechariah in the Gospel of John*, EBib NS 64 (Pendé: Gabalda, 2012).

72. The adverb πάλιν links the close pairing of the first of the fulfillment citations in 12:38 and 12:39–40, indicating that the shortened form of the citation formula appearing with the latter is to be understood in terms of its fuller expression as given with the former. Isaiah is conspicuously one who consistently "speaks" (see 1:23; see also the references to speaking in the first and the third citation formulas in John 19, helping to frame the citations that appear between 12:38 and 19:37). At the same time, Isaiah is one whose word is "fulfilled" (a first reference, linking 12:38–40 with the fulfillment formulas that follow).

(12:38–40).⁷³ Five citations, all five introduced with a formula marked by the same periphrastic construction (by the words "it stands written"),⁷⁴ follow after the first of the Gospel's three references to a saying of Isaiah;⁷⁵ five additional citations sharing not a formula marked by the words "it stands written" but one marked instead by the words "in order that the Scripture/the Word that stands written in their law might be fulfilled"⁷⁶ follow after the second and third of the Gospel's three references to a saying of Isaiah,⁷⁷ which themselves follow fast on the heels of Jesus's first reference, in 12:23, to the onset of his much-anticipated "hour."⁷⁸ Thus the fulfillment formulae appearing in 12:38–40 mark neither the beginning of the Gospel's second half⁷⁹ nor the actual beginning of the Gospel's narrative of its final week.⁸⁰ Rather, the fulfillment formulae appearing in

---

73. John 6:45 cites Isa 54:13, but utilizes a formula that occurs nowhere else in the NT, notably refraining from invoking the name of Isaiah in order to preserve the distinctive function of 1:23 and 12:38–40. See Schuchard, *Scripture within Scripture*, 47–50. With no other OT citations in John is a prophet named.

74. Cf. "that stands written," 15:25.

75. The word order of the first of the five citation formulae (2:17) is the opposite of the four that follow (6:31, 45; 10:34; 12:14). The formula in John 7:37–38 ("just as the Scripture said") appears to intentionally distinguish its reference to the OT from those that are this essay's focus, where the actual words of the Gospel's *Vorlage* (or combination of texts) are reproduced somehow with the offering of the citation. Because John 7:37–38 is an explicit reference to a discrete OT text(s) but not with words reproduced (and so is not an "explicit citation" as defined above), it has been omitted from consideration.

76. The first two citations of the OT offered by Jesus in John 6:45 and 10:34 bear similarly distinguishing formulae (see "in the prophets," 6:45; and "in your law," 10:34; see further "in their law," 15:25).

77. Again (see 12:38–40), πάλιν marks the close pairing of the last of the fulfillment citations appearing in 19:36 and 19:37 (see Hengel, "Old Testament," 394), indicating again that the shortened form of the citation formula appearing with the latter is to be understood in terms of its fuller expression as given with the former (see Francis J. Moloney, "The Gospel of John: The 'End' of Scripture," *Int* 63 [2009]: 359) and helping again to frame. Because 17:12 is as an explicit reference to a discrete OT text(s) but not with words reproduced (and so is not an "explicit citation" as defined above) it too has been omitted from consideration. Because it appears in the narrative of the final week, its "Scripture" is likewise "fulfilled."

78. See further 12:27–33.

79. See, e.g., Thompson, "They Bear Witness to Me," 267–68.

80. Of course, both the beginning of the Gospel's second half and its final week closely relate to what is the focus of the fulfillment formulas.

12:38-40 *and* those that follow instead mark from the time of its onset to the time of its consummation the time of the fulfillment of all things, the time of Jesus's hour.[81] Six citations therefore precede in John 1–12 in anticipation of Jesus's hour;[82] seven follow to mark its fulfillment.

Therefore, in keeping with so much of the everyday technique of his day,[83] the form of the Fourth Evangelist's explicit citations of the Old Testament is explained best in terms of his purposeful redacting of the texts that he recalls from a consistently Greek source.[84] Consciously arranged within the Gospel's concentric design, keyed also to the arrival and the accomplishment of Jesus's hour, the rhetorician's citations are a product of his editorial activity that impressively reflects and persuasively furthers his compositional intention.[85] Carefully adapted to the eventual literary and theological contexts in which they appear, consistently complementing both these contexts and the context, the informing purpose, of the Gospel as a whole, the evangelist's citations effectively further not only the esthetic appeal but also the persuasive power of the Gospel's stylized design. The evangelist's chief purpose in citing the Old Testament is to elucidate the person and the work of Jesus, especially the death of Jesus. His principal goal in his late first-century sociocultural context is that the hearer of his Gospel would be persuaded steadfastly to believe that Jesus is the Christ, the Son of God, so that, believing, the hearer would have life in his name (20:30-31). If the enduring popularity of his Gospel is any indication of the success of his efforts, we may say with some confidence that the evangelist's intention for his Gospel was in the end accomplished.

---

81. See Schuchard, *Scripture within Scripture*, 86. See further Tabb, "Johannine Fulfillment," 496–97; and Hengel, "Old Testament," 393.

82. Cf. in John 1–10 Jesus's six anticipatory signs.

83. See Bynum, *Fourth Gospel*, 20–21, 105–9, 119–27, 136–37.

84. Arguing rightly against the alternative suggestion that the evangelist's citations recall on occasion a *testimonia* collection is Bynum, *Fourth Gospel*, 133–35.

85. The form in which the Old Testament is cited, observes Bynum, *Fourth Gospel*, 1, "is critical for understanding the particular role each of the citations plays in the development of the Johannine narrative. The form of scriptural citation in the FG, though admittedly complex, does not appear to be accidental or haphazard. Instead, it consistently demonstrates careful conciseness and clarity on the part of the author. The specific purpose that each citation carries within the narrative is closely related to the form in which it is cited." See further 18–19.

Illustration 1. The Explicit Citations of the Greek
Old Testament in the Gospel of John

1. The Citation and Its Greek Source Exhibit Word for Word Agreement

John 10:34	ἐγὼ εἶπα θεοί ἐστε
Psalm 81:6	ἐγὼ εἶπα θεοί ἐστε
John 12:38	κύριε, τίς ἐπίστευσεν τῇ ἀκοῇ ἡμῶν; καὶ ὁ βραχίων κυρίου τίνι ἀπεκαλύφθη;
Isaiah 53:1	κύριε, τίς ἐπίστευσεν τῇ ἀκοῇ ἡμῶν; καὶ ὁ βραχίων κυρίου τίνι ἀπεκαλύφθη;
John 19:24	διεμερίσαντο τὰ ἱμάτιά μου ἑαυτοῖς καὶ ἐπὶ τὸν ἱματισμόν μου ἔβαλον κλῆρον
Psalm 21:19	διεμερίσαντο τὰ ἱμάτιά μου ἑαυτοῖς καὶ ἐπὶ τὸν ἱματισμόν μου ἔβαλον κλῆρον

2. The Citation and Its Greek Source Exhibit Close But Not Exact Agreement

John 1:23	ἐγὼ φωνὴ βοῶντος ἐν τῇ ἐρήμῳ· εὐθύνατε τὴν ὁδὸν κυρίου
Isaiah 40:3	φωνὴ βοῶντος ἐν τῇ ἐρήμῳ ἑτοιμάσατε τὴν ὁδὸν κυρίου εὐθείας ποιεῖτε τὰς τρίβους τοῦ θεοῦ ἡμῶν
John 2:17	ὁ ζῆλος τοῦ οἴκου σου καταφάγεταί με
Psalm 68:10	ὁ ζῆλος τοῦ οἴκου σου κατέφαγέν με
John 6:31	ἄρτον ἐκ τοῦ οὐρανοῦ ἔδωκεν αὐτοῖς φαγεῖν
Psalm 77:24	καὶ ἔβρεξεν αὐτοῖς μαννα φαγεῖν καὶ ἄρτον οὐρανοῦ ἔδωκεν αὐτοῖς
John 6:45	καὶ ἔσονται πάντες διδακτοὶ θεοῦ
Isaiah 54:13	καὶ πάντας τοὺς υἱούς σου διδακτοὺς θεοῦ
John 15:25	ἐμίσησάν με δωρεάν
Psalm 68:5	οἱ μισοῦντές με δωρεάν (= 34:19)
John 19:36	ὀστοῦν οὐ συντριβήσεται αὐτοῦ
Exod 12:10, 46	ὀστοῦν οὐ συντρίψετε ἀπ' αὐτου
John 19:37	ὄψονται εἰς ὃν ἐξεκέντησαν
Zech 12:10	ἐπιβλέψονται πρός με ἀνθ' ὧν κατωρχήσαντο
(cf. Theod:	ἐπιβλέψονται πρός με εἰς ὃν ἐξεκέντησαν)

3. The Citation and Its Greek Source Do Not Exhibit Close Agreement

John 12:15	<u>μὴ φοβοῦ, θυγάτηρ Σιών·</u> <u>ἰδοὺ ὁ βασιλεύς σου ἔρχεται</u>, <u>καθήμενος ἐπὶ πῶλον ὄνου</u>
Zechariah 9:9	<u>χαῖρε σφόδρα θύγατερ Σιων</u> κήρυσσε θύγατερ Ιερουσαλημ <u>ἰδοὺ ὁ βασιλεύς σου ἔρχεταί</u> σοι δίκαιος καὶ σῴζων αὐτός πραΰς καὶ <u>ἐπιβεβηκὼς ἐπὶ</u> ὑποζύγιον καὶ <u>πῶλον</u> <u>νέον</u>
John 12:40	<u>τετύφλωκεν</u> <u>αὐτῶν</u> <u>τοὺς ὀφθαλμοὺς</u> <u>καὶ ἐπώρωσεν αὐτῶν τὴν καρδίαν</u>, <u>ἵνα μὴ ἴδωσιν τοῖς ὀφθαλμοῖς καὶ</u> <u>νοήσωσιν</u> <u>τῇ καρδίᾳ</u> <u>καὶ</u> <u>στραφῶσιν</u>, <u>καὶ ἰάσομαι αὐτούς</u>
Isaiah 6:10	<u>ἐπαχύνθη γὰρ ἡ καρδία τοῦ λαοῦ τούτου</u> καὶ τοῖς ὠσὶν αὐτῶν βαρέως ἤκουσαν <u>καὶ</u> <u>τοὺς ὀφθαλμοὺς</u> <u>αὐτῶν</u> <u>ἐκάμμυσαν</u>, μήποτε <u>ἴδωσιν</u> <u>τοῖς ὀφθαλμοῖς καὶ</u> τοῖς ὠσὶν ἀκούσωσιν <u>καὶ τῇ καρδίᾳ</u> <u>συνῶσιν</u> <u>καὶ</u> <u>ἐπιστρέψωσιν</u>, <u>καὶ ἰάσομαι αὐτούς</u>
John 13:18	<u>ὁ τρώγων</u> <u>μου</u> <u>τὸν ἄρτον ἐπῆρεν ἐπ' ἐμὲ</u> <u>τὴν πτέρναν αὐτοῦ</u>
Psalm 40:10	<u>ὁ ἐσθίων ἄρτους</u> <u>μου</u> <u>ἐμεγάλυνεν ἐπ' ἐμὲ</u> <u>πτερνισμόν</u>

Illustration 2
The Concentric Structure of the Gospel of John

1. Prologue (1:1–18)

2. The First Framed Half of the Gospel (1:19–10:42)

   N.B.: In John 1:19–2:11, an initial six-day-long week of days is followed by a first Passover (2:13)

   <u>Across the Jordan, where John is baptizing, Jesus comes, many hear John's testimony regarding Jesus, and they believe in him there (1:19–51).</u>

   N.B.: In 1:23, the Baptist is the first testifier to testify to the testimony of the first testament.

   <u>Across the Jordan, where John was baptizing, Jesus comes, many recall John's testimony regarding Jesus, and they believe in him there (10:40–42).</u>

3. The Second Framed Half of the Gospel (11:1–20:31)

   <u>A troubled Thomas is featured and a dead man rises (John 11).</u>

   The first twenty-four-hour day (Saturday/Sunday) of a final six-day-long week of days appears in John 12 and includes:

   An evening meal (12:2) and foot service (cf. 1:27)/Jesus's anointing for burial (12:3, 7)

   Judas the betrayer (12:4–6)

   The onset of Jesus's hour (12:23, 27)

   N.B.: A framed final week (see esp. 12:3, 7 and 19:38–42) begins and ends in strikingly similar ways (no intervening days are narrated from the anticipatory beginning of Sat/Sun to the finality of Thu/Fri).

   The final twenty-four-hour day (Thursday/Friday) of a final six-day-long week of days appears in 13:1–19:42 and includes:

   An evening meal and foot service (13:2, 4–17)

   Judas the betrayer (13:2, 21–30; 18:1–5)

   The consummation of Jesus's hour (17:1)

   Jesus anointed and buried (19:38–42)

   <u>A dead man rises and a troubled Thomas is featured (John 20).</u>

   N.B.: In John 12–19, a final six-day-long week of days ends with a final Passover

4. Epilogue (21:1–25)

N.B.: Jesus the Lamb
Unnamed disciple
Andrew/Peter
Philip/Nathanael
Jesus's mother
Nicodemus

N.B.: Andrew/Philip
Beloved Disciple
Peter
Jesus's mother
Jesus the Lamb
Nicodemus
Nathanael

Illustration 3. The Explicit Citations of the Greek Old Testament within the Concentric Structure of the Gospel of John

The Citation and Its Greek Source	The Person(s) Citing the OT	The Formula Utilized to Mark the Citation
1. Prologue (1:1–18)		
2. The First Half of the Gospel (1:19–10:42)		
1:23 (Isa 40:3)	the Baptist	καθὼς <u>εἶπεν Ἠσαΐας ὁ προφήτης</u>
2:17 (Ps 68:10)	the disciples	γεγραμμένον ἐστίν
6:31 (Ps 77:24)	the crowd	καθώς ἐστιν γεγραμμένον
6:45 (Isa 54:13)	Jesus	ἔστιν γεγραμμένον <u>ἐν</u> τοῖς προφήταις
10:34 (Ps 81:6)	Jesus	οὐκ ἔστιν γεγραμμένον <u>ἐν τῷ νόμῳ ὑμῶν ὅτι</u>
3. The Second Half of the Gospel (11:1–20:31)		
12:14–15 (<u>Zech 9:9</u>)	narrator	καθώς ἐστιν γεγραμμένον
12:38 (Isa 53:1)	narrator	ἵνα ὁ λόγος <u>Ἠσαΐου τοῦ προφήτου</u> πληρωθῇ <u>ὃν εἶπεν</u>
12:39–40 (Isa 6:10)	narrator	<u>πάλιν εἶπεν Ἠσαΐας</u>
13:18 (Ps 40:10)	Jesus	ἵνα ἡ γραφὴ πληρωθῇ
15:25 (Ps 68:5)	Jesus	ἵνα πληρωθῇ ὁ λόγος ὁ <u>ἐν τῷ νόμῳ αὐτῶν</u> γεγραμμένος <u>ὅτι</u>
19:24 (Ps 21:19)	narrator	ἵνα ἡ γραφὴ πληρωθῇ ἡ λέγουσα
19:36 (Exod 12:10, 46)	narrator	ἵνα ἡ γραφὴ πληρωθῇ
19:37 (<u>Zech 12:10</u>)	narrator	καὶ <u>πάλιν</u> ἑτέρα γραφὴ λέγει
4. Epilogue (21:1–25)		

Quotations of Zechariah in the Fourth Gospel

William Randolph Bynum

1. Two Zecharian Quotations in the Fourth Gospel

It is well known that Zechariah, particularly what is commonly called Second Zechariah (Zech 9–14),[1] had a significant impact on the writers of the four gospels, as well as on the authors of various other New Testament books.[2] The Fourth Gospel (FG) indeed exhibits an unmistakable preference for Second Zechariah,[3] for the only two explicit citations in the FG from the Minor Prophets, or Book of the Twelve,[4] are from this part of Zechariah. The first is in 12:15, citing Zech 9:9 at the triumphal entry, and the second is in 19:37, citing Zech 12:10b at the end of the crucifixion episode.[5] It is evident that, at a minimum, John was in some sense including the Zech 9–14 material in his meditation on the significance of the passion of Christ. But further, if this is seen as a deliberate literary *inclusio*, John has bracketed his passion narrative by these "bookends," as it were,

---

1. See Wm. Randolph Bynum, *The Fourth Gospel and the Scriptures*, NovTSup 114 (Leiden: Brill, 2012), 28–31, regarding the question of the literary unity of Zechariah.

2. Raymond E. Brown, *The Gospel according to John*, 2 vols., AB 29–29A (Garden City, NY: Doubleday, 1966–1970), 1:954, gives a summary of allusions to Zech 9–14 in the FG, as well as Matthew, Mark, and Rev 1:7. Cf. Kurt Aland et al., eds., *The Greek New Testament*, 4th rev. ed. (Stuttgart: Deutsche Bibelgesellschaft, 1994), 888, 900, regarding allusions and verbal parallels to Zechariah in the NT.

3. See Maarten J. J. Menken, "The Minor Prophets in John's Gospel," in *The Minor Prophets in the New Testament*, ed. Maarten J. J. Menken and Steve Moyise, LNTS 377 (London: T&T Clark, 2009), 79–96, for a discussion of the specific quotations of Zechariah, as well as allusions to the same in the FG.

4. Note also that the only other prophetic work explicitly named in FG is Isaiah, in 1:23; 6:45; 12:38, 40.

5. Cf. the allusion to Zech 13:7 in John 16:32.

demonstrating the significant influence of Second Zechariah on his theological interpretation of the entire passion of Christ. As George Brooke reminds us, "All texts reflect a dialogue with other texts,"[6] so it is quite clear that John was interacting at some level with the oracles of Zechariah as he wrote to his audience about the suffering and death of Christ.

The idea of a specific Zecharian *inclusio* is strangely absent from most commentary on citations in the Johannine passion,[7] though there are indicators regarding the concept in general. For example, Raymond Brown does briefly discuss the "paschal lamb" motif of 19:36, which "forms an excellent inclusion with the Baptist's testimony given at the beginning of Jesus' ministry (1:29): 'Here is the Lamb of God who takes away the world's sin.'"[8] Later, Brown mentions John's general use of "inclusion" as a literary characteristic, and in so doing references 19:36–37 together: "This is a way of packaging sections by tying together the beginning and the end."[9] However, in the latter case he does not discuss exactly which section these verses are ending, or mention any relationship between those verses and the citation of Zechariah in 12:15, though he does mention that 19:36–37 "echoes John the Baptist's description of Jesus' mission."[10] Thomas Brodie has a similar thought in viewing 19:35–37 as referring to the entire "central drama of divine self-giving" in the FG, and the "lamb who takes away the sin of the world" in 1:29.[11] Alicia Myers is certainly not off the mark in seeing the double citation of 19:36–37 as "forming an *inclusio* with the previous double citation in Jn 12.38-40,"[12] but does

---

6. George J. Brooke, *The Dead Sea Scrolls and the New Testament: Essays in Mutual Illumination* (London: SPCK, 2005), 93.

7. See, however, Bruce G. Schuchard's insightful chapter in the present volume, "Form versus Function: Citation Technique and Authorial Intention in the Gospel of John," particularly his discussion of the concentric structure of the FG, and his related observation that the first and last of the narrator's six citations are from Zechariah alone.

8. Brown, *John*, 1:953.

9. Raymond E. Brown, *The Gospel and Epistles of John: A Concise Commentary* (Collegeville, MN: Liturgical Press, 1988), 18.

10. Ibid., 96.

11. Thomas L. Brodie, *The Gospel according to John: A Literary and Theological Commentary* (Oxford: Oxford University Press, 1993), 555.

12. Alicia D. Myers, *Characterizing Jesus: A Rhetorical Analysis on the Fourth Gospel's Use of Scripture in Its Presentation of Jesus*, LNTS 458 (London: T&T Clark, 2012), 169.

not specifically tie 19:37 with the citation from Zechariah in 12:15. Frédéric Manns would agree with Myers in tying these two double citations together as an *enchaînement*,[13] but also does not tie the two Zecharian citations together. Without denying their potential relationship to the double citation of 12:38–40 and to other scriptural citations in the FG, it is the purpose of this chapter to explore the dynamics of the specific Zecharian material cited in the FG and how these two citations shaped, to a significant extent, John's perception of the meaning of Christ's passion and its fulfillment of Scripture.

The two citations are obviously placed at critical transition points at the beginning and the end of the passion narrative, the first ending the presentation of the signs that Jesus performed and introducing the passion, and the second finalizing the crucifixion episode. If these verses are included not simply as two coincidentally relevant citations from the Zechariah material, but as a deliberate reflection by the author on the entire context from which they are drawn, then it is quite possible that the content of Zech 9–12, synthesized and symbolized as it were in the citations of 9:9 and 12:10, plays a significant role in shaping the content of the account of the passion week in John 12–19.

2. Zecharian Parallels

In the Zecharian material itself, there are striking literary parallels between 9:9 and 12:10 that begin to point us toward a connection between the two verses. First of all, both verses come near the beginning of their respective oracles, the first oracle beginning with 9:1 and the second with 12:1. Though the textual history of Zech 9 may be complex, since it is uniquely poetic in character in contrast to chapters 10–14, when viewed in a synchronic perspective, it fits well within its present context and flows with Second Zechariah's "inner coherence."[14] Both oracles begin with the words "The burden of the word of the Lord" (משא דבר־יהוה). Whatever position one might take regarding the textual history of this material and the interrelationship of its various sections,[15] the common introductory phrase

---

13. Frédéric Manns, "Zacharie 12.10 Relu en Jean 19.37," *LASBF* 56 (2006): 309.

14. See Carol L. Meyers and Eric M. Meyers, *Zechariah 9–14*, AB 25C (New York: Doubleday, 1993), 31.

15. Cf. Heiko Wenzel, *Reading Zechariah with Zechariah 1:1–6 as the Introduction to the Entire Book*, CBET 59 (Leuven: Peeters, 2011), 197–204, in particular, regarding

connects chapters 9–11 together as an oracle in the mind of the redactor, and 12–14 together as a following oracle.[16]

As to content, the beginning verses of both oracles pronounce judgment on the enemies of Judah with chapter 9 listing specific names (9:1–7), and chapter 12 speaking in general regarding "all peoples" and "all nations" that gather against Jerusalem and Judah (12:3, 9). Both passages then express support for Judah itself with positive actions on God's part (9:8–17 and 12:4–9). Both 9:9 and 12:10 can also be seen as central transition points in their respective passages. Paul Redditt, for example, sees Zech 9, which "announces God's future united kingdom and an earthly king,"[17] in a chiastic structure, with verses 9–10 at the center of the chiasmus.[18] Zechariah 9:9–10 is a high point for Jerusalem, he says, "where God presents the city its new king."[19]

There is a contrast in content between 9:9 and 12:10 at that point, however. While 9:9 calls for rejoicing over the coming king, 12:10a transitions from the promise of divine protection to the pouring out of "a spirit of grace and supplication" that leads to mourning. This mourning is a result of looking upon the one who has been pierced.

If one attempts to look further in identifying actual historical situations behind the two passages, the references are nebulous. It is not clear who is envisioned as the future king in chapter 9,[20] but his characteristics are indeed named: righteous, saved or saving,[21] and humble. The identity of the "pierced one" of 12:10 is even more historically obscure, and seemingly out of reach for modern scholarship. However, the decidedly transhistorical characteristics of Second Zechariah need not obscure the

---

the unity of Zech 1–14, and a holistic reading and interpretation of the entire book in the light of 1:1–6.

16. In addition, it provides continuity with Malachi, which begins with the same phrase.

17. Paul L. Redditt, *Zechariah 9–14*, IECOT (Stuttgart: Kolhammer, 2012), 16.

18. Ibid., 36.

19. Ibid., 14.

20. Ibid., 29, sees Zech 9 fitting well in the late sixth century BCE, "while hopes for Zerubbabel or some other Davidide to rule over Jerusalem, Judah, and Ephraim were alive."

21. See the interesting constructions here between MT צדיק ונושע הוא עני and LXX δίκαιος καὶ σῴζων αὐτός, πραΰς. Cf., e.g., Lancelot C. Brenton's English translation of the LXX text: "a Saviour"; NETS: "salvific is he"; NIV: "having salvation."

intended underlying message of eschatological hope in the two passages, and in the whole of Second Zechariah.

The contrast continues as the verses following 9:9 speak of God's actions on behalf of Judah, while the verses following 12:10 record a national mourning by Judah itself over the one who has been pierced. Further, though both the joy of the king's arrival and the mourning over the pierced one are the response to God's initiative on behalf of his people, yet the mourning of 12:10b is the result of an unfortunate and negative action on the part of the people, when they recognize the significance of what they have done in piercing this unnamed person. In the larger context, however, even the mourning that is described by Zechariah appears to be a significant part of the process of God's plan for the future of the nation leading to purification in 13:1-6, refinement through fire in 13:9, and ultimately to united worship in 14:16-21.

If there is truly an "overall integrity" to the six chapters of Zech 9-14,[22] it is not unreasonable to suppose that John sees a specific connection between his citations of 9:9 and 12:10 in terms of God's actions on behalf of his people, restored relationship (cf. the prominent theme of a double "return" in Zech 1:3), and eschatological hope. John's meditation on Christ's passion is in dialogue with these two oracles, and draws on the truth lying at the heart of them both. These two key verses can be seen together as making an important two-pronged statement about his interpretation of the passion of Christ. When they are viewed in the light of their Zecharian context,[23] there is a fitting flow with the Johannine passion narrative. Further, when they are compared and contrasted in terms of introductory formula, form, and purpose, there is additional confirmation that the specific placement of these two citations is not accidental, and offers additional insights into the FG's interpretation of the passion narrative.

---

22. So Meyers and Meyers, *Zechariah 9-14*, 34, for whom "there is a linkage in every chapter with every other chapter of this prophetic work." Cf. also William Hendriksen, *Exposition of the Gospel according to John*, NTC (Grand Rapids: Baker, 1954), 190, who categorized the entire "fourth division" of Zechariah (9-14) as comprising "predictions and promises regarding the future of Zion, and the rejection and subsequent glory of its Shepherd-King."

23. See Wenzel, *Reading Zechariah*, 2, who states, "This research argues for reading Zechariah as one book."

3. Zechariah 9:9 in John 12:15

With the first of the quotations in John 12:15, John quotes Zech 9:9: καθώς ἐστιν γεγραμμένον· μὴ φοβοῦ, θυγάτηρ Σιών· ἰδοὺ ὁ βασιλεύς σου ἔρχεται, καθήμενος ἐπὶ πῶλον ὄνου ("just as it is written: 'Do not fear, daughter Zion! Look! Your king is coming, seated on a donkey's colt'").

3.1. Introductory Formula

The introductory phrase to the citation καθώς ἐστιν γεγραμμένον ("just as it is written," 12:14b) is noteworthy. First of all, it is the final occurrence of that type of phrase in the FG, paralleling similar expressions in 2:17; 6:31, 45; and 10:34.[24] Following this citation, the introductory formula for subsequent citations changes quite dramatically to the phrase "so that the word/Scripture might be fulfilled," or similar constructions.[25] Thus the introductory formula of 12:15 forms a turning point in John's use and understanding of his scriptural citations.

This use of an introductory formula is deliberate, both for rhetorical and for theological reasons, indicating the manner in which John perceives the relevance and meaning of those particular citations for his Gospel. Up to and including 12:15, the focus is on the fact that "it is written." It is evident that chapters 2–12 of the FG record the "signs" that Jesus performed

---

24. See also 1:23, "just as Isaiah the prophet said," as well as phrases with similar intent in 7:38 and 7:42.

25. See John 12:38-40; 13:18; 15:25; 19:24; 19:36-37. For further discussion regarding the introductory formulae in the FG, see D. A. Carson, "John and the Johannine Epistles," in *It Is Written: Scripture Citing Scripture*, ed. D. A. Carson and H. G. M. Williamson (Cambridge: Cambridge University Press, 1988): 245-64; Bruce G. Schuchard, *Scripture within Scripture: The Interrelationship of Form and Function in the Explicit Old Testament Citations in the Gospel of John*, SBLDS 133 (Atlanta: Scholars Press, 1992), xi-xvii, 72-74, 141-42, 151-56; Hans Hübner, "New Testament Interpretation of the Old Testament," in *From the Beginnings to the Middle Ages (Until 1300)*, vol. 1 of *Hebrew Bible/Old Testament: The History of Its Interpretation*, ed. Magne Saebo (Göttingen: Vandenhoeck & Ruprecht, 1996), 358-62; Christopher D. Stanley, "The Rhetoric of Quotations: An Essay on Method," in *Early Christian Interpretation of the Scriptures*, ed. Craig A. Evans and James A. Sanders, JSNTSup 148 (Sheffield: Sheffield Academic, 1997), 44-58; Paul Miller, "They Saw His Glory and Spoke of Him," in *Hearing the Old Testament in the New Testament*, ed. Stanley E. Porter (Grand Rapids: Eerdmans, 2006), 130-33.

that pointed both to his divine power and the reality of his person. John's use of "it is written" as introduction to scriptural citation indicates that the Scriptures themselves have already pointed ahead to the ministry of Christ. "It [Scripture] is a proleptic announcement of what is to come that carries the stamp of divine authority."[26] During this period of his ministry, Jesus's actions in John's viewpoint are flowing completely in harmony with the Scriptures, affirming and continuing divine revelation.

Francis Moloney points out that this series of citations indicates to the audience (that is, the original Jewish audience depicted in each episode) who Jesus truly is in a moment of revelation. "In the midst of misunderstanding and inability to understand who Jesus is and what he is doing during his public ministry Scripture provides the correct explanation to 'the Jews,' whose sacred text is cited."[27] John appears to be saying that those actions on Jesus's part should come as no surprise to an audience even reasonably knowledgeable of the Scriptures (original audience or reading audience alike), for Jesus was continuing to do and to say exactly what those Scriptures had indicated all along. As Myers explains, "In this way, the evangelist vividly illustrates that it is the *same* God who acts on behalf of Israel in Scripture who acts in and through this Jesus."[28]

After 12:15, and continuing through chapter 19, the focus is on the reality "that the Scripture might be fulfilled." Though John does not specify exactly why he begins to use the alternative introductory formulae that he does, his abrupt change in form at this point must be seen as significant. In the absence of explanation it seems that either he saw the use of such formulae as self-evident, or perhaps assumed his audience would need no explanation from their own literary background. Such a transition as this could indicate that, up to and including 12:15, Jesus was doing "written" things in the sense of continuing in the flow of prior revelation, conforming to the Scriptures, and affirming their truth. Now, in contrast, scriptural citations in the passion narrative begin to take previously written scriptural material to a level of fulfillment that is beyond parallel. That is not to say that what Jesus did as recorded in the previous signs material was ordinary or mundane by any means, and certainly not

---

26. Miller, "They Saw His Glory and Spoke of Him," 131.
27. Francis J. Moloney, "The Gospel of John: The 'End' of Scripture," *Int* 63 (2009): 357–66.
28. Myers, *Characterizing Jesus*, 131 (emphasis original).

of any less importance.²⁹ They were not simply preliminary indicators, but rather an integral and significant aspect of his ministry. However, the change in introductory formula indicates that a change in perception and perspective is now taking place between what Jesus continued to do that had already been written, compared to what was now coming to a new and unique depth of development and fulfillment in the events recorded in the passion narrative. The change seems to indicate that Jesus is now playing a unique role in the unfolding of salvation history and bringing the Scriptures to an unprecedented significance by his fulfilling sacrifice for humanity's salvation. These scriptural citations now shed new light on the events of Christ's passion, as the passion events also open up new depths of meaning and interpretation for the verses that are cited. Martin Hengel says, "No Evangelist in the passion narrative emphasizes the need for Scripture to be fulfilled and the kingship of Jesus as much as John does"; the FG is "narrated Christology" that is "grounded throughout in the Old Testament."³⁰ Further, Paul Miller reminds us, "The true meaning of Scripture cannot be found within the text itself, but only in its fulfillment in Jesus and in the sending of the Spirit."³¹

The triumphal entry of Jesus into Jerusalem is a most significant transition episode in the FG. It is followed by the summary statement in 12:37 expressing the irony of unbelief in the presence of such signs as Jesus had already performed, and affirmed by the scriptural citations in 12:38–40. The previous use of the introductory formula "it is written" heightens and augments the irony of unbelief. The unthinkable has been done: the very signs that were in complete harmony with what was already written in Scripture were misunderstood and rejected. An added dimension of fulfillment then begins with the subsequent introductory formula from 12:38 on, "that it might be fulfilled." Now for the FG, not only do the Scriptures reveal who Jesus truly is, but they are indeed fulfilled.

---

29. Note the final use of the word "signs" in 20:30.

30. Martin Hengel, "The Prologue of the Gospel of John as the Gateway to Christological Truth," in *The Gospel of John and Christian Theology*, ed. Richard Bauckham and Carl Mosser (Grand Rapids: Eerdmans, 2008), 271.

31. Miller, "They Saw His Glory and Spoke of Him," 131.

3.2. Form

An adequate perspective regarding the form of citation is an important piece in an overall understanding of John's purposes in quoting Scripture. If he were presenting a direct and precise quotation from a contemporary textual tradition, it would reveal quite a different mind-set than if he were modifying or manipulating a scriptural form to fit his theological agenda. A discussion of the textual form is thus vitally related to the development of one's perspective on John's handling of his sources, his rhetorical strategy, and his credibility in the presentation of Jesus.

The form of citation in 12:15 is very concise and simple, characterized by the venerable A. T. Robertson as simply "from Zech. 9:9 shortened,"[32] by Rudolf Schnackenburg as "heavily abbreviated,"[33] by Moloney as "very loose,"[34] and by D. A. Carson as "an abridgment of Zechariah 9:9."[35] Gleason Archer and Gregory Chirichigno describe it as a "conflate quotation" that draws from Isa 35:4 for the opening phrase, that equals MT and LXX in the second phrase, and offers "a briefer summary" (than Matt 21:5) in the final phrase.[36] It preserves the key words and phrases, "paring the quotation down to its bare essentials,"[37] says J. Ramsey Michaels, and to G. K. Beale and Carson, "it appears that the quotation is shortened in John to include only what is relevant to the actual context."[38] Jo-Ann Brant offers a picturesque comment, stating that this citation (and the previous one from Ps 118) is "shaved" in order to "emphasize the acclamation of Jesus

---

32. A. T. Robertson, *Word Pictures in the New Testament* (New York: Harper & Brothers, 1932), 5:222.

33. Rudolf Schnackenburg, *The Gospel according to St. John*, trans. Kevin Smyth (New York: Crossroad, 1982), 2:376.

34. Francis J. Moloney, *The Gospel of John*, SP 4 (Collegeville, MN: Liturgical Press, 1998), 358.

35. D. A. Carson, *The Gospel according to John*, PNTC 4 (Grand Rapids: Eerdmans, 1991), 433.

36. Gleason L. Archer and Gregory Chirichigno, *Old Testament Quotations in the New Testament* (Eugene, OR: Wipf & Stock, 2005), 130.

37. J. Ramsey Michaels, *The Gospel of John*, NICNT (Grand Rapids: Eerdmans, 2010), 677.

38. Andreas J. Köstenberger, "John," in *Commentary on the New Testament Use of the Old Testament*, ed. G. K. Beale and D. A. Carson (Grand Rapids: Baker Academic, 2007), 473.

as 'King.'"³⁹ Menken sees it as based on a LXX text and reworked by the Fourth Evangelist.⁴⁰ Myers characterizes the quotation as "a *paraphrastic version of Zech. 9.9*" that "does not match any known form of Zech. 9.9."⁴¹

There is no doubt that here John is indeed quoting Zech 9:9. Both the formal introduction to the quotation, "just as it is written," and the very wording of the quotation itself point without question to that referent. However, the form of the quotation is not easily identifiable. The question regarding the source from which it was drawn, whether quoted from a particular written source, influenced by the dynamics of orality in the era, or quoted loosely from memory, has been debated often, and that debate need not be recited nor continued here.⁴²

It is important to note, however, that renewed confidence in recent years in the reliability of the FG,⁴³ together with an improved understanding of the scriptural text and the history of its development in the late first century CE, offer the possibility of an increased understanding of the way in which John cites the Scriptures, and in this case Zechariah. Admittedly, the historical and geographical accuracy of the author of the FG that would lead one to take him seriously as a historical witness⁴⁴ does not of necessity say anything about his scriptural citations. It would at least suggest, however, that he is not carelessly mishandling or misquoting his

---

39. Jo-Ann A. Brant, *John*, PNTC (Grand Rapids: Baker Academic, 2011), 191.

40. Menken, "Minor Prophets," 85.

41. Myers, *Characterizing Jesus*, 156, 159.

42. A number of proposals have been offered in addition to those cited here, including deliberate substitution of one phrase for another, compound citation, reflection of an independent knowledge of Hebrew, citing a more concise textual tradition, and drawing from a LXX text corrected toward a Hebrew text that is more concise than MT. For further discussion, see Bynum, *The Fourth Gospel*, 128–131; Myers, *Characterizing Jesus*, 155–63; Schuchard, *Scripture within Scripture*, 72–76.

43. See, e.g., Craig L. Blomberg, *The Historical Reliability of John's Gospel* (Downers Grove, IL: InterVarsity Press, 2001). See also C. Stephen Evans, "The Historical Reliability of John's Gospel: From What Perspective Should It Be Assessed?" in *The Gospel of John and Christian Theology*, ed. Richard Bauckham and Carl Mosser (Grand Rapids: Eerdmans, 2008), 91–119. Cf., however, Mark W. G. Stibbe, *John's Gospel*, NTR (London: Routledge, 1994), 53, who holds that "John's gospel is the product of a creative, historical imagination."

44. See John B. Gabel, Charles B. Wheeler, and Anthony D. York, *The Bible as Literature, an Introduction*, 3rd ed. (Oxford: Oxford University Press, 1996), 227. See also D. Moody Smith, *The Fourth Gospel in Four Dimensions: Judaism and Jesus, the Gospels, and Scripture* (Columbia, SC: University of South Carolina Press, 2008), 133–43.

scriptural texts. If he was a careful and accurate writer in other areas, then it is at least probable that he used the same care in citing sacred writings. If, as Myers well states, "Scripture works with the evangelist's rhetoric to persuade his audience of the accuracy of his portrayal of Jesus,"[45] then one would be hard pressed to argue for mishandled citations in the FG that would offend the sensibilities of his contemporary reading or listening audience.[46] Also, if it is possible that John, in comparison with the Synoptics, was acquainted in other areas with "alternative traditions that are arguably historical,"[47] it is a parallel possibility that he was familiar with textual traditions that were reliable as well.

Further, it is evident that John was "firmly within the Jewish tradition and was as well informed on the scriptures as any of the other gospel writers.... Many episodes and many terms in John's gospel presuppose a fairly intimate familiarity with Jewish thought."[48] This indicates that his use of the Jewish sacred writings would demonstrate sensitivity to contemporary Jewish practice, and would reveal a vital element of his strategy for proclaiming Jesus. On the other hand, one must admit that his christological interpretation and creative reshaping of the traditions available to him would not of necessity bind him to a specific practice. In cases such as these, where a New Testament writer is citing the Scriptures in a form that is not readily apparent or that does not exactly parallel well-known MT or LXX forms, the answer to the source of the quotation is certainly not a simple one. However, in John's use of Scripture to persuade his audience regarding the reality of Jesus, it is a safe assumption that he would not have used a spurious or inaccurate citation that would have needlessly offended his audience, and thus detracted from his credibility or damaged his case.

In the era in which he wrote, it is apparent that neither Judaism[49] nor the Christian church was concerned about having a single, precise form of the scriptural text. R. Timothy McLay's description of the "pluriformity

---

45. Myers, *Characterizing Jesus*, 2.

46. See, e.g., Menken, *Old Testament Quotations*, 207, "the [editorial] changes [in John's cited texts] are legitimate insofar as they stay within the boundaries of the common practices of explanation and alteration of texts in John's Jewish milieu"; Schuchard, *Scripture within Scripture*, xv–xvii, 151–56.

47. Smith, *Fourth Gospel in Four Dimensions*, 118.

48. Gabel, Wheeler, and York, *Bible as Literature*, 228.

49. Dennis Stamps's call for precision in defining terms related to Judaism in the first century CE is well taken. See Stamps, "Use of the Old Testament," 14–16. However, in light of the difficulty of precisely identifying the audience of the FG and the

(multiple forms) of the biblical text in the time of the early church"[50] clearly indicates that there was no single, universally accepted text of the Scriptures in that era. According to Eugene Ulrich, it is apparent that there existed "multiple literary editions of biblical books and passages" with no two manuscripts of any biblical book that were identical.[51] The writings that were moving toward canonical status at the time were considered no less sacred than they are today, yet their textual form was not yet standardized. As McLay puts it,

> There are numerous textual witnesses to any particular book that later became canonized.... There would have been no such thing as a biblical text in the context of the early church.... There are a wide variety of textual variants, ranging from single words or morphemes to whole sentences and paragraphs, when one compares the ancient texts for any book of Scripture.[52]

Brooke explains: "We are now just beginning to realize ... that in the first century C.E., while there is a move towards some kind of standardization of the Hebrew text form, there remains plenty of evidence for a plurality of text types extant in Palestine during the first centuries B.C.E. and C.E."[53]

In the specific case of the Book of the Twelve that is before us in the two citations we are considering, extant evidence illustrates the general truth regarding biblical manuscripts of the era in demonstrating more than a single literary edition. John would have had the possibility of various textual traditions available to him in a scriptural textual world characterized by pluriformity, and his use of those Scriptures would have been in keeping with contemporary rhetorical practices.[54]

---

author's relationship to his audience, perhaps it is justifiable here to simply use the generic term "Judaism."

50. R. Timothy McLay, "Biblical Texts and the Scriptures for the New Testament Church," in *Hearing the Old Testament in the New Testament*, ed. Stanley E. Porter (Grand Rapids: Eerdmans, 2006), 38.

51. Eugene Ulrich, "The Bible in the Making: The Scriptures at Qumran," in *The Bible at Qumran: Text, Shape, and Interpretation*, ed. Peter W. Flint (Grand Rapids: Eerdmans, 2001), 57.

52. McLay, "Biblical Texts," 43–44. Yet there also "would have been a variety of written books (texts) and collections of books (like the Torah) that were accorded the status of Scripture."

53. Brooke, *Dead Sea Scrolls*, 92–93.

54. See Bynum, *Fourth Gospel*, 19–25.

The significant amount of variation in the citation in comparison to known textual forms allows for a number of possible explanations in addition to textual pluriformity.[55] As mentioned above,[56] these include John's desire simply to present an abbreviated and concise quotation that avoids any ambiguity, his citing an alternative and more concise Greek textual tradition that was available to him, or his personal translation of an abbreviated Hebrew text.

Perhaps the most glaring variation from known textual forms is John's substitution of the opening phrase, "Rejoice greatly," with that of "Do not fear." It is quite possible that "rejoicing" seemed completely incongruous with John's reflection on the coming suffering and death of Jesus, or even on the current oppressive political situation, and so perhaps the change does not reflect an alternative text. His substitution of a fitting and well-known phrase, "Do not fear," could reflect his interaction with other passages in addition to the cited verse from Zechariah, such as Isa 40:9; 41:10; 44:2; or Zeph 3:16.[57] However, such a substitution would not have been offensive to his audience, and would have been quite in keeping with first-century quotation of sacred works.

3.3. Purpose

John uses this citation to explain Jesus's finding and sitting on a donkey as he entered Jerusalem. This action follows the proclamation of the crowd, and is Jesus's response to that proclamation. As the crowd proclaims him king, Jesus responds by finding a donkey and riding on it into the city.

In John's perception, it is evident that Jesus himself was not simply passively paralleling Scripture, but rather deliberately moving to flow with and fulfill the promise spoken by Zechariah. F. F. Bruce concludes: "It is probable to the point of certainty that our Lord himself had the oracle

---

55. See also Menken, "Minor Prophets," 81–85, for further discussion of possible explanations.

56. See n44.

57. A number of scholars have indicated similar possibilities. See, e.g., C. K. Barrett, *The Gospel according to St. John*, 2nd ed. (Philadelphia: Westminster John Knox, 1978), 418–19; Brown, *John*, 1:458; Wim Weren, "Jesus' Entry into Jerusalem," in *The Scriptures in the Gospels*, ed. C. M. Tuckett, BETL 131 (Leuven: Leuven University Press, 1997), 126–27.

in mind, and deliberately arranged to fulfil it."[58] As John portrays Jesus's active participation in that fulfillment, it speaks of the Lord's deep awareness of his own messiahship in the FG, as well as his high view of the truth of Scripture as expressing the will of the Father.[59] It also speaks of the significant part that Zech 9–14 played in Jesus's understanding of his role.[60] Thus Jesus is quoted earlier in 10:35, "and the Scripture cannot be broken" (NASB).

Jesus appears to be affirming in some sense as legitimate the enthusiasm of the crowd in their acceptance of his entry into Jerusalem. Indeed, John sees their reception of Jesus as a continued testimony to his power to raise one from the dead (see 12:17). However, it is possible at the same time that Jesus is critiquing that jubilation and setting some parameters for it by this symbolic peaceful action of riding a donkey instead of a warhorse.[61] Jesus says nothing directly to contradict the acclamation of the crowd, but instead moves to modify it by his actions. If he perceives the response of the crowd as a superficial celebration turning into nationalistic enthusiasm, he is challenging that viewpoint and breaking the mold by riding on a small and humble donkey.[62] By Jesus's silent action, the reader is left to wonder what his inner thoughts might have been.[63]

Bruce, however, does see Jesus's action as one of critique:

> They [the crowd] had their own clear ideas of what the King of Israel would do; Jesus, without repudiating the title which they gave him, repudiated the military and political ideas which they associated with it by his following action.... Jesus' riding into Jerusalem on a donkey was an acted parable designed to correct the misguided expectations of the pilgrim crowds and to show the city its true way of peace.[64]

---

58. F. F. Bruce, *The Gospel of John* (Grand Rapids: Eerdmans, 1983), 260.

59. James Montgomery Boice, *The Gospel of John* (Grand Rapids: Zondervan, 1985), 806.

60. Steve Moyise, *Jesus and Scripture* (Grand Rapids: Baker Academic, 2010), 105. See also Craig A. Evans, "Jesus and Zechariah's Messianic Hope," in *Authenticating the Activities of Jesus* (ed. Bruce Chilton and Craig A. Evans; Leiden: Brill, 1999), 373–88.

61. Cf. Jesus's avoidance of being proclaimed king in John 6:15.

62. Brodie, *John*, 409–10.

63. Stibbe's viewpoint of the portrayal of Jesus by John as an "elusive hero" with "intentional obscurity" is well taken. See Stibbe, *John's Gospel*, 30–31.

64. Bruce, *John*, 259–60.

Carson also views it as having the effect of "damping down nationalist expectations."[65] Herman Ridderbos sees this action on Jesus's part as an acceptance of kingship that nonetheless expresses the peaceful nature of that kingship.[66] Whatever his thought regarding the action of enthusiastic reception, Jesus's action made it quite evident that he was contrasting his entry into Jerusalem with that of others who would enter a city on a warhorse with a proud and haughty attitude to demonstrate their conquest. A. R. Faussett writes that such an image "contrasts beautifully with the haughty Grecian conqueror who came to destroy, whereas Messiah came to save."[67]

Looking at the grammatical structure of the acclamation of Jesus by the crowd, the second word of verse 14, δέ ("but," an "adversative and copulative Particle"[68]), could be taken either as a continuation of the thought of the crowd, or as a critique of the same. Even if our inclination is to accept it as a continuation, it may also express a deeper dimension of the concept than what the crowd understood, as it is filled with additional content from Zechariah. Jesus may be accepting the crowd's acclamation in one dimension, while moving to critique it or at least deepen it at another level. "By sitting on the ass, in fulfilment of Zech 9:9," Pryor writes, "he accepts the title king-Messiah, but rejects the political associations."[69]

In contrast, Brant sees Jesus in harmony with the crowd, while the disciples misunderstood: "While Jesus and the crowd act in consort, the disciples are represented as out of step with the action."[70] John's writing here allows for that interpretation as well. John may have seen in the spontaneous response of the people a truer perception of the meaning of Jesus's entry than the response evident in the misunderstanding of the disciples.

Perhaps it is also in some sense a "confession" on the part of the author regarding the misunderstanding of the disciples (see also 2:22; 14:26; 20:9). At the very least, it is an admission of a former ignorance that has

---

65. Carson, *John*, 433.

66. Herman N. Ridderbos, *The Gospel according to John: A Theological Commentary*, trans. John Vriend (Grand Rapids: Eerdmans, 1997), 423–24.

67. A. R. Faussett, "Zechariah," in *The Classic Bible Commentary*, ed. Owen Collins (Wheaton, IL: Crossway, 1999), 857.

68. LSJ 371.

69. Pryor, *John*, 134. In response to Pryor, however, "king" by definition includes some political associations, though indeed Jesus is moving to modify the crowd's assumptions in that regard. See quotation from Elizabeth Achtemeier below.

70. Brant, *John*, 191.

now been corrected by postresurrection meditation on the event, perhaps alluding to the illumination of the Spirit mentioned in 14:26 and 16:12–15.

John does not delve into the depth of understanding or misunderstanding that the crowd might have had at this point. He simply indicates that the disciples themselves had the wrong idea as the event unfolded, and only later understood the true meaning, which is now offered to the audience of the FG. However, John's continued discussion in chapter 12 does reveal the inability of the crowds present at the time to comprehend fully the nature of Christ's messiahship (see 12:34, 37), as Myers has aptly pointed out: "The next appeal to Scripture in v. 34 and the eventual rejection of Jesus in vv. 37–50 confirm their inability to understand completely."[71]

It is evident as well that John is alluding to more than a single verse to support his perception regarding the triumphal entry. By citing Zech 9:9, he is recalling the context of Zechariah's encouragement for the postexilic audience in Jerusalem to rejoice over the arrival of their humble king, who is seated on a donkey. This is not an isolated prooftext excised from Zech 9, but one that carries with it a significant divine promise from the context.[72] Certainly such an insightful person as the author of the FG would have understood clearly the section of Scripture from which this citation was drawn, for indeed the entire context must be kept in mind, if the full force of the citation is to be realized.[73] Thus Ridderbos proclaims: "When Jesus mounts a donkey, he fulfills not just this element but the entire prophecy."[74]

Carson, for example, sees three things that stand out in Zech 9 in the coming of Israel's gentle king: the cessation of war, the proclamation of peace to the nations, and the blood of God's covenant that signals release for the prisoners.[75] In Zechariah's viewpoint, this peaceful ruler was coming not to impose military discipline as a conqueror, but to demonstrate humility and compassion for the needs of his people, and to lift their spirits to the hope and restoration that lie ahead. As a result of postresurrection meditation on the event by the disciples,[76] the triumphal entry of

---

71. Myers, *Characterizing Jesus*, 158.

72. The number of fanciful and allegorical interpretations of this passage from early Christian writers is perhaps not surprising. See Alberto Ferreiro, ed., *The Twelve Prophets*, ACCS OT 14 (Downers Grove, IL: InterVarsity Press, 2003), 258–63.

73. Carson, *John*, 433.

74. Ridderbos, *John*, 423.

75. Carson, *John*, 433.

76. See John 12:16.

Christ into Jerusalem is seen by the FG as fulfillment of this arrival of the royal personage and the accompanying call for celebration.

Redditt believes that Zech 9:1–6a has a specific objective in view: "to sketch the borders of the coming new kingdom of God."[77] The prophet was envisioning a future "politico-spiritual reality"[78] that would both broaden the borders of Israel on all sides and include God's control of the entire area. Verses 9–10, then, envision the role of the new king in Jerusalem, says Redditt, affirming Marvin Sweeney's argument that Zech 9–11 and 12–14 function to "explain how Yhwh's statements concerning the restoration of Zion envisioned in Zech 1:7–8:21 would be realized."[79] This arriving king is described as "righteous, liberated, and humble," through whom God will bless the entire land.[80] And if the Zecharian context is taken into account, the rule of this king will extend much further than the borders of Palestine as he "commands peace to the nations" and establishes dominion "from sea to sea, and from the River to the ends of the earth" (Zech 9:10 NRSV). Elizabeth Achtemeier agrees that the use of the oracle of Zech 9 by the gospel writers carries with it the context of Zech 9. However, she sees the humility of this figure in the prophetic oracle not in the use of a donkey per se, but in the total dependence on God for his defense, his office, and his reign. "His is a kingship of total powerlessness, upheld by an unseen but Divine Warrior, who possesses all power."[81]

One question that naturally arises at this point is how much understanding John might be assuming on the part of his audience regarding the full context of Second Zechariah. First of all, the indicators in the FG regarding the audience to which it is directed are somewhat ambiguous. The variety of opinions on the matter indicates the ambiguity of the clues available in the FG, and the wide range of possible conclusions that one might draw from them. Suggestions include a primarily Jewish audience, a mainly gentile Christian audience, Jewish opponents to the gospel in dialogue with the Johannine community, Jewish and gentile Christians, or simply a broad, general Christian audience.[82] The lack

---

77. Redditt, *Zechariah 9–14*, 38.
78. Ibid., 38–43.
79. Ibid., 44, citing Marvin A. Sweeney, *The Twelve Prophets*, BO (Collegeville, MN: Liturgical Press, 2000), 2:574.
80. Redditt, *Zechariah 9–14*, 44–45.
81. Elizabeth Achtemeier, *Nahum–Malachi*, IBC (Atlanta: John Knox, 1986), 154.
82. See, respectively, (1) Severino Pancaro, *The Law in the Fourth Gospel: The*

of scholarly consensus on the issue allows us plenty of latitude to draw our own conclusions from the indicators that are present. It is possible to safely assume a quite diverse group of Jewish and non-Jewish listeners, Christian believers, and not-yet-believers.[83] One could see validity in Andreas Köstenberger's viewpoint that John ultimately envisioned a "universal readership," while his original audience "seems to have consisted primarily of Diaspora Jews and proselytes."[84]

And, of course, how one might see the possible audience of the FG is closely connected to how one would also view the purpose for John's writing. If one assumes a diverse audience, understanding of the Zecharian citation by John's audience could have ranged from no understanding of the citation whatsoever to a familiarity with both the citation and its meaning as situated in the context of Second Zechariah. Though it is quite reasonable to assume a significant understanding on John's part of both the immediate context of his citations as well as the full meaning of Zech 9–14, we are left to wonder at the level of understanding of his audience.[85] However, whatever the level of understanding may have been with a particular person or group in the audience of the FG, we are not far off the mark to believe that the author himself expected a significant level of understanding or, at a minimum, was calling his audience into a recognition of the importance of this cited Scripture.

Further, it is not an impossible task to ponder the function of a particular citation in the narrative and the anticipated effect on the intended audience. It is doubtful that the popular crowd that was receiving Christ at the actual event of the triumphal entry would have had a full understanding of the Zecharian context. With enthusiasm over Lazarus's raising occupying

---

Torah and the Gospel, Moses and Jesus, Judaism and Christianity according to John, NovTSup 42 (Leiden: Brill, 1975), 531; (2) Martin Hengel, *The Johannine Question*, trans. John Bowden (London: SCM, 1989), 119; (3) D. A. Carson, "John and the Johannine Epistles," in Carson and Williamson, *It Is Written*, 248; (4) Thomas L. Brodie, *The Quest for the Origin of John's Gospel* (Oxford: Oxford University Press, 1993), 11; (5) Richard Bauckham, "The Audience of the Fourth Gospel," in *Jesus in Johannine Tradition*, ed. Robert T. Fortna and Tom Thatcher (Louisville: Westminster John Knox, 2001), 101–3.

83. See Bynum, *The Fourth Gospel*, 12–15.

84. Andreas J. Köstenberger, *John*, BECNT (Grand Rapids: Baker Academic, 2004), 8.

85. Stamps may have a point in declaring that "assessing the level of audience understanding and perception is virtually impossible" ("Use of the Old Testament," 17).

the forefront of their thinking, it is a matter of speculation what further messianic expectation may have been in the minds of the people (see 12:17–19). However, popular messianic expectation, varied though it may have been in that era, still in broad outline may not have been antithetical to the full context of Second Zechariah. On the other hand, it is quite possible that John may be seeing the fervor of the crowd as misplaced nationalistic expectations of the Messiah in line with the disciples' own misunderstanding of the significance of the event[86] and later corrected by thoughtful reflection.

This first citation from Zechariah became for John an impetus for reflection on Jesus's triumphal entry that would carry him, the disciples, and the audience of the FG to a new level of understanding of Jesus's messiahship. That deepened level of spiritual perception is continued in the citation of 19:37, the second half of John's Zecharian *inclusio*.

4. Zechariah 12:10 in John 19:37

In this final scriptural citation of the FG, John closes the crucifixion episode with these words: καὶ πάλιν ἑτέρα γραφὴ λέγει· ὄψονται εἰς ὃν ἐξεκέντησαν ("And again another Scripture says, 'They will look on him whom they pierced'").

4.1. Introductory Formula

This citation is introduced with a unique formula: καὶ πάλιν ἑτέρα γραφὴ λέγει. Citing Adolph Schlatter, Brown sees it as a "fixed rabbinic formula for introducing another citation."[87] It is unique both in the form of the entire phrase and in the fact that it is the only introductory formula in the FG passion narrative that uses a verb in the present active indicative. It does not stand alone, however, in that the phrase καὶ πάλιν indicates clearly that it shares in some sense the force of the introductory formula of 19:36: ἵνα ἡ γραφὴ πληρωθῇ, which, as noted previously, is the common form for citations in John's passion narrative.

The textual provenance of the citation in 19:36 raises a number of issues that need not be dealt with here.[88] Nonetheless, the fact that 19:37

---

86. Köstenberger, *John*, 372.
87. Brown, *John*, 1:938.
88. See discussion of this verse in Bynum, *Fourth Gospel*, 119–27, as well as in Myers, *Characterizing Jesus*, 168–69.

shares the introductory formula with verse 36 calls for some explanation. As noted above in dealing with the citation of Zech 9:9 in 12:15, the unique introductory formulae in the passion narrative suggest a new depth of development and fulfillment of the Scriptures.

William Hendriksen gives a minimalistic viewpoint of the fulfillment of this citation in 19:37: "For the present—here in 19:37—all that is meant is that the spear thrust fulfilled the prophecy."[89] Brant goes further, noting that the narrator provides a prophecy to explain the events:

> The clear purpose of the fulfillment formula is to end with the chord that has been struck throughout the crucifixion narrative (18:9, 32; 19:24, 28). While the agents of the particular events may have their own motives and think that they act according to their own intent, events unfold according to a divine plan.[90]

James Montgomery Boice also speaks of a remarkable, complicated, and improbable fulfillment: "Moreover, it was the exact opposite of these two prophecies that the soldiers set out to fulfill.... Yet they ended up fulfilling the prophecies."[91]

Here there is profound irony in John's presentation: unbeknownst to those who carried out the military orders for his death, their very action is presented by John as the fulfillment of Scripture. By citing Scripture, John has given depth to the event of the crucifixion that transcends the mere putting to death of a common criminal. Both the fact that Jesus's legs were not broken as the legs of the other two criminals were and the looking on the crucified Jesus by those present at the cross, present the final outcome of a long-foretold reality. These are not, as they might have seemed to some, simply spontaneous superficial human actions of the moment, but, quite the contrary, are the fulfillment of ancient divinely spoken words that the characters in the text were in some sense "scripted" and "fated" to perform.[92]

4.2. Form

This statement from the middle of the verse in Zech 12:10 is remarkable for the form in which it is cited. This citation parallels the citation in John

---

89. Hendriksen, *Exposition*, 439.
90. Brant, *John*, 255.
91. Boice, *John*, 1386–87.
92. Myers, *Characterizing Jesus*, 170.

12:15 in terms of brevity and conciseness. It shares not a single word with the traditional LXX form of the phrase, which reads: καὶ ἐπιβλέψονται πρός με ἀνθ' ὧν κατωρχήσαντο. On the other hand, it shares considerable content with the traditional MT form of the text, והביטו אלי את אשר־דקרו, and yet does not equal it exactly.

Numerous suggestions for the particular form of this citation have been given. Jerome, for example, indicated that John had quoted from the Hebrew: "Look at this instance from Zechariah where the Evangelist John quotes from the Hebrew, 'They shall look on him whom they pierced'"; and he minimizes the differences with the Septuagint and Latin versions, "And yet, the divergence of language is atoned for by oneness of spirit."[93] David Brown is convinced that John's citation is not taken from the LXX, "which here is all wrong, but direct from the *Hebrew*."[94]

Though Michaels may be right in saying that this quotation "seems to be based on someone's (not necessarily the Gospel writer's) fairly literal translation of the Hebrew,"[95] the form of the citation raises more issues than are apparent at first glance. It does indeed indicate Hebrew influence, perhaps from John's own translation, from a consonantal text somewhat at variance from MT tradition, or from a variant vocalization tradition. Robertson states rather glibly that it is a "correct translation of the Hebrew of Zech. 12:10, but not like the LXX."[96] Similarly, Hendriksen notes that "the words of the prophet are quoted here not according to the LXX, but *more nearly* according to the original Hebrew."[97] Miller sees this citation as one instance in which John quotes "from the Hebrew against the Greek."[98] To Leon Morris, the most natural understanding of this citation is "that John knew and used the Hebrew."[99] Schnackenburg leans toward an "intentional alteration" on the part of the author in order to "fit the text

---

93. Jerome, *Epist.* 57.7 (quoted from Joel C. Elowsky, ed., *John 11–21*, ACCS NT 4A [Downers Grove, IL: InterVarsity Press, 2007], 330).

94. David Brown, "John," in *The Classic Bible Commentary*, ed. Owen Collins (Wheaton, IL: Crossway, 1999), 1147 (emphasis original).

95. Michaels, *John*, 976.

96. Robertson, *Word Pictures in the New Testament*, 5:306. See also Bynum, *Fourth Gospel*, 2–5, 163–67, regarding the comparison of this citation with the Hebrew text of Zech 12:10.

97. Hendriksen, *Exposition*, 439 (emphasis added). Hendriksen is assuming that the "original Hebrew" is equal to MT.

98. Miller, "They Saw His Glory and Spoke of Him," 128.

99. Morris, *John*, 727n109.

Christologically."¹⁰⁰ In their explanation of the great difference between the MT and LXX versions of the verse, Archer and Chirichigno simply reflect traditional views that maintain the MT's first person pronominal ending "to me" and view the LXX as misreading the Hebrew "they pierced" as a result of ד/ר confusion.¹⁰¹ Menken concludes that the citation represents "an independent early Christian translation into Greek of the Hebrew Text."¹⁰² Myers sees John once again exercising "*paraphrasis*, incorporating the passage in such a way that its scriptural origins remain clear even as he adapts it for his narrative context."¹⁰³

This citation definitely shows Hebrew influence yet at the same time allows for other possibilities. It could reflect an independent non-Septuagint rendering, another Greek version such as Theodoret or Theodotion, or a citation from an edited or corrected version of the Old Greek.¹⁰⁴ Interestingly enough, when this citation is compared to the Minor Prophets Scroll (or "R"), containing the oldest extant Greek fragments of the Twelve, there is a striking similarity of characteristics.¹⁰⁵ It is quite possible that John quoted from R or from a similar manuscript. Pluriform textual traditions of the era in both Hebrew and Greek would have presented various possibilities to John. In light of the diversity of his audience, perhaps it is best to say that this citation (and indeed all his scriptural citations) are in harmony with both Greek and Hebrew textual traditions that would have been acceptable to his entire audience, whether Jewish or non-Jewish. As Schuchard suggests, "The evangelist only cites those texts that both the synagogue and the earliest church of his day would have readily recognized as Scripture."¹⁰⁶ Further, though the complexity of forms in John's citations, together with the pluriformity of textual traditions of his day, make it difficult to identify a consistent source of citation, John's translated form is "invariably close to the Hebrew."¹⁰⁷ Whether John's source is a Greek or Hebrew Bible, his citations, including Zech 12:10, are entirely

---

100. Schnackenburg, *John*, 3:293.
101. Archer and Chirichigno, *Old Testament Quotations*, 163.
102. Menken, "Minor Prophets," 87.
103. Myers, *Characterizing Jesus*, 169.
104. Bynum, *Fourth Gospel*, 156–67.
105. Ibid., 167–69.
106. See earlier in this volume his essay "Form versus Function," n15.
107. Again, see Schuchard, "Form versus Function," n15.

in step with the contemporary Jewish handling of Scripture in the context of the pluriform textual traditions of the era in both Hebrew and Greek.[108]

4.3. Purpose

This citation contrasts with that of 12:15 in its portrayal of an enigmatic figure[109] that has been pierced, which in its original context leads Israel to nationwide mourning.[110] Thus the FG moves from the first Zecharian citation that calls for celebration, to the second, which would seem to call for mourning. Rather than contradictory, these two may be seen as complementary, for it is not unusual for an *inclusio* to demonstrate contrast.[111]

In Zech 12, the death of the pierced one brings national mourning for Judah, but the element of mourning in John is subdued. One may assume such sadness on the part of the one who has observed the piercing (19:35) together with his fellow disciples, as predicted by Jesus in 16:20–22. In John's passion narrative, however, the element of mourning is not specifically highlighted, though the pierced Jesus is indeed mourned and buried by Joseph of Arimathea and Nicodemus, and Mary's subsequent weeping is also mentioned in 20:11–15.

The very brevity of John's citation supports the suggestion that the element of mourning has not been emphasized. With John's knowledge of the Scriptures, he easily could have continued the citation of Zech 12:10 with the words, "and they will mourn for him." Interestingly, the element of mourning is included in the allusions to the same verse found in Matt 24:30 (καὶ τότε κόψονται πᾶσαι αἱ φυλαὶ τῆς γῆς) and Rev 1:7 (καὶ κόψονται ἐπ' αὐτὸν πᾶσαι αἱ φυλαὶ τῆς γῆς). In contrast, John ends his brief citation with the focus on looking upon the pierced one. Though the mourning is not contradictory to the FG's account of the crucifixion, the deliberate exclusion of that element from the citation compels us to use caution before including it.

---

108. It may be added as well that in the light of all the textual issues raised in this verse, John's particular citation carries as much or more textual certainty than any other extant form of the verse.

109. Regarding a pierced Messiah and Zech 12:10, cf. b. Sukkah 52. See also David C. Mitchell, "Messiah bar Ephraim in the Targums," *AS* 4 (2006): 545–53.

110. Zech 12:11–14.

111. See, e.g., m. Naz. 1:2; 9:5, which include references to the examples of Samson (1:2) and Samuel (9:5).

In the same vein, it might be tempting to read into John's citation the element of eschatological judgment,[112] as is evident in the citations of Matthew and Revelation. His use of the verb in the future tense could suggest such an interpretation, and one could assume that his citation of Zech 12:10 shares the theology of Matt 24:30 and Rev 1:7. Though it is evident that these three references share a common background, it is not necessarily true that they are citing the text with the same theological assumptions. It is important not to overlay additional content that might be incongruous with the flow of the Johannine understanding of the issue. However true it may be that "all humanity will have to look at the pierced Messiah at the last judgment ... to receive either final deliverance or final punishment,"[113] this does not seem to be John's primary emphasis here.

Such content has traditionally been included in commentary on the verse.[114] Judgment in the FG, when seen in the light of its "peculiar kind of eschatology"[115]—that is, an eschatology already initiated but not necessarily already realized—does indeed mean receiving the consequences of acceptance or rejection of Christ (see, e.g., 3:17–20, 36; 9:39). It is judgment that is already begun in the present, as in 5:24 and 12:31, for example. However, it is primarily focused on the offer of salvation, and not on condemnation, whether final or not. As the FG concludes the crucifixion episode by drawing the audience's attention to the pierced one, it makes no evident reference to guilt and condemnation. Instead, Boice sees rightly the offer of salvation: "This was John's purpose in recording these verses: that you might look to Jesus and trust Him. There is salvation in such a believing look."[116]

One need not categorically exclude all thought of eschatological judgment and condemnation on John's part.[117] However, it would be much more in harmony with the Gospel's previous references to salvation and judgment[118] to see its reference here to "looking upon the pierced one" as,

---

112. See Ferreiro, *Twelve Prophets*, 271–73, where much of the ancient commentary on Zech 12:10 is focused on final judgment.

113. Köstenberger, *John*, 554.

114. See Elowsky, *John 11–21*, 329–31.

115. Gabel, Wheeler, and York, *Bible as Literature*, 228.

116. Boice, *John*, 1388.

117. Schnackenburg, *John*, 3:294, e.g., wants to maintain both elements of "salvation or destruction."

118. See John 3:17; 16:8–11.

first of all, a literal fulfillment in the gaze of the actual persons present at the crucifixion. That would include the soldiers who were present, one of whom pierced Jesus's side, as well as the eyewitness, the "one who saw this" of verse 35. Second, it can be seen as a call for the entire audience, contemporary to the FG and future, to participate in an extended and continued fulfillment by gazing upon the crucified Christ. This pierced one is also, at the time of the writing of the FG and of the reception of the same by the audience, the resurrected Christ and ascended Lord.

"Seeing," in the sense of spiritual perception, is such a prominent theme in the FG that there is no need to build a case for it here.[119] Whatever might have been the understanding in the minds of the original audiences of the events of triumphal entry and crucifixion, it is obvious by the ἰδού of 12:15, the ἴδωσιν of 12:40, and the ὄψονται of 19:37 (as well as the ἑωρακώς of 19:35), all based on the same root verb, that there is a focus on, even a specific call for, "seeing," "observing," and "beholding" the figure of Christ. Here the *inclusio* of 19:37 with previous Johannine material extends to the first chapter of the FG and the call to "behold" in 1:29, 36, and to "come and see" in 1:39.

The ὄψονται ("they will look") of 19:37 is a verb that can indicate a perception of truth deeper than that of simply seeing, in the sense of "behold, perceive, observe ... discern."[120] Well beyond the physical looking of those present at the crucifixion, this "seeing" and "looking" is best understood as a directive on John's part to gaze upon the crucified Christ in transformative contemplation. Nor need it be seen as unidirectional in a vision that simply leads to faith, but as interactive, as both vision and faith lead toward one another in mutually enriching dynamics.

John's call to "see" is also in harmony with the context of Zech 12, where God has promised to pour out upon his people a "spirit of grace and compassion" that leads to looking upon the pierced one in recognition of what has been done. The full import of John's view of the crucifixion is also in keeping with the larger context, including Zech 13 and the "fountain for cleansing," as well as chapter 14 and the renewal of united worship.

It is not the purpose of this chapter to attempt a full treatment of the theological meaning of Jesus's death. However, it is evident at a minimum that John considered Jesus the paschal lamb referred to in Exod 12:10, 46,

---

119. Cf. Schnackenburg, *John*, 3:293, who connects the "seeing" of this reference with John 3:14; 8:28; and 12:32 regarding Jesus's being lifted up.
120. LSJ 1245.

and Num 9:12, the righteous one referred to in Ps 34:20 of whom not a bone would be broken, and the one who is to be looked upon for salvation. In this, John would be in agreement with Paul's statement in 2 Cor 3:18 regarding contemplation of Christ with "unveiled faces," changed from glory into glory, as well as the statement in 1 John 3:2 that "we will be like him, because we will see him just as he is." Brant argues that "John makes it possible to gaze on Jesus's body upon the cross without feeling his humiliation or needing to look away.... John treats the crucifixion as the epitome of the good death."[121] The truth of the FG's witness regarding the crucifixion is a saving truth that leads the audience to salvation in relationship to Christ. Anastasia Scrutton convincingly argues for revelation as salvation in the FG:

> Toward the end [of the FG] it becomes clear that revelation is the means of salvation, and knowledge of God the substance of salvation itself, ... our experiential knowledge of God in Christ *is* our salvation.... The individual's potential is fully realized only through fellowship with God, involving the individual's experience of God's saving revelation.[122]

If one accepts the validity of her argument, then the citation of 19:37 is a climactic key verse in leading the audience to the experience of God's revelation in Christ as the pierced one is looked upon and contemplated.[123]

5. The Purpose of the Two Citations Together

The citation of Zech 9:9 in John 12:15 finalizes the FG's use of the introductory formula "it is written." Similarly, the citation of Zech 12:10 in John 19:37 brings to an end not only the scriptural citations of the passion narrative, "that the scripture be fulfilled," but indeed all of the FG's scriptural citations as it closes the crucifixion episode and launches the reader into the burial and resurrection events.

---

121. Brant, *John*, 257.

122. Anastasia Scrutton, "The Truth Will Set You Free," in Bauckham and Mosser, *The Gospel of John and Christian Theology*, 363, 365, 367.

123. Cf. also Bruce, *John*, 14: "The revelation of the Father which he imparts means the salvation of the world: the revelation and the salvation are consummated together in Jesus' laying down his life on the cross."

When taken together as an *inclusio*, the two citations demonstrate John's dialogue with Zechariah as he encloses the passion narrative in the hope, the joy, and the irony of Zech 9–12. When seen in the light of the burial and resurrection of Jesus, the two citations are closely related both to one another and to the climactic resurrection narrative, carrying the audience beyond the mourning of death and burial into the rejoicing over seeing the resurrected Lord. Here the author is doing much more than calling the reader's attention to two potentially sensational and newsworthy events. He is directing the gaze of the reader, both ancient and modern, to the transforming power of the triumphal king who comes, who is crucified, and who is now the resurrected Lord and Lamb of God "who takes away the sin of the world" (1:29).

In viewing the events of Christ's passion in the light of Zechariah, John grasps the essential meaning of Zech 9–14, which promises divine hope and salvation for postexilic Judah along with a call for renewed relationship to God, and applies it to the events of Christ's entrance into Jerusalem, his death, and resurrection. Thus, in his view, God has truly returned; the promised humble king has arrived; the new era of his lordship has begun; the era of renewal envisioned by Zechariah has come. All the direction and hope given to Judah through the prophetic word of Zechariah are now finding deep fulfillment in Christ. At the same time, Christ is now seen much more clearly through the light shed on the events of his entry into Jerusalem and subsequent passion by the writings of Zechariah. Those writings, which directed the audience of Judah to rejoice in the reception of their coming humble and peaceful king, now continue to direct the audience of the FG to gladly receive Christ. At the same time, they encourage them to look with transformative contemplation upon Christ the pierced one.

Both citations are a call to lift one's gaze, to look, to see with deep perception, and to contemplate the person of Christ. In both instances, the physical scene before its original eyewitnesses, as well as its imagined reality by the audience of the FG, is a given, but the meaning of these events is not so apparent at first glance. It requires a theological interpretation to see the enduring spiritual significance for believers of the figure of Christ entering Jerusalem and then "lifted up" on the cross. In this, the two citations are complementary, giving a depth to one another that neither of them would have had standing alone.

In the pivotal event of the triumphal entry of Jesus into Jerusalem, the "signs" of Jesus come to a close and his passion begins. That beginning is signaled by a citation from Zechariah calling on Daughter Zion to look to and rejoice over her king who comes in a particularly symbolic manner. At the crucifixion of Jesus, the passion comes to a close with another citation from Zechariah that focuses on the gaze of ancient Judah upon the pierced one, and the contemporary gaze of the FG's audience upon the pierced Jesus. Both citations with their call to "behold" and "see" flow with the call of the FG to "behold the Lamb of God" (1:29, 36), to look for salvation to the one who is "lifted up" (3:14–15), as they direct the audience to "behold your coming king" and "look upon the pierced one" who has indeed "made the Father known to us" (1:16, 18). These two citations well reflect the prominent theme in the FG of "seeing and believing" (e.g., 1:7; 3:26–36; 14:9–11; 20:8, 29). By virtue of the universality of the FG, that audience must include all future believers as well as the original diverse readers to whom John was writing. Even those who "have not seen" (20:29) in a literal sense are now blessed as they come to faith and continue to renew their faith[124] in spiritual experience by their life-giving gaze upon this pierced one.

---

124. See Bruce M. Metzger, *A Textual Commentary on the Greek New Testament*, 2nd ed. (New York: United Bible Societies, 2000), 219, regarding alternative readings of John 20:31.

Quotations with "Remembrance" Formulae in the Fourth Gospel

Michael A. Daise

Research on the Fourth Gospel's biblical quotations has perhaps come of age. Begun by August Franke in the late nineteenth century,[1] it surfaced as a brief skirmish between Alexander Faure and Friedrich Smend in the early twentieth century[2] before coming into its own as a palpable subfield of Johannine studies with Edwin Freed's *Old Testament Quotations in the Gospel of John* in 1965.[3] Since then, it has yielded no less than six full monographs or major book sections, and, with the recent adoption of new approaches, it shows little sign of having yet run its course.[4]

---

1. August H. Franke, *Das Alte Testament bei Johannes: Ein Beitrag zur Erklärung und Beurtheilung der johanneischen Schriften* (Göttingen: Vandenhoeck & Ruprecht, 1885), 255–316.

2. Alexander Faure, "Die alttestamentlichen Zitate im 4. Evangelium und die Quellenscheidungshypothese," *ZNW* 21 (1922): 99–121; Friedrich Smend, "Die Behandlung alttestamentlicher Zitate als Ausgangspunkt der Quellenscheidung im 4. Evangelium," *ZNW* 24 (1925): 147–50.

3. Edwin D. Freed, *Old Testament Quotations in the Gospel of John*, NovTSup 11 (Leiden: Brill, 1965).

4. Works (or parts of works) treating all or a large portion of the quotations in John since Freed are Günter Reim, *Jochanan: Erweiterte Studien zum alttestamentlichen Hintergrund des Johannesevangeliums* (Erlangen: Verlag der Ev.-Luth. Mission, 1995), 1–96 (the first part is a reprint of *Studien zum alttestamentlichen Hintergrund des Johannesevangeliums*, SNTSMS 22 [Cambridge: Cambridge University Press, 1974]); Bruce G. Schuchard, *Scripture within Scripture: The Interrelationship of Form and Function in the Explicit Old Testament Citations in the Gospel of John*, SBLDS 133 (Atlanta: Scholars Press, 1992); Andreas Obermann, *Die christologische Erfüllung der Schrift im Johannesevangelium: Eine Untersuchung zur johanneischen Hermeneutik anhand der Schriftzitate*, WUNT 2/83 (Tübingen: Mohr Siebeck, 1996); Maarten J. J. Menken, most of whose articles are revised and collected in *Old Testament Quota-*

The issues traditionally addressed in this research can be parsed into some ten questions, not all applying to every citation. How many (that is, which) loci in the Fourth Gospel are to be counted as quotations? What segments of the Fourth Gospel's text represent those quotations? What bearing do introductory formulae have on these references? What biblical passages are cited? From what versions (and/or mediating traditions) have they been drawn—HB,[5] LXX, the Synoptic Gospels, targumim—and what might those sources indicate about the evangelist's provenance? How do the Johannine renderings compare to their source texts and original contexts? How can differences between the two be explained? What implications do the quotations carry for the Fourth Gospel's narrative (including

---

tions in the Fourth Gospel: Studies in Textual Form, CBET 15 (Kampen: Kok Pharos, 1996); Jaime Clark-Soles, *Scripture Cannot Be Broken: The Social Function of the Use of Scripture in the Fourth Gospel* (Leiden: Brill, 2003), 207–315; and, most recently, treating only the quotations from John 1:23 to John 12:15, Ruth Sheridan, *Retelling Scripture: "The Jews" and the Scriptural Citations in John 1:19–12:15*, BIS 110 (Leiden: Brill, 2012). Sheridan gives an insightful review of research in this subfield, albeit omitting Franke, on 12–37.

Sheridan marks the shift to new approaches to have begun with Obermann, turning on an interest in how the quotations function in the Fourth Gospel's narrative (*Retelling Scripture*, 27–37). Using this as a point of departure, Obermann investigates the hermeneutical concepts by which the Fourth Evangelist christologically appropriated the quotations (and by which he conceived of Scripture); Clarke-Soles considers how those quotations (and Jesus's words) were utilized socially to effect "something for and to" the Johannine community; and Sheridan herself explores how those quotations are employed rhetorically to construct "the Jews" as narrative characters in John 1–12. See Obermann, *Die christologische Erfüllung der Schrift*, 35 (see also 64–69); Clarke-Soles, *Scripture Cannot Be Broken*, 1, 8–9; Sheridan, *Retelling Scripture*, 46–48. One might also note the contribution by Adam Kubiś, *The Book of Zechariah in the Gospel of John*, EBib n.s. 64 (Pendé: Gabalda, 2012), 27–315, published in the same year as Sheridan's volume. It engages recent interest in intra- and intertextuality by treating portions of a single biblical book (Zechariah) as part of a larger reception history of the passages in question—for quotations in John this means Zech 14:8 at John 7:38; Zech 9:9 at John 12:15; and Zech 12:10 at John 12:37. For Kubiś's forebears in this approach, see 13–16.

5. The abbreviation HB (for Hebrew Bible) is used rather than MT (for Masoretic Text), so as to account for the non-Masoretic textual attestations found among the Judaean desert manuscripts. For a summary of these texts, see James VanderKam and Peter Flint, *The Meaning of the Dead Sea Scrolls: Their Significance for Understanding the Bible, Judaism, Jesus, and Christianity* (San Francisco: HarperSanFrancisco, 2002), 103–53.

sources) and theology? How does the Johannine interpretation of these passages (and its method) compare with cognate understandings? And what do these quotations signal about the evangelist's awareness of the Jewish Scriptures? The continued relevance (and even the fundamental utility) of such queries have been questioned by some advocates of newer approaches.[6] But, without issuing an apologetic for them here, this chapter proceeds on a contrary assumption, namely, that significant work on these issues remains to be (and in some cases must be) done.[7]

One of the bases for this assumption concerns quotations that share features among themselves. Certain citations, which have heretofore been examined individually, share common lexical and thematic characteristics that suggest they should be revisited as clusters. Four, for instance, share the factor of having been fulfilled during Jesus's crucifixion (John 19:23–24/Ps 22:19; John 19:28–30/Pss 42:3 [?]; 63:2 [?]; 69:22 [?]; John 19:36/Exod 12:10, 46; Num 9:12; Ps 34:21; and John 19:37/Zech 12:10). Three are the only ones whose introductory formulae explicitly ascribe them to Isaiah (John 1:23/Isa 40:3; John 12:38/Isa 53:1; and John 12:40/Isa 6:10). And three are the only ones cast as being "remembered" (ἐμνήσθησαν) by Jesus's disciples (John 2:17/Ps 69:10; John 12:13/Ps 118:25–26; and John

---

6. Sheridan, *Retelling Scripture*, 22–25; Kubiś, *Book of Zechariah*, 13–15.

7. To note just one line of reasoning, Sheridan suggests that the several HB text types found at Qumran, along with non-Qumran targumim, signify that "the search for the 'original' source text of John's OT citations may in fact be in vain" (*Retelling Scripture*, 24). In fact, however, those text types expand the amount of work remaining on that question. When Freed revived this subdiscipline in 1965, his inclusion of the few Qumran texts available at the time (1QS 4:20–21; 8:14; 9:20; CD 2:12; 1QH 4[Suk(enik) 17]:25–26; 12[Suk 4]:11; 13[Suk 5]:23–24, 33, 35; 15[Suk 7]:6–7; 16[Suk 8]:16; 20[Suk 12]:11–13) implied that knowing such text types should play an important role in this research (see *Old Testament Quotations*, 1, 22, 89, 104). And his successors who have been interested in these older questions (that is, up through Menken and Obermann) have to a greater or lesser degree followed suit. Their effort, however, remains unfinished, for two reasons: first, the *editiones principes* of the Judean desert texts were not fully published until several years after Menken and Obermann wrote (1996); and second, even when parallels to the Fourth Gospel's quotations were published and available before that time, they were not always taken into account by Johannine scholars working on those quotations. These factors were presented with further detail in a preliminary report by Michael A. Daise, "Quotations in John and the Judaean Desert Texts" (paper presented to the Johannine Literature section of the SBL, International Meeting, University of St. Andrews, St. Andrews, Scotland, 8 July, 2013).

12:15/Zech 9:9). The affinities among these groupings have been noticed, but broaching them as groupings—rather than as discrete verses—has yet to be done. This chapter offers a beginning for such collective exploration by examining the last of these clusters, that is, the three citations accompanied by "remembrance" formulae: John 2:17/Ps 69:10; John 12:13/Ps 118:25–26; and John 12:15/Zech 9:9.[8] It proceeds in two steps. First, each of these quotations will be introduced, with special attention given to the inclusion of John 12:13/Psalm 118:25–26 among them. Second, the literary structure formed by these quotations will be examined for the theological resonance it carries for the Fourth Gospel's portrait of Jesus's public ministry. In order to develop the second step, the first must be reduced simply to rehearsing the textual relationships that exist between the Johannine renderings and their biblical counterparts. As such, it by no means engages the full *status quaestionis* on these quotations.

1. Three Quotations with "Remembrance" Formulae

1.1. "Zeal for Your House Will Consume Me," John 2:17/Psalm 69:10

John 2:17 cites Ps 69:10 as a prophecy that is fulfilled by Jesus's cleansing of the temple and remembered as such by his disciples. After Jesus drives out the livestock, upends the exchange stands, and commands the pigeon sellers to take their goods away and not make his Father's house "a house of merchandise" (John 2:13–16), his actions are said to have been interpreted by his disciples through a recollection of Ps 69:10a: "His disciples remembered that it is written, 'Zeal for your house will consume me'" (John 2:17).

Determining the versions from which this and other quotations have been drawn has been a task fraught with debate. An apt starting point for one's thinking on it may perhaps be found in the earliest detailed essay on the matter, Franke's "Urtext und Septuaginta."[9] Bracketing references whose versions he believed were indeterminable—and keeping in mind the possible brokerage of quotations through the Synoptics—Franke ascribed most quotations to the LXX (John 1:23/Isa 40:3; John 2:17/Ps 69:10; John 6:31/Exod 16:4; Ps 78:24; John 6:45/Isa 54:13; John 10:34/Ps 82:6; John

---

8. Inasmuch as discussion of these quotations will constantly toggle between HB and LXX versions, with but a few exceptions only the HB numbering will be used for the psalter.

9. This appears in part 3 of Franke, *Das Alte Testament*, 282–93.

12:38/Isa 53:1; John 12:40/Isa 6:10 [for which he ultimately concluded "no certain result"]; John 19:24/Ps 22:19; John 19:36/Exod 12:46 [cf. Num 9:12]; Ps 34:21), conceded two to the HB (John 13:18/Ps 41:10; John 19:37/ Zech 12:10), and on the basis of those two—as well as on the more allusive use of Scripture throughout the rest of the Gospel—he argued that the influence of the Hebrew should be sought even in passages whose main text was clearly cited from the LXX.¹⁰ Whether one agrees with Franke's specific conclusions or not, his nuanced position can serve as a compass needle of sorts, from which one can move further toward the HB, the LXX, the Synoptics, other mediating traditions, or any combination of these, as each quotation is examined in its own right.

With regard to John 2:17/Ps 69:10, the LXX of the line cited by John follows the HB closely, having the grammatical (but not necessarily the semantic) difference of reading an aorist (κατέφαγέν με) for the Hebrew perfect (אכלתני). The Johannine rendering, then, could just as well reflect an independent translation of the HB as it might a re-presentation of the LXX. That its word choices match the LXX (given other options)¹¹ tilts the balance toward the latter; but that the evangelist elsewhere cites from the former (per Franke) bids restraint from too clear-cut a conclusion.¹²

Whichever the version, the language of the quotation has been modified in two ways: the conjunction ὅτι (or כי) has been removed and the aorist κατέφαγεν ("consumed")—or perfect אכלתני ("has consumed")—has been rendered as a future, καταφάγεται ("will consume").¹³ Further,

---

10. Ibid., 283–90 (quotation on 284).

11. See Menken, *Old Testament Quotations*, 39.

12. So Schuchard, *Scripture within Scripture*, 22, 31–32; and Menken, *Old Testament Quotations*, 39–49.

13. Several factors ostensibly ameliorate these differences. The future tense, as C. K. Barrett has noted, "is a possible rendering of the Hebrew perfect"; *The Gospel according to St. John*, 2nd ed. (Philadelphia: Westminster, 1978), 28. And further, alternate readings in both the LXX and the Fourth Gospel remove the variations: several witnesses to John 2:17 attest ὅτι at the beginning of the clause (P⁶⁶, P⁷⁵, W [in a later addition to the manuscript], 050); and two witnesses to LXX Ps 68:10 read καταφάγεται for κατέφαγεν (Vaticanus and Sinaiticus). The prospect that the future tense is a rendering of the Hebrew perfect, however, encounters the same difficulty as the hypothesis that it represents an attempt to make the passage appear as fulfilled prophecy, namely, that in similar Johannine quotations the biblical verbal tenses (including preterites) are retained (e.g., John 12:38/Isa 53:1; 12:40/Isa 6:10; 13:18/Ps 41:10; 15:25/Ps 35:19 or Ps 69:5; 19:24/Ps 22:19); see Menken, *Old Testament Quotations*, 40; over against Rudolf

this quotation may be referenced again a few verses later, at John 2:22c. In the next pericope Jesus is asked by the Jews to justify his actions in the temple, and he responds by saying that, if they destroy "this sanctuary" (τὸν ναὸν τοῦτον), he will raise it in three days. The following commentary explains that with these words he was referring, not to the edifice in Jerusalem, but to his body; and it then forecasts that after the resurrection his disciples would remember and believe both Jesus's reply at this juncture and "the Scripture": "When, therefore, he was raised from the dead, his disciples remembered [ἐμνήσθησαν] that he said this, and they believed the Scripture [τῇ γραφῇ] and the word [τῷ λόγῳ] which Jesus spoke" (John 2:22; the full pericope is John 2:18–22). The "Scripture" in this last clause (v. 22c) may denote the whole Bible in general, an individual but unspecified verse in it,[14] or the quotation of Ps 69:10 at John 2:17.[15] To the extent it may be the last of these options, John 2:22 should be kept in view when interpreting that quotation.

1.2. John 12:13 as a Quotation

Before introducing John 12:13/Ps 118:25–26, a word about its inclusion as a quotation, since it has been omitted from consideration by at least two exegetes: by Maarten Menken, because it is not accompanied by an introductory formula;[16] and by Bruce Schuchard, because it represents, "not a reference to the Old Testament per se, but simply a rendering of a popular Jewish festal greeting derived from Ps 118(117)."[17] For several reasons this reference is deemed integral to the discussion of quotations here. Most fundamentally, it meets a criterion that should be weighed heavily when defining a quotation: the proximity of the Johannine render-

---

Bultmann, *The Gospel of John: A Commentary*, trans. George R. Beasley-Murray (Philadelphia: Westminster, 1971), 124n3; Freed, *Old Testament Quotations*, 10, 117; and Raymond E. Brown, *The Gospel according to John*, 2 vols., AB 29–29A (Garden City, NY: Doubleday, 1966–1970), 1:124. Further, the variant LXX and Johannine readings may, in fact, reflect later scribal attempts to harmonize the two texts (see Alfred Rahlfs, ed., *Septuaginta: Id est Vetus Testamentum graece iuxta LXX interpretes*, 2 vols. [Stuttgart: Deutsche Bibelgesellschaft, 1979], ad loc.).

14. Brown, for instance, suggests Ps 16:10 as a passage intimating resurrection (*John*, 1:116).

15. See Bultmann, *John*, 128; as well as Brown, *John*, 1:116.

16. Menken, *Old Testament Quotations*, 11–13.

17. Schuchard, *Scripture within Scripture*, xiv, 76n31.

ing to its source text. "Blessed is the one who comes in the name of the Lord" at John 12:13c follows LXX Ps 117:26a verbatim; and, allowing the *qere* אדוני for יהוה, it does the same with the HB counterpart.[18] Further, this reference is treated by the evangelist (or redactor) in the same way as other quotations are done. As is the case with other citations, John 12:13/ Ps 118:25–26 is polyvalent, that is, the verbatim re-presentation of LXX 117:26a at John 12:13c is preceded and followed by anomalies that likely result from a conflation of Ps 118:25–26 with other passages.[19]

Moreover, John 12:13/Ps 118:25–26 furnishes a critical context for interpreting the citation that immediately follows, John 12:15/Zech 9:9. In John, unlike Matthew, Jesus sits on a colt in fulfillment of Zech 9:9, not

---

18. Noteworthy here are references, typically numbered among the quotations, that similarly follow their source texts word for word: John 10:34/LXX Ps 81:6; John 12:38/LXX Isa 53:1; and John 19:24/LXX Ps 21:19. Obermann also advocates this feature for John 12:13/Ps 118:25–26 (and for John 1:23/Isa 40:3) as one manifestation of a larger criterion for quotations that he sets alongside introductory formulae: that a word formulation carries characteristics that cause it to be seen as "an alien testimony" (*eine fremde Aussage*); *Die christologische Erfüllung der Schrift*, 73.

19. Among undisputed quotations, for instance, the citation at John 1:23 is thought by some to be a merger of Isa 40:3ab with any one or combination of passages: Isa 40:3c; LXX Prov 4:25–26; 9:14–15; 13:13a; 15:21; 20:24; LXX Sir 2:2, 6; 6:17; 37:15; 38:10; 39:24; 49:8–9 (see Freed, *Old Testament Quotations*, 4–7); the quotation at John 6:31 has been narrowed by Georg Richter to a merger with Exod 16:4; Exod 16:15; Ps 78:24; and/or Neh 9:15/2 Esd 19:15, in Hebrew or in Greek ("Die alttestamentlichen Zitate in der Rede vom Himmelsbrot Joh 6,26–51a," in *Studien zum Johannesevangelium*, ed. J. Hainz, BU 13 [Regensburg: Pustet, 1977], 202); and the quotation at John 19:36 is surmised to have combined any two or more of Exod 12:10, 46; Num 9:12; or Ps 34:21. With regard to John 12:13/Ps 118:25–26, if "hosanna" is not a conflation of HB Ps 118:25a (הושיעה נא; so Marie-Émile Boismard and Arnaud Lamouille, *L'Évangile de Jean*, vol. 3 of *Synopse des quatres évangiles en français*, 2nd ed. [Paris: Cerf, 1987], 109), it may reflect a merger with either HB Jer 31:7d, "Save, Lord [הושע יהוה], your people" (Franke, *Das Alte Testament*, 271) or HB Ps 20:10a, "Lord, save [הושיעה] your king" (cf. also Ps 20:8; Freed, *Old Testament Quotations*, 70–71, following the commentary on Matt 21:9 by Charles Cutler Torrey, *Four Gospels: A New Translation*, 2nd ed. [New York: Harper & Brothers, 1947], 295). As for "the king of Israel," which follows in this quotation, it may reflect a conflation with either a messianized (albeit putative) targumic paraphrase of Gen 49:10c, such as occurs in Tg. Onq. Gen 49:10; Tg. Ps.-J. Gen 49:10; and Frg. Tg. Gen 49:10 (so Joseph Blenkinsopp, "The Oracle of Judah and the Messianic Entry," *JBL* 80 [1961]: 56–59), or Zeph 3:15c, "The king of Israel [מלך ישראל/βασιλεὺς Ισραηλ], Yahweh, is in your midst" (Brown, *John*, 1:458).

before, but after the crowd hails him as "the one who comes in the name of the Lord";[20] and as such it (with other features of the text) raises the question of whether in doing so Jesus was accepting or correcting that crowd's recitation of Ps 118. If he was accepting it, the quotation at John 12:13/Ps 118:25–26 reflects the Fourth Gospel's royal Christology, along with the quotation at John 12:15/Zech 9:9. If he was correcting it, the quotation at John 12:13/Ps 118:25–26 serves as a foil to that royal Christology, over against the quotation at John 12:15/Zech 9:9.[21] Whichever view one takes, addressing John 12:15/Zech 9:9 requires comparable attention to John 12:13/Ps 118:25–26; and for the point at issue here this means that John 12:13/Ps 118:25–26 is omitted from consideration only at one's hermeneutical peril.[22]

Finally, the Fourth Gospel itself seems to pair John 12:13/Ps 118:25–26 with John 12:15/Zech 9:9 as two parts of a single unit. This occurs in the commentary at John 12:16. After Jesus is greeted with the recitation of Ps 118:25–26, then rides into the city in a way that alludes to Zech 9:9, he is said in that commentary to have been remembered by the disciples with respect to both: "His disciples did not recognize these things at first; but when Jesus was glorified, then they remembered that these things had been written about him and that they did these things to him" (John 12:16). The clause "that these things had been written about him" speaks of Jesus fulfilling Zech 9:9 by riding into Jerusalem at John 12:14–15. As for the clause "that they did these things to him," which follows, the pronoun "they" may grammatically refer either to the crowd reciting Ps 118:25–26 at John 12:13 or to Jesus's disciples. But, inasmuch as the disciples have done nothing at this juncture to which this clause can refer, the antecedent of the pronoun is likely the crowd.[23] As such, this second clause most likely

---

20. Compare the sequence in John 12:12–16 with that in Matt 21:1–11.

21. An extended defense of the position that Jesus is correcting the crowd's greeting is offered by Brown, *John*, 1:461–63, who was anticipated by Edwyn C. Hoskyns, *The Fourth Gospel*, ed. F. N. Davey, 2nd ed. (London: Faber & Faber, 1947), 420–22. Advocating (or at least inclined toward) the position that Jesus is endorsing that greeting is Barrett, *John*, 416–19. The two positions were somewhat bridged by Alfred Loisy, who suggested that, though mistaken, the crowd contributed "unconsciously [*inconsciemment*] to the fulfillment of the prophecy"; *Le Quatrième Évangile, Les Épitres dites de Jean*, 2nd ed. (Paris: Nourry, 1921), 366–68.

22. Schuchard, in fact, does engage issues attending John 12:13/Ps 118:25–26 in his discussion of John 12:15/Zech 9:9 (*Scripture within Scripture*, 76–78).

23. In Synoptic parallels the disciples do, in fact, act at this juncture by procuring

refers to the recitation of Ps 118:25–26 by the crowd at John 12:13; and so, inasmuch as the acts associated with both references are coupled by the commentary as having been "remembered" by the disciples, it seems the evangelist (or redactor) himself viewed them as a piece. To the extent this is the case, the one ought not be engaged without the other. On this and the previously stated bases, then, John 12:13/Ps 118:25–26 is here included as one of the quotations attended by "remembrance" formulae.

1.3. The Quotation of Psalm 118:25–26 at John 12:13

As has now partly been rehearsed, John 12:13/Ps 118:25–26 is cited by Passover pilgrims as Jesus approaches Jerusalem for that occasion. When they hear he is coming, they take palm branches and exit the city, reciting this adapted excerpt from Ps 118: "And they took palm branches and went out to meet him and were crying out, 'Hosanna! Blessed is the one who comes in the name of the Lord, the king of Israel'" (John 12:12–13).[24]

The core text cited is Ps 118:26a, "Blessed is the one who comes in the name of the Lord"; and as was the case with John 2:17/Ps 69:10, since the LXX of this verse follows the HB closely, it could theoretically have been drawn from either of those versions. In favor of the LXX is its verbatim repetition of the Greek. Supporting the HB is the cry ὡσαννά at John 12:13b, which is plausibly (if not indisputably) explained as a condensed transliteration of the Hebrew imperative הושיעה נא in HB Ps 118:25a or of similar constructs in HB Jer 31:7d or HB Ps 20:10a.[25] The LXX, by contrast, translates (rather than transliterates) the construction as σῶσον δή for the first passage, ἔσωσεν for the second, and σῶσον for the third.[26] A further factor to be weighed in this matter is the version that best accounts for the anomaly that follows the core text cited, "the king of Israel." As already

---

the donkey for Jesus: Matt 21:1–11; Mark 11:1–10; Luke 19:28–40. In John, however, it is Jesus who does this (John 12:14). Barrett insists, nonetheless, that the clause "that they did these things to him" at John 12:16 simply betrays a Johannine "awareness" of Synoptic tradition (*John*, 419). His position, however, begs the question.

24. The rendering of the last line follows Rudolf Schnackenburg, who argues that, even if the initial καί read in some manuscripts is original (א [original and second corrector] B L Q W Ψ 579), it likely functions epexegetically (*The Gospel according to St. John*, trans. K. Smyth [New York: Crossroad, 1982], 2:525n43).

25. See n. 19. Brown adds that the term may derive from the Aramaic equivalent, הושענא (*John*, 1:457).

26. The LXX equivalent to HB Jer 31:7 is LXX Jer 38:7.

mentioned, that phrase has been ascribed either to a putative targumic paraphrase of Gen 49:10c or to Zeph 3:15c;[27] and whether it is one, the other, or a third option will have a bearing on the version deemed to have been used for the base text itself.

As already noted, the Johannine rendering has been modified in two ways. First, in place of the parallel appeals for deliverance in Ps 118:25 is the single word "Hosanna" (ὡσαννά)—if not still a cry for salvation,[28] perhaps a greeting or shout of praise.[29] Second, the acclamation "Blessed is the one who comes in the name of the Lord" from Ps 118:26a does not lead into Ps 118:26b, "We have blessed you from the house of the Lord." Rather, it is followed by the appositive "the king of Israel."

1.4. The Quotation of Zechariah 9:9 at John 12:15

Finally, the quotation of Zech 9:9 at John 12:15 is cited as commentary on what Jesus does in response to the greeting in John 12:13. While the multitude rehearses Ps 118, Jesus finds a colt and sits on it; and as he does the evangelist (or redactor) declares that in so doing he fulfilled Zech 9:9. "And having found a young donkey, Jesus sat upon it, as it is written, 'Do not fear, daughter (of) Zion; behold, your king comes, sitting upon a foal of a donkey.'" With the exception of the nominative θυγάτηρ for LXX θύγατερ,[30] the words "daughter (of) Zion; behold, your king comes" in this rendering precisely follow their counterparts in LXX Zech 9:9. As is the case with the other two quotations, however, those LXX counterparts themselves follow the HB verbatim, leaving the version of the base text open to further question. Cues in the Johannine rendering support one or the other;[31] but here,

---

27. See n. 19.
28. Bultmann, *John*, 418n1.
29. Brown, *John*, 2:457; Schnackenburg, *John*, 2:375.
30. As with the attestations of κατεσθίειν at John 2:17/Ps 69:10, alternate readings in both the LXX and the Fourth Gospel remove these differences: for John 12:15, the vocative θύγατερ is attested in ℵ, Γ, Θ, Ψ, *family1* (1, 118, 131, 209, 1582), *family13* (13, 69, 124, 174, 230, 346, 543, 788, 826, 828, 983, 1689, 1709), 700, 892 (in a later addition), 1241, 1424, the lectionary 844, and the Majority text; for LXX Zech 9:9, the nominative θυγάτηρ is attested in Sinaiticus. Like the case at John 2:17, these may simply reflect later scribal attempts to harmonize the two texts. And this likely also applies to the omission of the dative σοι ("to you") at LXX Zech 9:9c in 534.
31. Like the LXX, for instance, the Johannine rendering employs the term πῶλος to convey "foal" for Zech 9:9e. Like the HB, however, the present participle καθήμενος

as with John 12:13/Ps 118:25–26, determining whether it is HB, LXX, or a mix is as dependent on explaining the quotation's modifications as it is on comparing its language to the biblical sources.

If those modifications were few in the previous two quotations, they are many in this one. Aside from the possibilities for deviating from either version generated by the ambiguous θυγάτηρ/θύγατερ Σιών,[32] the Fourth Gospel's rendering omits, replaces, and abbreviates significant elements of the verse. Omitted are the exhortation "shout, daughter (of) Jerusalem" at Zech 9:9b, the description of the king as "righteous and victorious" at Zech 9:9d, the description of the king as "humble"—along with the following conjunction—at Zech 9:9e, and the dative "to you" at Zech 9:9c.[33] The exhortation "rejoice greatly" in Zech 9:9a is replaced with the singular imperative "do not fear," and the description "riding" (ורכב) or (LXX) "mounted" (ἐπιβεβηκώς) in Zech 9:9e is replaced with "sitting" (καθήμενος). Further, the prolix "upon a donkey, upon a colt, a foal of donkeys" at Zech 9:9ef is shrunken to "upon a foal of a donkey."

2. Quotations with "Remembrance" Formulae and Jesus's Public Ministry

From this vantage point several lines of inquiry might be pursued.[34] This discussion, however, will proceed literary-critically and theologically, and will observe that in their current placement these "remembered" quotations create a literary structure that carries pneumatological implications

---

("sitting"), unlike the perfect participle ἐπιβεβηκώς in the LXX, is of the same tense as ורכב at Zech 9:9e; and, further, the Johannine phrase "a foal of a donkey" (πῶλον ὄνου) is reminiscent of the plural בן־אתנות ("a foal of donkeys") at HB Zech 9:9f.

32. The issue concerns whether the indeclinable Σιών has a genitival ("the daughter of Zion") or appositional ("daughter Zion") relationship to the term θυγάτηρ/θύγατερ before it, and the several options that play out when each possibility is set against the other and the HB בת־ציון.

33. The elements of Zech 9:9 here are translated from the HB, but apply to their LXX counterparts as well.

34. Exegetically, for instance, certain problems raised by individual quotations find wider contexts for resolution when these three citations are engaged collectively. And with regard to tradition- or redaction-criticism the appearance of "remembrance" formulae only in the temple episodes at John 2:13–22 and the entry into Jerusalem at John 12:12–19 suggests that at one point they all may have circulated as a piece.

for the Fourth Gospel's Christology. It develops by noting three features of these quotations.

2.1. An *Inclusio* of "Remembrance" Formulae

The first feature is that they form an *inclusio* to Jesus's public ministry in the Fourth Gospel. The "remembrance" formulae attending the quotation at John 2:17 and the logion in John 2:19 (at John 2:22ab) occur during the Passover that inaugurates that ministry; and the "remembrance" formula attending the quotations at John 12:13 and 12:15 (that is, at John 12:16) occurs during the Passover that concludes that ministry.[35] Inasmuch as motifs embodied in the components of an *inclusio* resonate with one another over the text that stretches between them, such a structure here suggests that the themes embodied in these quotations do the same across the Book of Signs, chapters 1–12 of the Fourth Gospel.

2.2. Johannine Pneumatology

Second, these quotations are tethered to Johannine pneumatology. More precisely, in light of the full context of the Fourth Gospel's narrative, they are recalled by the disciples after Jesus's resurrection (not at the time of their fulfillment)—and this, due to an illumination wrought by the Spirit. The operative locus is John 14:25–26, where Jesus is cast as telling this to his disciples during his Farewell Discourse: "These things I have spoken to you while abiding with you. But the Paraclete, the Holy Spirit, whom the Father will send in my name, that one will teach you all things and will remind you [ὑπομνήσει ὑμᾶς] of all that I said to you."

The items to be recalled according to these verses are not passages of Scripture per se, but teachings of Jesus: "he will … remind you of all that I [Jesus] said to you." Two factors, however, suggest both are meant. First, the "remembrance" formulae in question blend the two. The formula at John 2:22ab refers not to a biblical quotation, but to Jesus's logion at John 2:19;

---

35. This is noted by Alicia D. Myers, *Characterizing Jesus: A Rhetorical Analysis on the Fourth Gospel's Use of Scripture in Its Presentation of Jesus*, LNTS 458 (London: T&T Clark, 2012), 155–56. Because she does not read the "remembrance" at John 2:17 to be postresurrection, however, she sees the connection between John 2:22 and John 12:16 to be "just a bit more pronounced" than that between John 2:17 and John 12:16 (156n60).

yet, besides being lexically and thematically associated with the formulae at John 2:17 and 12:16 (which do refer to biblical quotations), it is immediately followed by a line (John 2:22c) that treats the disciples' later belief in this logion alongside their tandem belief in "Scripture": "When, therefore, he was raised from the dead, his disciples remembered [ἐμνήσθησαν] that he said this [the logion at John 2:19], and they believed the Scripture [τῇ γραφῇ] and the word [τῷ λόγῳ] which Jesus spoke."

Second, two (if not all three) of the recollections in the "remembrance" quotations are dated to the same time at which the Spirit was to remind the disciples of these matters, that is, after the resurrection. This is beyond question for John 2:22ab and 12:16, where the disciples are said to have remembered "when [Jesus] was raised from the dead" and "when Jesus was glorified," respectively. As for John 2:17, no such statement appears, and this has been taken by some to indicate a recollection that occurred "in the actual situation" rather than after the resurrection.[36] Elements of the context in which this formula is set, however, suggest otherwise: that it is lexically and thematically tied to the other "remembrance" formulae, which do date their quotations after the resurrection; that it lies in close proximity to one of those formulae, John 2:22ab; and (as noted above) that its quotation may be one and the same with the "Scripture" mentioned at John 2:22c, which is explicitly made an object of the disciples' faith after the resurrection. All such factors suggest that the lack of a chronological marker at John 2:17 may rather be due to ellipsis, the deliberate omission of words that are expected to be understood and supplied from elsewhere. More precisely, the formula at John 2:17 may lack postresurrection language simply because the evangelist expected that datum to be inferred from John 2:22ab (and perhaps from John 12:16).[37] To the extent this is the

---

36. Schnackenburg, *John*, 1:347; and more recently, Myers, *Characterizing Jesus*, 144. Slightly buttressing (but by no means establishing) this view is the reading "*Then* the disciples remembered" (τότε ἐμνήσθησαν) in two Latin manuscripts (a, e) and the lemma on John 2:12–25 added to Origen's *Comm. Jo.* (listed in the apparatus to NA^{27} but not NA^{28}).

37. Among commentators supporting such a reading are Bultmann, *John*, 124, 418; and Brown, *John*, 1:123. Myers further argues for the disciples' immediate (rather than postresurrection) remembrance at John 2:17 on the premises (1) that the disciples' instantaneous response to Jesus's action in the temple at this juncture corresponds to the Jews' similarly instantaneous reaction against it at John 2:18–19 and (2) that the pattern of characters making instant connections between Jesus and Scripture occurs elsewhere in the narrative (John 1:50–51; cf. John 1:23, 29, 36, 45;

case, the recollection given the disciples in the "remembrance" quotations at John 2:17, 22, and John 12:12–16 is part of the recollection they were promised to receive from the Spirit at John 14:25–26. As Gary Burge, following Allison Trites, puts it, "This phenomenon of recollection may have centered on the OT as well as on Jesus' words, and thus, as Trites believes, may account for the numerous fulfillment texts in John."[38] As such, the quotations with "remembrance" formulae are tied to the Fourth Gospel's pneumatology.

2.3. A New Creation

Finally, these quotations carry two themes that, when combined, connote mythic conceptions of cosmogony—specifically temple and kingship. The convention in question derives from the ancient Near Eastern practice of associating a new creation with a monarch's accession to the throne;[39] and, as such (among other things), it mythically depicts that king establishing a new order by building a new temple. The full implications of this tradition for John cannot be worked out here,[40] but it can at least be noted

---

Characterizing Jesus, 144). Against these premises it can be reiterated that the most salient parallels to the "remembrance" formula at John 2:17 are the "remembrance" formulae at John 2:22ab and John 12:16, and the pattern in those cases consists of characters (the disciples) making connections between Jesus and Scripture after the resurrection.

38. Gary M. Burge, *The Anointed Community: The Holy Spirit in the Johannine Tradition* (Grand Rapids: Eerdmans, 1987), 212; Allison A. Trites, *The New Testament Concept of Witness*, SNTSMS 31 (Cambridge: Cambridge University Press, 1977), 120. As Burge further notes, in this regard Trites specifically links the Spirit's recollection (among other passages) to John 2:17/Ps 69:10; John 12:13/Ps 118:25–26; and John 12:15/Zech 9:9.

39. Examples of the cosmogonic pairing of kingship and temple building (inter alia) are drawn by Richard J. Clifford, for instance, from the Sumerian Eridu Genesis, the minor Akkadian cosmogonies, the Enuma Elish, the Egyptian Urhügel, the Canaanite Baal Cycle (though perhaps not as a cosmogony), the communal laments in the Psalter, and Second Isaiah (*Creation Accounts in the Ancient Near East and in the Bible*, CBQMS 26 [Washington, DC: Catholic Biblical Association of America, 1994], 42–43, 71–73, 90–93, 105–6, 119–20, 126, 152–58, 172–76).

40. Likewise, two debated exegetical positions must be assumed rather than argued. One was noted above: that John 12:13/Ps 118:25–26 represents an articulation of (rather than a foil against) the Fourth Gospel's royal Christology. The other concerns John 2:17/Ps 69:10—specifically, the force of the verb "consume" in the quota-

that these same motifs attend the quotations that the disciples are made to "remember" by the Spirit in John 2 and 12. The quotations of Ps 118:25–26 and of Zech 9:9 at John 12:12–16 disclose to those disciples that at his last Passover Jesus was hailed by and came to the "daughter (of) Zion" as "the king of Israel." And the quotation of Ps 69:10 at John 2:17, as well as Jesus's own logion at John 2:19, apprise them that at his first Passover Jesus was "zealous" for the purity of the temple and would by that same zeal raise a new sanctuary in its place through his resurrection.

By virtue of the *inclusio* of "remembrance" formulae, these motifs reverberate with one another across the Book of Signs; and as such they dovetail with another cosmogonic theme permeating the Gospel: the reenactment of the Genesis creation.[41] As the Genesis creation occurred "in the beginning" and accounts for the existence of all things, so Jesus as the divine Logos was "in the beginning" with God and in that capacity served as the agent through whom "all things came into being and apart from [whom] nothing came into being that has come into being" (John 1:1–3; cf. Gen 1:1). As the Genesis creation consisted in God working until its completion, so Jesus, as the one who heals on the Sabbath, is the Son of the Father who "is working until now" on a new order (John 5:17; cf. Gen 2:2–3). As the Genesis creation was completed in six days with God resting on the Sabbath, so Jesus, as the high priestly Son who "has accomplished the work" the Father gave him to do, cries "It is finished" on the sixth day of the week and rests buried in the grave on "the Great Sabbath" (John 17:3; 19:28–31; cf. Gen 2:1).[42] And, as in the Genesis creation the Lord God

---

tion "zeal for your house will consume me." Over against many exegetes who espouse the contrary, this discussion does not read that term to mean "experience reprisal," as if to signify that Jesus's actions in the temple provoked an enmity which, in turn, caused his demise (so, e.g., Bultmann, *John*, 124; Schnackenburg, *John*, 1:347; Brown, *John*, 1:124; Boismard and Lamouille, *Jean*, 109). Rather, it understands that term to mean "possess": Jesus acted as he did in the temple, because his ardor for that institution took control of his emotions at that moment. And, insofar as that ardor also precedes Jesus's logion at John 2:19, it is taken to be proleptic of the zeal with which he would later raise the "sanctuary of his body" at his resurrection.

41. Some of the following motifs are drawn from or coincide with a more extensive (if at points overdone) reflection on the Genesis creation in John offered by Martin Hengel, "Die Schriftauslegung des 4. Evangeliums auf dem Hintergrund der urchristlichen Exegese," *JBT* 4 (1989): 273–74, 283–86; Hengel, "The Old Testament in the Fourth Gospel," *HBT* 12 (1990): 30–31, 33–34.

42. For Jesus accomplishing his Father's work Hengel also cites John 4:34 and

breathes "the breath of life" into the nostrils of the first man, so in John the risen Christ does to the new humanity of his followers by "breathing" the Holy Spirit onto his disciples (John 20:22; Gen 2:7).[43] Resonating as they do between chapters 2 and 12, the cosmogonic ideas of temple and kingship in the "remembrance" quotations blend with these Genesis motifs, so as to identify the new order created by Jesus with a new monarchy established by him. With Ps 118:25–26 and Zech 9:9 at John 12:12–16, Jesus, as the agent of this new creation, is cast as the "king of Israel," whose enthronement will coincide with its onset. And with Ps 69:10 at John 2:17 and the logion at John 2:19, Jesus, as that "king of Israel," will inaugurate his reign in this new order by zealously raising the sanctuary of his body from the dead at his resurrection.

Synthesizing all three features of these quotations into a whole, one can conclude the following. First, inasmuch as these quotations are the only ones attended by "remembrance" formulae—and appear at the opening and closing Passovers of the Book of Signs—they form an *inclusio*, whose themes resonate with one another across Jesus's public ministry. Second, by virtue of such "remembrance" formulae these quotations represent part of the pneumatological illumination that the disciples were regarded to have received after Jesus's resurrection. And finally, inasmuch as the themes revealed through these quotations reflect cosmogonic ideas of temple and monarchy, they enhance motifs of the Genesis creation that permeate the narrative, and with them they mythically connote Jesus's public ministry to have effected a new order, with Jesus acceding to its throne at his resurrection.

John 5:36; and with regard to the scene of Jesus's death at John 19:28–30, he references Reim, writing, "The double reference ὅτι ἤδη πάντα τετέλεσται ἵνα τελειωθῇ ἡ γραφή at 19:28 and the last cry τετέλεσται at 19:30 are indeed likely to be understood to mean that God's creative and salvific work, whose beginning is described at Gen 1:1, and taken up at John 1:1, 'achieves its aim with Jesus' work unto death on the cross'" (Hengel, "Die Schriftauslegung," 285; cf. Reim, *Jochanan*, 99).

43. Hengel underscores the likelihood that Jesus's "breathing" on the disciples in John alludes to God doing the same to Adam in Genesis by noting that the verb in question, ἐμφυσᾶν, is not only used in both instances, but also is otherwise a *hapax legomenon* to New Testament literature (Hengel, "Die Schriftauslegung," 273–74; Hengel, "Old Testament," 30–31).

3. Conclusion

Quotations in the Fourth Gospel enjoy a long history of research and have acquired fresh interest from exegetes interested in new methodological standpoints. The questions those quotations have traditionally raised, however, still merit attention and can be broached meaningfully, if citations with common characteristics are revisited as clusters. One such cluster consists of the quotations depicted as being "remembered" by Jesus's disciples; and reconsidering them as such suggests (among other possible conclusions) that they function as a postresurrection means by which the Spirit illumined Jesus's disciples to cosmogonic aspects of his ministry.

Part 2
Social and Rhetorical Perspectives

Scripture Cannot Be Broken: The Social Function of the Use of Scripture in the Fourth Gospel

Jaime Clark-Soles

In *Scripture Cannot Be Broken: The Social Function of the Use of Scripture in the Fourth Gospel*, I contend that the author of the Fourth Gospel deploys Scripture in order to achieve certain goals for his or her sectarian community. What I wrote then still largely inheres:

> To inquire after John's use of Scripture is not to ask an unusual question. But to inquire after the *social function* of John's use of Scripture *is*. Oddly, those who have worried about the social history of the Johannine community have not addressed the way John uses *Scripture* to do something *for* and *to* his community, while those who have attended to the issue of Scripture in John have shown little interest in a flesh and blood community living sometime in the late first century C.E.[1]

Certainly much impressive work has been done in the area of John and Scripture in the past decade, including this current volume,[2] but I would

---

1. Jaime Clark-Soles, *Scripture Cannot Be Broken: The Social Function of the Use of Scripture in the Fourth Gospel* (Leiden: Brill, 2003), 1.

2. I would also highlight the creative new work in John's use of Scripture vis-à-vis rhetorical criticism (Alicia D. Myers, *Characterizing Jesus: A Rhetorical Analysis on the Fourth Gospel's Use of Scripture in Its Presentation of Jesus*, LNTS 458 [London: T&T Clark, 2012]); orality and performance (Jonathan Draper, "Practicing the Presence of God in John: Ritual Use of Scripture and the *Eidos Theou* in John 5:37," in *Orality, Literacy, and Colonialism in Antiquity*, ed. Jonathan Draper [Atlanta: Society of Biblical Literature, 2004], 155–70); reception history (Marcus Öhler, "Who Was John the Baptist? From John 1:19–28 to Heracleon," in *"For It Is Written": Essays on the Function of Scripture in Early Judaism and Christianity*, ed. Jan Dochhorn, ECCA 12 [New York:

welcome further conversation about John's use of Scripture from a sociological angle.

The Fourth Gospel reflects a sectarian outlook, in the sociological sense of the word. Surprisingly, sociologists of religion, even those who study sectarianism, have not comprehensively addressed how sacred texts function among sectarian groups. I have attempted to remedy the lacuna by devising a theoretical framework for analyzing the social function of scriptural use among sectarian groups. In what follows, I will briefly introduce this framework and exemplify its application to John 12:37–41 and 15:25.

1. What Sects Must Do to Succeed

1.1. Methodology Part A: Sociology of Religion

In developing my comprehensive taxonomy about how Scripture might function for sectarian groups, I drew on the work of scholars in various branches of sociology, especially the sociology of religion, sociology of sectarianism, and the production of culture. Those scholars include Nancy Ammerman, William Sims Bainbridge, Rodney Stark, Benton Johnson, Robert Wuthnow, Brian Wilson, and Marsha Witten.

Sects need to do certain things to form and persist. Sects are engaged in the production of culture, a production in which Scripture can play a key role and which is fundamentally shaped by the need to distinguish the sectarian culture from various external cultures, especially a parent tradition. After considering all of the scholarship, I developed a heuristic taxonomy that outlines the potential functions Scripture might serve in the life of a sect (see table 1).

Table 1. Categories of Potential Scriptural Functions within Sects
    A. Breaking Away
        1. Creating "them"
        2. Degrading "them"
    B. Formation of Sect

Lang, 2011], 101–18); the historical Jesus (Steve Moyise, *Jesus and Scripture: Studying the New Testament Use of the Old Testament* [Grand Rapids: Baker Academic, 2011); and Christology (Francis Moloney, "The Gospel of John: The 'End' of Scripture," *Int* 63 [2009]: 356–66).

    1. Etiology
    2. Show sect's founder to have special insight regarding Scripture
    3. Defining "us"
  C. Creating a Distinct Way of Life
    1. Ethical behavior
    2. Ritual practice
    3. Language and rhetoric
    4. Use of sacred texts
    5. Roles of authoritative leaders
    6. Definition of the future
  D. Opposition from the Parent Religion
    1. Named opponents
    2. Those who break Scripture
  E. Opposition from within the Sect: Dealing with Defection
    1. Reward sticking with the sect
    2. Castigate potential and actual deserters
  F. Opposition from Without (The "World" or Some Part Thereof)
  G. Judgment against Opponents
  H. Growing the Sect
    1. Proselytizing
    2. The next generation

1.2. Methodology Part B: Comparative Social History

In addition to sociology, I employed the comparative method of social history. I found it useful to have both an ancient group, in this case the Qumran community, and a modern group, in this case the Branch Davidians, with which to compare the community of the Fourth Gospel. This comparative method serves us doubly. First, it tends to validate or invalidate claims made about the nature of the Fourth Gospel community. If one discovers a feature of the Fourth Gospel community that would seem to make sense given its status as a "breakaway" group, one can test one's hypothesis by asking whether the feature appears in other breakaway groups. If it does not, then one must account for the dissimilarity; if it does, then one must account for the similarity. Second, much more is known about the life of the Qumran and Branch Davidian communities than the Fourth Gospel community. The better known may shed light on the lesser known.

2. Examples from the Fourth Gospel

2.1. Ann Swidler

Of particular relevance for informing the passages I have chosen as examples is the work of both Ann Swidler and Harold Garfinkel. Ann Swidler analyzes the interaction between culture and social structure in two different situations that she refers to as "settled lives" and "unsettled lives." In settled lives, culture and action reinforce one another, whereas in unsettled lives culture serves to create new strategies of action.[3] The culture in which settled people live is "given" and requires little thought, though it does require some choice because established cultures can tolerate diversity in a way that ideological movements cannot. Hence, in settled lives, there are "gaps between the explicit norms, world-views, and rules of conduct individuals espouse and the ways they habitually act."[4] This does not generally constitute a problem, however, because people "know" how to act within the culture. In settled cultures, "ideology ... has gone underground, so pervading ordinary experience as to blend imperceptibly into commonsense assumptions about what is true."[5]

In unsettled periods, on the other hand, "ideologies—explicit, articulated, highly organized meaning systems (both political and religious)—*establish* new styles or strategies of action. When people are learning new ways of organizing individual and collective action, practicing unfamiliar habits until they become familiar, then doctrine, symbol, and ritual

---

3. Two points must be made here: first, "unsettled lives" may refer to individuals or groups; second, the distinction between culture's role in maintaining strategies of action or creating new ones should not be seen in completely dichotomous terms, because, admittedly, "even the most fanatical ideological movement, which seeks to remake completely the cultural capacities of its members, will inevitably draw on many tacit assumptions from the existing culture" (Ann Swidler, "Culture in Action: Symbols and Strategies," *ASR* 51 [1986]: 278), a point worth remembering when one undertakes an investigation of the use of Scripture among groups who stand over against a dominant cultural form (so the Qumranians deny the validity of other Jewish groups, the Fourth Gospel community denies the validity of "the Jews," and the Branch Davidians deny the validity of any groups outside the Branch Davidians who call themselves "Christian").

4. Ibid., 280.

5. Ibid., 281.

directly shape action."⁶ These groups do not tolerate the ambiguities, multiplicities, and even profound inconsistencies, which "settled lives" do. "In conflict with other cultural models, these cultures are coherent because they must battle to dominate the world-views, assumptions, and habits of their members."⁷ Sects fall into the category of unsettled lives and are in opposition at least to a parent tradition that can be viewed as a settled culture. It is important to note, however, that at their formation, for these high-ideology unsettled cultures, "much of their taken-for-granted understanding of the world and many of their daily practices still depend on traditional patterns."⁸ The position and influence of Scripture constitutes part of those "traditional patterns," while it simultaneously serves as a tool for establishing new strategies of action.

2.2. Harold Garfinkel

The process of developing a group identity involves distancing the community from other groups, defining the community over against authentic or constructed opponents. In creating an "us," leaders capitalize on the benefits of creating a "not-us," the "other." In his article "Conditions of Successful Degradation Ceremonies," Garfinkel explains, "Communicative work directed to transforming an individual's total identity into an identity lower in the group's scheme of social types is called a 'status degradation ceremony.'"⁹ There are at least three *dramatis personae* in this performance: the denouncer, the denounced, and the group the denouncer is trying to persuade (which Garfinkel designates "witnesses"). The denouncer must

---

6. Ibid., 278.
7. Ibid., 279.
8. Ibid.
9. Harold Garfinkel, "Conditions of Successful Degradation Ceremonies," *AJS* 61 (1956): 420. The denunciation can occur through a variety of media including writing or personal presence. Whether or not it is successful depends on a number of factors, which Garfinkel addresses on 424; e.g., "Whether the denunciation must be accomplished on a single occasion or is to be carried out over a sequence of 'tries,' factors like the territorial arrangements and movements of persons at the scene of the denunciation, the numbers of persons involved as accused, degraders, and witnesses, status claims of the contenders, prestige and power allocations among participants, all should influence the outcome." I am not interested in deciding whether the degradation "worked" in the historical sense but rather in providing a framework that defines how one undertakes the work of degradation.

present himself or herself as an authentic representative of the group. The primary task of the denouncer consists of proving not that the denounced has somehow changed but rather that the character presently described is the *essential* character, which may previously have escaped notice. The rhetoric of denunciation typically employs irony to highlight the disparity between what the denounced *seemed* to be and what he or she is now proved to be in reality. The reconsideration and "redefinition of origins of the denounced"[10] also figures largely in that rhetoric.

A successful degradation ceremony requires the following: First, the denounced and that which is being blamed on the denounced (what Garfinkel calls the "event") must be "removed from the realm of their everyday character and be made to stand as 'out of the ordinary.'"[11] Second, the denounced and the event must be seen in terms of types rather than unique occurrences so that a certain uniformity regarding both is engendered: "Any sense of accident, coincidence, indeterminism, [or] chance … should be inconceivable."[12] Having been convinced of the typed nature of the denounced, the group must then think in dialectical terms such that they "should not be able to contemplate the features of the denounced person without reference to the counterconception";[13] character traits are further clarified when held to the light of their opposites (note the Johannine Jesus's dualistic language: children of light vs. children of darkness, etc.). Having set the situation up this way, the denouncer aims to have the group in such a position that no real choice is involved when regarding the denounced; rather, morality constrains the group to believe that the need for denunciation is obvious, if not commonsensical.

The denouncer must enjoy some sort of authority and must show that he shares the same essence as the witnesses and that he speaks for the whole group. "What the denouncer says must be regarded by the witnesses as true on the grounds of a socially employed metaphysics whereby witnesses assume that witnesses and denouncer are alike in essence.… For bona fide members it is not that these are the grounds upon which we are *agreed* but upon which we are *alike*, consubstantial, in origin the same."[14] The denouncer must draw attention to the group's "ultimate values," speak

---

10. Ibid., 422.
11. Ibid.
12. Ibid.
13. Ibid., 422–23.
14. Ibid., 423n12.

on behalf of those values, and be viewed as one who maintains those values. The last requirement involves drawing boundaries, separating the denounced from the denouncer and the group. The denouncer must establish distance between the witnesses and the denounced so much so that "the denounced person must be ritually separated from a place in the legitimate order, i.e., he must be defined as standing at a place opposed to it. He must be placed 'outside,' he must be made 'strange.'"[15] Successful degradation reinforces "group solidarity" and "binds persons to the collectivity."[16] John 8 (with Jesus's insistence that his opponents are children of the devil) and 13 (where we learn about Judas's satanic commitments) exemplify this process fully, but we see aspects of it in John 15 as well.

With respect to my larger project, all of the sociological and comparative material informs the exegesis of the direct scriptural citations in the Fourth Gospel, of which there are nineteen (see table 2).

Table 2. Direct Citations according to the Author of the Fourth Gospel

Fourth Gospel	Indicator	Situation in Narrative
1:23	καθὼς εἶπεν Ἠσαΐας ὁ προφήτης "as the prophet Isaiah said"	John the Baptist says it
2:17	γεγραμμένον ἐστίν "it was written"	Disciples recall a relevant scriptural passage
6:31	καθώς ἐστιν γεγραμμένον "as it is written"	Jews quote it to Jesus in a challenge
6:45	ἔστιν γεγραμμένον ἐν τοῖς προφήταις "it is written in the Prophets"	Jesus quotes it to Jews
7:38	καθὼς εἶπεν ἡ γραφή "as the Scripture has said"	Jesus quotes it to the Jews
8:17	ἐν τῷ νόμῳ δὲ τῷ ὑμετέρῳ γέγραπται "in your law it is written"	Jesus quotes it to Jews

---

15. Ibid., 423.
16. Ibid., 421.

10:34	ἔστιν γεγραμμένον ἐν τῷ νόμῳ ὑμῶν "it is written in your law"	Jesus quotes it to Jews
12:13, 15–16	ταῦτα ἦν ἐπ' αὐτῷ γεγραμμένα "these things had been written of him"	Narrator indicates that disciples remembered citations
12:14–15	καθώς ἐστιν γεγραμμένον "as it is written"	Narrator explains Jesus's actions
12:38	ἵνα ὁ λόγος Ἠσαΐου τοῦ προφήτου πληρωθῇ ὃν εἶπεν "this was to fulfill the word spoken by the prophet Isaiah"	Narrator explains Jewish disbelief
12:39–40	εἶπεν Ἠσαΐας "Isaiah said"	Narrator explains Jewish disbelief
12:41	ταῦτα εἶπεν Ἠσαΐας "Isaiah said this"	Narrator regarding Isaiah's vision
13:18	ἵνα ἡ γραφὴ πληρωθῇ "it is to fulfill the Scripture"	Jesus regarding Judas
15:25	ἵνα πληρωθῇ ὁ λόγος ὁ ἐν τῷ νόμῳ αὐτῶν γεγραμμένος "it was to fulfill the word that is written in their law"	Jesus regarding Jewish rejection
17:12	ἵνα ἡ γραφὴ πληρωθῇ "that the Scripture might be fulfilled"	Jesus in prayer regarding Judas
19:24	ἵνα ἡ γραφὴ πληρωθῇ "this was to fulfill what the Scripture says"	Narrator regarding Jesus's clothes
19:28	ἵνα τελειωθῇ ἡ γραφή "in order to fulfill the Scripture"	Narrator regarding Jesus's thirst
19:36	ἵνα ἡ γραφὴ πληρωθῇ "that the Scripture might be fulfilled"	Narrator regarding Jesus's bones

19:37	καὶ πάλιν ἑτέρα γραφὴ λέγει· ὄψονται εἰς ὃν ἐξεκέντησαν.	Narrator regarding the piercing of Jesus's side
	"And again another passage of Scripture says, 'They will look on the one whom they have pierced.'"	

The vast majority of those instances have controversy between Jesus and his opponents as their context. Chapter 12 is no exception.

2.3. Example 1: John 12

> John 12:37–41: τοσαῦτα δὲ αὐτοῦ σημεῖα πεποιηκότος ἔμπροσθεν αὐτῶν οὐκ ἐπίστευον εἰς αὐτόν, ἵνα ὁ λόγος Ἠσαΐου τοῦ προφήτου πληρωθῇ ὃν εἶπεν· κύριε, τίς ἐπίστευσεν τῇ ἀκοῇ ἡμῶν; καὶ ὁ βραχίων κυρίου τίνι ἀπεκαλύφθη; διὰ τοῦτο οὐκ ἠδύναντο πιστεύειν, ὅτι πάλιν εἶπεν Ἠσαΐας· τετύφλωκεν αὐτῶν τοὺς ὀφθαλμοὺς καὶ ἐπώρωσεν αὐτῶν τὴν καρδίαν, ἵνα μὴ ἴδωσιν τοῖς ὀφθαλμοῖς καὶ νοήσωσιν τῇ καρδίᾳ καὶ στραφῶσιν, καὶ ἰάσομαι αὐτούς. ταῦτα εἶπεν Ἠσαΐας ὅτι εἶδεν τὴν δόξαν αὐτοῦ, καὶ ἐλάλησεν περὶ αὐτοῦ. ("Although he had performed so many signs in their presence, they did not believe in him. This was to fulfill the word spoken by the prophet Isaiah: 'Lord, who has believed our message, and to whom has the arm of the Lord been revealed?' And so they could not believe, because Isaiah also said, 'He has blinded their eyes and hardened their heart, so that they might not look with their eyes, and understand with their heart and turn and I would heal them.' Isaiah said this because he saw his glory and spoke about him.")

Here the narrator himself indicates a scriptural quotation[17] and intrudes with an explanation. This time he attempts to explain the apparent resistibility of Jesus's message on the part of "the crowd" (ὁ ὄχλος). As a character in the narrative, the crowd is difficult to define precisely.[18] At 12:34 the crowd initiates a conversation on Jesus's messiahship. He responds by exhorting them to "believe" (v. 36). It is the crowd, then, that is logically indicated by the third person plural language in the passage that follows.

---

17. NA[26] lists 12:27 as the next direct quote, but the author himself does not indicate this.

18. See R. Alan Culpepper's treatment of the crowd in *Anatomy of the Fourth Gospel: A Study in Literary Design* (Philadelphia: Fortress, 1983), esp. 131–32.

This passage quite clearly indicates that the crowd did not believe in Jesus (τοσαῦτα δὲ αὐτοῦ σημεῖα πεποιηκότος ἔμπροσθεν αὐτῶν οὐκ ἐπίστευον εἰς αὐτόν, "Although he had performed so many signs in their presence, they did not believe in him"), a statement that contradicts those made in 7:31 (ἐκ τοῦ ὄχλου δὲ πολλοὶ ἐπίστευσαν εἰς αὐτόν, "Yet many in the crowd believed in him") and 7:40–41 (ἐκ τοῦ ὄχλου οὖν ἀκούσαντες τῶν λόγων τούτων ἔλεγον· οὗτός ἐστιν ἀληθῶς ὁ προφήτης· ἄλλοι ἔλεγον· οὗτός ἐστιν ὁ χριστός, "When they heard these words, some in the crowd said, 'This is really the prophet.' Others said, 'This is the Messiah'"). Their stance vis-à-vis Jesus is not the only perplexing issue; one also wonders who constitutes this "crowd." In 12:9 they are presented as Jews (ὁ ὄχλος πολὺς ἐκ τῶν Ἰουδαίων), and our present passage contributes to such a characterization by saying, ὅμως μέντοι καὶ ἐκ τῶν ἀρχόντων πολλοὶ ἐπίστευσαν εἰς αὐτόν, ἀλλὰ διὰ τοὺς Φαρισαίους οὐχ ὡμολόγουν ἵνα μὴ ἀποσυνάγωγοι γένωνται ("Nevertheless, many, even of the authorities, believed in him. But because of the Pharisees they did not confess it, for fear that they would be put out of the synagogue," v. 42). All of these "characters," that is, the crowd, the authorities, and even the Pharisees, have been characterized in earlier chapters as suffering divisions among themselves on account of Jesus's identity and validity.[19] The author seems to collapse the groups so that there is overlap among the crowd, the Jews, the Pharisees, and the authorities. The author displays ambivalence toward those from the group who believe: he can characterize these people as "believing," but then go on to exclude them categorically from the group of believers (that is, at 12:37 he does not indicate that "some" did not believe, but rather simply says, "they" did not believe), only to claim a few verses later that "many, even of the authorities, believed in him" (v. 42), but ultimately reveals disappointment with them by qualifying that belief thus: ἀλλὰ διὰ τοὺς Φαρισαίους οὐχ ὡμολόγουν ἵνα μὴ ἀποσυνάγωγοι γένωνται ("But because of the Pharisees they were not confessing, lest they be put out of the synagogue," v. 42b).[20] The progression from initial belief to hostility occurs also in chapters 6 and 8 and probably indicates the trouble the sect

---

19. See the crowd at 7:43, the Pharisees at 9:16, the "Jews" at 10:19, and the authorities, especially represented by Nicodemus, at 7:45–52.

20. Raymond E. Brown offers an argument about these "crypto-Christians" in which he reaches the conclusion that these people remain outsiders in the eyes of the Johannine community (*The Community of the Beloved Disciple* [New York: Paulist, 1979], 89).

had with defectors. Before we leave the crowd, it should be noted that, in typical Johannine fashion, "the crowd" serves as yet another witness (ἐμαρτύρει οὖν ὁ ὄχλος, 12:17) to Jesus.

It might strike the reader of the Fourth Gospel as odd that Jesus's message could, in fact, remain resistible. Twice Jesus seems to indicate that he expects the crowd to believe. In a prayer delivered to his Father just before he raises Lazarus, Jesus thanks his Father for having heard him. He declares ἐγὼ δὲ ᾔδειν ὅτι πάντοτέ μου ἀκούεις, ἀλλὰ διὰ τὸν ὄχλον τὸν περιεστῶτα εἶπον, ἵνα πιστεύσωσιν ὅτι σύ με ἀπέστειλας ("I knew that you always hear me, but I have said this for the sake of the crowd standing here, so that they may believe that you sent me," 11:42). Again, in 12:36 Jesus exhorts the crowd: ὡς τὸ φῶς ἔχετε, πιστεύετε εἰς τὸ φῶς, ἵνα υἱοὶ φωτὸς γένησθε ("While you have the light, believe in the light, so that you may become children of light"). Immediately after that (12:37) the author informs the reader that, in fact, "they" did not believe in him. This is a strange predicament for him who "knew what was in everyone" (2:25) to find himself. The author makes some attempt to account for Jesus's resistibility by claiming that "the word spoken by the prophet Isaiah" was thus "fulfilled" by the unbelief of the crowd that Jesus had just evangelized. So clearly does the author want to make this point that he immediately repeats his argument, but draws on a different scriptural text the second time. He says, "For this reason they *could not* believe [οὐκ ἠδύναντο], because Isaiah also said, 'He has blinded their eyes and hardened their heart, so that they might not look with their eyes, and understand with their heart, and turn, and I would heal them.'" Moreover, the motif is already stated candidly in 2:23–25 and illustrated by Nicodemus.

The fact that John reiterates this point so emphatically should make us ask why. As previously noted, it is not enough to imagine compulsion on the author's part, since his work seems to argue against such a simple explanation. The question of Jesus's resistibility probably arose either from the community itself, seeking to understand how God's message could remain uncompelling for so many of their contemporaries, or the question was put to them by their Jewish contemporaries in the form, "If this person was who you say he was, then why does the majority of your Jewish brothers and sisters remain unconvinced?" Most likely the "answer" given served both the bolstering of the insiders and an apology regarding outsiders. That one might build a case for a social reality driving this apology is supported by at least two observations. First, before one writes it off as mere tradition, she would do well to note that the Synoptics nowhere use

Isa 53:1. In fact, the only other occurrence of the text appears in Romans 10:16 (and then only the first part of the verse), where Paul expressly addresses the very question we imagine the Johannine sect to have asked, or been asked, namely, how to explain the unbelief of the majority of Jews. Paul writes, "But not all have obeyed the good news; for Isaiah says, 'Lord who has believed our message?'" Paul then goes on to explain that the Jews' disbelief serves a definite and intentional function in God's salvific plan. So the only other appearance of the text occurs in a situation much like the one we imagine for John 12:38–40.

Furthermore, the second text John quotes, Isa 6:10, is used differently in the Synoptics. There it always serves a part in the explanation for the obscure nature of Jesus's parables. John, who has no parables, groups this text with Isa 53:1 to explain the disbelief of those whom the Johannine community would have expected to have believed. If this understanding of the presence of these scriptural texts is accurate, then one can readily imagine the function served for the sect. First, the authority of Scripture as well as the contention that scripture refers to the evangelist's contemporary community is affirmed; the author claims that "because" (ὅτι) Isaiah said so, the crowd could not believe. (Matthew places more blame on Jesus's parable audience, stating that they simply "did not" perceive, listen, or understand, unlike John's crowd, who "could not" believe.) Scripture is clearly a locus of authority for the group. Second, the author of the Fourth Gospel not only quotes Isaiah but even explains why the prophet was moved to say such a thing in the first place, namely, ὅτι εἶδεν τὴν δόξαν αὐτοῦ, καὶ ἐλάλησεν περὶ αὐτοῦ ("because he saw his glory, and he spoke about him"). The author clearly indicates that hoary Scripture actually applies and finds its telos in Jesus. Third, this use of Scripture may be characterized as a rhetorical technique that, if it does not "effect" inclusion or exclusion, certainly "validates" the experience of the community and draws clear boundaries between insiders and outsiders. That is, there are those, indeed the majority, who have not joined the group. Why not? The answer according to John and Paul is: "Do not be troubled, all is going according to plan, as you can see by referring to Scripture." This passage provides a good example of Garfinkel's phenomenology of degradation rituals. The opponents are different in essence; they are those who are "not chosen."

A successful sect must offer heavy rewards to balance the sacrifices made by its members. The second scriptural quote implies a reward for the sectarians, namely, "healing": καὶ ἰάσομαι αὐτούς. The association between healing, salvation, and sin, especially the sin of faithlessness, is heavily attested in the Old Testament and is assumed by some New Testament authors as well. It is particularly a favorite metaphor of the psalmist and the prophets and applies both to individuals and to the collective Israel. In Ps 40:5 (MT 41:4), the author entreats God: ἐγὼ εἶπα κύριε ἐλέησόν με ἴασαι τὴν ψυχήν μου ὅτι ἥμαρτόν σοι ("As for me, I said, 'Lord, have mercy on me; heal my soul because I have sinned against you'").[21] The prophets, especially Jeremiah and Isaiah, frequently use this language. After proclaiming Israel's faithlessness, God says, ἐπιστράφητε υἱοὶ ἐπιστρέφοντες καὶ ἰάσομαι τὰ συντρίμματα ὑμῶν ("Return, O faithless children, I will heal your faithlessness," Jer 3:22). Later Jeremiah implores God: ἴασαί με κύριε καὶ ἰαθήσομαι σῶσόν με καὶ σωθήσομαι ("Heal me, O Lord, and I shall be healed; save me, and I shall be saved," Jer 17:14).[22] Isaiah, from whom the author has taken both quotations in this passage, demonstrates an inseparable link between healing and salvation from sin. Isaiah 53:5 can speak of a certain salvific figure thus: αὐτὸς δὲ ἐτραυματίσθη διὰ τὰς ἀνομίας ἡμῶν καὶ μεμαλάκισται διὰ τὰς ἁμαρτίας ἡμῶν παιδεία εἰρήνης ἡμῶν ἐπ'αὐτόν τῷ μώλωτι αὐτοῦ ἡμεῖς ἰάθημεν ("But he was wounded for our transgressions, crushed for our iniquities; upon him was the punishment that made us whole, and by his bruises we are healed"). Isaiah 61:1, which serves a programmatic function at the inauguration of Jesus's ministry in Luke, announces: πνεῦμα κυρίου ἐπ'ἐμέ οὗ εἵνεκεν ἔχρισέν με εὐαγγελίσασθαι πτωχοῖς ἀπέσταλκέν με ἰάσασθαι τοὺς συντετριμμένους τῇ καρδίᾳ κηρύξαι αἰχμαλώτοις ἄφεσιν καὶ τυφλοῖς ἀνάβλεψιν ("The spirit of the Lord God is upon me, because the Lord has anointed me; he has sent me to bring good news to the oppressed, to bind up the brokenhearted, to proclaim liberty to the captives, and release to the prisoners"). The author of the Fourth Gospel has adopted Isaiah's vision of God as one who "hardens hearts" and one who "heals hearts."

The quote from Isa 6:10 is the first mention of heart (ἡ καρδία) in the Fourth Gospel. As we have noted, that Scripture citation helps to explain the resistibility of Jesus's message and implies reward for the faithful sectarians. If the sectarians are to identify themselves with the disciples in the narrative, then the reward implied in the present passage unfolds more fully to them in the succeeding narrative. Καρδία is first mentioned at 12:40 as part of the quote. After that it occurs five more times, always with reference

---

21. Cf. Ps 102:2–3 (MT 103:2–3): εὐλόγει ἡ ψυχή μου τὸν κύριον καὶ μὴ ἐπιλανθάνου πάσας τάς ἀνταποδόσεις αὐτοῦ τὸν εὐιλατεύοντα πάσαις ταῖς ἀνομίαις σου τὸν ἰώμενον πάσας τάς νόσους σου.

22. See also Lam 2:13; Hos 6:1; 14:5.

to Jesus's disciples. Immediately after our passage, the reader learns that the devil puts it into Judas's heart (καρδία) to betray Jesus. Three times we learn that the disciples are troubled, afraid, and sorrowful in heart (14:1, 27; 16:6). The final word once again acknowledges their pain but points toward the promise of joy: καὶ ὑμεῖς οὖν νῦν μὲν λύπην ἔχετε· πάλιν δὲ ὄψομαι ὑμᾶς, καὶ χαρήσεται ὑμῶν ἡ καρδία, καὶ τὴν χαρὰν ὑμῶν οὐδεὶς αἴρει ἀφ' ὑμῶν ("So you have pain now; but I will see you again, and your hearts will rejoice, and no one will take your joy from you," 16:22). In addition to healing, then, the disciples in the narrative and the sectarians receive inalienable joy.

That healing and salvation are synonymous is indubitable to any reader of the Synoptics, and I will not belabor the point here. Rather, it bears reminding the reader of John's own connection between healing and salvation as indicated by 3:14, where the author alludes to Moses's lifting up the serpent in the wilderness to indicate what effect Jesus's crucifixion will have. The author does not explain what transpired in the Moses event but assumes that the reader knows. In fact, Moses's raising the serpent brought healing: καὶ ἐποίησεν Μωυσῆς ὄφιν χαλκοῦν καὶ ἔστησεν αὐτὸν ἐπὶ σημείου καὶ ἐγένετο ὅταν ἔδακνεν ὄφις ἄνθρωπον καὶ ἐπέβλεψεν ἐπὶ τὸν ὄφιν τὸν χαλοῦν καὶ ἔζη ("So Moses made a serpent of bronze, and put it upon a pole; and whenever a serpent bit someone, that person would look at the serpent of bronze and live," Num 21:9). That is, it brought life and salvation, two of the author's favorite words. All of these, healing, salvation, and joy, are no small rewards for the insiders.

Finally, in his concluding remarks on the pericope, the author implies that there are some potential sectarians who remain on the fringe for fear of being put out of the synagogue. The author has no patience for such people and contrasts Isaiah's seeing Jesus's glory and voicing that glory with those who have seen but do not voice it, because they are more concerned with human glory than Jesus's. Such a presentation would serve both to call the fence-sitters to complete allegiance and to keep in place those already wholly aligned with the group. We are once again reminded of the sect as a high ideology group characterized by unsettled lives prone to apostasy. Those in settled lives are wary of joining due to the heavy social dislocation involved.

2.4. Example 2: John 15

> John 15:25: ἀλλ' ἵνα πληρωθῇ ὁ λόγος ὁ ἐν τῷ νόμῳ αὐτῶν γεγραμμένος ὅτι ἐμίσησάν με δωρεάν. ("It was to fulfill the word that is written in their law, 'They hated me without a cause.'")

All would agree that John evinces a concern for love. Of 142 occurrences of ἀγαπάω in the New Testament, half occur in the Fourth Gospel and in the Johannine Epistles (thirty-seven and forty-one times, respectively). Ἀγάπη is a particularly Johannine word; the Fourth Gospel harbors seven of the nine Gospel appearances.[23] Of the twenty-five occurrences of φιλέω in the New Testament, half (thirteen) appear in the Fourth Gospel. But John is even more disproportionately concerned with hate, which is showcased in 15:18–25.[24] Hatred (μισέω) of Jesus forms an *inclusio* in the passage, which has verses 18 and 25 as its brackets. The first part of the passage alludes to the world's hatred of the disciples and the second part to hatred of the Father; the hatred of both the disciples and the Father is tied to the hatred of Jesus. The world hates the disciples on account of Jesus's name, because they do not know the Father (v. 21). Whoever hates Jesus also hates the Father (vv. 23–24).

In addition to the author's explicit treatment of hate, close attention to the author's use and nonuse of Scripture corroborates the point. John, for all his attention to love, is the only gospel writer *not* to have Jesus quote Lev 19:18, "You shall love your neighbor as yourself." Either John did not know the tradition, which, given its appearance in all of the other gospels plus both Paul and James, seems unlikely, or the author knew it and chose to omit it for some particular reason.[25] If the Fourth Gospel community

---

23. The adjective ἀγαπητός, which occurs sixty-one times in the NT, never appears in the Fourth Gospel. The "beloved disciple" of the Fourth Gospel is always referred to with the verb. See, e.g., 21:7: ὁ μαθητὴς ἐκεῖνος ὃν ἠγάπα ὁ Ἰησοῦς ("that disciple whom Jesus loved").

24. Of the twenty-five occurrences of μισέω in the gospels, twelve occur in the Fourth Gospel (3:20; 7:7 [twice]; 12:25; 15:18 [twice], 19, 23 [twice], 24, 25; 17:14). Of those twelve, seven occur in ch. 15. Outside the Gospels and Acts, μισέω occurs only fifteen times (Rom 7:15; 9:13; Eph 5:29; Titus 3:3; Heb 1:9; 1 John 2:9, 11; 3:13, 15; 4:20; Jude 1:23; Rev 2:6 [twice]; 17:16; 18:2); notice that of those fifteen, one-third occur in 1 John.

25. The argument somewhat approximates that surrounding the Bethlehem tradition in which some scholars suggest, improbably, that the author simply did not know the tradition, whereas others argue for the author's intentional omission. So Raymond Brown states, "The objection raised against Jesus being the Messiah indicates that there was no knowledge in Jerusalem that Jesus had actually been born in Bethlehem, an indication that is hard to reconcile with Matt ii 3 where 'all Jerusalem' is upset by the birth of the child. Some commentators would transfer the ignorance of Jesus' birth at Bethlehem from the crowd to the evangelist. They maintain that the silence of John in not giving a rebuttal to the objection in vs. 42 means that the author did not know the

was indeed sectarian, as I argue, then the group's boundaries preclude any possibility of love for outsiders. The sect is a persecuted minority, whose very survival depends on separation from, not sympathy or collusion with, its opponents. As the language throughout the Fourth Gospel indicates, there is an "us" (represented in the text by the disciples who "remember Jesus's words" and "understand") and there is a "them," which indicates all who are "not us." The fact that the author is concerned primarily with the boundary between his group and those outside his group helps to explain why the boundaries between all of those in the Gospel who are "not us" remain so ill-defined; that is, the distinction between "the Jews," the Pharisees, the crowd, Nicodemus, the world, Judas, and so on is not always clear.

John is the only evangelist to omit the "love" quote of Lev 19:18, and the only author in the entire New Testament who includes the "hate" quote: "they hated me without cause," which the author claims derives from "what is written in *their* law." In fact, the sentence ἐμίσησάν με δωρεάν never appears in the LXX; rather, the phrase οἱ μισοῦντές με δωρεάν appears twice (Pss 68:5 and 34:19 [MT 35:19]). Although the author once again (cf. 10:34) claims to quote from the law (νόμος), in actuality he does not quote (he paraphrases), and the "text" is not from the law (it is a psalm[26]).

Though it offers the most concentrated attention to hate, chapter 15 is not the first time the author has addressed it. Already at 3:20 "hate" identifies which camp a person inhabits: "For all who do evil hate the light and

---

tradition of Jesus' birthplace as it is found in Luke and Matthew" (*The Gospel according to John*, 2 vols., AB 29–29A [Garden City, NY: Doubleday, 1966–1970], 2:330). Paul D. Duke also attests to the debate: "Though no one doubts irony's presence here, scholars debate its actual locus. Some say the author has in mind the tradition of Jesus' birth in Bethlehem. Others say John neither knows nor cares about that tradition, the ironic point being that Jesus is the Christ precisely in *spite* of his Galilean origin, because he is really from God" (*Irony in the Fourth Gospel* [Atlanta: John Knox, 1985], 67). On 174n11, Duke provides a bibliography of those who consider John knowledgeable about the Bethlehem tradition (Barrett, Brown, Bernard, Culpepper, Hoskyns, Morris, and Schlatter), those who dissent from this view (Bultmann, Lindars, de Jonge, and Meeks), and those who remain neutral (Dodd and Schnackenburg).

26. Jonathan G. Campbell's observation regarding Pauline literature obtains: "Secondly, it appears that Moses was viewed as a prophet and the Torah as the prophetic work par excellence, with the corollary that all his godly successors and their writings could be viewed as analogous, if secondary. The latter factor explains the flexibility evident in the terminology employed in the likes of 1 Cor 14:21, citing Isa 28:11, 12 as part of 'the law'" (*The Use of Scripture in the Damascus Document 1–8, 19–20*, SJ 228 [Berlin: de Gruyter, 1995], 17).

do not come to the light, so that their deeds may not be exposed." While this may sound like conventional wisdom or proverbial language, for John it is technical language, so that "hating the light" signifies hating Jesus.[27] Those who hate Jesus are further defined as those who "effect bad things" (ὁ φαῦλα πράσσων, 3:20).[28] In stark contrast, followers of Jesus, defined as "those who come to the light," are those who "do the truth" (ὁ δὲ ποιῶν τὴν ἀλήθειαν, 3:21).

The next time readers hear of "hate," at 7:7, they are both reminded of what they have learned in 3:20 and are taught something additional. They find Jesus explaining to his unbelieving brothers: "The world cannot hate

---

27. The word φῶς is particularly Johannine, occurring twenty-three times as opposed to seven times in both Matthew and Luke, and once in Mark. Of the twenty-three appearances in the Fourth Gospel, all but one (5:35) refer to Jesus. See, e.g., ἦν τὸ φῶς τὸ ἀληθινόν, ὃ φωτίζει πάντα ἄνθρωπον, ἐρχόμενον εἰς τὸν κόσμον ("The true light, which enlightens everyone, was coming into the world," 1:9); πάλιν οὖν ὐτοῖς ἐλάλησεν ὁ Ἰησοῦς λέγων· ἐγώ εἰμι τὸ φῶς τοῦ κόσμου· ὁ ἀκολουθῶν ἐμοὶ οὐ μὴ ἠεριπατήσῃ ἐν τῇ σκοτίᾳ, ἀλλ᾽ ἕξει τὸ φῶς τῆς ζωῆς ("Again Jesus spoke to them, saying, 'I am the light of the world. Whoever follows me will never walk in darkness but will have the light of life,'" 8:12). In 9:5, Jesus indicates that he will not always be in the world: ὅταν ἐν τῷ κόσμῳ ὦ, φῶς εἰμι τοῦ κόσμου ("As long as I am in the world, I am the light of the world") and, as is often the case, the Gospel goes on to verify this when Jesus's hour comes and he returns to the Father. The end of the so-called Book of Signs finds the last references in the Fourth Gospel to Jesus as the "light": ὡς τὸ φῶς ἔχετε, πιστεύετε εἰς τὸ φῶς, ἵνα υἱοὶ φωτὸς γένησθε. ταῦτα ἐλάλησεν Ἰησοῦς, καὶ ἀπελθὼν ἐκρύβη ἀπ᾽ αὐτῶν ("'While you have the light, believe in the light, so that you may become children of light.' After Jesus had said this, he departed and hid from them," 12:36); and ἐγὼ φῶς εἰς τὸν κόσμον ἐλήλυθα, ἵνα πᾶς ὁ πιστεύων εἰς ἐμὲ ἐν τῇ σκοτίᾳ μὴ μείνῃ ("I have come as light into the world, so that everyone who believes in me should not remain in the darkness," 12:46). Jesus's words in 12:46 indicate a closure of his activity as the light that shines in the darkness (σκοτία) that was announced in the prologue: καὶ τὸ φῶς ἐν τῇ σκοτίᾳ φαίνει, καὶ ἡ σκοτία αὐτὸ οὐ κατέλαβεν ("The light shines in the darkness, and the darkness did not overcome it," 1:5), thus forming an *inclusio* for the Book of Signs.

28. The only other time πράσσω occurs is in a passage much like the present one, which distinguishes between two types of people, namely, those who do (ποιέω) good and those who accomplish (πράσσω) the bad: μὴ θαυμάζετε τοῦτο, ὅτι ἔρχεται ὥρα ἐν ᾗ πάντες οἱ ἐν τοῖς μνημείοις ἀκούσουσιν τῆς φωνῆς αὐτοῦ καὶ ἐκπορεύσονται οἱ τὰ ἀκαθὰ ποιήσαντες εἰς ἀνάστασιν ζωῆς, οἱ δὲ τὰ φαῦλα πράξαντες εἰς ἀνάστασιν κρίσεως ("Do not be astonished at this; for the hour is coming when all who are in their graves will hear his voice and will come out—those who have done good, to the resurrection of life, and those who have done evil, to the resurrection of condemnation," 5:28–29).

you, but it hates me, because I testify against it that its works are evil," and they are thereby reminded that "Jesus haters" do "evil works"; but they also learn that "the world" (ὁ κόσμος) falls into the camp of "Jesus haters." Thus they are surprised neither by Jesus's announcement in 15:18–25 that the world hates him nor that people fall into two and only two distinct categories, here, "those who belong to the world" (ἐκ τοῦ κόσμου, 15:19)[29] and "those who do not belong to the world." In this passage Jesus identifies the latter as his disciples. There are two related principles at work in Jesus's words: (a) one can only love and be loved by that to which one *belongs*, and (b) one can belong to only one group. So the world must love its own (15:18); the disciples are not the world's own but rather are Jesus's own, as the reader already knows from 13:1: "having loved his own who were in the world, he loved them to the end" (cf. 1:11). Therefore, the disciples must be hated by the world. The world's hatred is inevitable, but Jesus encourages the disciples in two ways. First, he identifies with their experience. Second, he shows foreknowledge of what the future holds such that his credibility is high; so, if it is the case that what he says about the world's hatred comes to pass, it should also be the case that comforting promises (of an advocate, of eternal life, etc.) will likewise be fulfilled. So, just when the disciples begin to undergo their persecution, they should, ideally, remember that Jesus predicted this and be encouraged by the promise that they should expect to be honored by Jesus.

As often happens, Jesus quotes himself and correctly here. When he says at 15:20, "Remember the word that I said to you, 'Servants are not greater than their master,'" he is referring back to 13:16, though in that context Jesus uses the maxim to enjoin the disciples to act in a certain way toward one another rather than endure the ignominy of the world. The effect of this middle section of 15:18–26 is to list numerous ways in which the disciples are united with Jesus against the world; they are his own, so that which holds true regarding the world's attitude toward him obviously holds true for them: the world hates them, the world persecutes them, and the world will not keep its word.

---

29. In "derivation," Leander E. Keck argues that "indeed, this Gospel relies repeatedly on one preposition—ἐκ (of, from)—to express not only its Christology but also its anthropology and soteriology" ("Derivation as Destiny: 'Of-ness' in Johannine Christology, Anthropology, and Soteriology," in *Exploring the Gospel of John: In Honor of D. Moody Smith*, ed. R. Alan Culpepper and C. Clifton Black [Louisville: Westminster John Knox, 1996], 274).

Jesus then turns his attention from the relationship between the disciples and the world back to the relationship between the world and himself and, in doing so, largely repeats material he has stated earlier in the Gospel: (1) the world does not know the Father (see 16:3) who sent Jesus;[30] (2) had the world been ignorant of Jesus, it would not be culpable (see 9:41); (3) it hates Jesus and his Father; and (4) it does not heed Jesus's words (see 14:24). Four times in 15:18–25 the author indicates the world's hatred of Jesus and his father: in verses 18, 23, 24, and finally in verse 25, where Jesus announces that all of this hatred is in accordance with the word that is written in *their* law.[31] Surely the irony is thick when Jesus quotes from "their" law. Throughout the Gospel one has seen a battle raging about the proper interpretation of Scripture. The opponents and Jesus confront one another at every turn regarding it, with the opponents claiming that Scripture must be fulfilled, such that Jesus cannot be the Messiah, because he breaks the Sabbath (ch. 9), he does not come from Bethlehem (ch. 7), and so on. The irony throughout lies in the fact that Scripture, rightly understood, *is* fulfilled in Jesus, though the opponents cannot see this, because, as Jesus says to them, "You search the Scriptures, because you think that in them you have eternal life; and it is they that testify on my behalf" (5:39). The opponents long to see Scripture fulfilled; when Jesus fulfills it, they cannot see it. They long to fulfill Scripture; when they do so, they are blind to its ramifications. At 15:25, Jesus declares that they have achieved their goal; they have, indeed, fulfilled *their* law, but in the most tragic of ways: "It was to fulfill the word that is written in their law, 'They hated me without a cause.'"

This is a sophisticated move on the author's part. Unlike Qumran, where the opponents are characterized forthrightly as "lawbreakers," John grants, ironically, that the opponents are, indeed, fulfillers of the law, but not in the way they imagine themselves to be. What does this scriptural citation do for the late first-century Johannine community? The author intends his community to identify with the disciples/Jesus/Father, so the citation warns the members of John's community to *expect* the world's

---

30. Jesus is often described as the one whom God has "sent" (ἀποστέλλω; πέμπω), and God is often described as the one who sent (ἀποστέλλω; πέμπω) Jesus. See, e.g., 3:17, 34; 5:36, 38; 6:29, 57; 7:29; 8:42; 10:36; 11:42; 17:3, 8, 18, 21, 23, 25; 20:21.

31. The author already indirectly indicated the world's hatred of Jesus at 3:20 and directly at 7:7.

hatred and persecution, and it provides a theodicy for those already experiencing it.

The use of Scripture in this passage draws definite boundaries between insiders and outsiders. The opponents, here called "the world," are degraded and shown to be, as Garfinkel suggests, something essentially different from the followers of Jesus. Simultaneously the opponents are degraded and the sectarians elevated. This is done in both obvious and subtle ways. When Jesus makes such statements as, "If you belonged to the world, the world would love you as its own," and "Because you do not belong to the world, but I have chosen you out of the world, therefore the world hates you" (15:19), he degrades the world as hostile toward him and elevates the disciples as those he has "chosen out of the world"; his disciples are both "chosen" and separate from "the world."

The author, therefore, degrades the opponents and elevates the sectarians by associating them with their respective forebears who have been placed in their distinct categories. But the passage also reveals a slightly more subtle method of elevating the disciples: for every negative and degrading characteristic Jesus ascribes to the opponents, the author has depicted the disciples in opposite terms. The world "hates" the disciples and Jesus, whereas the disciples "love one another" (cf. 13:35) and Jesus (e.g., 14:15; 15:17; 17:26; 21:15, 16, 17). The world loves its own, whereas the disciples are not the world's own (17:14). The world persecutes on account of Jesus (cf. 16:2), whereas the disciples are persecuted on account of Jesus's name (see 16:2). The opponents do not keep Jesus's word (cf. 14:24), whereas the disciples do (esp. 17:6, "they have kept your word"; see also 14:15, 21, 23; 15:10). The opponents do not know God (see 16:3), whereas the disciples do (14:7). The opponents' response to viewing Jesus's works is hatred of Jesus and his Father (10:38–39), whereas the disciples respond with belief (cf. 2:11), and so on.

Finally, the scriptural citation provides the ultimate degradation of the opponents, because not only do they hate Jesus, they hate him for no reason at all. That is to say, by means of the scriptural citation, Jesus summarizes the point he has made throughout the Gospel: though the opponents claim to hate him on account of his words and deeds, in actuality they are never able to make their case viable. The only reason they hate Jesus is because their father is the devil (8:44); they are, in their very *essence*, opponents of Jesus. The Johannine community is supposed to identify with the disciples, Jesus, and God in the narrative such that the text, by depicting the disciples' and Jesus's opponents in a degrading light, depicts the Johannine community's own opponents in the same light. Simultaneously, then, John has used the scriptural citation to mark a boundary between insider and outsider, to degrade the opponents, and to elevate the sectarians. Furthermore, the scriptural citation evinces the practice of setting boundaries by means of literary and rhetorical techniques to effect inclusion or exclusion; those "outside" the group are those who "fulfill Scripture" by hating Jesus "without a cause."

The author also bolsters the confidence of the Johannine sectarians by showing Jesus's special insight regarding Scripture. The opponents lord scripture over Jesus and the disciples in the narrative and John's first-century community, but the community is shown the errors of the opponents' ways. The opponents *think* they know what Scripture means, but Scripture cannot be understood apart from knowledge of and belief in Jesus (5:39), knowledge and belief that only the Johannine community possesses. As always in the Fourth Gospel, Jesus wields Scripture truly and effectively, leaving his scriptural opponents looking obtuse. This would go some distance in convincing the Johannine sectarians that they had the upper hand, despite appearances and experiences that may indicate otherwise. The invocation of Scripture by Jesus at 15:25 demonstrates that Jesus is a locus of authority: he alone properly understands Scripture, and he and the community serve as its telos.

3. Conclusion

When one applies systematically the method proposed in this paper to all of the scriptural citations, one finds that Scripture serves a stunning array of functions for the author of the Fourth Gospel as evidenced in table 3. Note that I have plotted our examples on the chart in bold.

Table 3. Functions of Scriptural Citations in the Fourth Gospel
- A. Breaking Away: Creating and Degrading "Them" (2:17–18; 10:22–39; **12:38–43; 15:25**)
- B. Formation of Sect
    1. Etiology: celebrate the origins of the community; ground the community in the hoary past (12:13–15)
    2. Show sect's founder to have special insight regarding Scripture (11:22–39; 13:18; **15:25**; 19:28)
    3. Defining and elevating "us"

a. Those who receive revelation through "remembrance" (2:22; 12:13–15; 13:18; **15:25**)
  b. Those who see, know, understand, believe; those who "get" the author's irony (7:37–52)
C. Creating a Distinct Way of Life
  1. Ethical behavior
  2. Ritual practice
  3. Language and rhetoric (2:22; 7:37–52; 10:22–39; 12:13–15; **12:38–43**.; 13:18; **15:25**)
  4. Use of sacred texts
    a. The sectarian community as Scripture's telos (1:23; 2:17; 12:13–15; **12:38–43**; 13:18; **15:25**; 19:24, 36, 37)
    b. Scripture validates the sect's views (7:38–39)
  5. Roles of authoritative leaders
    a. John the Baptist: important but subordinate to Jesus (1:23)
    b. Jesus
      i. The leader is righteous, chosen by God, admirable (2:17; 10:22–39; 12:13, 15)
      ii. Unjustly persecuted (10:22–39; **15:25**)
      iii. Privy to special insight (10:22; 13:18; **15:25**)
      iv. Warrants fidelity and belief; salvation depends on one's stance toward him (**12:38–43**)
  6. Definition of the future
D. Opposition to and from the Parent Tradition
  1. Named opponents (10:22–39; 13:18; **15:25**; 19:24, 28, 36, 37)
  2. Those who break Scripture or fail to understand it (2:17–18; 5:39–47, 10:22–39)
E. Opposition from within the Sect: Dealing with Defection
  1. Reward sticking with the sect (John 6; **12:38–43**)
  2. Castigate potential and actual deserters (13:18; **12:38–43**)
  3. General remarks (19:24, 28, 36, 37)
F. Opposition to and from Without (**12:38–43; 15:25**)
G. Judgment against Opponents: Jesus's word, not Scripture, is used for this in the Fourth Gospel (see 5:24)
H. Growing the Sect
  1. Proselytizing
  2. The next generation

John, believer, preacher, storyteller, and minister, already knew what scholars of New Testament and sociology are only now beginning to study and take somewhat seriously: Scripture is powerful for all who lend it authority.

A Voice in the Wilderness:
Classical Rhetoric and the Testimony
of John (the Baptist) in John 1:19–34*

Alicia D. Myers

After the work of George Kennedy, interest in the light that classical rhetoric can shed on the New Testament has boomed among certain interpreters.[1] While initially the majority of this work was limited to dissecting the arguments found in the Pauline Epistles, the rhetorical nature of the gospels is now also being acknowledged.[2] The Gospel of John, in particular, is ripe for rhetorical exploration with its numerous discourses and clear persuasive intent expressed in 20:30–31. Andrew Lincoln, Harold Attridge, and George Parsenios have noted a number of connections between John and

---

* This essay is a revised and expanded version of a presentation offered at the 2012 Society of Biblical Literature annual meeting in Chicago: "A Voice in the Wilderness: The Testimony of John in Rhetorical Perspective."

1. George A. Kennedy, *New Testament Interpretation through Rhetorical Criticism*, SR (Chapel Hill: University of North Carolina Press, 1984). There is an important distinction between scholars who examine the rhetoric of John in light of contemporary methods of rhetorical criticism and the approach of this particular essay, which focuses on *classical* rhetoric. "Classical rhetoric" focuses on the rhetorical techniques outlined by various orators and authors in the ancient Mediterranean world, including (but not limited to) the instructional works of the *progymnasmata* (rhetorical textbooks for teaching secondary students); Quintilian's *Institutes of Oratory*, Cicero's *De oratore*, *Rhetorica ad Herennium*, and *Topica*; and Aristotle's *Rhetoric* and *Poetics*. The rhetorical techniques outlined in these and other similar works are used and adapted throughout the preserved literatures of the ancient Mediterranean world.

2. See the call for continued exploration into the rhetoric of the gospels by C. Clifton Black, "Kennedy and the Gospels: An Ambiguous Legacy, a Promising Bequest," in *Words Well Spoken: George Kennedy's Rhetoric of the New Testament*, ed. C. Clifton Black and Duane F. Watson, SRR 8 (Waco: Baylor University Press, 2008), 63–80.

juridical rhetoric while Jo-Ann Brant emphasizes the Gospel's epideictic, or praising, nature.[3] These scholars suggest that the discourses alone are not the only places in which one can find rhetorical aspects of the Gospel. Instead, the entire narrative construction incorporates rhetorical components that resonate with expectations surrounding the creation of narratives in the ancient world.[4] While many of these components may come out with special force in Jesus's speeches and dialogical exchanges, they are nevertheless present throughout this ancient biography (*bios*), including the way it shapes its characters and events, and the way it uses Scripture to do so.[5] Examining the Fourth Gospel in light of classical rhetoric, then, provides another way forward in the discussion of the use of Scripture in John that is the focus of this present volume. Since the Gospel incorporates various techniques from classical rhetoric in service of its larger argument about Jesus's identity, it should not be surprising that its use of Scripture also reflects familiarity with these techniques—either through explicit instruction or through general literary and rhetorical exposure.[6]

---

3. Andrew T. Lincoln, *Truth on Trial: The Lawsuit Motif in the Fourth Gospel* (Peabody, MA: Hendrickson, 2000); Harold W. Attridge, "Argumentation in John 5," in *Rhetorical Argumentation in Biblical Texts: Essays from the Lund 2000 Conference*, ed. Anders Eriksson et al., ESEC 8 (Harrisburg, PA: Trinity Press International, 2002), 188–99; George L. Parsenios, *Rhetoric and Drama in the Johannine Lawsuit Motif*, WUNT 258 (Tübingen: Mohr Siebeck, 2010), esp. 34–47; Jo-Ann A. Brant, *John*, PCNT (Grand Rapids: Baker Academic, 2011), 12.

4. For in-depth discussion of these rhetorical connections, see Alicia D. Myers, *Characterizing Jesus: A Rhetorical Analysis of the Use of Scripture in the Fourth Gospel's Presentation of Jesus*, LNTS 458 (London: T&T Clark, 2012), esp. 22–77; Jerome H. Neyrey, "Encomium versus Vituperation: Contrasting Portraits of Jesus in the Fourth Gospel," in *The Gospel of John in Cultural and Rhetorical Perspective* (Grand Rapids: Eerdmans, 2009), 3–38.

5. For more on the Gospel's genre, see Richard A. Burridge, *What Are the Gospels? A Comparison with Graeco-Roman Biography*, 2nd ed. (Grand Rapids: Eerdmans, 2004); Myers, *Characterizing Jesus*, 22–39.

6. It is impossible to *prove* the amount of education this, or any NT author, received. It is clear, however, that the author (or authors) of John received *some* education resulting in literacy and general awareness of rhetorical conventions. Jerome Neyrey makes the argument that the author must have had access to a good deal of education, reaching at least the level of the *progymnastic* exercises, since the narrative displays familiarity with a variety of rhetorical topics (*topoi*) and techniques ("The 'Noble' Shepherd in John 10: Cultural and Rhetorical Background," in *The Gospel of John in Cultural and Rhetorical Perspective* [Grand Rapids: Eerdmans, 2009], 309). Nevertheless, John does not demonstrate the rhetorical polish of professional rheto-

Exploring the inclusion of intertexts in classical rhetoric can thus shed light on both how Scripture is employed in the Gospel as well as its various functions.

The present chapter is an exercise in just this sort of method. Consulting the rhetorical handbooks of Aristotle, Cicero, Quintilian, and several *progymnasmata*, I will demonstrate how John's use of Scripture compares to various expectations surrounding the use of intertexts in classical rhetoric. I will provide a brief overview on the use of intertexts in classical rhetoric before exploring John 1:19–34 as a test case. As a recognized source of authority, Scripture repeatedly surfaces in the Gospel to further its plot, reinforce its cosmological perspective, and endorse its arguments concerning Jesus's identity and the resulting identities of those who accept and reject him. Reflecting its juridical nature, the Gospel establishes Scripture—and its various representatives—as witnesses speaking on behalf of Jesus, who operates as both defendant and judge (5:19–47). Demonstrating epideictic features, these scriptural intertexts further the Gospel's praise of Jesus as the Son of God, who successfully completes his mission as God's agent (20:30–31; 21:24–25). This essay will focus on John 1:19–34 in particular, and its citation of Isa 40:3 by the divinely commissioned witness, John (the Baptist).[7] The association between John (the Baptist) and Isa 40 is well established outside John's Gospel, but our author employs this well-known intertext to enhance the persuasiveness of John's testimony and sharpen the characterizations outlined in the Gospel's prologue (1:1–14). As the herald of Jesus's ministry, John invokes Scripture and speaks with the Isaianic voice. By incorporating this scriptural *exemplum*, John figuratively takes on Isaiah's prophetic mantle, initiating the Gospel's blending of their voices into one: a voice whose divine origins reach across time to

---

ricians and authors, nor is it clear that it was ever his aim to do so having written a biography in common (and, some would suggest, rudimentary) Greek. See, for example, the recent debate concerning the most rhetorically nuanced gospel author, Luke: Michael W. Martin, "Progymnastic Topic Lists: A Compositional Template for Luke and Other *Bioi*?," NTS 54 (2008): 18–41; Osvaldo Padilla, "Hellenistic Paideia and Luke's Education: A Critique of Recent Approaches," NTS 55 (2009): 416–37.

7. The Gospel of John does not use the Synoptic moniker "the baptizer" in its discussion of John (cf. Matt 3:1; Mark 1:4). Indeed, even though John's baptismal work is described, it is not the primary focus of the Gospel's presentation of his character. For the sake of clarity in this essay, I will refer to John with the aside (the Baptist) when context demands.

support Jesus's identity as God's Son and persists in the confession of the Gospel community.

1. Classical Rhetoric and Intertexts: A Brief Overview

While scholars have begun exploring the relationship between John and classical rhetoric, less interest has been shown among those examining John's use of Scripture. This reflects a larger sentiment that while classical rhetoric might be helpful in other aspects, it does not provide much assistance in intertextual studies because handbooks give little to no explicit instruction on the proper incorporation of quotations. Thus, while handbooks may describe the use of authoritative sources as "testimony" in passing, Christopher Stanley concludes, "This is as far as the ancient sources take us."[8] Although Stanley is right to note the lack of clear instruction on the precise methods of quotations, this conclusion overlooks the fact that ancient Mediterranean education is based on a foundational practice of imitation or mimesis. The significance of mimesis in education reflects broader mimetic assumptions in the ancient world, which influence ethical and identity formation, rhetorical performances, literary compositions, and interpretations of history. Imitation of expected norms, or great personages, was believed to shape a person, particularly if they were young. Moreover, such imitation invited favorable comparisons when the imitation was performed well. As a part of the larger mimetic program of ancient Mediterranean society, therefore, students were instructed to imitate and adapt past masters for their own rhetorical purposes, effectively reinforcing cultural codes in the young and demonstrating erudition, credibility, authority, and virtue as they matured.[9]

---

8. Christopher D. Stanley, "The Rhetoric of Quotations: An Essay on Method," in *Early Christian Interpretation of the Scriptures of Israel*, ed. Craig A. Evans and James A. Sanders, JSNTSupp 148, SSEJC 5 (Sheffield: Sheffield Academic, 1994), 45.

9. There are significant gender overtones with the emulation of past virtuous figures and the mastering of rhetoric. As a masculine-centered culture, the alignment of perfection with masculinity is assumed, even when women were authors and/or topics. Maud W. Gleason argues that as a display of education (*paideia*), rhetorical performance "made boys into men" and showcased the superiority of the elite male (*Making Men: Sophists and Self-Presentation in Ancient Rome* [Princeton: Princeton University Press, 1995], xxi–xxii). Rather than relying on the display of material books to showcase education, elite men "display[ed] their level of culture … only by having absorbed books so completely that they could exhale them as speech" (xxiv). The

When outlining the various exercises and techniques for their readers, the authors of rhetorical handbooks and *progymnasmata* encourage the imitation of past masters whose works act as patterns to be followed. Thus, at the outset of his *progymnasmata*, Aelius Theon offers an extensive list of authors he considers to be worthy of imitation by students. He writes, "First of all the teacher should collect good examples of each exercise from ancient prose works and assign them to the young to be learned by heart" (*Prog.* 65–66).[10] These examples include Homer, Thucydides, Plato, Sophocles, and Demosthenes among others—each author or text being set apart as a paradigm for a particular exercise.[11] Theon also reports that a teacher must likewise create good examples of exercises, so that "molded [τυπωθέντες] by what they have learned, they [students] may be able to imitate [μιμήσασθαι]" (*Prog.* 71). Theon's language here is evocative, creating the picture of *typing* a young student in the same way that wax was poured into a mold to be set in an individual seal.[12] Theon describes *forming* students so that their imitation of laudable predecessors comes naturally, resulting in work of comparable (though perhaps not equal) quality.[13] It is not surprising, then, that Theon continues to incorporate examples from other well-known sources in outlining exercises for his readers in the main text of his *progymnasmata*. Plato provides examples of *chreia* (χρεία, "anecdotes"), Thucydides of a credible historical narrative, Isocrates of an *encomiastic topos* (praise topic), Homer of *ekphrasis* (ἔκφρασις, "vivid

---

ubiquity of these gender assumptions solidify the crucial role of intertexts in classical rhetoric since one's education was directly tied to the estimation of one's authority and character—both of which were intimately tied to evaluations of gender.

10. All quotations from the *progymnasmata* are taken from George A. Kennedy, *Progymnasmata: Greek Textbooks of Composition and Rhetoric*, WGRW 10 (Atlanta: Society of Biblical Literature, 2003) unless otherwise noted.

11. Theon, *Prog.* 65–72. Quintilian likewise includes a section on authors whom orators in training should read and how they should (and should not) imitate them (*Inst.* 10.1–2). Also see Fred W. Householder Jr., *Literary Quotation and Allusion in Lucian* (Morningside Heights, NY: King's Crown Press, 1941), which offers a list of ancient authors commonly cited as exemplars for students (56–64).

12. See Plato, *Tim.* 50c; *Leg.* 65e; *Soph.* 239d; *Theat.* 171e; *Rep.* 387c; 402d, for elaboration on the language of "typing" (τυπόω).

13. The overlap between this educational model and character—as in ethical—formation of students is intentional in the ancient Mediterranean world. See Aristotle, *Nicomachean Ethics*; Gleason, *Making Men*, esp. xvii–xxix; Myers, *Characterizing Jesus*, 55–61.

description"), and various famous individuals are listed as examples for *synkrisis* (συγκρίσις, "comparison") as well as encouragement to note with a comment (ἐπιφωνεῖν) when "other famous men have thought the same."[14] Theon is not alone in this practice, as Quintilian likewise incorporates a number of examples from his predecessors, especially Cicero. Once mastered, students could vary the form and style of the exercises as they best fit their own arguments. But the exemplary authors that undergirded their own education remained as a ready source of material to which they might appeal in constructing their own works. Noting the persistent appeal to well-known people in ancient literature in particular, Ruth Webb explains, there was

> [a] practical advantage of using familiar epic and legendary figures as the raw material for these exercises. The basic characteristics of the persons and actions involved were agreed, what really mattered was what the rhetor or his students could do with them and the possibilities for argument that they offered.... These stories are elements of a common cultural property, to be manipulated and exploited as a demonstration of the art of argumentation. Their utility for the purpose lies precisely in the fact that they are well known.[15]

Making use of "common cultural property," then, rhetors and their students demonstrated their own cultural astuteness, making lessons of the past relevant and underscoring their own interpretations in their contexts. Moreover, the handbooks themselves model appropriate incorporation of intertexts. In this way, one's education laid the groundwork for the use of quotations and allusions without needing additional instructions to belabor their significance.

Explicit quotations and more subtle allusions, therefore, surface as ubiquitous and convenient resources when constructing various exercises and techniques. The ability to construct and combine various references, both overt and muted, highlighted the skill of an author or performer, as well as complimented the audience when they were able to recognize

---

14. Theon, *Prog.* 98; 84; 106; 118; 112–15. On including a comment to add authority to *chreia* in particular, Theon encourages using the "witness of the famous whenever we say that a wise man or lawgiver or poet or some other renowned person agrees with the saying" (103).

15. Ruth Webb, "The *Progymnasmata* in Practice," in *Education in Greek and Roman Antiquity*, ed. Yun Lee Too (Leiden: Brill, 2001), 302.

such appeals. Authors and orators are encouraged to incorporate examples to orient an audience as well as beautify, clarify, vivify, and render a rhetorical work more plausible for their hearers. Intertexts are especially useful for identifying precedents for current events, characterizations, and arguments. Aristotle, for example, suggests employing historical examples (πράγματα) alongside fables because, he writes, "as a rule the future resembles the past" (*Rhet.* 2.20.8 [Freese, LCL]). According to Aristotle, these precedents become even more effective for an argument when they are from authoritative sources, such as those used for various types of examples and testimonies, which various rhetoricians classify as human, written, ancient, and divine.[16] Moreover, such intertexts are freestanding, seemingly independent from the context into which they are incorporated by a given author or rhetorician, especially if they are very old and well known. Explaining this line of thought further, Quintilian encourages his readers to employ

> opinions which can be attributed to nations, peoples, wise men, distinguished citizens, or famous poets. Even common sayings and popular beliefs may be useful. All of these are in a sense testimonies, but they are actually *all the more effective* because they are not given to suit particular Causes, but spoken or given by minds free of prejudice for the simple reason that they seem either very honorable or very true. (*Inst.* 5.11.36–37, emphasis added)[17]

---

16. In his discussion of testimony, Cicero writes, "When people see men endowed with genius, industry and learning, and those whose life has been consistent and of approved goodness, like Cato, Laelius, Scipio and many more, they regard them as the kind of men they would like to be. Nor do they hold such an opinion only about those who have been honored by the people with public office and are busy with matters of state, but also about orators, philosophers, poets, and historians. Their sayings and writings are often used as authority to win conviction" (*Top.* 20.78 [Hubbell, LCL]). For full discussion of these types of testimony, see Alicia D. Myers, "'Jesus Said to Them': The Adaptation of Juridical Rhetoric in John 5:19–47," *JBL* 132 (2013): 421–25; Myers, *Characterizing Jesus*, 98–104.

17. All translations of Quintilian's *Institutes of Oratory* are from Donald A. Russell, LCL (2001–2002). For an example of this technique, see Cicero, *Pro Caelio* 8.18, in which he quotes both his contemporary Marcus Crassus and a Latin adaptation of Euripides's *Medea* to describe Caelio's move to an apartment near the Forum. This move made it possible for him to begin his relationship with the infamous Clodia—the "Medea" who brought suit against Caelio for attempted murder. The intertextual links incorporate references to recent political events foreshadowing Caelio's troubles

The overlap between the use of "examples" and "testimony" is highlighted in several additional handbooks. Aristotle writes that people are "more ready to believe in facts for which many testify, and examples and tales resemble testimony" (*Prob.* 18.3.32–34 [Hett, LCL]). Pseudo-Cicero also notes the similarity between examples and testimony, writing, "Examples, they say, serve the purpose of testimony; for, like the testimony of a witness, the example enforces what the precept has suggested" (*Rhet. Her.* 4.1.2 [Caplan, LCL]).[18] Stanley is indeed correct that intertextual examples often function as "witnesses" or "testimonies" in ancient works. However, as we now see, this is not a meager finding. Rather, the pervasiveness of these intertextual connections emphasizes the force they bring to a variety of literatures and even iconic material representations. They swiftly incorporate gnomic mores, establish well-worn precedents, and embed culturally significant contexts that function as frequent and effective proofs in arguments and representations.

Much as they do in contemporary literature, intertexts in ancient works serve to create comparisons between the current topic and what has occurred before. This is most apparent in formal *synkrises*, which set an individual, an event, or a topic alongside a known counterpart from the past. These comparisons "amplify" positive and negative qualities by "setting the better or worse side by side" (Theon, *Prog.* 112).[19] Aristotle encourages the use of *synkrises* in encomiastic works in particular, writing, "And you must compare him [your subject] with illustrious personages, for it affords ground for amplification and is noble, if he can be proved

---

with Clodia as well as creating a negative characterization of Clodia through the *synkristic* equation of her and Medea.

18. Elsewhere Ps.-Cicero distinguishes the two, explaining: "The difference between testimony and example is this: by example we clarify the nature of our statement, while by testimony we establish its truth" (*Rhet. Her.* 4.3.5 [Caplan, LCL]). The flexibility of actual rhetorical practice, however, blurs such a distinction since an intertextual reference can serve either of these functions or both simultaneously, as we will see in John 1:19–34. Quintilian's distinction between testimony and example is more helpful; he divides them not as a result of their affects, but along the lines of source. Examples are "external" proofs brought from outside the case at hand, and therefore "technical" (requiring "skill" [τέχνη] to shape), while testimony is "internal" and nontechnical, recorded and introduced specifically for the present topic or case (*Inst.* 5.11.43–44).

19. For additional information on *synkrisis* and comparisons, see Myers, *Characterizing Jesus*, 47–49.

better than men of worth" (*Rhet.* 1.9.39 [Freese, LCL]). Theon repeats this sentiment: "It is not without utility also to make mention of those already honored, comparing their deeds to those of the person being praised" (*Prog.* 111). Quintilian discusses the use of well-known figures from the past in his category of "examples" (*exempla*), under which he classifies both comparisons (*similitudo*, παραβολή) and precedents (παραδείγματα). These are "technical" proofs in an argument because they are external to a case, "especially with reference to things which rest on the authority of history," and must be used with skill by the orator so that they apply to present events (*Inst.* 5.11.1, 43–44). In addition to arguing for similarity and difference, Quintilian explains that one great "virtue" of these references is that they bring "the object [or person] before our eyes not only plainly but also concisely and rapidly" (*Inst.* 5.11.82). Such a move unites the audience and author in their common cultural property, makes otherwise obscure figures known, and reinforces a rhetorician's interpretation of events and characters. As a result of their persuasive potency, well-known persons and events were manipulated for use in any number of specific rhetorical techniques, including detailed descriptions of settings or individuals (*ekphrasis*); reworded or combined with other intertexts to fit a new context (*paraphrasis, metalepsis*), and woven into speeches for new characters (*prosōpopoiia*). As Quintilian notes, all of these techniques effectively establish a comparative context for the argument being presented; moreover, they do so with the benefit of externality and the authority that only accepted narratives and traditions carry.[20]

This brief overview demonstrates the importance of intertexts in classical rhetoric even without explicit instructions on the use of quotations. Instead of spending time instructing their readers on how to use "quotations," rhetorical handbooks and *progymnasmata* turn to descriptions of incorporating larger traditions and well-known individuals. In a society based largely on oral transmission and communication, lack of attention to explicit (and especially written) quotations is not surprising. But this does not mean that intertexts were irrelevant for composition and arguments. Instead, our sources largely assume their importance, regularly illustrating the significance of references by weaving them into a number of techniques. Such widespread incorporation of allusions and quotations

---

20. Cf. the example taken from Cicero's *Pro Caelio* 8.18 in n17, as well as Alexander's mourning of Hepheasteon in imitation of Achilles's mourning of Patroclus in Arrian, *Anab.* 7.14.4 (Homer, *Il.* 23.140–54).

is indicative of an ancient educational system built on mimesis; as Aristotle reminds us, the ancients believed that "the future resembles the past." Shaping one's rhetoric to reflect and reinterpret that past demonstrates awareness and understanding of the cultural repertoire, adding authority, vividness, and credibility to the argument at hand without getting bogged down in the details of "proper citation." Instead of justifying the dismissal of ancient rhetoric for the study of the use of Scripture in John (or the NT in general), then, such an attitude highlights the potential insight classical rhetoric can provide. It is with this lens that we now turn to our test text from the Fourth Gospel: the testimony of John (the Baptist) in John 1:19–34.

2. The Testimony of John

John 1:19–34 contains a number of scriptural references. As in the Synoptics, a version of Isa 40:3 is quoted to describe the ministry of John, although this time it appears on John's own lips rather than in an aside by a narrator (Matt 3:3; Mark 1:2–3; Luke 3:4–6). Other scriptural connections surface in the priests and Levites' questioning of John in 1:19–28—is he the Christ, Elijah, or perhaps the prophet like Moses from Deut 18:15–19? John (the Baptist) employs additional scriptural images from Israel's exodus narratives when he identifies Jesus as the "Lamb of God" in verses 29 and 36, and from Isaiah when he describes Jesus as the "Chosen One" in verse 34.[21] All of these references continue the narrator's tactic of situating the Gospel in the larger context of Israel's sacred story, which was initiated in the opening words of the prologue with "in the beginning" (Gen 1:1). The flowing cadence of the prologue continues to imitate the opening chapter of Genesis bringing in images of light, life, "becoming" (γίνομαι), and "begetting" (γεννάω).[22] In this way, the opening of John's Gospel reflects other lofty and encomiastic *prooimia* (prologues) in

---

21. Space prevents full exploration of the text-critical issue in v. 34 here. See Tze-Ming Quek, "A Text-Critical Study of John 1.34," *NTS* 55 (2009): 22–34.

22. A variety of chiastic structures have been proposed, most often with vv. 12–13 functioning as the fulcrum of these eighteen verses. See R. Alan Culpepper, "The Pivot of John's Prologue," *NTS* 27 (1981): 1–31; Jeffrey L. Staley, *The Print's First Kiss: A Rhetorical Investigation of the Implied Reader in the Fourth Gospel*, SBLDS 82 (Atlanta: Society of Biblical Literature, 1988), 53–57; Mary Coloe, "The Structure of the Johannine Prologue and Genesis 1," *ABR* 45 (1997): 40–55.

ancient Greco-Roman literatures, and reflects instructions to reach back across broad stretches of time in historical narratives.[23] With this imitation of Gen 1, John's Gospel emphasizes its own importance, as well as the importance of the Gospel's protagonist. According to John's Gospel, the incarnation of the Word in the person of Jesus marks another creation moment for the believing community and the cosmos. The prologue, then, has a programmatic function: setting the stage, establishing expectations, and summarizing the authoritative vantage point of the narrator for the remainder of the narrative. As the mimetic foundation for this program, Israel's Scriptures continue to play prominently. Yet, as Judith Lieu notes, rather than employing a litany of overt quotations to indicate fulfillment, the Gospel of John often weaves Scripture more subtly behind the scenes to create the fabric of its story of Jesus. In this way, the narrator encourages his audience to find connections between Jesus's identity, the events and persons involved in his ministry, and Scripture that become clear in the hindsight that the Spirit, and the Johannine community, provide (cf. 2:22; 12:15–16; 1 John 1:1–4).[24]

Completing his mimetic invocation of Genesis the narrator continues his prolonged introduction of his protagonist, this time by building a bridge to his physical entrance by means of the one who was "sent by God" to "testify to the light" whose "name was John" (1:6–8). In terms from classical rhetoric, John 1:19–34 surfaces in the midst of the larger, transitional section of 1:15–2:12, which uses climax (κλῖμαξ) or gradation (*gradatio, ascensus*) to shift focus from the witnessing John to the subject of his witness: Jesus.[25] This breakdown understands 1:16–18 to be the content of John's initial testimony, continuing his words from verse 15 since (1) there

---

23. Aristotle explains that *prooimia* are helpful to a wide variety of genres, writing that they should secure the goodwill of an audience by giving necessary knowledge and engage their attention through "astonishing" and/or important things (*Rhet.* 3.14.6–7). See also Peter M. Phillips, *The Prologue of the Fourth Gospel: A Sequential Reading*, LNTS 294 (London: T&T Clark, 2006), 37–45; Brant, *John*, 24–26. On the breadth of historical narratives, see Aristotle, *Rhet.* 3.16.4–7; Quintilian, *Inst.* 4.2.44–51; Theon, *Prog.* 22, 83; Lucian, *How to Write History*, 49–50.

24. Judith Lieu, "Narrative Analysis and Scripture in John," in *The Old Testament in the New Testament: Essays in Honor of J. L. North*, ed. Steve Moyise, JSNTSup 189 (Sheffield: Sheffield Academic, 2000), 144–63, esp. 161–62.

25. Using modern literary-critical categories, Catrin H. Williams uses the language of "focalization" to discuss this transition ("John [the Baptist]: The Wilderness on the Threshold," in *Character Studies in the Fourth Gospel: Narrative Approaches*

is no clear section break until verse 19 and (2) the three ὅτι clauses that follow encourage hearing these verses as a single unit.[26] Read together, the opening section of 1:15–2:12 creates a step sequence from the prologue's introduction of witness and subject, through the witness's activity, and on to the protagonist's revelation of glory in 2:11. A climax structure has a building effect, drawing an audience forward with growing tension or plot development. Quintilian describes climax as a rhetorical figure of speech that uses addition, "since it repeats what has already been said, and pauses on each earlier step before it proceeds to the next" (*Inst.* 9.3.55). In John 1:15–2:12, this structure can be diagramed as follows:

    A. John's Testimony: Jesus's Glory as the *Monogenēs* (1:15–18)
      A/b. John's Testimony and the Unnamed "One" (1:19–28)
        A/B. Jesus's Arrival during John's Testimony (1:29–34)
          a/B. Jesus's Collection, John's Lessening Voice (1:35–51)[27]
            B. Jesus's Glory Manifested (2:1–12)

Each section is related to the one that comes before, drawing the audience's focus squarely on Jesus and his glory just before he enters the temple, his "Father's house," in 2:13–25. The Gospel's use of this structure reflects the preference for building climax in classical rhetoric, and for overlapping sections of narratives with integrative links.[28] Indeed, John's Gospel cre-

---

to Seventy Figures, ed. Steven A. Hunt, D. Francois Tolmie, and Ruben Zimmerman, WUNT 314 [Tübingen: Mohr Siebeck, 2013], 53–55).

26. John 1:15–18 can be translated as follows: "John testifies concerning him and has cried aloud saying, 'This was the one about whom I said, "The one who is coming after me became before me, because he was my superior [πρῶτος], because from his fullness we all received grace upon grace, because the law was given through Moses, grace and truth came to be through Jesus Christ." No one has seen God ever yet [πώποτε]; the *monogenēs* [μονογενής] God, the one who is in the Father's bosom, that one showed the way.'" The thrice-repeating cadence of "because" encourages the recollection of John 1:15–18 in John (the Baptist's) repetition of v. 15 in v. 30. Brant notes that while this reading may be a surprise to contemporary interpreters, it was the standard way of reading John 1:15–18 until a shift in scholarship during the eighteenth century (*John*, 26–27). On *monogenēs*, see n. 32 below.

27. John is absent from the final "day" in 1:43–51, yet hints of his mission to "reveal" Jesus to Israel become preliminarily actualized with the gathering of Nathanael, the "true Israelite" (cf. 1:29–34). Also, as in 1:16, Moses's writing is again explicitly tied to Jesus in 1:45.

28. Quintilian, *Inst.* 9.4.123–29; Lucian, *How to Write History* 55–57. This does

ates a number of cyclical links as Jesus journeys to and from Jerusalem for Jewish pilgrimage festivals, especially Passover (John 2:13–3:21; 6:4–71; 12:9–19:42).[29] Frequently interlacing themes, vocabulary, and even events, the narrator encourages the audience to hear later sequences in light of earlier ones, blending scenes and privileging them with ironies that reinforce their reliance on the narrator's authority.

Scripture quotations and allusions also feature in these integrative links, contributing to the scriptural fabric of the Gospel described above. Thus, in 1:15–2:12, the audience repeatedly hears John's "voice" and watches him "make straight the way of the Lord" by facilitating his own disciples' transition to the tutelage of the Lord (cf. 6:45; Isa 54:13). The Gospel audience hears John's voice once more in 3:27–36, only to listen as he shifts the power of "voice" to Jesus (see 3:30), who will develop this motif throughout the remainder of his speeches (cf. 5:19–47; 10:1–18). John (the Baptist's) description of the "bridegroom's voice" in chapter 3 links the audience back to his quotation of Isaiah in 1:23 by recalling John's prophetic status and his connection to Isaiah. But it also continues the step pattern of 1:15–2:12 by diminishing his status in comparison to Jesus: the one whose voice has the power to call forth life instead of simply describe it (3:30–36). While a crucial character, then, John's significance centers on his right identification of Jesus rather than on his own prestigious following.[30] As a prophet like Isaiah, John declares the

---

not mean, however, that all narratives were arranged this way. Additional options for arrangements included chronological variations, by topics (*topoi*), dialogue, question and answer, and harmonizing themes (e.g., Theon, *Prog.* 87–91).

29. An outline of the Gospel of John in the preferred linear fashion of current, Western literature is especially difficult and has led to a number of compositional debates concerning the Gospel's construction. The rhetorical option for cyclical and looping narratives in the ancient world should caution contemporary readers against looking for clean, narrative progressions. Narratives that reach backward and forward created links, which aided in the memorization and performance of lengthy works, as well as maintained audience attention so that they trusted the performer and could be "led along by [their] own pleasure" rather than simply by facts (Quintilian, *Inst.* 9.4.129; on memorization see *Inst.* 11.2, esp. 11.2.37–39 on the importance of arrangement). See also Bruce W. Longenecker, *Rhetoric at the Boundaries: The Art and Theology of New Testament Chain Link Transitions* (Waco, TX: Baylor University Press, 2005).

30. Much, perhaps, to the chagrin of his followers as indicated in the exchange between John and his disciples in 3:22–36. See Neyrey, "He Must Increase," 124–26.

visitation of the divine Word among God's people, and his glory is tied to the recognition of this Word by others rather than in his own status (1:12–13, 29–42; cf. 12:37–38; Isa 53:1). Like his prophetic predecessors, John's witness in the wilderness gains the attention of the Jerusalem religious elite. Yet his prolonged "wilderness" location also serves as an indicator of his shrinking importance in relationship to the metropolis-bound Jesus, who repeatedly travels to Jerusalem to teach. Prior to each Jerusalem section, the audience is reminded of John's witness, once more by John himself (3:27–36), and then with references by Jesus (5:33–36), the Jews (10:40–42), and finally with a parallel appeal to Isaiah at the close of Jesus's public ministry (12:38–42). As John slips from view in the remaining narrative cycles, Jesus's voice dominates. The final flash of John comes not with his voice, but with that of Isaiah, whose vision of "glory" is narrated at the key transitional point of John 12:37–42: John/Isaiah connections bracket Jesus's public ministry. Each Jerusalem cycle, then, brings the content of John's witness to the ears of the Gospel audience once more, offers reprises of John's prophetic "voice," while consistently placing it in the service of Jesus. At John 12:38–42, John's voice is fully blended into that of Isaiah as a part of the narrative's larger presentation of Jesus as the consistent subject of Scripture.

The larger structures noted above inform our understanding of 1:19–34, and especially its use of Scripture. The climactic cyclical pattern effectively prioritizes John's witnessing activity in 1:19–34, reinforcing its significance by recalling it throughout the narrative as support for Jesus's identity in the face of ever-increasing conflict. The narrator introduces our passage as "the testimony of John" (τὰ μαρτυρία τοῦ Ἰωάννου) in verse 19 and emphasizes his words of confession (ὡμολόγησεν) throughout 1:19–34.[31] The narrator paints a juridical scene as the Jerusalem emissaries pepper the witness, John, with questions concerning his own identity as a result of his baptismal activities (1:25). It is up to John, therefore, to offer acceptable proofs justifying his actions in the Jordan; as we will see, his quotation of Isa 40:3 acts as one of these proofs. Yet in 1:19–34 there are actually *two* juridical sequences taking place: one at the level of the characters present in the immediate context and the other at the larger level of the entire Gospel, visible only to the Gospel audience in retrospect.

---

31. John 1:20 is especially emphatic about John's confession: "he confessed and did not deny, but he confessed." John's open confessions resonate with other uses of "confess/confession" (ὁμολογέω/ία) in the Gospel (9:22; 12:42).

On the first level, the Gospel audience listens in as the Jerusalem religious leaders aim to integrate John into their own scriptural schema of a baptizing prophet, with the references to Elijah and "the prophet" mentioned above. John, however, uses the opportunity to point to the identity of the "coming one" and thus enacts his consistent trait as a witness established in the prologue. Instead of aligning himself with Elijah or "the prophet," he borrows Isaiah's words to describe himself as "the voice in the wilderness." Such a description does indeed reflect John's actions (in John's Gospel he speaks rather than acts) and physical location (beyond the Jordan). On the second level, John's brief trial-like scene is a key piece of evidence in the Gospel as a whole—a scene of witness interrogation in a larger trial spanning the entire narrative and focusing on the identity of Jesus. Again, the reference to Isaiah is fitting since the identity of the prophetic voice serves to verify the one who speaks through it: the Lord. It is this same Lord who, as a result of his own identity as Creator, offers restoration and redemption to the exilic Judeans through the removal of their "sins" in Isaiah (Isa 40–55; cf. John 1:29–34). John's Gospel interprets this promise actualized in a new way in the coming of Jesus, who manifests God's glory as only the μονογενής (*monogenēs*) can (John 1:14–18, 51; 2:11; 12:38–42; Isa 6:1; 40:5).[32] Scripture operates at both juridical levels to support John (the Baptist's) answers to his interlocutors *and* to reinforce the Gospel's verdict of Jesus's identity (John 20:30–31).

Scripture also functions as a part of several overlapping, rhetorical techniques in John 1:19–34. Recording "the *testimony* of John" in dialogue form, the evangelist creates a *prosōpopoiia* (προσωποποιία, "speech in character") for both John and his questioners. The consistency of John's words with the prologue noted above conforms to the expectations surrounding *prosōpopoiia* in classical rhetoric that all created speech should be appropriate to both the character speaking and the situation of the narrative. Callis-

---

32. Turid Karlsen Seim suggests that *monogenēs* (μονογενής) can be translated as "uniquely-begotten," "only-begotten," or "begotten only" ("Descent and Divine Paternity in the Gospel of John: Does the Mother Matter?," *NTS* 51 [2005]: 361–75). The significance of this word is most clearly seen in light of ancient theories of conception and generation, *epigenesis* and *pangenesis*. As one "begotten" uniquely and by the Father (alone), Jesus is a physical manifestation of the divine *logos* (λόγος, "word, reason, order"). He brings God's glory to the earth undiluted and unmediated. Thus he can say "whoever has seen me has seen the Father" (14:9). See also Adele Reinhartz, "'And the Word Was Begotten': Divine Epigenesis in the Gospel of John," *Semeia* 85 (1999): 83–103.

thenes explains, "Anyone attempting to write something must not fail to hit upon the character, but must make speeches appropriate to the person and the circumstances."³³ John's speech corresponds seamlessly with his introduction, even repeating his words from 1:15 in 1:30 and inviting further integration of 1:16–18 through the rest of his testimony concerning Jesus as "the Chosen One" on whom God's Spirit rests (1:29–34). Moreover, the appeal to Isa 40:3 establishes expectations for future associations between John and Isaiah in the remainder of the Gospel, as well as integrating a tradition affiliated with John that is also found outside the Gospel. The overarching consistency, therefore, increases the credibility of John as a divinely commissioned witness, as well as of the narrative reporting his words.

John's *prosōpopoiia* also operates as a "nontechnical" proof in the narrative world of the Johannine trial sequence. Although crafted by the evangelist, *within the story* John's statements are a nontechnical proof because they are not manufactured by a prosecutor or defender, but presented as John's *own* responses.³⁴ As in any other courtroom, John stands as a witness; he is interrogated in the Gospel's trial of Jesus. However, John's introduction of Isaiah's words is a "technical" proof in the midst of his testimony (1:23). Corresponding to the discussion above, Isaiah functions an example (*exemplum*, παραδείματον) whose inclusion fashions a comparison (*synkrisis*, παραβολή, *similitudo*) between himself and John. The proof is "technical" because it is manufactured by John to apply to the current situation. Recall that as an external, well-known example, John's reference to Isaiah becomes "all the more effective" according to Quintilian, because it appears "spoken or given by minds free of prejudice for the simple reason that [it] seem[s] very honorable or very true" (*Inst.* 5.11.37). It also elevates the character John as speaker by highlighting his education (and virtue) with the effective integration of the well-known prophet into his argument. John demonstrates his awareness of the historical and scriptural example of Isaiah—a prophet par excellence in the tradition of Israel—and claims that he is operating according to the Isaianic paradigm set before him.

---

33. *FGrHist* 124 F 44, from John Marincola, "Speeches in Classical Historiography," in *Companion to Greek and Roman Historiography*, ed. John Marincola, BCAW (Malden, MA: Blackwell, 2007), 1:122. For more on *prosōpopoiia* and its overlap with *ēthopoiia* and "Dialogue," see Theon, *Prog.* 115; Quintilian, *Inst.* 3.8.49–54; 9.2.29–37; Cicero, *De or.* 3.53.205; Ps.-Cicero, *Rhet. Her.* 4.49.63; Myers, *Characterizing Jesus*, 51–54.

34. Quintilian, *Inst.* 5.1.1–3, 7.1–37. Quintilian relies on Aristotle's definitions from *Rhet.* 1.2.1–2.

Quintilian emphasizes the persuasive power of examples further when he describes them as the "most effective" type of comparative proof (*Inst.* 5.11.6). Pseudo-Cicero offers a similar conclusion, writing:

> [An example] renders a thought more brilliant when used for no other purpose than beauty; clearer when throwing more light upon what was somewhat obscure; more plausible when giving the thought greater verisimilitude; more vivid, when expressing everything so lucidly that the matter can, I may almost say, be touched by the hand. (*Rhet. Her.* 4.49.62 [Caplan, LCL])

By means of his invocation of Isaiah, then, John clarifies his identity claims by setting them alongside those of the scriptural prophet: he is the "voice," and his words point to the coming of "the Lord." This scriptural example, therefore, also vivifies John's argument by painting a picture of his ministry, not only with the visual language in the text of the quotation but also with the larger context in which this quotation is found. Coming from a pivotal point in the Book of Isaiah, Isa 40 offers comfort to those in Jerusalem with the promise of the coming of the Lord and revelation of his glory. Recalling the new exodus imagery of Isaiah, John establishes the paving of a new wilderness journey. In the Gospel, then, John takes on the role of Isaiah and brings the same word of "comfort" to the Jerusalem emissaries, as well as to the Gospel audience. Imitating, and indeed taking on Isaiah's "voice," John invites those who hear to evaluate his own character and ministry in light of that of Isaiah and, therefore, to understand Jesus's coming as the manifestation of "the Lord."

The comparison between John and Isaiah, therefore, is not a formal *synkrisis*, but rather the result of the comparative element of *exempla* described by Quintilian. Information concerning *synkrises* is nevertheless instructive for our understanding of John's comparative *exemplum*. While *synkrises*, or comparisons in general, could be used to demonstrate a subject's superiority or inferiority to another, they could also be employed to establish equality between two persons, events, or objects. While perhaps not as daring as arguing for superiority, equating oneself with a recognized figure from the past nevertheless also "amplifies" a person's qualities.[35] In

---

35. Ps.-Hermogenes writes, "Now sometimes we introduce comparisons on the basis of equality, showing the subjects we compare as equal, either in all respects or in most" (*Prog.* 19; cf. Theon, *Prog.* 108; Aphthonius, *Prog.* 31R–32R; Nicolaus, *Prog.*

the case of John 1:19–34, John (the Baptist) amplifies his identity and ministry by linking himself to Isaiah, suggesting that the same prophetic voice now articulates through him. John's persistent allusions to Isaianic motifs in 1:19–36 reinforce this identification as does the final reference to Isaiah in John 12:38–42; the voice who spoke through Isaiah in the past continues to speak the same message, now through the "sent one" named John (1:6–8, 33). In addition to establishing John's ministry as equally important (and legitimate) as that of Isaiah, this comparison also hints at the upcoming rejection he, and Jesus, will face as the Gospel's "voice" and its "Lord."[36] Quoting Isaiah again at the close of Jesus's public ministry, the narrator justifies Jesus's rejection by the people, as well as that of John, his witness and Isaianic stand-in. Isaiah and John's words, therefore, blend together in the Fourth Gospel to create *one*, consistent, prophetic voice that *continues* to "make straight the way of the Lord" in the face of Jesus's dismissal by other characters.[37]

The blending of Isaiah's and John's voices also has the effect of introducing an additional type of testimony, or authority, into the juridical sequences: "divine testimony." According to Cicero, testimony from the gods is inherently valuable and authoritative since "the surpassing virtue of the gods is the result of their nature, but the virtue of men is the result of hard work" (*Top.* 20.76 [Hubbell, LCL]).[38] Cicero includes the following as sources for divine testimony:

> First, the heavens themselves and all their order and beauty; secondly, the flight of birds through the air and their songs; thirdly, sounds and flashes of fire from the heavens, and portents given by many objects on

---

60; Cicero, *Top.* 3.11; 18.68; Quintilian, *Inst.* 5.10.86–87). For an example of a *synkrisis* demonstrating equality, see Sallust *Bell. Cat.* 54.

36. John 1:10–11; 3:24; 12:38–42; Isa 6:9–10; 53:1; Ascen. Isa. 5.1–16; Liv. Pro. 1.1–13.

37. The blending of Isaiah and John's voices is also noted by Sherri Brown ("John the Baptist: Witness and Embodiment of the Prologue in the Gospel of John," in *Characters and Characterization in the Gospel of John*, ed. Christopher W. Skinner, LNTS 449 [London: T&T Clark, 2013], 156); and Catrin H. Williams, both in her analysis of John (the Baptist's) character ("John [the Baptist]," 52, 60) and her contribution to this volume ("Scripture Remembered: Social Memory and Perceptions of Israel's Past in the Gospel of John").

38. For extended treatment of "divine testimonies," see James R. McConnell Jr., *The* Topos *of Divine Testimony in Luke-Acts* (Eugene, OR: Pickwick, 2014).

earth, as well as the foreshadowing of events which is revealed by the entrails (of sacrificial animals). Many things also are revealed by visions seen in sleep. (*Top.* 20.76–77 [Hubbell, LCL])

Quintilian likewise includes "divine testimonies" alongside quotations of famous poets, philosophers, and common sayings under the heading of "authority." Unlike human words and sayings, however, divine testimonies are especially significant since they are "rare" and are "derived from oracles" (*Inst.* 5.11.42).[39] As divinely commissioned prophets, filled with the same voice, both John and Isaiah offer divine testimonies as proof for their messages (1:29–34; 12:38–42; Isa 6:1). In keeping with Cicero's definition of divine testimony, John describes the dove-like flight of the Spirit descending on Jesus and the accompanying oracular utterance in 1:29–34. These divine portents demonstrate that John's testimony is not based on his own perspective, but on that of "the one who sent" him, whom the Gospel audience at least knows is God (1:6–8). John's ministry of baptism here does not usher in a period of repentance before Jesus's coming; rather, it creates an opportunity for a *moment of divine revelation* so that John himself can understand the baffling Jesus before him, the one standing in the midst and yet unknown by the religious leaders (1:28). In verse 30, John explains, "And I did not know him, but so that he might be revealed to Israel, *for this reason*, I came baptizing with water." Only with divine insight can John then fulfill his own prophetic mission and articulate the Isaianic voice that Jesus is the "Lamb of God," the "Chosen One." The allusion to Isaiah's vision of "glory" in John 12:41 likewise reinforces the validity of his witness, completing the blending of Isaiah's and John's voices in the service of Jesus: "Lord, who has believed *our* report?" (12:38). Moreover, by presenting the Logos—either preincarnate (12:41; Isa 6:1) or incarnate (1:30–33)—as the subject of both men's visions, the Gospel creates a consistent divine witness who interjects through these proph-

---

39. For Quintilian, appeals to the "Authority of the Gods" can function in either nontechnical or technical proofs. If this authority is internal to a case, it is a nontechnical proof and can legitimately be called "divine testimony." If, however, it is external, it must be shaped to fit the case and is, instead, a technical proof or an "Argument" (*Inst.* 5.11.42; cf. 5.7.36–37). In John 1:19–34, the vision and accompanying oracle John describes is internal to the case at hand—it was given as verification of John's personal encounter with Jesus. For this reason, they are "divine testimonies."

ets, as well as through Jesus's signs, to proclaim his identity as the "Son" (5:36–38).

The use of Scripture in 1:19–34, then, supports the overall rhetorical purpose of John's Gospel, that is, of pointing to Jesus's identity as "the Christ, the Son of God" (20:30–31). While the interlocutors from Jerusalem have their own scriptural agenda to establish John (the Baptist's) identity, *he* takes on Isaiah's mantle and claims Isaiah's voice in order to shift attention away from himself and onto the one he calls "the Lord," "the Chosen One," and the "Lamb of God." All of this is, of course, visible without the use of classical rhetorical categories. However, viewing the exchanges of 1:19–34 through the lens classical rhetoric expands our vision and connects us back to the expectations of ancient audiences, enabling us to hear better cues patterned for their ears. In this way, the *climax* cycles become more prominent and invite us to listen for the ebb and flow of the Gospel's structure, particularly with reference to John (and Isaiah). The speech (*prosōpopoiia*) crafted for John fits his character and is, therefore, more credible for ancient audiences; it employs a scriptural *exemplum* that demonstrates John's knowledge and virtue as well as vivifying his argument with a comparative context; and it ushers in a mixture of technical and nontechnical "testimonies" within his own prophetic witness, effectively blending his voice and that of Isaiah into one—consistent and with a divine source. As a result, John's testimony in 1:19–34 defies easy categorization as human or divine, written or spoken, ancient or recent, because it operates in *all these categories simultaneously*. The overall effect is a testimony that bridges boundaries, becoming a transcendent voice that still echoes among the Johannine believers, who enjoy the presence of the Spirit as their Paraclete (παράκλητος, 16:7–15; cf. 2:22; 7:39; 12:16). It is fitting, then, that in 1:15–18 John's words collapse into the present reality of the Gospel audience with the use of the emphatic first person plural "we all" (1:16). John's testimony ties God's past vocalizations through prophets to the incarnate Jesus, and his words become the confession of all the Johannine believers.

3. Conclusion

This chapter has outlined a new avenue for interpreting the use of Scripture in the Gospel of John—as well as in the New Testament as a whole. While previous scholars have dismissed the usefulness of classical rhetorical categories for such studies, the foundational role that mimesis plays in Greco-Roman education and society invites us to reconsider. Classical rhetoricians in the ancient Mediterranean world encouraged their students to imitate past masters and to incorporate their materials into a number of techniques and exercises as authoritative witnesses and *exempla*. While these rhetors may not have laid out many specific instructions on how to "quote a text," they have nevertheless provided models that illustrate the pervasive use of intertexts in the ancient world.

It is from these models that the present chapter has gained insight into the use of Scripture in John 1:19–34. The classical rhetorical categories utilized by the Gospel outlined here clarify *how* Scripture works in John 1:19–34 and provide contemporary readers glimpses into expectations from the Gospel's milieu. In this way, classical rhetoric can guide the interpretation of intertexts in the Fourth Gospel, giving readers a context from which to understand its pervasive use of Scripture. In the case of John 1:19–34, its larger context of 1:15–2:12 and the climactic cycles of the Gospel, the categories expose the depth of John's imitation of Isaiah and help modern readers decipher the weightiness of the testimony he offers based on ancient presuppositions. Blending John's ministry with that of Isaiah, the narrator continues building the argument begun in the prologue that Jesus is at the heart of Israel's sacred scriptural story. Moreover, through these prophets the Gospel crafts a consistent "voice" that transcends the limitation of a human lifetime, reinforcing divine providential direction in the person and work of Jesus Christ. Endorsed by *this* voice, the Johannine community is encouraged to continue listening for Jesus's voice—their shepherd and leader no longer physically present, yet speaking now through the traditions preserved and Spirit residing among the believers.

Whose Zeal Is It Anyway?
The Citation of Psalm 69:9
in John 2:17 as a Double Entendre

Benjamin J. Lappenga

The editorial comment in John 2:17 ("His disciples remembered that it was written, 'Zeal for your house will consume me'") interrupts the narrative flow between the account of Jesus's actions in the temple (vv. 14–16) and the inquiry by "the Jews"[1] as to what sign Jesus gives for acting as he does (v. 18). Interpreters disagree about the significance and function of the citation of Ps 69:9 in verse 17, but most agree that "will consume" (καταφάγεται) is a reference to Jesus's death, and nearly all agree that "zeal for your house" (ὁ ζῆλος τοῦ οἴκου σου) refers to the actions of Jesus described in verses 15–16. The present study argues that, while καταφάγεται does refer to Jesus's death, ὁ ζῆλος τοῦ οἴκου σου only initially references Jesus's actions

---

1. By "the Jews" (οἱ Ἰουδαῖοι), hereafter noted without quotation marks, I mean the literary construct used to designate Jesus's opponents in the Gospel of John. While it is true that "the tendency to standardize 'Jewish Opposition' reaches its fullest expression in the Fourth Gospel," the present study will argue that the presentation of "the Jews" in the text of John is a more nuanced phenomenon than simply a construct representing "the unbelieving world that prefers the darkness to the light" (Luke Timothy Johnson, "Anti-Judaism and the New Testament," in *Handbook for the Study of the Historical Jesus*, ed. Tom Holmén and Stanley E. Porter [Leiden: Brill, 2011], 1619–20). Important recent studies relating to the broader topic include Steve Mason's widely cited article ("Jews, Judaeans, Judaizing, Judaism: Problems of the Categorization in Ancient History," *JSJ* 38 [2007], 457–512); the collection of essays edited by Reimund Bieringer, Didier Pollefeyt, and Frederique Vandecasteele-Vanneuville (*Anti-Judaism and the Fourth Gospel: Papers of the Leuven Colloquium, 2000* [Assen: van Gorcum, 2001]); and Raymond E. Brown's discussion and the works cited in its bibliography (Raymond E. Brown, *An Introduction to the Gospel of John*, ed. Francis J. Moloney [New York: Doubleday, 2003], 157–75, 184–87).

and is to be viewed in hindsight as a double entendre. That is, although Jesus's actions are presented as a demonstration of zeal for the purity of the temple, the passage is crafted so that the focus falls on *the Jews'* ζῆλος that ultimately, but not inevitably, leads them to pursue Jesus's death.

This reading accounts for the observation that, as the narrative progresses, the increasing hostility of the Jews is portrayed in a manner consistent with instances of "ζῆλος for the temple" that are prominent in first-century Jewish literature. In other words, both the strategic ambiguity of the citation in the immediate context of 2:17–22 and the portrayal of the Jews' behavior in the ensuing narrative function as rhetorical devices that invite John's readers to evaluate the divergent actions of Jesus and the Jews in terms of "zeal."[2]

To make the case for this reading, I will briefly survey the concept of "zeal" in early Jewish texts before demonstrating that John's portrayal of the hostility of the Jews "in the temple" (ἐν τῷ ἱερῷ) consistently conforms to a pattern best classified as "zeal." Then I will offer a narrative-compositional (final-form) analysis of John 2:13–22 to show that a twofold understanding of the ζῆλος that will "consume" Jesus is appropriate, and thus the reference in 2:17 anticipates the portrayal of the Jews that unfolds throughout the narrative. Finally, after addressing some possible objections, including the complications introduced by John's use of Ps 69, I will make some suggestions about the implications of such a reading for the interpretation of the Gospel as a whole.

1. "Zeal for the Temple" in Early Jewish Writings

The emergence of "zealot" (ζηλωτής) as a "technical term for a model of piety rooted in zeal for God and the Law"[3] gives some sense of the importance of the concept of "zeal" for Jews living during the first century. It is also clear that its point of origin is the Scriptures: Jewish zeal for maintaining the divine glory is derived from the zeal of the Lord in relation to the people of Israel (קנאת יהוה/ζῆλος κυρίου; e.g., Exod 20:5; 2 Kgs 19:31; Ezek 16:38; 23:25; 39:25).[4] More specifically, numerous texts speak of zeal for the place of God's dwelling (with or without using the term קנאה/ζῆλος),

---

2. Reference to "John" throughout this essay is shorthand for the text of the Fourth Gospel in its final form and does not represent a claim regarding authorial intent.

3. David Rhoads, "Zealots," *ABD* 6:1044.

4. See further Albrecht Stumpff, ζῆλος, ζηλόω, κτλ, *TDNT* 2:878–84.

notably the zeal of Nehemiah (Neh 13:15–22),[5] Phinehas (Num 25:11), Elijah (1 Kgs 19:10, 14), and David (Ps 119:139; 2 Sam 7:13). To this list we may add the portrait of Phinehas in Sir 45:24 as "leader of the sanctuary"[6] and God's violent reaction to the desecration of the temple in Ezek 9:3–11 (cf. ζῆλος in LXX Ezek 5:13; 16:38, 42; 23:25; 36:6; 38:19).[7] Likewise, the Phinehas-inspired ζῆλος of Mattathias (1 Macc 2:24–26, 54, 58) traces its roots to the incident in which "[Antiochus and his forces] defiled the sanctuary" (ἐμόλυναν τὸ ἁγίασμα; 1 Macc 1:37; cf. 1:21–24; 4:36–58; 2 Macc 2:18–19; 5:15–27; 10:1–8).

Other early Jewish writings exhibit this same concern to "purge Jerusalem and make it holy as it was even from the beginning" (Pss. Sol. 17:30; cf. Jub. 30:15; T. Levi 16:1–5; As. Mos. 5:3–6; 6:1). Even for the Qumran community, whose relationship with the temple in Jerusalem is complex, zeal (קנאה) is directed not against pagan intervention but at grievances with Jewish practices.[8] For example, 1QH[a] 6:14 reads, "I become zealous against all those who practice wickedness and men of deceit" (קנאתו על כול פועלי רשע ואנשי רמיה), and in the Damascus Document, "the defilement of the sanctuary" is a prominent concern (טמא המקדש; CD 4:18; cf. 12:2). In Josephus and Philo, it is equally clear that zealous acts on behalf of the purity of the temple captured the hearts of the Jewish people (e.g., *Ant.* 12.271 [ζηλωτής ... τῆς τοῦ θεοῦ θρησκείας; "zealots ... for the worship of God"]; cf. *J.W.* 2.1–14).

---

5. J. Duncan M. Derrett refers to Nehemiah as the "most famous zealot after Phinehas himself" ("Zeal of the House and the Cleansing of the Temple," *DR* 95 [1977]: 92–93).

6. NRSV, following the Hebrew fragments. Greek Sir 45:24 has ἁγίων ("holy things") in place of "sanctuary"; see further William Klassen, "Jesus and Phineas: A Rejected Role Model," *Society of Biblical Literature 1986 Seminar Papers*, SBLSP 25 (Atlanta: Scholars Press, 1986), 492.

7. The promise of a restored temple in Ezek 37:26 (cf. chs. 40–48) likely informs John's portrayal of Jesus as "temple"; see further C. Hassell Bullock, "Ezekiel: Bridge Between the Testaments," *JETS* 25 (1982): 29.

8. See further Ethelbert Stauffer, "Historische Elemente im vierten Evangelium," in *Bekenntnis zur Kirche: Festgabe für Ernst Sommerlath*, ed. E. H. Amberg and U. Kuhn (Berlin: Evangelische Verlagsanstalt, 1960), 48n61: "The polemic against the desecration of the temple plays a major role in the Qumran movement, but there (unlike the Maccabees) it is not directed against pagan interventions, but against Jewish abuses" (my translation).

Of particular significance to the present study is the evidence regarding the expectation that those who enter the temple as foreigners or defilers can and should be immediately killed. For example, Philo writes: "For all men guard their own customs, but this is especially true of the Jewish nation.... Still more abounding and peculiar is the zeal of them all for the temple [ἡ περὶ τὸ ἱερὸν σπουδή], and the strongest proof of this is that death without appeal is the sentence against those of other races who penetrate into its inner confines."[9] Elsewhere Philo writes concerning those who "betray the honor due to the One" (καθυφίενται τὴν τοῦ ἑνὸς τιμήν; cf. John 5:23 [ὁ μὴ τιμῶν τὸν υἱὸν οὐ τιμᾷ τὸν πατέρα]; 8:49) that "those who have a zeal for virtue [τοῖς ζῆλον ἔχουσιν ἀρετῆς] should be permitted to exact the penalties offhand and with no delay" (*Spec.* 1.54–55). The Mishnah suggests that this kind of "lynch-law justice" extended to other acts of desecration and was not restricted to foreigners: "If a priest performs the Temple service in a state of impurity, his fellow priests do not take him to the court ... [rather they] take him outside the temple and smash his skull with logs."[10]

This sampling of texts does not prove that "ζῆλος for the temple" was a universally acknowledged term for all incidents of "lynch-law justice" or nationalistic fervor during the first century. However, they are suggestive of the way Jewish ζῆλος comes to expression in contexts in which the temple is in view, and they provide a literary context within which John's narrative may be placed.[11]

---

9. Philo, *Legat.* 210–212 (Colson, LCL).

10. M. Sanh. 9:6 (my translation, adapted from Lazarus Goldschmidt, *Der babylonische Talmud* [The Hague: Martinus Nijhoff, 1933–1935], 8:784). This text is discussed by Martin Hengel (*Die Zeloten: Untersuchungen zur jüdischen Freiheitsbewegung in der Zeit von Herodes I. bis 70 n. Chr.*, ed. Roland Deines and Claus-Jürgen Thornton, 3rd ed., WUNT 283 [Tübingen: Mohr Siebeck, 2011], 216).

11. A complete discussion of the *historical* context is not the immediate concern of this study, but the recent work of Joel Marcus may be applicable to the reading proposed here. Marcus argues that the Zealot party's occupation of the temple was likely to have been justified by prooftexting from Zech 14:21b ("no Canaanite [כנעני] will be in the house of the Lord"), and that Mark (11:17) and Josephus (*J.W.* 4.158–159, 262) draw on a deliberate misreading of כנעני as "Zealots" (קנאיו/Aramaic קנאנין) to support their antirevolutionary positions. If so, it is possible that these debates inform John 2:13–22: "John, like Mark, may be grafting features of the Zealots' temple occupation onto his tale of Jesus' earlier temple action" ("No More Zealots in the House of the Lord: A Note on the History of Interpretation of Zechariah 14:21," *NovT* 55 [2013]:

2. "Zeal for the Temple" in the Narrative of John

The pervasiveness of the temple as the setting for John's stories has often been noticed, and it seems clear from the pattern of explicit references to the temple location (e.g., 2:13; 5:14; 7:14, 28; 10:23; 11:56; 18:20) that John is not merely telling stories that happen to occur on the temple grounds. Margaret Daly-Denton has aptly dubbed the temple setting "a cave of resonant signification,"[12] and this resonance is understood by most interpreters to refer to the symbolic appropriateness of Jesus teaching in the house of his Father (cf. 12:49–50).[13] However, as Judith Lieu points out, "The irony of the Gospel is that Jesus' glory is never experienced in the Temple.... For John, the Temple is the supreme centre of 'the Jews.'"[14] The temple is where Jesus teaches openly, but it is also where he meets his ultimate rejection.

We will examine John 2:13–22 in detail below, but for now we observe that the hostility of the Jews may already commence in 2:18, when they demand that Jesus "prove his right to act as he did."[15] At the very least, the temple incident in John 2 is something of a quandary for the Jews. On the one hand, Jesus's action does not result in his immediate stoning or arrest (cf. 8:20, 59), because, as our survey of Jewish literature has suggested and will be argued below, Jesus's action was consonant with the kind of zeal for the purity of the temple the Jews themselves would welcome. But, on the other hand, there is a claim to prophetic authority that accompanies such activity, and the Jews require a sign (σημεῖον, 2:18).

This demand marks the beginning of a hostility that will only increase as Jesus speaks openly in the temple about his identity. In chapter 5, Jesus finds and addresses the man he healed "in the temple" (ἐν τῷ ἱερῷ, 5:14), and the man reports his healing to the Jews (ἀνήγγειλεν τοῖς Ἰουδαίοις, 5:15). The Jews "seek all the more to kill him," because Jesus violates the

---

26; cf. Helmut Schwier, *Tempel und Tempelzerstörung: Untersuchungen zu den theologischen und ideologischen Faktoren im ersten jüdisch-römischen Krieg [66–74 n. Chr.]*, NTOA 11 [Göttingen: Vandenhoeck & Ruprecht, 1989], 119–25).

12. Margaret Daly-Denton, *David in the Fourth Gospel: The Johannine Reception of the Psalms* (Leiden: Brill, 2000), 128; cf. Francis Moloney, "Reading John 2:13–22: The Purification of the Temple," *RB* 97 (1990): 436.

13. See, e.g., Marianne Meye Thompson, *John*, NTL (Louisville: Westminster John Knox, forthcoming), 71.

14. Lieu, "Temple and Synagogue," *NTS* 45 (1999): 68–69.

15. Rudolf Schnackenburg, *The Gospel according to St. John* (London: Burns & Oates, 1968), 1:248.

Sabbath (5:9–10, 18) and "makes himself equal with God" (5:18; cf. 5:23; Philo, *Spec.* 1.54–55). Then in chapter 7, Jesus goes up "into the temple" (εἰς τὸ ἱερόν) to teach (7:14), and asks the Jews (7:15) why they are trying to kill him (7:19; cf. 7:20, 25).

After speaking about "seeking glory" (7:18) and about the Sabbath (7:22–23), Jesus, still teaching "in the temple" (ἐν τῷ ἱερῷ, 7:28), incites the "lynch mob" impulses of the Jews ("They were seeking to seize him," 7:30). Likewise, the chief priests and Pharisees and their temple assistants attempt to "seize" Jesus in 7:32 and in 7:44. In light of the evidence discussed above regarding the relationship between the temple and "lynch-mob justice," it is not surprising that the disagreement between these parties in 7:45–52 involves a discussion about "the crowd" not "knowing the law" (7:49) and about the legality of "condemning" (κρίνω) someone without a hearing (7:51).[16]

In chapter 8, Jesus again teaches "in the temple" (ἐν τῷ ἱερῷ, 8:20), and attention is drawn to the possibility of Jesus's arrest (8:20) and to the agent of Jesus's death (8:22). In 8:37 and 40, Jesus states that the Jews seek to kill him because "my word makes no headway among you" (8:37). Then, after the most odious verbal exchange in the escalating hostility (8:42–56), the Jews "pick up stones to throw at him," but Jesus slips away "from the temple" (ἐκ τοῦ ἱεροῦ, 8:59).

In chapter 10, Jesus once again walks "in the temple" (ἐν τῷ ἱερῷ, 10:23). The Jews attempt to stone him for his claims about his relationship to the Father (10:29–32), and this time the charge is specifically called blasphemy (10:33). The pattern repeats in 10:36–39 before Jesus leaves the temple to go across the Jordan.

Then, in 11:45–57, three recurring elements appear together: the temple (11:48, 56), the Jews and other authorities (11:45–47, 54, 57), and the attempts to kill Jesus (11:53, 57). Here the Jews misunderstand Caiaphas's "prophecy" (11:51) to mean that killing Jesus will spare the nation (ἔθνος, 11:48, 50) *and the temple* (τὸν τόπον)[17] from destruction by the Romans because "everyone will believe in him" (11:48). John's editorial

---

16. Commentators usually focus on the attitudes of the ruling class to the uniformed masses that could be inferred in 7:49, but in light of the present study it is worth considering that John has the impulsive zeal of the "mob" in view.

17. Interpreters are nearly unanimous in understanding τόπος ("place") in 11:48 as a reference to the temple (cf. 4:20; Acts 6:13–14; 7:7; 2 Macc 5:19). Even if Chrysostom is correct that τόπος refers to Jerusalem (*Hom. Jo.* 64.3), the mention of Passover

comment in 11:51–52 ("[Caiaphas] did not say this on his own") points out the tragic irony: it is Jesus's (salvific) death on behalf of the Jews and the "scattered children of God" (11:52) that is in view. Thus Alan R. Kerr correctly notes that in 11:48 Caiaphas "is ready to destroy Jesus so as to preserve the Temple."[18] Kerr's observation underscores John's emphasis on the Jews' concern for the temple, and, as we will explore further below, highlights the close connection between the temple episode in chapter 2 and the Caiaphas episode in chapter 11.

In addition, when the temple assistants (οἱ ὑπηρέται; cf. 7:32, 45–46) finally do arrest Jesus in 18:12, Caiaphas's prophecy that "one man should die for the people" (εἷς ἄνθρωπος ἀποθάνῃ ὑπὲρ τοῦ λαοῦ, 11:50) is immediately restated (18:14). In fact, all of the signature elements of "zeal for the temple" (temple, purity, lynch-law justice) are recapitulated in this penultimate "consumption" scene. First, Jesus says, "I have always taught in the synagogue and in the temple [ἐν τῷ ἱερῷ], where all the Jews [οἱ Ἰουδαῖοι] come together" (18:20). Next, the Jews do not enter Pilate's quarters "lest they be defiled [μιαίνω]" (18:28).[19] And finally, in what appears to be a desperate lie (see 8:44, 55), the Jews insist that Jesus be tried because lynch-law justice is not permitted: "it is not lawful for us to kill anyone" (18:31).[20] It is at the end of this scene, when Pilate hands Jesus over to the Jews to be crucified (19:16), that the Jews' "zeal for the temple" comes to full expression.

(11:55; cf. 2:13) and the search for Jesus (11:56–57) still closely link this episode with the Jews' concern for the temple (cf. ἐν τῷ ἱερῷ, 11:56).

18. Alan R. Kerr, *The Temple of Jesus' Body: The Temple Theme in the Gospel of John* (London: Sheffield Academic, 2002), 85. Kerr looks to the episode in 11:45–53 to support his argument that a sacrificial "consumption" is in view in 2:17, and notes that the raising of Lazarus seems to be the more immediate cause of the hostility against Jesus, rather than the temple incident in 2:13–22.

19. Josephus, who is at pains to show that the rebel Zealots are not indeed those who have a genuine zeal, writes: "Ananus and his party ... went so far as to send [John of Gischala] as their delegate to the Zealots to arrange a treaty; for they were anxious on their side to preserve the Temple from pollution (μὴ μιᾶναι τὸ ἱερόν)" (*J.W.* 4.215 [Thackeray, LCL]). For other instances involving defilement, temple, and zeal, see *Ant.* 2.31; 7.92, 371; 9.155; 10.37; 11.300; 18.271; *J.W.* 1.39; 2.289; 4.201, 323; 5.402; 6.95; Philo, *Mos.* 2.158.

20. The similar wording in the closing sentence of Josephus's *Antiquities* (περὶ τῶν νόμων, διὰ τί κατ' αὐτοὺς τὰ μὲν ἔξεστιν ἡμῖν ποιεῖν, τὰ δὲ κεκώλυται, *Ant.* 20.268) suggests that the law of Moses is in view, rather than Roman law; see further J. Ramsey Michaels (*The Gospel of John*, NICNT [Grand Rapids: Eerdmans, 2010], 917).

3. "Zeal for Your House" in John 2:13–22

In light of this pattern, it is perhaps surprising that John would not use the term ζῆλος itself to describe the Jews' behavior (cf. 1QH^a 6:14; Josephus, *Ant.* 12.271; Philo, *Spec.* 1.54–55). John uses ζῆλος only in 2:17, and interpreters have rarely connected this occurrence to the behavior of the Jews, because it has seemed obvious that the quotation of Ps 69:9 refers to Jesus's actions.[21] In what follows, I will argue that, although at first glance ζῆλος in 2:17 refers to Jesus's zeal, John has cleverly structured the passage so that in hindsight (from the perspective of the resurrection) ζῆλος also refers to and anticipates the ensuing behavior of the Jews.

John's "cleansing" narrative (2:13–22) begins with an explicit reference to the Jews that is otherwise unnecessary: "the Passover *of the Jews* [τὸ πάσχα τῶν Ἰουδαίων] was near" (2:13; cf. τὸ πάσχα ἡ ἑορτὴ τῶν Ἰουδαίων in 6:4; but only πάσχα in 2:23; 11:55; 12:1; 13:1; 18:28, 39; 19:14). At least two preceding elements suggest that this reference in 2:13 functions as a prompt for the reader to consider the effect Jesus's actions in 2:14–16 might have on the Jews. First, the evangelist declares in the prologue that "his own did not receive him" (1:11), and immediately introduces "the Jews of Jerusalem" (1:19). Second, when the Jews' representatives express suspicions about the messianic and prophetic symbolism behind John's baptizing (1:20–22), John steers them toward Jesus (1:26–30). Therefore,

---

21. Steven M. Bryan has recently argued that "the zeal that consumes Jesus is not his own. In John's view, the psalmist of Ps 69 suffers at the hands of pious enemies motivated by their zeal for the temple and thus corresponds to Jesus, the righteous sufferer, attacked by 'righteous' enemies whose zeal for Herod's temple will ultimately lead to Jesus' death" ("Consumed by Zeal: John's Use of Psalm 69:9 and the Action in the Temple," *BBR* 21 [2011]: 481). Bryan's reading parallels my own in significant ways, but whereas Bryan preserves the either/or (the Jews' zeal, not Jesus's zeal), my reading locates within the ambiguity an opportunity for John's readers to evaluate rightly directed zeal. As will become clear below, I am also unconvinced by Bryan's suggestion that "in seeking to protect the temple the Jews arouse the judgment of God against the standing temple" (ibid., 494). Jane S. Webster writes of 2:17 that "the religious authorities are zealous in the protection of the temple and, because Jesus threatened it, they put him to death," but she misleadingly attributes this reading to scholars who do not in fact hold this view (Brown, Dodd, Schnackenburg, and Bultmann) and advocates a very different understanding of Jesus's "consumption" (*Ingesting Jesus: Eating and Drinking in the Gospel of John*, AcadB [Atlanta: Society of Biblical Literature, 2003], 47).

within the carefully constructed narrative, at the beginning of the "cleansing" passage (2:13–22) it is uncertain whether the Jews might look favorably on Jesus's actions (as John's disciples do at the announcement of the "lamb" in 1:36–37), or whether they may question the authority by which Jesus operates.

Then in 2:14–16 John narrates Jesus's actions themselves. Unlike the Synoptic accounts (Matt 21:12–13; Mark 11:15–17; Luke 19:45–46), where the incident in the temple follows Jesus's entry into Jerusalem and directly ushers in the set of events that culminate in Jesus's death, John narrates this event at the beginning of Jesus's ministry, and he does so in a way that accords with the kind of zeal for the purity of the temple the Jews themselves might welcome. Jesus's actions in his Father's "house" (τὸν οἶκον τοῦ πατρός μου, 2:16) are reminiscent of, for example, Nehemiah's efforts to cleanse the Lord's "house" in Neh 13:4–30 (e.g., LXX Neh 13:14 [ἐν οἴκῳ κυρίου]; cf. Pss. Sol. 17–18; T. Mos. 5:3–6:1).[22] It is striking, then, that both Jesus and the Jews show nothing but devotion to the "Father's house" (cf. 18:20). As we will see below, the only destruction John's Jesus has in mind is of a different temple altogether (v. 21).

Before returning to the question of how the Jews will respond (v. 18), in verse 17 John enigmatically reports that the disciples "remembered" (ἐμνήσθησαν; cf. v. 22) Ps 69:9a: "zeal for your house will consume me" (ὁ ζῆλος τοῦ οἴκου σου καταφάγεταί με; cf. MT: קנאת ביתך אכלתני; LXX: ὁ ζῆλος τοῦ οἴκου σου κατέφαγέν με). Until John clarifies in verse 22, it remains unclear whether the disciples call to mind this citation while witnessing the event itself, or whether the disciples reflect on this event later in light of the psalm. Either way, since the evangelist assumes that his readers know what happens to Jesus (see 1:11; 2:22; 3:14; 7:39; 8:21),

---

22. Full treatment of this issue is beyond the scope of this essay. Here it is enough to concur with the view popularized by E. P. Sanders that John's telling is best understood as a symbolic act (*Jesus and Judaism* [Philadelphia: Fortress, 1985], 71–76), but to accept the evidence presented by Craig A. Evans as a correction of Sanders's view that this symbolic cleansing included the destruction of the existing temple. Evans shows that the temple was indeed viewed by many as corrupt and in need of cleansing (e.g., Pss. Sol. 17–18; T. Mos. 5:3–6:1), and therefore John's portrayal of Jesus's actions as a symbolic cleansing without threatening the destruction of the existing temple is perfectly acceptable (Craig Evans, "Jesus' Action in the Temple and Evidence of Corruption in the First-Century Temple," in *Jesus and His Contemporaries: Comparative Studies*, AGJU 25 [Leiden: Brill, 2001], 319; see also Evans, "Jesus' Action in the Temple: Cleansing or Portent of Destruction?" *CBQ* 51 [1989]: 249).

presumably "zeal for your house will consume me" denotes the relationship between Jesus's behavior described in verses 14–16 ("zeal") and his impending death ("consume"). However, interpreters regularly fail to notice that if ζῆλος refers to Jesus's actions, the logic of the citation in verse 17 has to be manipulated: Jesus's zeal does not consume him but *leads to his being consumed* by another party.[23]

I will return to the matter of whose zeal is in view in Ps 69 below, but already the suspicion of a bait and switch arises. This is especially the case because rather than elaborating on Jesus's actions to explain the citation, John immediately follows the citation with the reaction of *the Jews* (ἀπεκρίθησαν οὖν οἱ Ἰουδαῖοι, v. 18). They respond much as they did toward John the Baptist in 1:19–26: "What sign do you show us that you do these things?" (2:18).

In fact, John next presents a statement about *the Jews* taking Jesus's life that reads as a parallel to the citation in verse 17: "Jesus answered them, '[You will] destroy this temple [λύσατε τὸν ναὸν τοῦτον]'" (v. 19).[24] John will report in verse 21 that Jesus spoke of the destruction of his body. But within the narrative, the Jews are thoroughly confused (v. 20), not least because *destroying* the temple would be the furthest thing from their minds (cf. 11:48: "If we permit him like this, all will believe in him, and the Romans will come and sweep away both our place [the temple] and our nation").

In verse 22 further clarification about the citation is provided. John repeats the exact phrase that introduced the citation in verse 17 (ἐμνήσθησαν

---

23. For example, Thompson affirms that "[Jesus's] passion for the house of God would lead to his demise," yet she interprets John's use of Ps 69 to mean that "Jesus will be consumed *by forces hostile to him*" (*John*, 74 [emphasis added]). Thompson writes elsewhere: "Whereas Psalm 69 speaks of 'many' who seek to 'destroy me,' so in the Gospel of John Jesus speaks of *those who destroy the temple*—an allusive prediction to his death by crucifixion" (Thompson, "'They Bear Witness to Me': The Psalms in the Passion Narrative of the Gospel of John," in *The Word Leaps the Gap: Essays on Scripture and Theology in Honor of Richard B. Hays*, ed. J. Ross Wagner, C. Kavin Rowe, and A. Katherine Grieb [Grand Rapids: Eerdmans, 2008], 276 [emphasis added]).

24. This imperative is most often understood as an ironic command ("Destroy!" cf. Isa 8:9; Amos 4:4) or a condition ("If you destroy"), but Lloyd Gaston argues that "the sense of the imperative is neither ironic nor concessive but future … 'you will destroy my body and in three days I will raise it up'" (Lloyd Gaston, *No Stone on Another: Studies in the Significance of the Fall of Jerusalem in the Synoptic Gospels*, NovTSup 23 [Leiden: Brill, 1970], 207; cf. 71). I am inclined to follow Gaston since his reading is perfectly acceptable on grammatical grounds and makes good sense in context, but my broader proposal does not suffer if one reads λύσατε as a command.

οἱ μαθηταὶ αὐτοῦ), but this time John clarifies when the disciples "remember" and what significance they find in these events. "After he was raised from the dead," the disciples not only remember Ps 69:9 (ὅτι γεγραμμένον ἐστίν, v. 17) and what Jesus said in verse 19 about raising up the "temple" in three days (ὅτι τοῦτο ἔλεγεν, v. 22), but they also *believe* "the Scripture and the word." The following annotated rendering of verses 17–22 draws attention to the parallelism in the passage and recapitulates my reading:

[A] 17 οἱ μαθηταὶ αὐτοῦ <u>remembered</u> [after the resurrection] that it was written,
   [B] ζῆλος for your house—[in hindsight, a passion shared by Jesus and the Jews] will consume me.
   18 <u>οἱ Ἰουδαῖοι</u> then said to him,
     "What sign can you show us for doing this?"
  19 <u>Jesus</u> answered them,
     "You will destroy this temple [λύσατε τὸν ναὸν τοῦτον],
          and <u>in three days I will raise it up</u>."
   20 <u>οἱ Ἰουδαῖοι</u> then said,
     "This temple [ὁ ναὸς οὗτος] has been under construction
        for forty-six years, and <u>you will raise it up in three days</u>?"
  21 But he was speaking of the temple of his body.
  22 After he was raised from the dead,
[A'] οἱ μαθηταὶ αὐτοῦ <u>remembered</u> that he had said this;
   [B'] and they believed the <u>Scripture</u> [i.e., "zeal for your house will consume me"]
       and the <u>word</u> that Jesus had spoken [the Jews will destroy the
          "temple" of Jesus's body because they fail to grasp Jesus's identity].

Given the parallelism, "the Scripture" is specified as "zeal for your house will consume me" (v. 17) and "the word" that gives significance to this Scripture is "[The Jews will] destroy this temple, and in three days I will raise it up" (v. 19).[25] This passage illustrates the way in which the

---

25. In John's Gospel, with the possible exception of 20:9, γραφή refers to a specific text, rather than Scripture as a whole (see 7:38, 42; 10:35; 13:18; 17:12; 19:24, 28, 36, 37).

disciples' later perspective informs the events that have taken place, as does the later reinforcement of the importance of "remembering" what is written (12:16) in light of what Jesus has said (14:26; 15:20; 16:4). Therefore, verse 22 strongly suggests that the disciples look back on this event and understand that, despite appearances, the ζῆλος that consumes Jesus is not Jesus's passion for the temple, but rather that of the Jews. As we have seen, this is precisely the way John narrates the behavior of the Jews in the ensuing narrative. Though it seems enigmatic, the delayed explanation of the citation in 2:17 is a rhetorical device that illustrates how events (or Scripture) can be properly understood only in light of the resurrection (or Jesus's word).[26]

Some of the particularities of this reading have yet to be defended, but if I am correct that Jesus's actions represent only one manifestation of "zeal" and that a double entendre can be detected, the stage is set for a sharp irony. The Jews' zeal for the protection and purity of the soon-to-be-destroyed temple (ὁ ζῆλος τοῦ οἴκου σου) is shared by Jesus himself. What goes wrong, in John's view, is not that the Jews demonstrate zeal for the temple. Rather, their zeal becomes misplaced, because they fail to comprehend Jesus's identity as the true locus of God's presence that cannot be destroyed (2:21; cf. 5:39–44; 9:40; 10:33). In this way, John has provided a device ("zeal for the temple") by which Jesus and the Jews are to be evaluated in the events that follow.

4. Possible Objections

4.1. A "Readerly Misunderstanding"?

One objection that could be leveled against this reading is that it is too subtle. It is of course a novel reading, but other instances of irony and "Johannine misunderstanding" perform important functions in the gospel. These include the Jews' misunderstanding of Caiaphas's prophecy

---

26. John is also, of course, inviting his readers to evaluate the events that follow from this same perspective (cf. 20:31). For a more complete analysis of "resurrection perspective" as a literary strategy in John's Gospel, see Richard B. Hays, "Reading Scripture in Light of the Resurrection," in *The Art of Reading Scripture*, ed. Ellen F. Davis and Richard B. Hays (Grand Rapids: Eerdmans, 2003). As Andrew Lincoln observes, "Scripture has to be understood in the light of the word of Jesus" (*Truth on Trial: The Lawsuit Motif in the Fourth Gospel* [Peabody, MA: Hendrickson, 2000], 55).

in 11:51, the disciples' later remembrance of Zech 9:9 in John 12:14–16,[27] and the references to a future time of clearer understanding in 10:16 and 12:32.[28] In addition, the notion that the Jews demonstrate a misguided zeal is made more explicit as it is extended to the disciples' future suffering in 16:2–3: "Indeed, an hour is coming when *all who kill you* will think that they are *offering worship to God*. And they will do this because *they do not know* the Father or me."

4.2. "I Lay It Down of My Own Accord"

Even if John's portrayal of the hostility of the Jews can fittingly be labeled "zeal," some might object that John makes it clear in 10:18 that Jesus lays down his own life ("No one takes it from me, but I lay it down of my own accord"). That is, given John's portrayal of Jesus as totally in control of all that transpires, understanding the citation in 2:17 to mean that *Jesus's own zeal* consumes him, fits John's emphases much better than does the suggestion that Jesus's enemies consume him.[29] In response, it should be noted that John's portrayal of the responsibility for Jesus's death is not one-sided, and to say that the zeal of the Jews will consume Jesus is indeed consistent with John's approach elsewhere. For instance, John notes in the prologue that although the "light" was unknown and rejected (1:10–11), in fact "the darkness did not overcome it" (ἡ σκοτία αὐτὰ οὐ κατέλαβεν,

---

27. The incident in 12:14–16, containing the only occurrence of the verb μιμνήσκομαι (v. 16) besides 2:17 and 22 (cf. ὑπομιμνήσκω in 14:26), shares many features with 2:17–22. As Lincoln writes, "They only remember and believe the word of Scripture in Ps 69:9 after the resurrection (cf. 2:17, 22), and they only remember and see the significance of Zech 9:9 after Jesus' glorification (cf. 12:16)" (*Truth on Trial*, 55). Likewise, R. Alan Culpepper has noted, "The ironies of the story, like the misunderstandings but more subtly, invite the reader to share the implied author's higher vantage point" (*Anatomy of the Fourth Gospel: A Study in Literary Design* [Philadelphia: Fortress, 1983], 181; see also Hays, "Reading," 221).

28. For other strategies by which John includes the reader, see Adele Reinhartz, *Befriending the Beloved Disciple* (London: Continuum, 2002), 100–103.

29. Daly-Denton writes, "The suggestion inherent in the image that Jesus is to fall victim to a force stronger than himself is difficult to reconcile with Johannine thought" (*David*, 125). Daly-Denton solves this dilemma by proposing that at a deeper level the quotation in 2:17 points to "the Father's acceptance of [Jesus's] death as a perfect sacrifice" (126), but it is not at all clear that John is much concerned with the idea of "sacrifice" per se.

1:5). In addition, John often reminds the reader that the Jews are trying to kill Jesus (5:18; 7:1, 7, 19; 8:37, 40), the people repeatedly attempt to arrest and stone Jesus (7:30, 44; 8:20, 59; 10:31, 39), and in 19:16 Pilate hands Jesus over to the Jews to be crucified (cf. 18:36). Thus it is not inconsistent to suggest that John ultimately presents Jesus as totally in control and laying down his own life, while also asserting that the quotation in 2:17 is a reference to the death of Jesus at the hands of the Jews.

4.3. The Use of Psalm 69 in the Narrative of John

Perhaps most important is the objection that because it is the *psalmist's* zeal that is spoken of in Ps 69, it must then be Jesus's zeal that the disciples "remember" in 2:17. Alan R. Kerr, noting that the specific nature of the zeal in Ps 69 itself is irretrievably unknown, helpfully lists eight possible interpretations of John 2:17 based on the various options for understanding ζῆλος/קנאה, οἶκος σου/ביתך, and κατεσθίω/אכל.[30] Kerr rightly concludes that the citation in 2:17 is deliberately multivalent, but notably missing from his eight options is the possibility that it is not Jesus's zeal.[31] Even if we grant that the psalmist should be understood to refer to his own zeal (though the emphasis on "those seeking my life" [ζητοῦντές μου τὴν ψυχήν, LXX Ps 69:3] should not be underestimated), *John's* purposes are another matter altogether.[32] The question, then, is whether John's regular practice

---

30. Kerr's possibilities include having passion for the rebuilding of the temple, striving to reestablish worship in a postexilic setting, and even expressing devotion to the people as the "house" of the Lord; see *Temple*, 83–84. Stephen Voorwinde also notes that in the original context of Ps 69 it is difficult to assess whether οἶκος/בית refers to the temple in a literal or metaphorical sense (*Jesus' Emotions in the Fourth Gospel: Human or Divine?*, LNTS 284 [London: T&T Clark, 2005], 129).

31. Kerr unintentionally supports my reading even as he attempts to sidestep the logic of the citation. He claims that Jesus's zeal, like the psalmist's zeal, "triggered a hostile reaction, a reaction that devoured him" (*Jesus' Emotions*, 129).

32. If the psalmist is referring to his passion for the temple, we might infer that he is somewhat alone in his devotion and that his zeal somehow kindles his enemies' hatred. There is no reason to suspect that the psalmist's enemies were likewise zealous for the temple, as is the case in Jesus's context (as we have seen above). Psalms scholars hold widely differing views about the historical background, but Alphonso Groenewald makes a strong case that Ps 69:10 witnesses to an "early post-exilic conflict which derives from the whole issue of whether the temple should be rebuilt or not" ("'Indeed—The Zeal for Your House Has Consumed Me!': Possible Historical Background to Psalm 69:10AB," in *Stimulation from Leiden: Collected Communications to*

of citing Scripture allows for the kind of change of subject from the original context that I am proposing.

Nothing like an exhaustive study of John's use of Scripture is possible here,[33] but two observations suggest that a change of subject should not be ruled out on the basis of John's usual practice. First, John has no qualms about straying from the textual traditions that appear to be the source of his quotations,[34] as the change from the aorist κατέφαγεν to the future καταφάγεται in 2:17 may already demonstrate.[35] Second, as noted above, the interpretive significance of scriptural quotations in John is regularly provided by Jesus's words or by the whole of John's narrative (e.g., 6:45; 7:38; 10:34; 13:18), rather than by the original context of a given passage.[36]

---

the XVIIIth Congress of the International Organization for the Study of the Old Testament, Leiden 2004, ed. Hermann Michael Niemann and Matthias Augustin, BEATAJ 54 [Frankfurt am Main: Peter Lang, 2006], 179).

33. In addition to the other essays in this volume, see Harold W. Attridge, "Giving Voice to Jesus: Use of the Psalms in the New Testament," in *Essays on John and Hebrews* (Tübingen: Mohr Siebeck, 2010), 320–30; Daly-Denton, *David*; Edwin D. Freed, *Old Testament Quotations in the Gospel of John*, NovTSup 6 (Leiden: Brill, 1965); Martin Hengel, "The Old Testament in the Fourth Gospel," *HBT* 12 (1990): 19–41; Maarten J. J. Menken, "The Use of the Septuagint in Three Quotations in John: Jn 10,34; 12,38; 19,24," in *The Scriptures in the Gospels*, ed. Christopher M. Tuckett (Leuven: Leuven University Press, 1997), 367–93; Günter Reim, *Studien zum alttestamentlichen Hintergrund des Johanessevangeliums*, SNTSMS 22 (Cambridge: Cambridge University Press, 1974); and especially Bruce G. Schuchard, *Scripture within Scripture: The Interrelationship of Form and Function in the Explicit Old Testament Citations in the Gospel of John*, SBLDS 133 (Atlanta: Scholars Press, 1992).

34. According to Menken, the quotations in 7:42; 8:17; 12:34 are free paraphrases, those in 1:23; 2:17; 6:31, 45; 7:38; 12:15; 15:25; 19:36 have been edited from the LXX to serve John's narrative/theological purposes, and those in 10:34; 12:38; and 19:24 are left intact from the LXX, because John had no need to change them ("Septuagint," 367).

35. The significance of John's apparent change from the aorist to the future (which could also simply be John's own translation of the Hebrew perfect [אכלת]) has been discussed ad nauseam and is of little consequence for our purposes here.

36. A more sophisticated version of the objection about the psalmist and Jesus might appeal to the "rules" of the ancient exegetical practice known as "prosopological exegesis." This was an exegetical technique commonly used by the church fathers (e.g., Justin, Tertullian, and Athanasius) with roots in classical literature (for a recent treatment of prosopological exegesis in the NT, including a discussion of John 2:17, see Matthew W. Bates, *The Hermeneutics of the Apostolic Proclamation: The Center of Paul's Method of Scriptural Interpretation* [Waco, TX: Baylor University Press, 2012],

Raising a more significant question than that of the original context, however, interpreters point to the citations of Ps 69 in John 15:25 (Pss 69:4; 34:19)[37] and John 19:28–29 (Ps 69:21) to argue that John uses Ps 69 to express Jesus's suffering and crucifixion in terms of the suffering of David.[38] For example, Marianne Meye Thompson writes of the citation in 2:17:

> Psalm 69 supplies two other quotations in the Gospel of John ... both pointing to the suffering of its speaker; namely, David, king of Israel who was maltreated, pursued, or deserted by his own people. As King of Israel, David's suffering prefigured the destiny of the Jesus, King of Israel.... Even though the quotation of Psalm 69:9 occurs at the outset of the Gospel rather than in the context of the passion narrative, neverthe-

---

esp. 243–47). From this perspective, the true identity of the "speaker" of Ps 69 is *Jesus* (irrespective of the "plain sense" of the text), so the speaker cited in John 2:17 cannot be "the Jews" or even a double entendre because the words of Ps 69:21 are unambiguously used of Jesus in John 19:28–29 (ἵνα τελειωθῇ ἡ γραφή λέγει <u>διψῶ</u> σκεῦος ἔκειτο <u>ὄξους μεστόν</u>; cf. LXX Ps 68:22: εἰς τὴν <u>δίψαν μου ἐπότισάν με ὄξος</u>). This is no real objection, of course, since at issue in my reading of John 2:17 is the *referent* of ζῆλος and not the speaker (με refers to Jesus). Intriguingly, however, at least one early interpreter of the Gospel of John *did* propose another speaker. Origen writes, "It is especially careless of Heracleon ... to think that the statement, 'The zeal for your house will devour me' is placed in the mouth of the powers which were cast out and destroyed by the Savior" (*Comm. Jo.* 10.222–223; trans. Ronald E. Heine, *Origen, Commentary on the Gospel according to John*, FC 80 [Washington, DC: Catholic University of America, 1989]). Heracleon's interpretation does the opposite of my proposal: he assumes that it is Jesus's zeal but that the "consuming" refers to the powers. Thus Heracleon places the quotation in the mouth of the powers, whereas my reading changes the referent of "zeal" and keeps the words in the mouth of Jesus. In light of the recent "rehabilitation" of Heracleon as an exegete (see esp. Ansgar Wucherpfennig, *Heracleon Philologus: Gnostische Johannesexegese im zweiten Jahrhundert*, WUNT 142 [Tübingen: Mohr Siebeck, 2002]), it is worth noting that already in the second century an interpreter with good narrative sensibilities put forward an alternative to the standard reading of this citation.

37. For the argument that Ps 69 is more likely in view in John 15:25 than Ps 34, see, e.g., Helen C. Orchard, *Courting Betrayal: Jesus As Victim in the Gospel of John*, LNTS 161 (Sheffield: Sheffield Academic, 1998), 184n86.

38. Much attention has been given to this particular use of Ps 69 in the early Christian tradition; see, e.g., C. H. Dodd's discussion about a possible corpus of *testimonia* that give witness to Jesus (*The Interpretation of the Fourth Gospel* [Cambridge: Cambridge University Press, 1953], 302). For the argument that zeal for the temple is the outstanding characteristic of David, see Daly-Denton, *David*, 128.

less it foreshadows and interprets Jesus' death: his passion for the house of God would lead to his demise.[39]

Thompson is right to draw attention to David's suffering, but it need not follow that it is Jesus's passion that leads to his demise. In John 15:25 the "enemies" of Ps 69 are unambiguously in view: "they hated me without cause" (ἐμίσησάν με δωρεάν; cf. οἱ μισοῦντές με δωρεάν, LXX Ps 68:5; MT Ps 69:4: שנאי חנם).[40] It is intriguing, then, that the passages that cite Ps 69:9 (John 2:17) and Ps 69:4 (John 15:25) both involve verbs that describe antagonism toward Jesus (κατεσθίω and μισέω), and both verbs have με as their object. In 15:25 *Jesus's opponents* are the subject of μισέω, and, if the present study is correct, in 2:17 Jesus's opponents are also the ones who do the "consuming."[41]

In fact, the rest of Ps 69:4 ("mighty are those who would destroy [צמת; LXX: ἐκδιώκω] me") seems to inform Jesus's words in John 2:19 ("[You will] destroy this temple").[42] As noted above, this echo in 2:19 is already anticipated by the parallel citation in 2:17. Thus while it may be said that John utilizes Ps 69 to interpret Jesus's suffering in terms of David's suffering (as Thompson emphasizes), John also uses the psalm to elucidate the nature of the opposition to Jesus. In other words, John's citation of Ps 69 relates to *the unbelief of the Jews* as much as it does *the suffering and death of Jesus*. It might even be said that, through the double entendre in 2:17, John in fact unites the two concerns of his source text. For Jesus, appropriating the psalmist's zeal culminates in laying down his own life in obedi-

---

39. Thompson, *John*, 74.

40. Although John has shifted from speaking of "the Jews" to speaking of "the world" (κόσμος) in chapters 14–16, in 15:25 Jesus is referring to those who are hostile to him and refuse him outright (cf. 15:24). As Raymond Brown puts it: "But those about whom Jesus is speaking here … are like 'the Jews' who would not believe that the blind man had been healed" (*The Gospel according to John*, 2 vols., AB 29–29A [Garden City, NY: Doubleday, 1966–70], 2:698).

41. The allusion/citation of Ps 69:21 in John 19:28–29 (διψῶ σκεῦος ἔκειτο ὄξους μεστόν … προσήνεγκαν αὐτοῦ τῷ στόματι; cf. εἰς τὴν δίψαν μου ἐπότισάν με ὄξος, LXX Ps 68:22) is of little consequence here, although Ulrich Busse makes a connection between 2:17 and Jesus's dying word (τετέλεσται, 19:30): "When Jesus dies … with the words, 'it is finished,' it could mean: The zeal for you, Father, has consumed me" (*Das Johannesevangelium: Bildlichkeit, Diskurs, und Ritual*, BETL 162 [Leuven: Leuven University Press, 2002], 97 [my translation]).

42. Cf. Thompson, "They Bear Witness to Me," 275–76.

ence to the Father. For the Jews, their unbelief causes this very same zeal to degrade into a misguided and ultimately violent zeal for the Jerusalem temple that blinds them to the temple that is Jesus.

5. Historical and Theological Implications

We have seen, then, that in John's narrative ὁ ζῆλος τοῦ οἴκου σου καταφάγεταί με comes to be understood not only as a reference to Jesus's zeal but also as a description of the zeal of the Jews. Through the use of this double entendre, John has presented the hostility of the Jews as a foil for the true model of zeal: Jesus's relationship to the Father. As Ulrich Busse has noted about what the disciples "remember" in 2:17, "The disciples see a time with Jesus before them that will be exclusively marked by his zeal for God's cause.... For [the disciples,] it will be interpreted by Jesus' zeal for the cause of God [as opposed to "the Jews"] in that they destroy the 'temple.'"[43] Jesus's cleansing of the temple shows that he has the same kind of passion that many Jews from Israel's storied past and in the first century have shown for the place where God's presence dwells. Viewed from this angle, John's Gospel aims to communicate how and why two manifestations of this hallmark Jewish attribute can produce results that are so diametrically opposed. The acceptance or rejection of Jesus's identity as the one sent from the Father is lived out in the pattern of the zeal of the Jews or the zeal of Jesus.

From a historical perspective, such a reading raises questions about the notion of "Christian zeal" in the late first century and beyond. I have argued that Jesus provides the model for true ζῆλος in the Fourth Gospel. But perhaps John's choice not to describe Jesus's instructions for the disciples in terms of "zeal" but rather "love" (e.g., 16:27) and even "peace" (14:27; 16:33) reflects a movement away from violent expressions of Jewish zeal such as that of the Jews in John and that of the Zealots of 68–70 CE. William Klassen has noted that such an impulse seems to be present in 4 Macc 6:27–29, where the model of zeal in the way of Phinehas (e.g., 1 Macc 2:26) is rejected in favor of a self-sacrificial martyrdom.[44] The letters of Paul (e.g., Rom 10:2; 2 Cor 11:2; cf. Titus 2:14) and the book of Acts (e.g., 21:20; 22:3) certainly show no resistance to describing Christ follow-

---

43. Busse, *Johannesevangelium*, 97 (my translation).
44. Klassen, "Phineas," 499.

ers as "zealots," but perhaps for John's first readers the negative connotations of "zeal" had begun to prevail (cf. 1 Clem. 4.7–6.4).[45]

In this light, the theological implications of this reading should not be overlooked. It is certainly appropriate to approach this text from a different critical framework (reader-oriented, literary/ideological), and to critique both John's portrayal of the Jews and especially the subsequent use of John's narrative to validate anti-Jewish sentiment and behavior. However, the narrative-compositional approach of the present study already challenges the prevailing view that John's perspective is irredeemably dualistic and polemical. As we have seen, the editorial comment in 2:17 prepares John's reader to recognize that because the Jews do not accept Jesus's claims about his identity, even their commendable ζῆλος for the place of God's dwelling is tragically crippled. When viewed from the perspective of misguided zeal, John's portrayal of the hostility of the Jews is not a portrait of hatred and alienation but rather a rhetorical device that emphasizes the importance of accepting Jesus's claims about his identity. That is, John's portrayal of the Jews' actions as "zeal for the temple" suggests a more sympathetic assessment of both the Jews and the temple cult than has traditionally (and often tragically) been construed.

Precisely in its ambiguity and subtlety, John's citation of Ps 69:9 in 2:17 serves an important function. It casts the decision for John's readers (cf. 20:31) not in terms of Jesus as the replacement of the temple or the Johannine community as a replacement of Judaism, but rather in terms of "zeal with understanding" (see Rom 10:2). This reading of "zeal" and "temple" in 2:13–22, like Stephen Motyer's reading of Jesus's incendiary remarks in 8:44, suggests that John employs "a strategy, rooted in the conditions of late first-century Judaism, which is designed to appeal to Jews to see Jesus as the Messiah, and is motivated by a deep commitment to the good of Israel."[46]

---

45. On Paul, see further Benjamin J. Lappenga, "Misdirected Emulation and Paradoxical Zeal: Paul's Redefinition of 'The Good' as Object of ζῆλος in Gal 4:12–20," *JBL* 131 (2012): 775–96.

46. Stephen Motyer, *Your Father the Devil? A New Approach to John and "the Jews"* (Carlisle, UK: Paternoster, 1997), xii. See also Brown, *Introduction*, 173–75.

The Testimony of Two Witnesses: John 8:17*

Ruth Sheridan

John 8:12–20 depicts Jesus engaged in a debate with the Pharisees over the validity of his self-testimony. After Jesus claims to be the "light of the world" (8:12), the Pharisees reply that Jesus testifies to himself, which automatically invalidates the content of his testimony (8:13). Jesus counters their concern with a concession: "even if I testify about myself, my testimony is true, because I know where I came from and where I go; but you do not know where I come from or where I go" (8:14). The Pharisees' purported lack of knowledge about Jesus's true identity corresponds to, and is made evident by, their predilection for judging "according to the flesh" (κατὰ τὴν σάρκα, 8:15a). Jesus, on the other hand, judges no one (8:15b). Jesus follows up with a parallel concession: "even if I judge, my judgment is true, because I am not alone, but I and the Father who sent me" (8:16). Both Jesus's knowledge of his origins and destiny and his awareness of God the Father's continual presence with him indicate that Jesus's testimony and judgment are "valid" or "true" (ἀληθής). Then, to substantiate his point, Jesus refers to a prescription from the Torah about proper judicial evidence, speaking to the Pharisees thus: "even in your law it has been written that the testimony of two witnesses is valid" (καὶ ἐν τῷ νόμῳ δὲ τῷ ὑμετέρῳ γέγραπται ὅτι δύο ἀνθρώπων ἡ μαρτυρία ἀληθής ἐστιν, 8:17). Jesus then applies this to his situation, telling them that, while he does "witness" to himself, the Father who sent him also "witnesses" to Jesus (8:18). When the Pharisees ask after the whereabouts of Jesus's "father," Jesus responds

---

* This is a revised version of a paper presented at the Johannine Literature section at the Society of Biblical Literature annual meeting, November 2012 (Chicago). I want to thank Tom Thatcher for inviting me to give the talk, and also Paul Anderson, Adele Reinhartz, Mary Coloe, and Jonathan Kaplan for their comments on an earlier version of this paper. Any remaining errors are, of course, my own.

by telling them that they know neither Jesus nor his Father, and that to know Jesus is to know the Father (8:19). This short pericope closes with the narrator's note that Jesus spoke thus in the temple treasury, but that it did not lead to Jesus's arrest (8:20). The purpose of this essay is to examine the significance of Jesus's reference to the Torah's stipulation about "two witnesses" alluded to in 8:17. I aim to assess its rhetorical contribution to the altercation between Jesus and his opponents in these verses (8:12–20) against the larger narrative context of John 7:1–8:59.[1]

1. Interpretive Issues

Scholarly discussions of John 8:17 have focused on only a few points. First, there is Jesus's curious introductory expression, "in your law it is written that" (καὶ ἐν τῷ νόμῳ δὲ τῷ ὑμετέρῳ γέγραπται ὅτι). The emphatic form of the pronoun has led to the suggestion that Jesus is distancing himself from the Jewish law—effectively stating that it is his opponent's law, and not his own.[2] But one could find such a view inconsistent with the Johannine author's appreciation of Scripture as authoritative and valid for the community, and of Jesus as the embodiment of the Torah.[3] A radical detachment from the Jewish law, inferred only from 8:17, does seem to strain credulity, pressing a Greek vocable into the service of a broader argument. However, Jesus's use of the second person pronoun is emphatic. The point being made appears to be that Jesus's testimony is valid because it proceeds from himself *and* from God (who is his co-witness); we could paraphrase it thus: "even the law that is yours, that you yourselves admit, stipulates that the testimony of two witnesses is valid."[4]

---

1. Various commentators read John 7–8 as a unit: Barnabas Lindars, *The Gospel of John*, NCB (London: Oliphants, 1972), 277; Peter F. Ellis, *The Genius of John: A Composition-Critical Commentary on the Fourth Gospel* (Collegeville, MN: Liturgical Press, 1984), 135; Bruce Malina and Richard Rohrbaugh, *Social Science Commentary on the Gospel of John* (Minneapolis: Fortress, 1998), 139; Craig S. Keener, *The Gospel of John* (Grand Rapids: Baker Academic, 2003), 1:703, among others.

2. Cf. C. H. Dodd, *The Interpretation of the Fourth Gospel* (Cambridge: Cambridge University Press, 1953), 82.

3. See Keener, *John*, 1:741 (Keener cites John 2:22; 7:38; 13:18; 17:12; 19:24, 28, 36–37; 20:9).

4. See Raymond Brown, *The Gospel according to John*, 2 vols., AB 29–29A (Garden City, NY: Doubleday, 1966–70), 1:341.

Second, commentators debate the content of Jesus's "testimony," that is, the exact words that provoke such offense in his listeners. Is the offense, requiring validation from another witness, found in Jesus's claim to be the "light of the world" (8:12)? Or is the subject of Jesus's self-testimony his laconic formulation "I and the One who sent me" (8:16)—an ostensible expression of the Divine Name?[5] Is it unspecified, an assumed summation of everything Jesus has already said thus far in the Gospel story? Parallels between chapters 5 and 7–8 of the Gospel might suggest that such is the case. Although it is not the purpose of this essay to resolve this question, I think it most likely that 8:12 forms the basis of Jesus's provocative claim, as it comes directly before the Pharisees' objections about Jesus's self-testimony. But, at the same time, Jesus's claim to be the "light of the world" is part of his frequent habit of making absolute self-assertions (see thus far in the narrative 6:35, 48), which could cumulatively form the provocation at this point.

The third issue concerns the possible Torah text to which Jesus alludes. Because the form of 8:17 is not a verbatim citation, the issue of John's source text remains an open question. There is no text in the LXX that corresponds exactly to John's δύο ἀνθρώπων ἡ μαρτυρία ἀληθής ἐστιν (8:17b). And so, although the text reads as an indirect quotation, it is yet "formed by the narrative shape and the language of the Fourth Gospel."[6] Nevertheless, there are three texts from the Torah that discuss the necessity of multiple witnesses. These texts are Deut 17:6; 19:15; and Num 35:30. Most Johannine commentators include a reference to one or all of these texts from the Torah when discussing John's possible source in 8:17b, but they typically refrain from arguing for John's reliance on one of these texts over another. The conclusion that "one cannot be certain of the textual form of [John's] cited text" is thus quite widespread in the secondary literature.[7] However, some distinctions can be made. For example, Maarten Menken has demonstrated that Deut 17:6 and Num 35:30 deal with the death penalty, whereas Deut 19:15 focuses on the task of the witnesses, and is thus more akin to John 8:17–20.[8] Below, I will assess the possibility that John

---

5. C. K. Barrett, *The Gospel according to St. John*, 2nd ed. (London: SPCK, 1978), 339.

6. Michael Labahn, "Deuteronomy in John's Gospel," in *Deuteronomy in the New Testament*, ed. M. J. J. Menken and Steve Moyise, NTSI, LNTS 358 (London: T&T Clark, 2007), 85.

7. Labahn, "Deuteronomy," 86.

8. Maarten J. J. Menken, *Old Testament Quotations in the Fourth Gospel: Studies in*

8:17 recontextualizes elements present in each of the three relevant Torah texts while nevertheless conceding that the popularity of Deut 19:15 in Second Temple Jewish sources suggests its influence in John as well (see CD 9:16-23; Mark 14:55-59; 2 Cor 13:11; 1 Tim 5:19; Heb 10:28).

Despite attention to these factors in the scholarly literature on John 8:17, the intertextual shape of John 7-8, particularly as evoked by the Torah's requirement of two witnesses in 8:17, has not received sufficient attention. This may be due to the indecisive status of 8:17 as a genuine "citation."[9] But it could also be due to another factor—the tendency of some scholars to dismiss the scriptural context of the law of two witnesses as irrelevant to Jesus's discourse in 8:12-20 due to its apparent redundancy. To be sure, scholars do not state this explicitly. Generally speaking, it *could* be inferred from the brevity of attention scholars give the relevant Torah texts when discussing John 8:17—but that alone would be an argument *ex silentio*. The logic of such an (unexpressed) assumption would be that, with respect to understanding John 8:12-20, whatever the Torah texts present about the rule of multiple witnesses is inconsequential because Jesus has already reinterpreted it to fit his situation. In John 8:12-20, Jesus responds to a situation in which he is positioned as the accused, and forced to testify about himself; but Jesus emerges out of the situation triumphant and vindicated, turning the tables on his accusers, and, with subversive irony, effectively judging them as lacking knowledge of God (8:18-19).[10] In light of the ironic reversal present in the narrative itself,

---

Textual Form (Kampen: Kok Pharos, 1996), 16. As we will see, Deut 19:15 deals with more than just the task of witnesses, so this distinction does appear reductive.

9. For example, in his monograph on the scriptural citations in John's Gospel, Menken does not analyze 8:17, because he considers it a "rephrasing of the content of an OT passage" rather than a "formulaic" quotation; see Menken, *Old Testament Quotations*, 17. For similar reasons, consideration of 8:17 is also absent from Bruce G. Schuchard, *Scripture within Scripture: The Interrelationship of Form and Function in the Explicit Old Testament Citations in the Gospel of John*, SBLDS 133 (Atlanta: Scholars Press, 1992), xiii-xiv; Andreas Obermann, *Die christologische Erfüllung der Schrift im Johannesevangelium*, WUNT 2/83 (Tübingen: Mohr Siebeck, 1996), 71-73; and Mogens Müller, "Schriftbeweis oder Vollendung? Das Johannesevangelium und das Alte Testament," in *Bekenntnis und Erinnerung: Festschrift zum 75. Geburtstag von Hans-Friedrich Weiss*, ed. Klaus-Michael Bull and Eckart Reinmuth (Münster: LIT, 2004), 135.

10. Cf. Jerome H. Neyrey, "Jesus the Judge: Forensic Processes in John 8:21-59," *Bib* 68 (1987): 509-42.

the context of the scriptural citation in 8:17 remains underexamined, perhaps on the unexpressed assumption that it adds nothing substantial to what is present in the text itself.

Sometimes the secondary literature evidences explicitly "dismissive" reasoning about the significance of the scriptural context of John 8:17. For example, Francis Moloney's commentary on the Gospel contains the unusual (and counterconsensus) argument that in John 8, Jesus is not "on trial."[11] Moloney argues that in John 5, "the Jews" effectively "trialled" Jesus and his claims, and that Jesus voluntarily assumed the role of defendant by adducing a series of "witnesses" on his behalf (John the Baptist, Moses, Scripture, Jesus's own words and works, etc.). But in John 8, when the Pharisees try to put Jesus on trial, demanding that he produce a witness who can validate his claims (cf. 8:13), Jesus does not capitulate; his words are not a "witness in the forensic sense" and there is "no trace of a trial."[12] Instead, what we have in John 8, according to Moloney, is an attempt on the part of the Pharisees to "control Jesus by means of their legal system."[13] For Moloney, Jesus's claim to be the "light of the world" (8:12) is also a claim "to personify, perfect, and universalize the light of the Temple and the light of the Law"—but the Pharisees' reference to Jesus's need for a validating, second witness to speak on his behalf represents, according to Moloney, a misguided "quibble."[14] While Jesus speaks of his origins with God, the Pharisees "control and condemn Jesus on the basis of the Mosaic Law," in "mundane" and "earthly" fashion no less.[15] But for Jesus, the "niceties" of the Mosaic law do not apply.[16] Rather, "Jesus' aggressive affirmation of his origins puts the validity of his witness outside the reach of the questioning of the Law."[17]

---

11. That John 7–8 represents Jesus's "trial" is an idea found in Andrew T. Lincoln, *Truth on Trial: The Lawsuit Motif in the Fourth Gospel* (Peabody, MA: Hendrickson, 2000); and, earlier, in Anthony E. Harvey, *Jesus on Trial: A Study in the Fourth Gospel* (London: SPCK, 1976). See also Barrett, *John*, 334. Challenging the "trial" thesis recently is Martin Asiedu-Peprah, *Johannine Sabbath Conflicts as Juridical Controversy*, WUNT 2/132 (Tübingen: Mohr Siebeck, 2001).

12. Francis J. Moloney, *John*, SP 4 (Collegeville, MN: Liturgical Press, 1998), 266.
13. Ibid.
14. Ibid.
15. Ibid.
16. Ibid., 267.
17. Ibid.

I have engaged with Moloney's comments at length here because they encapsulate a position about John 8:17–20 that inhibits a comprehensive dealing with the "Mosaic law" alluded to in 8:17. In short, and to put the matter somewhat sardonically, if we can paint the Pharisees in pejorative terms (here, for example, they "quibble" over legal "niceties," they are "mundane," "earthly" and "controlling"), then we need not tar ourselves with the same brush by stooping to a close reading of the original scriptural context for the legal allusion. Not only does this reasoning potentially import an anti-Jewish perspective, but it also (mistakenly, I think) elevates the Johannine Jesus to a status *above* the law (e.g., as "beyond" its "questioning"); yet it simultaneously asserts that Jesus "perfects" and "universalizes" the law. But if the law cannot bring the validity of Jesus's self-testimony into question, why does Jesus bother referring to the law of multiple witnesses, effectively conceding the point of his opponents and showing how he nevertheless applies it uniquely to himself? It would seem, rather, that Jesus's allusion to the Torah's rule of multiple witnesses *invites* the Gospel's reader to assess the original context(s) of that rule, and to weigh up the manner in which, and the extent to which, the Torah's context plays into John 8:12–20, and chapters 7–8 as a whole. Far from being asked to dismiss the scriptural intertext as evidence of the Pharisees' misguided reasoning, the reader is pulled into the world of the Scriptures in order to make a judgment about Jesus and the "trial" in which he stands. In the next section I will briefly address some methodological issues, proposing to read John 8:17 from the approach of "metaleptic intertextuality," while avoiding a presentation dense with jargon.

2. Metaleptic Intertextuality

Richard Hays's seminal work on scriptural echoes in the Letters of Paul is renowned for giving the field the methodological concept of "metaleptic intertextuality."[18] Hays's work relies extensively on literary critic John Hollander's work on textual "echoes."[19] Hays follows Hollander's focus on

---

18. Richard B. Hays, *Echoes of Scripture in the Letters of Paul* (New Haven: Yale University Press, 1989).

19. John Hollander, *The Figure of an Echo: A Model of Allusion in Milton and After* (Berkeley: University of California Press, 1981).

the "rhetorical and semantic effects" of allusions.[20] Eschewing the need to systematize his thoughts about allusions into a broad theory, for example, Hollander interprets how literary "echoes" function rhetorically within poems from the Renaissance and early modern eras.[21] Hollander is not concerned to ascertain the first audiences of the poems, nor the poet's "authorial intention"; rather, Hollander summarizes his view, and his approach, in the following lapidary statement: "the revisionary power of allusive echo generates new figuration."[22] In other words, allusions create new rhetorical salience, because the recontextualization of another text necessarily involves a revision of its meaning, whether slight or completely subversive. The task of the critic, as Hollander sees it, is to uncover the rhetorical dynamics of allusive recontextualization in a text.

Relying on Hollander's work, Hays uses the terms "overt allusion" and "allusive echo," adapting them for use in New Testament criticism. An allusive echo is more subtle and covert than an allusion, and much more subtle again than an explicit quotation.[23] An "echo" operates in the subliminal dimensions of consciousness where heightened indeterminacy reigns.[24] For Hollander, an echo is "metaleptic," suggesting that the semantic figuration of an echo falls outside the "frame," residing in what is left unsaid or suppressed ("transumed").[25] When a prior text is "echoed" in a later text, its entire allusive matrix is potentially carried over with it, and is incorporated within the frame of the new text.[26] Building on these insights, Hays states that "metalepsis" is "a rhetorical and poetic device in which one text alludes to an earlier text in a way that evokes resonances of the earlier text *beyond those explicitly cited*. The result is that the interpretation of a metalepsis requires the reader to recover unstated or suppressed correspondences between two texts."[27]

---

20. See Hays's review, *Echoes of Scripture*, 16–18.
21. Ibid., 19.
22. Cited in ibid.
23. Ibid., 23.
24. Ibid.
25. Cited in ibid., 20. Other uses of the term "metalepsis" can be found in literary criticism. See particularly Gérard Genette, *Narrative Discourse: An Essay in Method*, trans. Jane E. Lewin (Ithaca, NY: Cornell University Press, 1983), 234–37.
26. C. H. Dodd posited something similar for the NT's use of the OT in his *According to the Scriptures: The Substructure of New Testament Theology* (London: Collins, 1952).
27. See Richard B. Hays, *The Conversion of the Imagination: Paul As Interpreter*

Hays's work demonstrates that Paul's echoic references to Scripture obey exactly this kind of layered dynamic.

In elucidating his method, Hays depends on the hermeneutical presupposition of readerly competence. That is, in order for allusive echoes to be extrapolated successfully from a text, the reader in question must be able to recognize them, and, moreover, to situate them within a recognized literary "canon." Hays uses phrases like "the reader whose ear is able ... not only to discern the echo but also to locate the source"; "the task [of criticism] is to call attention to [the echoes] so that others might be able to hear"; and "consulting a concordance, we discover."[28] This suggests that Hays is not talking about authorial intention, but about the role that the reader has in semiosis—in making meaning. Empirically speaking, it is indisputable that readers will vary in literary competency, as a result of the divergent factors influencing real readers' lives. Hays indirectly addresses this issue by citing Hollander to the effect that, in the process of reconstructing suppressed echoes, "we must always wonder what our own contribution was—how much we are always being writers as well as readers of what we are seeing."[29] Does the reader/critic extract allusive echoes that are plainly "there," present in the text, or does she create them, fabricating them out of her own existing network of intertextual knowledge? Hays's work would suggest that it is a bit of both—but that it is primarily the reader who is responsible for identifying probable "intertextual" echoes.

Nevertheless, as we read through Hays's work, it is possible to observe that the creative and radical poetics of metaleptic intertextuality advanced by Hollander (which Hays initially espouses) give way ever so slightly to an author-centered hermeneutic. We could be excused for thinking that, here, Hays makes a concession to historically minded critics of the New Testament who would rather be assured that allusive echoes to the Old Testament are "scientifically" verifiable. To this end, Hays has famously developed methodological criteria to determine the likelihood that the scriptural echoes perceived in the New Testament match up with what the original, ancient authors of the New Testament understood and knew. Hays's list of seven criteria is well-known and is frequently rehearsed in

---

of Israel's Scripture (Grand Rapids: Eerdmans, 2005), 2; following Hollander, *Figure*, 113–32.

28. Hays, *Echoes of Scripture*, 21–22, 19, 24.
29. Ibid., 25.

scholarly articles.[30] There is no need to discuss his criteria in detail here, only to note that they depend on a sliding scale of probability, and that they aim to measure the degree to which intertextual echoes can be verified or falsified. As such, perceived Old Testament "echoes" need to have been "available" to a first-century author; they must display a reasonably high level of "verbal correspondence" with the New Testament text; they must be found frequently in the said New Testament text or in texts of Second Temple Judaism; they must cohere thematically with the New Testament text; and it must be plausible to suggest that the original audience of the New Testament text would have picked up these proposed intertexts.[31]

On one reading, Hays's concession to an audience-centered method shies away from the vaster implications of metaleptic interpretation suggested by Hollander's work on allusive echoes, and restrains the contemporary reader's agency to "co-create" the text from its intertextual field.[32] Nevertheless, Hays does point out that his criteria are only meant to function as a partial "corrective" to overly subjectivist readings that might be generated by metaleptic theory, and not as a preliminary constraining device on what can be validly inferred as allusive context.[33] On another reading, Hays's work is therefore not presumed to be as naive about "intertextuality" as his detractors argue; although conceivably a "limited version of intertextuality," Hays's adoption of Hollander's work for use in New Testament studies is "informed and subtle" and not "the traditional and much maligned author-centered quest for sources and influences."[34]

In my view, the value of metaleptic intertextual interpretation lies in its ability to open a three-way hermeneutical dialogue between the text, its allusive context, and the social location of a given, historically situ-

---

30. See, recently, the survey in Brittany E. Wilson, "Pugnacious Precursors and the Bearer of Peace: Jael, Judith, and Mary in Luke 1:42," *CBQ* 68 (2006): 436–56.

31. Hays, *Echoes of Scripture*, 24.

32. Thomas R. Hatina, "Intertextuality and Historical Criticism in New Testament Studies: Is There a Relationship?," *BibInt* 7 (1999): 36–37, is adamant that Hays's approach adds nothing to the debate on "intertextuality" in the poststructuralist tradition, and that, consequently, Hays could well dispense with the term, which he uses in a sense akin to "influence," or source criticism. Hatina's analysis of the "chasm" between "influence" and "intertextuality" in literary criticism is accurate and important.

33. Hays, *Echoes of Scripture*, 190–91.

34. Leroy Huizenga, *The New Isaac: Tradition and Intertextuality in the Gospel of Matthew*, NovTSup 131 (Leiden: Brill, 2009), 44.

ated reader/critic. The resulting production of different "readings" of the same text does not indicate the shortcomings of an ideological subjectivism at the heart of the method; rather, it illustrates the dynamic of multiple interpretive possibilities, as different scholars look to what is "transumed" in the allusive process, to what is left unsaid, uncited but (even "subliminally") implied in the recontextualization of a text. Moreover, in Hays's approach, the underlying assumption is that both the contemporary reader/critic *and* the first-century New Testament audiences interpret scriptural allusions *contextually*—that is to say, that they understand, and would have understood, scriptural allusions to mean *what they meant in their original scriptural context*. This approach admits that when metaleptic echoes are detected they are also changed and "transumed," but it does not, as a consequence, assume that connection with the scriptural matrix is lost.

3. Allusive Echoes: The Testimony of Multiple Witnesses in the Biblical Texts

In what follows, I will investigate the metaleptic transfer of meaning between the three Torah texts concerning the requirement for multiple witnesses and John 8:17–20. The first thing to notice is the apparent incongruity of the legal contexts of the three Torah texts when they are set side by side with John 8:12–20. In John 8, Jesus makes an ostensibly outrageous claim for himself (see 8:12), and the Pharisees object that his status as sole testifier to himself renders his testimony invalid—evoking the substance of the biblical rule of judicial evidence. But in John 8, Jesus is only making provocative claims, whereas the texts of Deut 17:6; 19:15; and Num 35:30 each concern criminal law and capital punishment, or at least the discernment between cases that may warrant, at worst, capital punishment. These cases are of the most serious kind: idolatry, homicide (accidental or intentional), vengeance, incitement to idolatry, and perjury. What could account for this incongruity? Is it possible to gain insight into John's narrative dynamic in 8:12–20 (or even chapters 7–8 more broadly) by analyzing what is metaleptically "transumed" in the allusion at 8:17? Are the evocations of criminality in any way carried over into the fabric of John 8—that is, is it, on a deeper reading, in fact not so incongruous a connection? Guided by the theory of the "subliminal" connections effected by allusions (see above), I would assent to what these questions imply, as we will see shortly.

3.1. Deuteronomy 17:6

Deuteronomy's first mention of the law of two or more witnesses (17:6) occurs in the context of the laws of governance (16:18–18:22), the purpose of which is to "democratize" power so that it is shared by judges and prophets, not simply concentrated in the hands of priests and kings.[35] The tribunal is to execute judgment after trials are held. The immediate context of Deut 17:6 concerns apostasy (17:2–7) and the procedures in the central sanctuary for cases too difficult to arbitrate in local courts (17:8–13). These two subsections (17:2–7 and 8–13) are related to each other by casuistic examples that increase in complexity: apostasy is apparently straightforward enough to be punished via the local courts (אל־שעריך, lit. "at your gates," 17:5), but ambiguous cases must rely additionally on priestly inquiry (see 17:9).[36]

The text begins with the case of any man or woman (ἀνὴρ ἢ γυνή, LXX 17:2) who is "found" (εὑρεθῇ) in one of the towns to have done "evil before the Lord your God" (ὅστις ποιήσει τὸ πονηρὸν ἐναντίον κυρίου τοῦ θεοῦ σου). This "evil" is specifically defined as transgressing the covenant (παρελθεῖν τὴν διαθήκην αὐτοῦ) by serving and worshiping other gods (17:2b–3a). The Hebrew verb translated by the Greek παρελθεῖν in 17:2b is from the root עבר and is formulated in quasi-technical language when predicated of God's covenant (בריתו לעבר). It conveys the sense of overstepping an uppermost limit, and is elsewhere explicitly related to the abrogation of the first commandment, against idolatry.[37] Deuteronomy 17:4–5 continues the conditional language already begun in verse 2: "and *if* it is told to you or you hear of it." The text is now addressed, in the second person masculine singular, to the implied reader, who is then provided with another conditional: and *if* by "thorough inquiry" he finds the charge to be "true" (MT: אמת; LXX: ἀληθῶς), then the accused is to be brought out

---

35. Richard D. Nelson, *Deuteronomy* (Louisville: Westminster John Knox, 2001), 213–14.

36. There is also some debate about whether 17:1 fits with the following text, or with what precedes it. Peter M. Craigie includes v. 1 (*The Book of Deuteronomy*, NICOT [Grand Rapids: Eerdmans, 1976], 248–51). Duane L. Christensen, *Deuteronomy 1:1–21:9*, 2nd ed., WBC 6A (Nashville: Nelson, 2001), 367, takes v. 2 as the beginning, linking it with Deut 21:1–9; 22:22; 24:7.

37. See Num 14:41; Deut 26:13; Josh 7:11, 15; 23:16; Judg 2:20; 1 Sam 15:24; 2 Kgs 8:12; 2 Chr 24:20; Jer 34:18; Isa 24:5; Hos 6:7; 8:1. See BDB s.v. עבר.

to the gates of the city and stoned to death. The reference to idolatrous practices as "abominations" in 17:4b (cf. Exod 8:26; Deut 7:25, 26; 32:16; 2 Kgs 23:13; Isa 44:19) further underscores the focus on the capital crime of idolatry as equivalent to transgressing the entire covenant (cf. v. 2).

But the accused cannot be executed without the hearing of "two or three witnesses" (MT: עַל פִּי שְׁנַיִם עֵדִים אוֹ שְׁלֹשָׁה עֵדִים; LXX: ἐπὶ δυσὶν μάρτυσιν ἢ ἐπὶ τρισὶν μάρτυσιν) that, satisfactorily and beyond dispute, would convict him or her of the reported crime (17:6a). The text formulates the stipulation in the positive case; in 17:6b, it is repeated in its corresponding negative formulation (MT: לֹא יוּמַת עַל־פִּי עֵד אֶחָד; LXX: οὐκ ἀποθανεῖται ἐφ' ἑνὶ μάρτυρι). This repetition reinforces the seriousness of executing a woman or man who may have been innocent. The "hand of the witnesses is to be the first raised against the person," if it is decided that the idolater is to be stoned (17:7a), followed by the "hand of all the people" (17:7b).

Deuteronomy 17:8–13 then moves on to the subject of ambiguous incidents. Whether cases of "homicide, civil law, or assault" are in dispute, the court is to repair to the central sanctuary where legal resolution of the case can occur. The cases in question do not merely concern idolatry, but appear broader, with capital and petty crimes included as examples. Once again, the second person singular pronominal forms are used (וְדָרַשְׁתָּ; or second person singular verb forms in Greek, ἐλεύσῃ, 17:9) to address the man in charge—he is to "go up" to the "place the Lord your God will choose" (17:8), where he will consult the "judge" and the priests (17:9a), and they will render the verdict (17:9b), quite possible in the temple locale in Jerusalem.[38] As in 17:5–6, where the consequent imperative was stated (death by stoning after a trial with witnesses), so in 17:10–13, the impera-

---

38. According to Deuteronomy's focus on centralization and on the temple, this central court was associated with the "shrine" of the temple; Julius Wellhausen, *Prolegomena zur Geschichte Israels*, 6th ed. (Berlin: Neudruck, 1927), 154–56; cf. Alexander Rofé, *Deuteronomy: Issues and Interpretation*, OTS (London: T&T Clark, 2002), 128–29. Although some scholars read it as a reference to a secular, central court of law, established solely for ambiguous juridical cases that would be too complex for local courts; see Jacob Milgrom, *Numbers* (Philadelphia: Jewish Publication Society of America, 1990), 506; Bernard M. Levinson, *Deuteronomy and the Hermeneutics of Legal Innovation* (Oxford: Oxford University Press, 1997), 128. Still others argue that a central court was possibly located at or near the central shrine in Jerusalem, but not identical to it. See Craigie, *Deuteronomy*, 251; Christensen, *Deuteronomy*, 373–74; Pamela Barmash, *Homicide in the Biblical World* (Cambridge: Cambridge University

tive is to carry out precisely the sentence mandated by the priests and the judge. If the verdict of the tribunal is not enacted (v. 11), then the person who obstructed the carrying out of the verdict is to be put to death (v. 12). Both subsections conclude with the refrain, "thus you shall sweep out the evil from your midst" (17:7c ["from Israel," v. 12]; cf. Deut 13:5; 19:29; 21:21; 24:7). The punishment of the "presumptuous man" functions as a deterrent for others who may be inclined to ignore the final verdict of the central tribunal (v. 13). In sum, Deut 17:8–13 mandates that ambiguous cases require a unique form of judgment to ascertain the truth of an allegation, and that this is to be carried out in, or near, the temple.[39]

3.2. Deuteronomy 19:15

Deuteronomy 19:15 is set within the context of 19:1–21, which deals with the establishment of the cities of refuge as well as the case of the proven perjurer. Like Deut 17:2–13, this unit can be divided into two neat subsections, with the text on multiple witnesses fitting roughly in between these two sections. Deuteronomy 19:1–13 concerns the creation of six cities of refuge to which the homicide might flee, and distinguishes between cases of manslaughter and murder, while Deut 19:16–21 concerns the procedure for trying a proven perjurer.[40] The text of Deut 19:15 reads, "a single witness shall not suffice to convict a person of any crime or wrongdoing in connection with any offense that may be committed. Only on the evidence of two or three witnesses shall a charge be sustained" (NRSV). Multiple witnesses are required for *any* case, not only capital offenses, and a *single* witness against an accused is not satisfactory to convict the

---

Press, 2005), 32; and Nelson, *Deuteronomy*, 242, who links the centralized court with YHWH's shrine.

39. How the discernment of the divine "witness" (or "judgment") is to take place is a moot point in the literature. Nelson, *Deuteronomy*, 215, considers the priests to have consulted oracles and lots. Christensen, *Deuteronomy*, 376, is against the theory that the Levites consulted lots or oracles (as in, for instance, Exod 22:7–10; 28:29–30; cf. 1 Sam 14:38–42; Num 5:11–31). Jeffrey H. Tigay, *Deuteronomy* (Philadelphia: Jewish Publication Society of America, 1996), 164, thinks likewise, suggesting that methods of reasoning were used instead of sacral means. Barmash, *Homicide*, 36, notes that the means is simply not known.

40. Also wedged between the two sections is a law against removing the ancient boundary marker in 19:14—a verse that has generated a lot of scholarship, but which will not be relevant to this analysis.

accused. That is, it is not mandated that "two witnesses" must appear, but that "two or three" witnesses are necessary for judicial evidence to be properly weighed—in other words, more than one witness must speak.

The case of the manslayer is developed in Deut 19:4–7. He is one who "might flee and live" (19:4): he might flee to the designated cities of refuge, but, upon trial, if it is determined that he killed his victim unintentionally, he will not be executed. The main criterion for determining manslaughter is the lack of premeditation. The manslayer has killed his neighbor "without intent" and without "first hating him" (19:4b; cf. v. 6b). This is reinforced by the second, contrasting case of the murderer, described in 19:11a. The latter is the man who "hates his neighbor, waits in ambush for him, and rises up against him to take his life, so that he dies" (MT: שנא לרעהו וארב לו וקם עליו והכהו נפש ומת; LXX: μισῶν τὸν πλησίον καὶ ἐνδρεύσῃ αὐτὸν καὶ ἐπαναστῇ ἐπ' αὐτὸν καὶ πατάξῃ αὐτοῦ ψυχήν; see Gen 4:8). The reference to the murderer "waiting in ambush" for his victim indicates his prior intent to kill, and the murderer's hatred for his victim is expressly given as the grounds for his premeditation. The murderer may flee to a city of refuge, but he will be taken from the city, tried, and executed by the "avenger of blood" (19:12).[41]

The cities of refuge appear to have been established with the potential rage of the "avenger of blood" in mind. In 19:5 we see that the manslayer can flee to one of the cities of refuge and "live." However, his life may be imperiled by the "great distance," since the "avenger of blood" in his "hot anger" might "overtake" the fleeing manslayer and kill him (19:6). "Therefore," the Israelites are commanded to set apart three cities (cf. 19:1–3)—and then three additional ones west of the Jordan, when their land is enlarged (19:7–9). The cities of refuge will prevent the shedding of "innocent blood" (MT: דם נקי; LXX: αἷμα ἀναίτιον) in the land of their inheritance (19:10). These verses are usually taken to mean that the "distance" to a central sanctuary would be "too great" (19:6) for a manslayer

---

41. The Hebrew reads גאל הדם ("redeemer of blood"), while the LXX has τῷ ἀγχιστεύοντι τοῦ αἵματος ("nearest blood relative"). While NETS and other LXX translations take this as "avenger," LSJ notes the LXX of Isa 11:11; Ruth 3:13; 4:4; Num 36:8; 2 Esd 2:62; Neh 7:64, supporting a definition of simple kinship (LSJ s.v. ἀγχιστεύω). The גאל הדם in the Hebrew Bible was responsible for a relative of the victim who avenges the killing (see Barmash, *Homicide*, 32). The term גאל could also refer to a relative who "redeemed" a relative from debt or slavery, or who "redeemed" the family line through marriage (see Lev 25:23, 47; Ruth 3:13).

to reach by foot, and that the cities were established so as to avoid the possibility of the "avenger of blood" catching and killing the fleer en route. Thus, the cities were to be set up "in the midst" (MT: בתוך ארצך; LXX: ἐν μέσῳ τῆς γῆς σου/ἐν τῇ γῇ σου, 19:2, 10) of the land, not established according to the traditional tribal boundaries.

Shifting from cases of capital offense to "any crime or wrongdoing … whatsoever," the text moves on to the importance of having multiple witnesses testify to an offense (19:15). While the original context of this requirement might have been for cases of homicide, where witnesses were needed to make the sometimes-fine distinction between intentional murder and unintentional manslaughter, the requirement is here expanded to fit both capital offenses and lesser criminal cases. Another element is then added in Deut 19:16 that was not present in Deut 17:6—the case of the "false witness," or perjurer. If it is proven that a man has testified *falsely* against an accused, then his punishment will be equivalent to that which he sought to bring upon the person against whom he falsely testified (19:19a). In line with this, Deut 19:16–21 concludes with the *lex talionis*: "life for life, eye for eye, tooth for tooth, hand for hand, foot for foot" (19:21).

The crime of perjury described in Deut 19:16 (MT: עד־חמס, "violent witness"; LXX: μάρτυς ἄδικος, "unjust witness") could be understood as an expansion on the ninth commandment (see Deut 5:20).[42] What is often overlooked in the scholarship on Deut 19:16 is that the hypothetical false witness arises to testify against someone accused of סרה (MT; LXX: ἀσέβειαν). While the Hebrew noun is often translated as "wrongdoing" (see NRSV), in accordance with the general picture given in 19:15, it is possible to translate סרה with a more specific referent, namely, the crime of "apostasy," defection to the worship of false gods.[43] Worthy of note is MT Deut 13:6, where דבר־סרה is used to mean "enticing" another person away from

---

42. Nelson, *Deuteronomy*, 238.

43. The term סרה is translated in the LXX by ἀσέβεια, which means "ungodliness," "impiety" (cf. Deut 9:4, 5; 18:22), "iniquity," "wrongdoing," or "injustice" (19:16); see J. Lust, E. Eynikel, and K. Hauspie, eds., *Greek-English Lexicon of the Septuagint* (New York: American Bible Society, 2004), s.v. ἀσέβεια. The verb ἀσεβέω primarily connotes acting impiously or profanely (Lev 20:12; Deut 17:13; 18:20; 25:2), and can be used to translate the Hebrew זיד, translated in English as "acting presumptuously." BDB defines סרה as "apostasy," "defection," or a "turning aside" (Deut 13:6; Isa 1:5; 31:6; Jer 28:16; 29:32). But it can also be "used apparently of any moral or legal offense" (see Deut 19:16; Isa 59:13). See BDB s.v. סרה.

worship of YHWH—that is, to commit apostasy through enticement; this crime involves not only apostasy in the first instance, but also abetting others to worship gods. The LXX translates the Hebrew using πλανάω (to "deceive," "lead astray"). This functions as an important intertext for John 7–8, as will be shown below. The hypothetical false witness of Deut 19:16 not only directly abrogates the ninth commandment against perjury but also violates the commandment against murder, by maliciously accusing someone of apostasy, and thereby working toward the execution of that person. The "false witness" is guilty of shedding innocent blood by design (see Deut 19:8–10), because the punishment for apostasy is death (see Lev 24:14; Deut 13:5). This time it is not the גאל הדם but the implied reader ("then *you* shall do") who is responsible for executing the convicted perjurer (19:19). In this way it is demonstrated that the crime of framing someone for apostasy is taken just as seriously as the crime of apostasy itself, and requires the same punishment.

In sum, to quote Laurence Welborn's grasp of the purpose of the text in Deut 19:15, "The requirement of multiple witnesses—three, or at least two—was meant *to protect the accused* from a single malicious witness intent on doing harm."[44] The purpose was not *only*, therefore, to engage multiple witnesses as a means of verifying the truth of the defense (as seems to be the immediate sense in John 8). Welborn finds this theme of protection pronounced in all the citations of Deut 19:15 in the literature of the Second Temple period, which he thinks includes John 8:17 (see CD 9:16–23; Mark 14:55–59; ; 1 Tim 5:19; Heb 10:28; and his text of concern, 2 Cor 13:1). I would add that Deut 19:15–16 is particularly alert to false accusations of apostasy and to the implication that the crime of falsely "crying apostasy" is as heinous as the act of apostasy itself. This nuance is to be detected in the wider context of John 8:17 in a way not immediately obvious in the other citations of Deut 19:15 listed above. But at the same time, as we will see, John's presentation of Jesus's reference to "two witnesses" in 8:17 does not exactly obey, and sometimes subverts, the logic of the motif in Deut 19:15 and the other scriptural texts.

---

44. Laurence L. Welborn, "By the Mouth of Two or Three Witnesses: Paul's Invocation of a Deuteronomic Statute," *NovT* 52 (2010): 207–20, esp. 210 (his emphasis, added for the purpose of highlighting how scholars reading 2 Corinthians against the grain of Deut 19:15's original context miss the central point of the passage and make Paul apply the text "against the accused").

3.3. Numbers 35:30

The final scriptural text mentioning the rule of multiple witnesses is Num 35:30.[45] Like Deut 19:1–13, the text of Numbers concerns the legislation surrounding murder, manslaughter, and the function of the cities of refuge.[46] Nevertheless, there are a number of significant literary differences between Num 35:30 and Deut 17:6; 19:15. Whereas in the Deuteronomic sources the requirement of multiple witnesses occurs in the center of the texts' respective structures, in Num 35 it occurs almost as an addendum to the longer discussion on Levitical towns (Num 35:1–5), the cities of refuge (35:6–15), and the distinctions between intentional murder (35:16–21) and unintentional manslaughter (35:22–28).[47] Only afterward—and almost as an afterthought—is the requirement of multiple witnesses legislated (35:30). Following on from this is a prohibition against accepting ransom for murder (35:31) and against "polluting" the land with "bloodguilt" (35:33–34). In Deut 17:6 and 19:15, the requirement of multiple witnesses was framed positively ("two witnesses are required") and reiterated negatively ("not on the basis of a single witness"). This is also the case in Num 35:30, but in this latter text it is limited to the capital offense of murder. All murderers (MT: כל־מכה־נפש; LXX: πατάξας ψυχήν) are not to be executed on the basis of a single witness but must have "the evidence of witnesses" to sustain the sentence.[48] Moreover, Num 35:30 adds: "the murderer shall be put to death," thus assuming that the killer in question is also a murderer, and not an accidental homicide.[49] The specific crimes of idolatry (see Deut 12:29–32; 17:2–7) and apostasy (cf. Deut 13:1–11) are absent from Num 35:1–34, and the reference to perjury (Deut 19:16) or

---

45. Canonically, this is not the last mention of the "two witnesses," but the first. Historically, it is possibly postexilic and therefore later than Deuteronomy. It is treated later here for that reason. One scholar asserting the probability of Num 35:30 as John's immediate source text is Johannes Beutler, *Studien zu den johanneischen Schriften*, SBAB 25 (Stuttgart: Katholisches Bibelwerk, 1998), 295–315.

46. The technical term "cities of refuge" is characteristic only of Numbers, not Deuteronomy. It is also found later in Josh 20:2 and 1 Chr 6:42, 52. See Philip Budd, *Numbers*, WBC 4 (Nashville: Nelson, 1984), 381.

47. It could have been appended from another legal code; see Baruch A. Levine, *Numbers 21–36*, AB 4 (New York: Doubleday, 2000), 558–59.

48. The text of Numbers is also different in that it only uses the plural "witnesses," implying multiple witnesses rather than directly stating "two" or "two or three."

49. Ibid., 565.

the temple as a central court of tribunal is also not attested. Numbers 35:30 is only concerned with the offense of intended homicide and the function of the cities of refuge in relation to the unintended homicide.

Numbers 35 differentiates between murder and manslaughter. In Num 35:16–21, intentional homicide is defined by the use of the specific verb "to strike" (MT: נכה; LXX: πατάσσω). If a person "strikes" another "so that he dies" with any object ("iron," 35:16; "hand-stone" [MT: באבן יד; LXX: λίθῳ ἐκ χειρός], 35:17; or "weapon of wood," 35:18), it is classified as intentional murder. The image is of one who takes a heavy object for use as a weapon and repeatedly strikes another person, "so that he dies." When the "avenger of blood" "meets" with the murderer, he is responsible for executing the murderer (35:19). Intentional murder is further defined by the emotions the killer harbors toward his victim, which signify that he acted with premeditation. If he "pushes" another from "hatred," or hurls an object at another, or "lies in ambush" for another, "so that he dies," then the killer is a murderer and should be put to death by the avenger of blood (35:21). Unintentional killing is defined largely by lack of motive, and by the lack of the verb "to strike." The same verb "to push" (cf. 35:20a) is used in 35:22a to describe the act of pushing someone suddenly, but "without hatred"—and this is classified as manslaughter. Likewise, if a person "hurls" an object without "lying in ambush," the death that accidentally results is not considered intentional homicide (35:22a). One might "handle" a stone object and "drop" it on another "so that he dies," but the parties may not have "hated each other" and no harm was meant—therefore it is accidental and constitutes manslaughter (35:23–24). The trial following an act of homicide is to be staged by the "congregation" (MT: העדה; LXX: συναγωγή; see Num 35:12, 24, 25). The "avenger of blood" is the executioner of those found guilty of intentional homicide (35:19b, 21b). In cases of possible manslaughter, the congregation is to "judge between" the slayer and the "avenger of blood" (35:24). The witnesses must make a judgment on the basis of the killer's intentions, since no forensic evidence is mentioned as important to the trial.[50] If the "avenger of blood" tries to enact vengeance despite a finding of manslaughter, the congregation is responsible for "rescuing" the manslayer from the "avenger of blood" by placing him in the city of refuge (35:25). If innocent of premeditated murder, the accused is returned to the city

---

50. Barmash, *Homicide*, 123–24. Cf. Deut 21:1–9.

of refuge (35:25a), where he is to live until the death of the high priest (35:25b). Possibly as a punitive measure as much as a protective one, the manslayer is to stay in the designated city of refuge—if he ventures outside the boundaries of the city, he is liable to be killed by the "avenger of blood" with impunity (35:27).[51] The shedding of blood—whether intentional or accidental—pollutes the land, and must be compensated for by human death.[52] In lieu of the execution of the manslayer is the natural death of the high priest, as "expiation" for the bloodguilt incurred by all manslayers resident in the cities of refuge.[53]

The sacredness of the land is an evident motif in Num 35. When bloodguilt is expiated, the land itself is also "expiated" (35:33). The land and its inhabitants are intricately intertwined; shed blood flowing into the earth "pollutes" the land and jeopardizes the well-being of its inhabitants, threatening their exile from the land.[54] Polluted land, therefore, must be expiated by shedding the blood of the killer—either actually through the role of the "avenger of blood" or symbolically through the death of the high priest. Compared to Deut 17:2-13 and 19:1-21, Num 35 makes more prominent the role of the "avenger of blood" as the instrument of God's decree. Numbers 35 also makes comparatively more of the consequences for unatoned bloodshed in the land. The blood of the victim murdered intentionally was said to "cry out" for vengeance (cf. Gen 4:10), and "bloodguilt" would then attach to the slayer and his family, literally "dancing around their heads" (2 Sam 3:28-29) for generations (2 Sam 21:4-6; 2 Kgs 9:26).[55] God, as the first and ultimate "kinsman" of humanity (who are made in God's image; cf. Gen 1:27; 9:6), requires that murder be requited; drawing as it does on these theological traditions, Num 35 presents God as humanity's "avenger of blood" and agent of justice.[56]

---

51. See Milgrom, *Numbers*, 510.

52. Budd, *Numbers*, 384; Martin Noth, *Numbers*, trans. James D. Martin, OTL (London: SCM, 1968), 656.

53. Timothy R. Ashley, *The Book of Numbers*, NICOT (Grand Rapids: Eerdmans, 1993), 225.

54. See Levine, *Numbers*, 560.

55. Ibid., 509.

56. Ibid., 510.

4. Reading John 8:17 in Light of the Scriptural Texts

The rule of multiple witnesses occurs in a limited number of highly specific scriptural contexts dealing with offenses such as murder, idolatry, apostasy, and perjury. Citations of the rule in various New Testament and Dead Sea Scroll texts indicates that authors respected this contextual meaning, and did not fabricate a "prooftexted" secondary meaning for the rule. We can assume that, for John's first readers, a complex network of metaleptic resonances drawn from the scriptural texts—and from these serious themes—would have been activated.[57] This is precisely what makes John 8:17 and its surrounding context so intriguing, since Jesus's appropriation of the legal stipulation occurs not in the midst of his criminal "trial," but in the context of Jesus's "trial" regarding his learning (7:16–18), his "origins" and destiny (8:21–23; 56–58), and his identity (7:25–31). With the citation of the rule of multiple witnesses in 8:17, Jesus's "christological trial" is configured within the semantic bounds of Deut 17:6; 19:15; and Num 35:30. The themes of apostasy, idolatry, and false witness found in these texts are evoked in John 8:17, resonating throughout the unit of John 7:1–8:59 as a whole.

The first metaleptic resonance between John 7–8 and the scriptural texts concerns the locale of Jesus's trial/debate with the Pharisees. Recall that Deut 17:8–13 stipulated that, for ambiguous cases of any kind, the central tribunal, probably a court located in or around the temple precincts in Jerusalem, must take charge of the matter. In John's Gospel, Jesus's public teaching is frequently taking place in the temple or in the temple precincts.[58] In John 7–8, Jesus is present in the temple for the feast of Sukkoth (7:2), and he delivers his teaching there (cf. 8:20). The presence of the "chief priests and Pharisees," and their dialogue with the "guards" (7:45) over Jesus's planned arrest (7:45–49), adds to the tense atmosphere surrounding Jesus's trial in these chapters. The divisions and debates among the various groups listening to Jesus, and their conflicting assessments of

---

57. Even if we could say for sure that Deut 19:15 represented the most likely form for John's citation in 8:17, the fact that *each* instance of the rule concerns criminal law means that later citations of the rule itself carried with them a broad network of nuances relating to these themes that would have been identifiable. Hence arguing for one of the three texts over another as the most likely of John's sources is not germane to this essay.

58. See Judith Lieu, "Temple and Synagogue in John," *NTS* 45 (1999): 51–69.

his claims (cf. 7:40–44), contribute to the presentation of Jesus's trial as colored by ambiguity. It is necessary that Jesus be present in the temple for his ambiguous case to be resolved. Jesus is not portrayed ambiguously; rather, his *claims* are ambiguously received and his audiences demand that they require fuller explication. The reason that Jesus's claims touch a nerve—and require additional testimony (cf. 8:13)—is that they come close to absolute statements identifying Jesus with God, thus approaching idolatry in the minds of his interlocutors (8:12, 24, 28, 58).[59] The crime of idolatry looms large in the context of Deut 17:16 (cf. 17:1–3), and is a relevant intertext for John 7–8. In early rabbinic Judaism, idolatry was closely connected to blasphemy—a connection that is discernible in John's narrative (see 5:16–18; cf. 7:19–24).[60] To declare oneself "God" (5:18; cf. 10:33) or "Son of God," and so to invite self-worship, was thought to be an example of blasphemy touching on the idolatrous (cf. b. Sanh. 61a–b; cf. y. Ta'an. 2:1/24, fol. 65b). This may be paralleled in the view of Jesus as one who "leads the people astray" (πλανάω, 7:12, 47)—a word referring to the incitement to idolatry in the LXX, as we have seen, and which translates the Hebrew סרה.[61] In the view of "the Jews"/"the Pharisees" in John 7–8, Jesus could therefore be seen as one who *entices* others to idolatry, effectively inviting their worship.[62] In doing so, Jesus leads the people away from the law of Moses (cf. 9:28) and from the divine commandment against idolatry. Against the backdrop of Deut 17:6, Jesus's presence in the temple in John 7–8 is a sign of the ambiguity of the legal case in which he is embroiled, on trial for blasphemy and (incitement to) idolatry—what could be termed, against the scriptural context, apostasy.

---

59. See Chris Keith, *The* Pericopae Adultera: *The Gospel of John and the Literacy of Jesus*, NTTSD 38 (Leiden: Brill, 2009), 175–201.

60. See Peter Schafer, *Jesus in the Talmud* (Princeton: Princeton University Press, 2007), 106.

61. This view of Jesus apparently circulated in the context of Jewish-Christian disputes. The same Greek word is found in Justin Martyr's *Dialogue with Trypho* (pars. 69, 108). For a discussion, see Barrett, *John*, 313.

62. Cf. Deut 13:6, 19:15. In b. Sanh. 43a Jesus is seen as an enticer, as one who was justly executed for inciting self-worship (which equates to the idolatry of *others*). For a theory on the early dating of this basic text (also found in m. San. 6.7), see David Instone-Brewer, "Jesus of Nazareth's Trial in the Uncensored Talmud," *TynBul* 62 (2011): 269–94. In the Mishnah we see a distinction between private apostasy and the public enticement of others to idolatry, which parallels the order of offenses in Deut 13—a text with much affinity to Deut 17:2–13.

Deuteronomy 19:1–21 adds another two details to this texture. The first is the context of murder, manslaughter, and the laws of asylum in which the requirement for multiple witnesses is embedded. In an ironic reversal, Jesus comes across not as the accused in John 7–8, but as the judge—more precisely, as the one who hands down the verdict: eventual death in sin (7:34; 8:21). "The Jews"/the Pharisees—not Jesus—stand trial for murder, or at least for unjustly desiring the murder of an innocent man (cf. 8:43–44), a portrayal in keeping with the Gospel's overwhelmingly negative characterization of Jewish authority figures.[63] It is at this point that the criterion for murder (rather than manslaughter) stated in Deut 19 becomes relevant. Murder is defined by motive and by action: by harboring hatred for another, by waiting in ambush for the victim, and by "rising up" to kill the victim. In John, Jesus's enemies are depicted as seeking to kill him (7:1) in the temple, where they lie in wait for him, on the lookout to take hold of an opportunity to arrest him (7:30, 32, 44); at the conclusion of John 8, they take matters into their own hands, attempting to stone him to death (8:59). The presentation could not be more subversive: Jesus and, with him, the implied reader of the Gospel are the multiple witnesses of the murderous behavior of Jesus's adversaries in the narrative.

Second, as argued above, in Deut 19:15–21, *falsely* testifying against another to accuse him of apostasy is considered to be as serious as apostasy itself. The idea of false versus true testimony pervades John 7–8. In John 8:13 Jesus is accused of testifying falsely against himself and, indirectly, against God. Of course, this does not quite fit the context of Deut 19:15–21: Jesus is not trying to "frame" himself, so that if he is found guilty of trying to have himself killed through self-perjury, he will himself be killed. When reading John 8:17 in light of Deut 19:15–21, we are able to perceive another characteristically Johannine irony: Jesus's self-testimony is presented to the reader as true and valid because of Jesus's heavenly origins, but the testimony of the Pharisees *against Jesus* as a blasphemer, deceiver, and inciter to idolatry are thereby also presented as patently false to the implied reader. The Pharisees thus appear as the actual "false witnesses," accusing Jesus of crimes of which he is not guilty, and effectively rendering themselves guilty of perjury. Subtle allusions to the status of Jesus as the "false prophet" of Deut 18:20–24 could also be reworked in

---

63. The literature on Johannine anti-Judaism is vast. An overview of the topic can be found in my *Retelling Scripture: "The Jews" and the Scriptural Citations in John 1:19–12:15*, BIS 110 (Leiden: Brill, 2012), 37–46.

John 7–8, with Jesus's eventual death at the hands of "the Jews" in John 18–19 an apparent confirmation of his "false" prophecy (cf. Deut 18:20).[64]

The text of Num 35:30 adds a third metaleptic layer. If the subversive logic of John's portrayal of Jesus's "trial" in chapters 7–8 is read against the backdrop of Num 35:30, then the attempts of "the Jews" to execute Jesus in 8:59 (who is, according to the Gospel, innocent) would draw "bloodguilt" upon them. The criterion for willful homicide in Num 35 is close to Deut 19, but it differs from the latter in that it frequently uses the verb "to strike" to refer to murderous acts, and in that it specifies the instruments of killing. One of the instruments listed is a "hand-stone" (LXX: λίθῳ ἐκ χειρός; John 8:59: λίθους). While "the Jews" do not actually end up killing Jesus (they manipulate Pilate to authorize a Roman execution), they do attempt to stone Jesus twice (8:59, with violence, as the verb βάλλω suggests; 10:31–39). On each occasion Jesus eludes them. The effect of reading Num 35:30 and Deut 19:12 as intertexts is that they subvert the order of allegations raised. It is not Jesus who must be tried, but "the Jews," for they are depicted as murderous without due cause, passing judgment on a "man from God" (8:42), who himself "judges no one" (8:15).

Yet if Jesus's enemies acquire "bloodguilt" in the process, who would function as Jesus's "avenger of blood" according to the text of Num 35? Biblical law mandates that the nearest kin (husband, brother, uncle) perform this duty. Jesus's kin are mentioned infrequently in the Gospel (2:1; 7:3–8), but his male kin seem too detached from him and too mistrustful of his purposes to act in Jesus's interest in this regard. Jesus stands in a unique, filial relationship with God, his "Father" (1:1–2, 17–18); the metaleptic implication is that God acts not only as Jesus's second witness but also as his "avenger of blood." The Gospel does not openly present God as the "avenger of blood" for Jesus, avenging the execution of Jesus upon "the Jews," but many other early Christian texts did not hesitate in postulating that the punishment meted out to "the Jews" as a people was merited by their deicidal killing of Jesus.[65] The more explicit early Christian tradi-

---

64. See Paul Anderson, "The Having-Sent-Me Father: Aspects of Agency, Encounter, and Irony in the Johannine Father-Son Relationship," *Semeia* 85 (1999): 33–57.

65. See, possibly, 1 Thess 2:14–15; Matt 27:25b (the crowd of Jews accepts the "bloodguilt" for Jesus's death; compare Judas's fear over having, through perjury, betrayed "innocent blood" in Matt 27:4). In the late antique Christian writings, John Chrysostom is the most thoroughgoing in sentencing "the Jews" collectively to divine punishment for having killed Jesus. Chrysostom's idea is that "the Jews" (as a people)

tion of the apparent punishment of "the Jews" for deicide may be implicitly present in the subtext of John 7–8. Indeed, the dative singular used in the emphatic position in 8:21 (ἐν τῇ ἁμαρτίᾳ ὑμῶν ἀποθανεῖσθε) is found as an unemphasized plural in 8:24 (ἀποθανεῖσθε ἐν ταῖς ἁμαρτίαις ὑμῶν). C. K. Barrett claims that this may allude to "the fate of unbelieving Judaism in the disaster of A.D. 66–70."[66] Leon Morris refers approvingly to the accusation against "the Jews": "If there is any significance in the singular ἁμαρτίᾳ, it will be to concentrate attention on the sin of all sins, that of rejecting Jesus, of failing to believe in him."[67]

The ironic subversion present in the narrative of Jesus's trial in John 7–8, with judgment eventually falling on Jesus's accusers, is thus also at play in the scriptural allusion to the testimony of multiple witnesses in 8:17, and the potentially anti-Jewish interpretations that the contextual implications spawn should not be ignored. This reading has suggested that the "charges" for which Jesus stands accused in his trial relate to apostasy, blasphemy, and/or idolatry. The view that Jesus is a "deceiver" (πλανᾷ τὸν ὄχλον, John 7:12) resonates with the texts of Deut 13; 17:2–7; 29:18, 25–28, that speak of the apostate and enticer; while the warning of Jesus in 8:21 (cf. 7:34) that the Jews will "die in their sins" reconfigures the vengeance motif of Deuteronomy and Numbers, with the "Father" of Jesus acting as "avenger of blood." The accusation of "false witness," which are brought against Jesus (8:16–18) by the fact that he has no second witness to verify his testimony, is ironically subverted with reference to the law against perjury in Deut 19:16: it is, rather, Jesus's opponents who judge him falsely. Together, the three scriptural texts provide contextual cues for John 7:1–8:59, for the forensic tone of its dialogue, and the narrative of Jesus's "trial" projected within it.

"slew" Christ (see *Adv. Jud.* 1.4.5; 1.6.3; 1.7.2, 5; 2.3.8; 3.6.8; 4.3.6; 5.9.5; 6.2.6, 10; 6.5.4) or "crucified" him (1.2.1; 1.3.3–4; 1.5.1; 4.3.6; 5.1.7; 5.3.7; 6.1.7; 6.3.5; 6.4.7). As such they now suffer the "punishment" of degradation, "bondage," and exile (5.5.1, 8; 5.4.3; 5.5.1; 5.8.5; 5.10.6–7; 6.1.1–2; 6.2.1; 6.2.8; 6.3.2 [2x]). See John Chrysostom, *Discourses against the Judaizing Christians*, trans. Paul W. Harkins, FC 68 (Washington, DC: Catholic University of America Press, 1979).

66. Barrett, *John*, 341. He thinks that this is not "the primary thought" of the passage, but according to the argument of this article, it could certainly be the secondary, intertextual meaning of the passage.

67. Leon Morris, *The Gospel according to John*, rev. ed., NICNT (Grand Rapids: Eerdmans, 1995), 395n33.

PART 3
MEMORY AND SCRIPTURE IN JOHN

Patriarchs and Prophets Remembered: Framing Israel's Past in the Gospel of John

Catrin H. Williams

Over the past few decades the study of "John and Scripture" has been approached from a variety of perspectives and with a wide range of methodological tools. The textual form and function of the explicit quotations in John's Gospel have, inevitably, received most attention to date, but a number of scholars are now venturing beyond the relative comfort zone of direct—and largely identifiable—quotations to explore the interpretative mechanisms at work within a narrative also saturated with a rich deposit of scriptural concepts and motifs. There is also a growing recognition that discussion of John's engagement with the Scriptures cannot be undertaken in isolation from the broader context of Jewish exegetical activity during the late Second Temple period. Situating John's Gospel within this context helps to sharpen awareness of its preference for some scriptural texts over others and of John's familiarity with exegetical techniques and insights that emerged several centuries after the original texts were composed.

Much progress has also been made since the introduction of "intertextuality" into the study of "the Old Testament in the New," not least because intertextual analysis challenges the interpreter to formulate a well-defined method in the study of the relationship between texts. This is a vital task when investigating John's Gospel, because it often proves difficult to isolate the exact source(s) of its scriptural references and to evaluate their precise function within a new Johannine context. However, two significant factors are often overlooked when intertextuality becomes the overarching framework for the study of John's "use" of Scripture. First, whereas intertextual studies focus largely on the *literary* relationship between *written* texts, it is increasingly being acknowledged that first-century texts like John's Gospel emerged from a media environment in which both orality and textuality were important factors in the composition and reception of texts and traditions. This is not to deny that John betrays close familiarity with scriptural texts that circulated in written form, but the likely impact of the performative context in which such texts were "heard," often in dialogue with, and filtered through, the oral-textual matrix of Jewish exegetical traditions, should also be taken into account. Second, with the rise of audience-oriented approaches to New Testament texts, the dialogical function of John's use of Scripture, particularly in relation to the Gospel's original readers/hearers, demands closer scrutiny. It calls in particular for an investigation of the communicative force of appeals to Israel's past within the Gospel narrative, particularly because these appeals may disclose important clues about strategies for shaping the collective identity of the audience.

This essay will examine the communicative dynamics of John's appeal to Scripture by focusing on its presentation of three well-known scriptural figures: Moses, Abraham, and Isaiah. These characters have been selected because of the significance afforded to them as individuals who bear witness to Jesus: Moses wrote about him (1:45; 5:46), Abraham rejoiced at seeing his day (8:56), and Isaiah saw his glory and spoke about him (12:41). These figures, all of whom feature exclusively in the first half of the narrative, are usually noted by scholars in discussions of the salvific significance of Israel's story within John's Gospel or, more commonly, the contribution of their depictions to the Gospel's distinctive Christology,[1] which invariably include such questions as: How does Jesus's gift of life relate to the gift of the law through Moses? Did Abraham and Isaiah see the preexistent or the earthly Jesus? These questions are certainly not unimportant for this essay, but its primary aim is to determine the intended effect of the explicit signaling of these prophetic and patriarchal figures on John's readers/hearers. Furthermore, while these figures are sometimes linked to direct quotations (1:23; 6:32; 12:38–40), they are also—more characteristically—referred to in isolation from identifiable verses or longer scriptural passages. In these cases it is, as noted by Tom Thatcher, more likely that John is drawing on the collective memory of these foundational characters and evoking wider commemorative frameworks associated with them. This is

---

1. "Christological witnesses" is a term often used with reference to the Johannine depiction of Moses, Abraham, and Isaiah. For a recent, but much broader, application of this designation, see Sanghee Michael Ahn, *The Christological Witness Function of the Old Testament Characters in the Gospel of John*, PBM (Milton Keynes: Paternoster, 2014).

not to deny that written texts were often the basis for such memories, "yet it is the memories themselves, not the texts on which they are based, that are 'cited' for the audience's consideration."[2]

For the purpose of investigating the function(s) of Moses, Abraham, and Isaiah within John's call to Israel's past, particularly the role played by them in the formation of collective memory and identity, the essay will draw on insights from a range of social memory theories. These are theories that are now beginning to make their mark on investigations into the reception of the Jewish Scriptures in the New Testament writings.[3] One of the distinctive contributions of "social memory" to the task at hand is that it offers a new theoretical framework for analyzing the interplay between past and present and of the communicative patterns reflected in a text like John's Gospel. Though bearing some resemblance to redaction-critical methods of studying the sociohistorical origins of texts,[4] social memory theories emphasize the role of "memory" in the formation and maintenance of group identity. Therefore, before examining how memories of Moses, Abraham, and Isaiah have been formed within the Johannine collective memory, it is necessary to outline the key features and interpretative potential of social memory theories.

1. Social Memory: Frameworks, Keying, and Framing

Building on the work of the French sociologist Maurice Halbwachs, contemporary social memory studies offer insights into the workings of memory by investigating how communities and individuals interpret the past in the light of present social realities.[5] Halbwachs himself argued that

---

2. Tom Thatcher, "Cain and Abel in Early Christian Memory: A Case Study in 'The Use of the Old Testament in the New,'" *CBQ* 72 (2010): 750; cf. Philip F. Esler, "Collective Memory and Hebrews 11: Outlining a New Investigative Framework," in *Memory, Tradition, and Text: Uses of the Past in Early Christianity*, ed. Alan Kirk and Tom Thatcher, SemeiaSt 52 (Atlanta: Society of Biblical Literature, 2005), 158–59.

3. Esler, "Collective Memory," 151–71; Rafael Rodríguez, *Structuring Early Christian Memory: Jesus in Tradition, Performance, and Text*, LNTS 407 (London: T&T Clark, 2010); Thatcher, "Cain and Abel," 732–51.

4. Holly E. Hearon, "The Construction of Social Memory in Biblical Interpretation," *Enc* 6 (2006): 348; Samuel Byrskog, "A New Quest for the *Sitz im Leben*: Social Memory, the Jesus Tradition, and the Gospel of Matthew," *NTS* 52 (2006): 319–21.

5. Maurice Halbwachs, *Les Cadres sociaux de la mémoire* (Paris: Alcan, 1925); Halbwachs, *La Topographie légendaire des évangiles en terre sainte: Étude de mémoire*

memory is socially constructed, in that groups and individuals remember the past through their reliance on "social frameworks." Social groups determine what is remembered and how it is remembered.[6] He defined "collective memory" as a fluid, variable, and selective phenomenon relating closely to the identity of a group; it entails the construction of a shared past that is continuous with the present and, at the same time, serves to unite the group.

Contemporary theorists readily acknowledge the significance of Halbwachs's focus on the ways in which a group's representation of the past is shaped by present concerns and experiences, but memory, it is argued, should not be categorized as "an entirely malleable construction in the present" or, alternatively, as "the authentic residue of the past." Rather, it involves a "fluid negotiation between the desires of the present and the legacies of the past."[7] It is a case of perpetual dialogue between the past and the present, "at times attributing greater force to the remembered past and at times to the remembering present."[8]

Of particular relevance is the strategy described by Barry Schwartz as commemorative "keying," one that involves the mapping of present events and figures onto those belonging to the past.[9] Current experiences or situations are paired with archetypal images or symbolically significant patterns from the past, so that, for example, in the case of several New Testament texts, "figures of memory" (*Erinnerungsfiguren*) integral to the mnemonic framework of ancient Judaism are used to explain, even shape, the present.[10] Keying allows the past to act as a "frame" for the present,

---

collective (Paris: Presses Universitaires de France, 1941); Halbwachs, *La Mémoire collective* (Paris: Éditions Albin Michel, 1997).

6. Maurice Halbwachs, *On Collective Memory*, ed. and trans. Lewis A. Coser (Chicago: University of Chicago Press, 1992), 38.

7. Jeffrey K. Olick, "Products, Processes, and Practices: A Non-Reificatory Approach to Collective Memory," *BTB* 36 (2006): 13; cf. Jeffrey K. Olick and Joyce Robbins, "Social Memory Studies: From 'Collective Memory' to the Historical Sociology of Mnemonic Practices," *ARS* 24 (1988): 128–30.

8. Werner H. Kelber "The Works of Memory: Christian Origins as Mnemohistory—A Response," in Kirk and Thatcher, *Memory, Tradition, and Text*, 234.

9. Barry Schwartz, *Abraham Lincoln and the Forge of National Memory* (Chicago: University of Chicago Press, 2000), 18–20; cf. Schwartz, "Frame Image: Towards a Semiotics of Collective Memory," *Semiotica* 121 (1998): 1–4.

10. Jan Assmann, *Das kulturelle Gedächtnis. Schrift, Erinnerung und politische Identität in frühen Hochkulturen* (Munich: Beck, 1992).

providing coherent models for interpreting present experiences. Furthermore, if present situations inevitably affect what is seen, and looked for, in the past, the memory of an already salient past functions as an important orienting symbol for the present, molding and framing collective values and goals.[11] Thus, commenting on the mirror- as well as lamp-like quality of memory, Schwartz notes:

> The past is matched to the present as a model *of* society and a model *for* society. As a model *of* society, collective memory reflects past events in terms of the needs, interests, fears, and aspirations of the present. As a model *for* society, collective memory performs two functions: it embodies a *template* that organizes and animates behavior and a *frame* within which people locate and find meaning for their present experience. Collective memory affects social reality by *reflecting, shaping*, and *framing* it.[12]

Another notable feature of "keying" and "framing" is that the past is frequently streamlined through a process of schematization: a cluster of harmonized elements are tied together to form "conventional plot structures and mnemonic patterns" within a newly constructed framework.[13] "One of the most remarkable features of human memory is our ability to mentally transform essentially unstructured series of events into seemingly coherent *historical narratives*."[14] Differences between mnemonic entities are minimized in this process in order to secure the highlighting of analogous features to the exclusion of all others.[15] Accordingly, in their capacity as archetypal figures, landmark individuals or events can provide a unified and coherent image of the past.

---

11. Barry Schwartz, "Memory as a Cultural System: Abraham Lincoln in World War II," *ASR* 61 (1996): 910; Schwartz, "Frame Image," 26–27.

12. Schwartz, *Abraham Lincoln*, 18.

13. Byrskog, "New Quest," 325.

14. Eviatar Zerubavel, *Time Maps: Collective Memory and the Social Shape of the Past* (Chicago: Chicago University Press, 2003), 13.

15. Cf. Tom Thatcher, "Cain the Jew the AntiChrist: Collective Memory and the Johannine Ethic of Loving and Hating," in *Rethinking the Ethics of John: "Implicit Ethics" in the Johannine Writings*, ed. Jan G. van der Watt and Ruben Zimmermann, Contexts and Norms of New Testament Ethics 3, WUNT 291 (Tübingen: Mohr Siebeck, 2012), 357–58.

Social memory of a common past is also a vital component in the definition and preservation of the collective identity of a group. "When we remember, we represent ourselves to ourselves and to those around us. To the extent that our 'nature'—that which we truly are—can be revealed in articulation, we are what we remember."[16] Groups are able to acquire and maintain a collective identity through shared memories of a (constructed) common past; this enables them to make sense of their common heritage, but also to reinforce those beliefs and values from which group cohesion is forged so that "present lines of conduct can be formulated and enacted."[17] Archetypal or foundational figures certainly belong to the past, but they are also made to embody the normative values that distinguish the group in the present. In the words of Schwartz, they serve as a model *for* society as well as a model *of* society.

This essay will now examine the techniques and strategies used in John's Gospel in its evocation of selected memories about Moses, Abraham, and Isaiah. If their depiction as pivotal witnesses to Jesus belongs to a distinctively Johannine schematization of Israel's past, what does the narrativization of that schema reveal about the normative and rhetorical function of Moses, Abraham, and Isaiah in John's commemorative narrative? Moreover, how is their memory reconfigured in the light of present realities (model *of* society), and to what extent do they function as orienting symbols or templates for Johannine beliefs and commitments in the present (model *for* society)? To address these questions, the central features of John's presentation of these three scriptural figures will now be considered.

2. Remembering Moses

Moses traditions have influenced John's Gospel in a variety of ways. Several veiled allusions to Moses can be detected in the narrative, many of which are widely regarded as part of an attempt to depict Jesus as the prophet like Moses (Deut 18:15–18).[18] Nevertheless, to examine the

---

16. James Fentress and Chris Wickham, *Social Memory*, NPP (Oxford: Blackwell, 1992), 7.

17. Schwartz, *Abraham Lincoln*, 18; cf. Alan Kirk, "Social and Cultural Memory," in Kirk and Thatcher, *Memory, Tradition, and Text*, 17–19.

18. See Wayne A. Meeks, *The Prophet-King: Moses Traditions and the Johannine Christology*, NovTSup 14 (Leiden: Brill, 1967), 301–8; John Lierman, "The Mosaic Pat-

mnemonic strategies and communicative techniques used in evoking Israel's past, it is essential to focus, above all else, on the seven distinct passages that make explicit reference to Moses (John 1:17; 1:45; 3:14; 5:45–47; 6:32; 7:19–23; 9:28–29).[19]

Moses makes his first, and arguably most ambivalent, appearance toward the end of the prologue: "The law was given through Moses; grace and truth came through Jesus Christ" (1:17). The exact force of the comparison is difficult to determine, but despite the lack of an adversative δέ between both clauses, an element of contrast is strongly suggested by the swift movement from Moses as the mediator of God's gift of the law (ἐδόθη) and, possibly, from the earlier evocation of its ability to supply grace (1:16), to the clear focus on Jesus as the embodiment (ἐγένετο) of grace and truth (1:17; cf. 1:14). This reevaluation amounts to a reconfiguration of an integral aspect of Jewish collective memory about Moses and about the giving of the law on Sinai as a unifying and orienting "primary event."[20] In its Johannine context, the Sinai theophany is measured against a new foundational event—the coming of the incarnate Logos—which is collectively recalled by its participants ("we" in 1:14, 16) through their recognition and confession of Jesus as the manifestation of God's glory, grace, and truth. The Johannine understanding of the law as God's gift (1:17) nevertheless remains undescribed in the prologue. Its function as a witness leading to the "truth" in Jesus is certainly explicated in the Gospel narrative (1:45; 5:39, 45–47; cf. 3:14), but as far as the prologue is concerned, the emphasis is not so much on what the law—and Moses as its mediator—can offer but rather on what cannot be achieved.

The introduction of Moses (1:17) after a series of tightly connected statements (1:14–16) is unexpected.[21] It is likely, however, that the persistence of his memory in relation to divine revelation and the gift of the law reflects a sociohistorical setting in which the continuing relevance of that

---

tern of John's Christology," in *Challenging Perspectives on the Gospel of John*, ed. John Lierman, WUNT 2/219 (Tübingen: Mohr Siebeck, 2006), 211–14.

19. The additional reference to Moses in the *pericope adulterae* (John 7:53–8:11) will not be considered in this essay.

20. Schwartz, "Memory as a Cultural System," 911.

21. The abruptness of the reference is one of the reasons why several commentators regard 1:17–18 as John's own commentary on what formed the original conclusion of an already existing hymnic passage (Rudolf Bultmann, *Das Evangelium des Johannes*, 18th ed., KEK 2 [Göttingen: Vandenhoeck & Ruprecht, 1964], 53n5; Jean Zumstein, *L'Évangile selon Saint Jean*, CNT 4A [Geneva: Labor et Fides, 2014], 1:51).

memory was being contested[22] but at the same time would not allow Moses to become a figure of oblivion.[23] The concrete signaling of Moses (1:17) picks up on allusions to the Sinai theophany that shape much of what is stated about the "glory" (cf. Exod 33:18, 22) and "grace and truth" (34:6) manifested by the incarnate Word (1:14–16).[24] But what is the function of these scriptural allusions in the prologue? No overt reference is made to an actual revelation of God's glory in Israel's past, no indication that the Sinai revelation *foreshadows* or is a type of that which came through the Word made flesh, and no hint that Jesus *fulfills* what was originally promised to Moses. The strategy of "keying" provides some valuable assistance in this regard. Keying does not necessarily work with a model of foreshadowing or fulfillment; it interprets present realities by *enacting* elements tied to landmark events and figures from the past. "Mnemonic keying does not operate on the principle of analogy, but rather on the principle of identification," and it can involve the collapsing of the temporal distance between two eras in order to "solidify the connection" between them.[25] The Sinai event becomes the archetypal-theophanic model for articulating the significance of the revelation of the incarnate Word, but the two "events" are assimilated in such a way that the focus is on the *fullness* of the grace and truth now embodied in Jesus, not on whether these divine qualities were already manifested in the distant past.[26]

---

22. See Stefan Schapdick, "Religious Authority Re-Evaluated: The Character of Moses in the Fourth Gospel," in *Moses in Biblical and Extra-Biblical Traditions*, ed. Axel Graupner and Michael Wolter, BZNW 372 (Berlin: de Gruyter, 2007), 188–89.

23. According to Warren Carter ("The Prologue and John's Gospel: Function, Symbol, and the Definitive Word," *JSNT* 39 [1990]: 35–38), the function of the prologue in relation to the sociohistorical context of the Gospel suggests that it addresses a situation of "competing claims regarding God's knowability and presence" (37).

24. See, e.g., Anthony Tyrrell Hanson, "John 1.14–18 and Exodus 34," in *The New Testament Interpretation of Scripture* (London: SPCK, 1980), 97–109; Craig A. Evans, *Word and Glory: On the Exegetical and Theological Background of John's Prologue*, JSNTSup 89 (Sheffield: Sheffield Academic, 1993), 79–82.

25. Thatcher, "Cain the Jew," 362; cf. Thatcher, "Cain and Abel," 750–51. The murmuring of "the Jews" (6:41, 43), which recalls the behavior of their ancestors in the wilderness (Exod 16:2), provides another striking example of keying through a process of enactment. See further Judith Lieu, "Narrative Analysis and Scripture in John," in *The Old Testament in the New Testament: Essays in Honour of J. L. North*, ed. Steve Moyise, JSNTSup 189 (Sheffield: Sheffield Academic, 2000), 148.

26. See Andrew T. Lincoln, *The Gospel according to St John*, BNTC (London: Continuum, 2005), 75, 107–8.

Mnemonic detachment from Moses continues in the last verse of the prologue, where he is again evoked, albeit implicitly, in the statement, "No one has ever seen God" (1:18). As in 1:17, the emphasis falls on the second part of the verse and its explication of the claim of the believing community (1:14): they have experienced the theophanic manifestation of Jesus as the embodiment of God's glory on earth. In this respect, the uncompromising and starkly phrased denial of any vision of God (other than in and through Jesus) in 1:18 (θεὸν οὐδεὶς ἑώρακεν πώποτε) amounts to what social memory approaches describe as a reconstructed fragment of memory that casts all possible exceptions into oblivion. Regardless of Moses's reputation as one who spoke with God "face to face" (Exod 33:11; Deut 34:10; cf. Num 12:8; Sir 45:3), or even *because* of later Jewish speculation that his ascent of Sinai was an ascent to heaven to receive a direct vision of God (e.g., 2 Bar. 4:1–7; 4 Ezra 14:3–6), such traditions are excluded from the Johannine collective memory in order to emphasize the veiled character of God's revelation in the past. Jesus is the exclusive revealer of God, and so the law cannot be the source of God's revelation nor can Moses serve as its mediator.

If the prologue discloses a minimal sense of attachment to Moses, and the role of the law is largely left undefined, some clarification is provided when Philip, in one of many scenes dominated by the importance of testimony to Jesus (1:19–51), announces to Nathanael, "We have found the one about whom Moses in the law and also the prophets wrote, Jesus, son of Joseph, from Nazareth" (1:45). This first example of John's positive reconfiguration of the law depicts Moses as a faithful witness to Jesus in his capacity as the writer of the scriptural books ascribed to him. The contours of Moses's reconstructed memory may be outlined in Philip's declaration, but important details are lacking. While it is possible that specific instances of Moses's written testimony are implied (e.g., Deut 18:15–18), the pairing of "the law" with "the prophets" points to a more comprehensive signal of the witnessing function of the Scriptures. How the "present reality" of Johannine belief in Jesus influences constructions of memory is explored quite differently here from the prologue (1:17[–18]), in that Moses, and his direct association with the law, is recognized as a phenomenon that cannot be tied solely to the past.

Another strategy for appropriating the past is encountered in the scene where Jesus explains the significance of his mission to Nicodemus (3:14) by comparing his lifting up (on the cross) to the wilderness incident in which Moses lifted up the bronze serpent on a pole (Num 21:7–9).

Moses's association with the law is not signaled on this occasion, nor, as we shall see, is his naming integral to the comparison,[27] but the opportunity is taken to highlight his intermediary function, earlier linked to the giving of the law (1:17), in relation to the specific historical event of God's act of healing the Israelites bitten by snakes. The correspondence (καθώς ... οὕτως) established between these two events provides a good example of "keying" or "frame-imaging," although, different from the prologue (1:14–16), the keyed events are not merged but explicitly juxtaposed as belonging to two different eras. A tight correlation is thus established between two events now regarded as mutually illuminating;[28] the elevation of the serpent is a type or foreshadowing of Jesus's crucifixion, whereby the scriptural memory frame is compressed and its vocabulary harmonized with that of the "present" event through the use of the verb ὑψοῦν (rather than ἱστάνται, LXX Num 21:9).[29] The intended correspondence, therefore, is not between Moses and Jesus,[30] but between the effects of the two acts of "lifting up" and, implicitly, the two acts of "seeing" the one who is elevated. It is also a connection that involves contrast: gazing at the serpent led to physical healing, but seeing Jesus will lead to eternal life (3:15; cf. 6:40). Far more clues are provided in this comparison about the significance of the interplay between past and present as far as the Johannine memory of Moses is concerned.

The next explicit reference to Moses (5:45–47) is, as in the serpent comparison, somewhat unexpected, even though it occurs in a scene of confrontation in which Jesus appeals to a series of witnesses who have testified on his behalf (5:31–40). Faced with the refusal of his interlocutors to believe that he has been sent by God (5:41, 43), Jesus uses their allegiance to Moses as the authoritative figure par excellence within Judaism (cf. 7:19–23) to turn the tables on them by identifying Moses as their accuser. In a severely worded reconstruction of their collective memory,

---

27. Stan Harstine, *Moses as a Character in the Fourth Gospel: A Study of Ancient Reading Techniques*, JSNTSup 229 (London: Sheffield Academic, 2002), 55.

28. See Kirk, "Social and Cultural Memory," 16.

29. See Jörg Frey, "'Wie Mose die Schlange in der Wüste erhöht hat ...' Zur frühjüdischen Deutung der 'ehernen Schlange' und ihrer christologischen Rezeption in Johannes 3,14f.," in *Schriftauslegung im antiken Judentum und im Urchristentum*, ed. Martin Hengel and Hermut Löhr, WUNT 73 (Tübingen: Mohr Siebeck, 1994), 182–83, 193.

30. See, most recently, John Ashton, *The Gospel of John and Christian Origins* (Minneapolis: Fortress, 2014), 13.

Jesus undermines the position of his opponents. He informs them that their rejection of him reverses their belief in Moses as Israel's intercessor before God (see Exod 32:11–13; Deut 5:5; Jub. 1:20–21), a belief that undergirds the reference to Moses in connection with the bronze serpent (Num 21:7) and probably accounts for Jesus's aside to "the Jews" as to how this archetypal figure molds their present: he is the one "on whom you have set your hope" (5:45). Jesus explains that Moses, now brought center stage in his capacity as one whose writings testify about Jesus (5:46–47; cf. 1:45), can also accuse those who do not accept his testimony. Because Jesus is the interpretative key to the Scriptures, believing Moses should lead to belief in Jesus. This is, in other words, a different but deliberate attempt at controlling the memory of Moses, one whose contours are clearly made to conform to the Johannine worldview.

John's most overt attempt at asserting mnemonic control over Moses centers on a textualized form of memory, when "the crowd" evokes a scriptural quotation, "He gave [ἔδωκεν] them bread from heaven to eat" (cf. Ps 78[77]:24; Exod 16:4, 15), to support their request for Jesus to provide a Moses-like authenticating sign that will repeat the provision of manna in the wilderness (6:30–31). The crowd seeks to establish a close link between Jesus and Moses, but their interpretation is disputed, indeed corrected, by Jesus: "Very truly, it was not Moses who gave [δέδωκεν] you the bread from heaven, but it is my Father who gives [δίδωσιν] you the true bread from heaven" (6:32). In some respects, Jesus's textual-exegetical intervention amounts to a form of "keying," one that strengthens the correlation between past and present through modification and transformation. For this particular representation to work as an effective memory frame, it is important to recognize God as the giver of "bread from heaven" in the past (Exod 16) as well as in the present,[31] leaving Moses once again to fulfill the role of mediator (1:17; 3:14; 5:45–47).[32] What is

---

31. See Maarten J. J. Menken, *Old Testament Quotations in the Fourth Gospel: Studies in Textual Form*, CBET 15 (Kampen: Kok Pharos, 1996), 54–55; Alicia D. Myers, "'The One of Whom Moses Wrote': The Characterization of Jesus through Old Testament Moses Traditions in the Gospel of John," in *"What Does the Scripture Say?" Studies in the Function of Scripture in Early Judaism and Christianity*, ed. Craig A. Evans and H. Daniel Zacharias, LNTS 470 (London: T&T Clark, 2012), 2:16.

32. See Menken, *Old Testament Quotations*, 56–63, for the view that John 6:32 (see also 1:17–18; 3:13; 5:45–47) reflects John's response to a Moses-centered form of Jewish piety.

also striking, but frequently overlooked, is that continuity between the two gifts is secured through the identification of their past (δέδωκεν ὑμῖν) and present recipients (δίδωσιν ὑμῖν). The contrast between the two God-given "events" is, nevertheless, made more explicit here than in Jesus's earlier correlation of two acts of elevation (3:14), because the inclusion of the adjective ἀληθινός in his description as the "true" bread of heaven, the one who gives life to the world (6:33), accentuates the superiority of the gift of bread over the one that could provide no more than physical sustenance in the wilderness.

The cluster of four references to Moses in John 7:19–23 returns to the question of the law, this time prompted by Jesus's assertion to "the Jews" that his authority stems from God (7:17–18). Their unspoken appeal to Moses's teaching about true and false prophecy may temper the abruptness of Moses's introduction by Jesus into the dialogue, "Did not Moses give you [δέδωκεν ὑμῖν] the law?" (7:19).[33] The wording of this challenge resembles the distinctive interplay in Jesus's declaration about the bread from heaven (6:32), again blurring the distinction between past and present recipients and accentuating the continued relevance of Moses as lawgiver—curiously, not mediator (1:17)—to those who rely on the law. The wording is often interpreted as indicating that the Johannine Jesus distances himself from the law, but neither here nor in 5:45–47 does he contrast Moses's authority with his own.[34] What he does, on both occasions, is communicate with his dialogue partners on their own terms of acknowledgment of Moses's elevated status in relation to the law.[35] No memory of Moses is reshaped at this point, but his interlocutors' inconsistent behavior is highlighted because their rejection of Jesus amounts to their failure to keep the law (7:19). The emphasis on what Moses has given to the Jews (δέδωκεν ὑμῖν) continues with reference to circumcision (7:22), despite the fact that the ritual was actually a gift by the patriarchs. Moses was the one responsible for providing a record of it in his writings (Gen 17:10–12), and as a result his authoritative status gives added force to Jesus's argument.[36] That Jesus continues to address them in their own "language" is demonstrated by the legitimation of his Sabbath healing (5:2–16) based on

---

33. Lincoln, *John*, 248–49.
34. See Lieu, "Narrative Analysis," 159.
35. For the view that, before the inclusion of John 6, 5:47 was originally followed by 7:15, see Ashton, *John*, 16–17.
36. See Martin Hasitschka, "Die Führer Israels: Mose, Josua, und die Richter," in

the legal principle that if the Sabbath law can be overridden to deal with circumcision (cf. m. Šabb. 18:3; 19:2), how much more so to heal a whole person. Accordingly, if Moses can act as their accuser because they do not have the proper key to the Scriptures (5:46-47), Jesus's opponents are now faced with a related, though legally based, challenge that claims Moses for the Johannine side.

The increasingly complex web of references to Moses reaches its conclusion in a scene where appeal to this landmark figure is made not by Jesus but by hostile Jewish adversaries ("the Pharisees") in their confrontation with the blind man (9:28-29) whose healing also takes place on the Sabbath (9:14, 16). The healed man's taunt that they may also wish to become Jesus's disciples (9:27) prompts the Pharisees to introduce Moses into the dialogue as a way of asserting their own collective identity (9:28) and to justify their refusal to accept Jesus (9:29). By referring to themselves as "disciples of Moses" they use the name and authority of their teacher— in a hitherto unprecedented way—to distance themselves further from Jesus's disciple and indeed from Jesus himself.[37] It is also a self-designation that dovetails with their stringent obedience to the law, prompting them to accuse Jesus of sinful violation for healing on the Sabbath (9:16, 23; cf. 5:10, 16; 7:23). Their common identity marker ("disciples of Moses") is underpinned, it is claimed, by their collective memory of Moses as the one to whom God has spoken (9:29; cf. Num 12:8); group cohesion is thus created through shared knowledge (οἴδαμεν) of Moses's privileged status but also by a shared lack of knowledge (οὐκ οἴδαμεν) of Jesus's origins (πόθεν).

What can be learned, therefore, about the function of Moses as a figure of memory in John's appeal to, and interpretation of, this foundational figure from Israel's past? This brief examination of the relevant passages has demonstrated that all explicit references to Moses share some salient features, but there is little to suggest a consciously sequential unfolding of

---

Alttestamentliche Gestalten im Neuen Testament: Beiträge zur biblischen Theologie, ed. Markus Öhler (Darmstadt: Wissenschaftliche Buchgesellschaft, 1999), 127.

37. Martinus C. de Boer, "The Depiction of 'the Jews' in John's Gospel: Matters of Behavior and Identity," in *Anti-Judaism and the Fourth Gospel: Papers of the Leuven Colloquium, 2000*, ed. R. Bieringer, D. Pollefeyt, F. Vandecasteele-Vanneuville (Assen: Van Gorcum, 2001), 275-76; Schapdick, "Religious Authority Re-evaluated," 204. Jan Assmann ("Collective Memory and Cultural Identity," *NGC* 65 [1995]: 130-31) notes that collective memory is often expressed positively or negatively through "a kind of identificatory determination," with knowledge characterized by the "sharp distinctions made between those who belong and those who do not."

his ascribed role within a well-defined commemorative framework. Moses is evoked with the aid of some striking mnemonic techniques, and as I have argued, theoretical insights relating to the strategy of "keying" prove helpful in determining how the past relates to the present with reference to Moses, from the virtual merging of past and present events (1:14–16) to their juxtaposition for the purpose of correlation and contrast (1:17; 3:14; 6:32).

Determining how Moses is remembered in John's Gospel also depends, to a large extent, on whose memory is being evoked within the narrative. At least two forms of collective memory can be detected, and it cannot be assumed that mnemonic features in one "version" can simply be superimposed on the other. Thus, on the one hand, from the (narrativized) Jewish perspective of those who enter into debate with Jesus or his followers, Moses is consistently evoked as an authoritative figure who is held in high esteem; he is the one in whom they pin their hopes (5:45) and to whom they show allegiance as disciples (9:28) because of his status as lawgiver (7:19, 22–23) who has spoken with God (9:29). On the other hand, the Johannine collective memory of Moses consists of many layers and is a more complex phenomenon. He is presented as a faithful witness to Jesus, one who wrote about him in the books of the law (1:45; 5:46). Indeed, the mnemonic profiling provided by "the Jews" is severely challenged when Jesus recasts Moses in the role of accuser rather than advocate due to their refusal to accept his testimony about Jesus (5:45–47). Johannine belief in Jesus as the exclusive revealer of God does, nevertheless, lead to a far-reaching reevaluation of Moses's significance in relation to divine revelation (1:17) and salvation (3:14; 6:32).

Whether these two constructed mnemonic representations of Moses overlap with each other in any way is a question left unaddressed within the Gospel narrative. Certainly there is much that separates both sets of memories, not least due to their emergence from radically different interpretations of the purpose of the law written and given by Moses. His importance for Jewish collective identity is acknowledged, indeed accentuated, by Jesus in debates with his Jewish interlocutors (3:14; 5:45–47; 6:32; 7:19–23); what is rejected is the notion that the gift of the law brings life. Moses is principally remembered in the Johannine collective memory for having written about Jesus, and while it could be inferred, on the basis of that memory, that a "true" disciple of Moses is at the same time a disciple of Jesus,[38] no

---

38. Lincoln, *John*, 78.

indicators are given in the narrative that discipleship of Moses is to be (re)-claimed by the Johannine side as part of its collective identity. Moses may not have been deleted from the Johannine memory, but his role—precisely in his capacity as giver/writer of the law—has been redefined in a way that allows continuity with the past insofar as it speaks to the present.

3. Remembering Abraham

If explicit references to Moses are scattered in a largely self-contained manner throughout the first half of John's narrative, all eleven references to the patriarch Abraham occur in one extended dialogue between Jesus and those described as "the Jews who had believed in him" (8:31–59). This encounter can be divided into three parts: appeal to descent from Abraham is made by those who reject Jesus's offer of freedom (8:31–36), which prompts a debate on kinship and paternity (8:37–37), before the scene concludes with an exchange about the relationship between Abraham and Jesus (8:48–59). To determine the interrelationship of these three parts, attention will be given to ways John draws on a selection of traditions about Abraham in order to develop a distinctively Johannine representation of the patriarch. The intended impact of that portrayal on hearers/readers of the text will also be considered.[39]

After Jesus declares that by remaining in his word they will know the truth that makes them free, his dialogue partners state: "We are descendants of Abraham and have never been slaves to anyone" (8:33). They instantly draw attention to a collective memory that centers on a key aspect of Jewish collective identity, but curiously, they link their descent from Abraham to a claim of unbroken freedom. Though it likely focuses on spiritual rather than political freedom,[40] the uncompromising character of this claim (cf. 1:18) suggests that it operates according to what theorists identify as social memory's selective processes in reconstructions of the past: some subjects are remembered, others are forgotten, so that a

---

39. See further Catrin H. Williams, "Abraham as a Figure of Memory in John 8.31–59," in *The Fourth Gospel in First-Century Media Culture*, ed. Anthony Le Donne and Tom Thatcher, LNTS 426 (London: T&T Clark, 2011), 205–22.

40. On Jewish traditions linking Abraham with freedom, see Tineke de Lange, *Abraham in John 8,31–59: His Significance in the Conflict between Johannine Christianity and Its Jewish Environment* (Amsterdam: Amphora, 2008), 123–27.

group's collective memory is made to serve the image that it seeks to project of itself, that is, a durable and unchanging image of its past.[41]

If memories involve reconstructions of the past, they often prove to be sites of contestation. In his response, Jesus challenges his audience's claim to Abrahamic descent and freedom. The assertion that they have never been enslaved is disputed because, whatever its basis, those who commit sin are slaves to sin (8:34). Due to their failure to accept his word, Jesus then confronts the other component of their collective memory, their self-identification as "the seed of Abraham." Whereas their *physical* descent from the patriarch is acknowledged (8:37), its incompatibility with their behavior is highlighted. A deliberate shift can be identified from the language of physical descent (σπέρμα, 8:37) to that of spiritual kinship (τέκνα, 8:39). To warrant the designation "children of Abraham" they need to imitate their ancestral father by acting like him: "If you are really the children of Abraham, you would be doing the works of Abraham" (8:39). The aim at this point is not so much to contest but to appeal to their memory of Abraham as the ancestor whose behavior should be emulated. The emphasis is on how retrieving the past should shape present actions rather than on how present realities can transform the memory of the past. This evocation of Abraham (8:39) is indeed an example of how present challenges can be keyed—through hoped-for reversal of behavior—to an archetypal image or pattern from the past.[42]

What is particularly noteworthy is Jesus's call to the Jewish interlocutors to do "the works of Abraham" (8:39). This concise phrase acts as a mnemonic signal for a wide range of deeds and attributes for which the patriarch is remembered in late Second Temple Judaism, including his opposition to idolatry, and his status as a model of righteousness, hospitality, and receptiveness to God's word. John in fact draws on a form of metonymic referencing that has the capacity to recall a vast network of associations relating to Abraham's "works." Nevertheless, the remainder of Jesus's statement (8:40) appears to focus on one particular aspect of the patriarch's works; in a highly condensed remark, the attempt to kill Jesus is contrasted with the behavior of the one whom they maintain is their father: "This is not what Abraham did [ἐποίησεν]." Given the widespread focus on hospitality as one of Abraham's most memorable virtues

---

41. Halbwachs, *La Mémoire collective*, 135–42; Assmann, *Das kulturelle Gedächtnis*, 42–43.

42. See Schwartz, "Frame Image," 1–4; Thatcher, "Cain and Abel," 732–51.

(cf. Josephus, *Ant.* 1.196–917; T. Ab. Rec. A 1:1–2; 3:7–9), the event being recalled at this point is probably the patriarch's reception of the three heavenly messengers by the oaks of Mamre (Gen 18:1–8). It would follow, then, that Abraham is cited to his descendants as an archetypal example of how they should be responding to Jesus, who himself claims to be the heavenly messenger sent by God. However, even if the veiled reference to "what Abraham did" (8:40) is intended as an allusion to the Mamre event, it does not necessarily exhaust the range of "works" previously mentioned by Jesus. Other "works," or aspects of a particular "work," may later be recalled with the aid of different mnemonic cues when Abraham comes into view again, later in John 8, as a figure of memory.

Explicit references to Abraham cease at this point, with the Jews stating: "We have one father, God himself" (8:41). Abraham has, nevertheless, not been forgotten, because the tracing of their lineage to God stands not as a replacement for, but rather as an affirmation of, their Abrahamic ancestry. Asserting their belief in the one God of Israel is an unspoken expression of pride in their Abrahamic status, particularly in view of the frequent praise of the patriarch in Jewish tradition for his rejection of idolatry (Jub. 11:16–17; Apoc. Ab. 1–8; Josephus, *Ant.* 1.154–157). Jesus, however, states that the only decisive criterion to become a child of God is to recognize him as the one sent by the Father. This amounts to a denial of the notion that descent from Abraham is synonymous with descent from God; only through belief in Jesus, not because of an ethnic identity tied to Abrahamic status, can one claim God as Father.

To understand how this reconfiguration "works" in the text, it needs to be set within the wider framework of its contestation of paternity and origins (8:37–47). It can also be considered in the light of social memory approaches to how a group establishes its origins or beginnings, with common ancestry often forming the "social cement" holding descendants together.[43] "Membership in a group inevitably entails a common perception of when it was 'born.'"[44] The key to the debate on origins in John 8, and elsewhere in the narrative, is undoubtedly the contrast it establishes between the horizontal/temporal and vertical/spatial axes within which it operates. On the question of "origins," the different notions of descent from God are tied to these different

---

43. Zerubavel, *Time Maps*, 55–81; cf. Byrskog, "New Quest," 333.
44. Zerubavel, *Time Maps*, 457; cf. Zerubavel, *Ancestors and Relatives: Genealogy, Identity, and Community* (Oxford: Oxford University Press, 2012).

axes. On the one hand, Jesus's interlocutors are presented as expressing a profound sense of connectedness to an ancestor, which means that their self-understanding is tied to Abrahamic descent and possesses a horizontal/temporal perspective. On the other hand, because they reject Jesus, their origins with God, which *they* link to their status as children of Abraham, is denied. The Johannine contestation of their collective memory involves a recasting of origins, one that belongs to the vertical/spatial axis and is set out in the spoken word of Jesus. He announces that he has come from God (8:42), declaring what he has seen in the Father's presence (8:38) and the truth that he has heard from him (8:40, 46). However, because of their deeds—attempting to kill Jesus and failing to accept his word (8:37, 43)—the origins of Jesus's audience is traced to the devil, who is described as a murderer from the beginning and the father of lies. As a result, they cannot claim descent from God, because only those who hear the words of God, revealed through his Son, is "of/from God" (ἐκ τοῦ θεοῦ, 8:47).

From the perspective of John's readers/hearers, the language and structure of John 8 is undoubtedly molded to evoke a response from them. Both the explicit either/or scenario set out in this encounter, and the failure of Jesus's opponents to respond to his warning that one's origins are evident from one's actions, are designed to encourage the audience to place themselves firmly on the side of "true disciples" (8:31). They must believe in Jesus as God's heavenly envoy and accept his revelation to receive the status of children of God (cf. 1:12–13; 11:52).

This new perspective on the question of "origins" from God also invites the question: where does it leave Abraham and his descendants? To a certain degree, Abrahamic and divine lineage are allowed to stand side by side, in a manner resembling the debate on discipleship (Jesus and/or Moses) in John 9. Certainly, Jesus's dialogue partners in John 8 are told: if Abraham were truly your father, you would not reject Jesus; if God were truly your Father, you would believe in Jesus. However, to infer from this "juxtaposition" that a true child of Abraham is at the same time a child of God[45] is to make a connection on which the text is silent. What is asserted is that descent from God "begins" with faith in Jesus; neither physical ancestry nor continuity with the past is the necessary requisite to claim

---

45. Mary B. Spaulding, *Commemorative Identities: Jewish Social Memory and the Johannine Feast of Booths*, LNTS 396 (London: T&T Clark, 2009), 147.

God as Father. Abraham is remembered as an ancestor whose behavior should be reproduced by his descendants, but the precise contours of his role as a figure of memory still await further definition.

Significant shifts occur in the final part of this encounter (8:48–59). All traces of belief in Jesus have disappeared, and the wider group described as "the Jews" explicitly takes over as the voice of opposition. Jesus's offer of salvation, now defined as deliverance from death, prompts the group to use Abraham as a screen through which to challenge Jesus: *even* the patriarch and the prophets could not avoid physical death (cf. T. Ab. Rec. A 8:9). The memory of Abraham's mortality also prompts them to ask, "Are you greater than our father Abraham?" to which he responds: "Abraham, your father, rejoiced that he would see my day; he saw [it] and was glad [καὶ εἶδεν καὶ ἐχάρη]" (8:56). This is not a new memory formulated from a "blank page," but one assembled from a wealth of Jewish traditions. Abraham's rejoicing is widely attested, with reference to the blessings promised by God (Jub. 14:21; Apoc. Ab. 10:15) and, more specifically, the gift of a son (Jub. 15:17) and the promise of a "holy seed" from the sons of Isaac (16:17–19). None of these memories of Abraham's joy is accompanied by an overt reference to "seeing," although the association between divine blessings and Abraham as the recipient of visionary experiences is well documented. Because the use of the aorist εἶδεν (8:56) points to a particular event during Abraham's lifetime as the setting for what "he saw," its most likely context is a variety of Jewish traditions about the covenant between the pieces (Gen 15), during which Abraham is said to have been granted visions of the future and the end times (4 Ezra 3:14; Apoc. Ab. 24:2).

If widespread traditions about the patriarch provide the raw material for Jesus's declaration (8:56), they are now constructed to form a christologically marked reconfiguration of the memory of Abraham. The linking together of his "rejoicing" and "seeing" attests the mosaic-like character of memory:[46] fragments of the inherited past are pieced together to produce a new mnemonic framework aligned to present realities. The new reality, as set out in 8:31–59, is belief in Jesus as the heavenly revealer of God, so that the reason for Abraham's joy is neither the birth of Isaac nor the promise of the holy seed but Jesus himself. He has become the focal

---

46. Barbie Zelizer, "Reading the Past against the Grain: The Shape of Memory Studies," *CSMC* 12 (1995): 224.

point of Abraham's visionary experiences. Some Jewish traditions state that Abraham, on this occasion, saw the hidden things already existing in heaven (2 Bar. 4:3–4), which, from John's perspective, could suggest a vision of the preexistent Jesus. The emphasis, however, is on seeing Jesus's "day" (8:56), which implies a vision whereby Abraham "sees" the earthly mission of the Son.

The statement about Abraham's rejoicing at seeing Jesus's day spells out what, up to this point, has been a vaguely defined role for the patriarch. The earlier call to do "the works of Abraham" (8:39), with its capacity to invoke a variety of deeds and attributes, as well as the ambiguously phrased "this is not what Abraham did" (8:40), create a sense of anticipation that is somewhat left hanging in the air. Only now, in 8:56, are Jesus's earlier, open-ended remarks elucidated for the readers/hearers of the text: the paramount "work" to be reproduced by all "true disciples" who remain in Jesus's word (8:31) is the acceptance of his true identity and mission; they should rejoice that they are seeing his day. For that reason, Abraham's joyful response upon "seeing" Jesus becomes an archetypal "orienting symbol"[47] or model *for* Johannine believers.

The gulf separating Jesus and "the Jews" does, however, become more evident as the mnemonic battle over Abraham intensifies. Their conviction that Abraham is greater than Jesus leads them to ask how he could allege to have seen the patriarch, to which he responds: "Very truly, I say to you, before Abraham was, I AM" (8:58). The use of the present tense (ἐγώ) εἰμί (rather than the aorist ἤμην) reinforces the role of this pronouncement as Jesus's claim to an absolute form of being, one closely aligned to what social memory theorists define as "frames that relate past, present, and future" and that profess "to reveal or describe ultimate reality."[48] Jesus's claim to disclose "ultimate reality" articulates how his identity and mission transcend all earthly categories. It also amounts to an intersection of the Johannine horizontal and vertical axes, since the time-bound existence (γενέσθαι) attributed to Abraham is unequivocally contrasted with the timeless form of existence (ἐγώ εἰμί) professed by Jesus.

John 8:31–59 provides a new commemorative narrative on Abraham that appeals to, recasts, but also contests a selection of memories about him in Scripture and Jewish tradition. Because the collective identity of

---

47. Schwartz, "Memory as a Cultural System," 910.
48. Olick, "Products, Processes, and Practices," 7.

the Johannine Christians stems from a redefinition of their memory of origins, Abraham's significance as "father" is considerably diminished; nowhere are believers called "children of Abraham" because descent from God—traditionally associated with Abrahamic origins—is available exclusively through Jesus. In the light of the new reality of Johannine belief in Jesus, this landmark figure from the past emerges as a witness, whose "work" par excellence is his joyful response upon "seeing" Jesus's mission. His affirmation of the Gospel's christological claims becomes, in Johannine terms, the only valid form of memory of Abraham but it also sets him up as a model to be emulated by all "true disciples."

4. Remembering Isaiah

Isaiah may not receive as much mnemonic exposure as Moses and Abraham if measured in terms of the number of references to the prophet in John's Gospel. Nevertheless, his importance as a scriptural witness to Jesus cannot be denied. Quotations from what "Isaiah said" (εἶπεν Ἠσαΐας) frame the beginning (1:23) and end (12:38, 39, 41) of the narrative about Jesus's ministry (1:19–12:50), so that, on both occasions, the unusually explicit naming of the prophet alerts attention to Isaiah and his spoken testimony.

Isaiah is first mentioned in the opening testimony of John the Baptist, who sets out his own designated role with the aid of Isa 40:3: "I am the voice of one crying out in the wilderness, 'Make straight the way of the Lord,' as the prophet Isaiah said" (1:23).[49] This identification with the herald who proclaims God's message of salvation and disclosure of his glory (Isa 40:3–5) is not forged by a narrator's explanatory comment (cf. Mark 1:2–3; Matt 3:3; Luke 3:4) but by the Baptist himself (ἐγώ). This makes him the only character in John's Gospel to appropriate the words of Scripture for the purpose of self-description. And although the Greek text prevents us from drawing firm conclusions, the formula "as the prophet Isaiah said" may also be intended as part of the Baptist's speech rather than as John's parenthetical remark. Given the emphasis on witness and confession within this opening scene (1:20), the Baptist's self-testimony acquires

---

49. On the textual form and significance of the quotation (LXX Isa 40:3) in John 1:23, see Bruce G. Schuchard, *Scripture within Scripture: The Interrelationship of Form and Function in the Explicit Old Testament Citations in the Gospel of John*, SBLDS 133 (Atlanta: Scholars Press, 1992), 1–15; and Menken, *Old Testament Quotations*, 21–35.

validity by highlighting Isaiah as his reliable co-witness.[50] It also attests the mnemonic keying of his testimony to that of a divinely appointed witness from the past, so that the Baptist not only *embodies* the voice in the wilderness but also, through his testimony, *enacts* Isaiah's prophetic words about making straight the way of the Lord. Further traces of this keying to Isaiah can be detected, as we shall see, in the Baptist's assertion that his testimony to Jesus stems from what he *has seen* (1:34).

The close Johannine association between seeing and testifying undergirds the next—and final—appearance of Isaiah, where his testimony is recalled through two quotations (Isa 53:1; 6:10) as part of a summary assessment of the unbelief encountered by Jesus during his ministry (12:38–40). To explain how these quotations are subjected to christological interpretation, John remarks: "Isaiah said these things because he saw his glory and spoke about him" (12:41). The scriptural setting for this remark is undoubtedly Isaiah's call-vision (Isa 6:1–13), which forms the wider context of the immediately preceding quotation from Isa 6:10 (John 12:40), while the reference to the prophet having "seen his glory" relates specifically to Jewish interpretative renderings of his encounter with the enthroned "Lord" as a vision of the divine δόξα (LXX Isa 6:1; cf. T. Isa. 6:1).

Pinpointing the event that provides the setting for this vision of glory is not, however, the primary purpose of 12:41, but to explain how Isaiah's experience and prophetic words can be read with reference to Jesus. This christologically marked statement is widely interpreted by scholars as centered on Isaiah's vision of the preexistent Jesus, but there are several indicators that it focuses heavily, if not primarily, on Isaiah as having seen the manifestation of divine glory in Jesus's earthly life.[51] As the centerpoint of reflections on the negative response to Jesus's ministry (12:37–43), Isaiah's testimony ("Isaiah said these things," 12:41a) results from his vision of Jesus's future glory ("he saw his glory," 12:41b), which is what enabled him to speak about Jesus's mission in the world ("he spoke about him," 12:41c). What underpins this explanation is the juxtaposition of two

---

50. Catrin H. Williams, "John (the Baptist): The Witness on the Threshold," in *Character Studies in the Fourth Gospel*, ed. Steven A. Hunt, D. Francois Tolmie, and Ruben Zimmermann, WUNT 314 (Tübingen: Mohr Siebeck, 2013), 52.

51. Nils Alstrup Dahl, "The Johannine Church and History," in *The Interpretation of John*, ed. John Ashton, 2nd ed., SNTI (Edinburgh: T&T Clark, 1997), 154–55. This aligns the presentation of Isaiah in John 12:37–41 with the Jewish understanding of his role as a visionary prophet who can see the future (cf. Sir 48:24-25).

quotations (Isa. 53:1; 6:10) for which several distinctive verbal and thematic links can be identified in their wider contexts.[52] According to LXX Isaiah, the prophet sees the "glory" (δόξα) of the Lord in his temple vision (6:1) and also speaks, in the fourth Servant Song (52:13–53:12), of the glorification (δοξασθήσεται) of the servant (52:13). Of particular significance is the additional link between Isaiah "seeing" the glory of the Lord (Isa 6:1, 5: εἶδον) and the "seeing" of the glorification of the servant (ἰδού, 52:13; cf. 52:15, where many nations and kings will see [ὄψονται] the servant). If John 12:41, as seems likely, acts as a commentary on both Isaiah quotations, two "events" or "acts" of seeing are subsumed under the one reference to glory to create a single, mosaic-like memory frame: Isaiah's vision of Jesus as the glorious figure in the temple is also the occasion for the prophet to see, ahead of time,[53] the glory manifested by Jesus during his earthly life, and whose rejection ultimately leads to his glorification on the cross.[54]

What do John's reflections in 12:37–41 reveal about the Johannine *function* of Isaiah as a figure of memory? The comment that Isaiah "saw his glory" relates closely to the preceding remarks, filtered through an Isaianic lens, on the relationship between signs and faith, blindness and unbelief. Because the signs act as a vehicle for the disclosure of Jesus's glory (2:11), a contrast is established between Isaiah, who truly "saw" the glory of Jesus, and those who, despite seeing the signs with their eyes, lacked the capacity to do so at a deeper level (12:37–38) because of the blinding of their eyes and the hardening of their heart (12:39–40). The closest Johannine counterpart to the assertion that Isaiah "saw his glory" is the confession, in the prologue, attributed to those who have witnessed Jesus as the unique manifestation of God's glory in human form ("we have seen his glory," 1:14). As a result, Isaiah's vision operates as a "reflective symbol"[55] keyed

---

52. Craig A. Evans, "Obduracy and the Lord's Servant: Some Observations on the Use of the Old Testament in the Fourth Gospel," in *Early Jewish and Christian Exegesis: Studies in Memory of William Hugh Brownlee*, ed. Craig A. Evans and William F. Stinespring (Atlanta: Scholars Press, 1987), 230–32; Jörg Frey, "'Dass sie meine Herrlichkeit schauen' (Joh 17.24): Zu Hintergrund, Sinn, und Funktion der johanneischen Rede von der δόξα Jesu," *NTS* 54 (2008): 385–86.

53. This interpretation of John 12:41 relates closely to the description of Abraham's joyful response upon seeing Jesus's day (8:56), where the aorist εἶδεν once again denotes a specific event as the context for Abraham's "vision."

54. See Frey, "Dass sie meine Herrlichkeit schauen," 386.

55. Schwartz, "Frame Image," 26.

to present experiences of (or obstacles to) seeing Jesus as the embodiment of God's glory on earth. This serves, in short, as a key identity marker for all Johannine believers.

This refraction of Isaiah's testimony through a Johannine framework continues in 12:42–43. In what appears at first glance to act as a qualification of John's earlier evaluation of the negative response to Jesus's ministry (12:37–41), it is stated that many of the authorities believed in him, but (ἀλλά) they failed to disclose openly their belief in Jesus because of the Pharisees and due to their fear of being cast out of the synagogue (12:42). A stinging indictment follows their failure to make a public confession of faith: "they loved human glory more than the glory of God" (12:43; cf. 5:44; 7:18). That this assessment deliberately plays on δόξα as meaning "honor/esteem" as well as "glory/splendor" is suggested by its proximity to the comment that Isaiah saw "his glory." Those who hover on the fringes of belief give preference to honorable status over offering public witness to Jesus,[56] who is the revelation of the glory of God. Contrary, therefore, to Johannine Christians, for whom Isaiah's vision of glory serves as a mnemonic pattern and source of encouragement in the face of opposition with synagogue Jews, the failure to confess Jesus is tantamount to a rejection of Isaiah's prophetic testimony.

5. Conclusion

The gathering together of Moses, Abraham, and Isaiah through a mnemonic lens discloses clear affinities but also notable differences with regard to the methods and aims of their evocation within John's commemorative framework. There is no doubt that, by focusing on *how* John recalls, gives prominence to, and also forgets certain elements from Israel's past, the characterizations of Moses, Abraham, and Isaiah differ from each other in quite significant ways. Moses is evoked, usually briefly, at various points in different narrative settings, and most of the references to him are bound

---

56. For the view that the kind of scenario outlined in John 12:42–43 reflects a sociohistorical situation similar to the one behind John 8:31–36, see Andrew T. Lincoln, *Truth on Trial: The Lawsuit Motif in the Fourth Gospel* (Peabody, MA: Hendrickson, 2000), 92, 283–85; and Michael Theobald, "Abraham—(Isaak—) Jakob. Israel's Väter im Johannesevangelium," in *Israel und seine Heilstraditionen im Johannesevangelium: Festgabe für Johannes Beutler SJ zum 70. Geburtstag*, ed. Michael Labahn, Klaus Scholtissek, and Angelika Strotmann (Paderborn: Schöningh, 2004), 175–83.

together by the highlighting of his role and status as writer and giver of the law (1:17, 45; 5:45–47; 7:19–23; 9:28–29). Abraham's mnemonic image emerges as a more coherent entity, since John, through the cumulative effect of reconfiguring Abraham within one extended scene (8:31–59), constructs a distinctive collective memory that involves the application, contestation, and recasting of Abrahamic memories held by those who claim descent from the patriarch, and thus from God. Finally, in a more textually based form of memory, great value is placed on the spoken testimony of Isaiah to frame the narrative of Jesus's public ministry (1:23; 12:37–40).

As to *why* John evokes the memory of these three scriptural characters, the answer can be found, to a large degree, in their ascribed role as reliable and enduring witnesses to Jesus, set within a unified schematization of the past that is shaped in/by the present. As is characteristic of such schematized patterns, John produces a highly monochromic image of these three figures, providing nothing more than the essential details required for their remembrance. If the task of collective memory is to establish and articulate a collective sense of identity, it is significant that the commemorative contours of Moses, Abraham, and Isaiah are formulated to accord with that which binds together all Johannine Christians: belief in Jesus as the exclusive source of God's revelation and salvation. This extends to normative significance in the case of Abraham and Isaiah, both of whom function as paradigmatic witnesses—or lamp-like exemplars—to be emulated by others, whether in joyful response upon "seeing" Jesus (8:56; cf. 20:20) or through recognition of Jesus as the manifestation of God's glory (12:41; cf. 1:14). John does not specify whether Moses, like Abraham and Isaiah, "saw" Jesus and his mission, although this may well be implied by the notion that Moses wrote about him (1:45; 5:46). Nevertheless, there is certainly less focus within the narrative on Moses as providing a mnemonic template for potential and actual believers, no doubt because the emphasis falls mainly on his reputation as the mediator of the law, which from a Johannine perspective has been stripped of its significance as the locus of God's revelation (1:17; 9:28) and the source of eternal life (3:14; 6:32).

What binds all three witnesses together is that they are commemorated in John's Gospel as individuals privileged to have been able to testify to that which has remained hidden until the coming of Jesus. More specifically, their testimonies relate directly to the identity and mission of the *earthly* Jesus. In order for Moses, Abraham, and Isaiah to function as rhetorically effective embodiments of the core values of Johannine Christians, the witness of these authoritative figures must be aligned, in the closest possible terms, to the conviction that Jesus of Nazareth is the definitive revelation of God. This alignment certainly establishes continuity with the past, but from a Johannine perspective it also marks new "beginnings,"[57] because whatever preceded those beginnings must be absorbed into a new mnemonic framework held together by belief in Jesus. For this reason, Moses, Abraham, and Isaiah are counted in John's Gospel as figures from Israel's remembered past who had already foreseen the remembering present.

---

57. See Zerubavel, *Time Maps*, 66–68, 89–95.

Sympathetic Resonance:
John as Intertextual Memory Artisan

Jeffrey E. Brickle

> It is not the literal past that rules us.... It is images of the past.... Images and symbolic constructs of the past are imprinted, almost in the manner of genetic information, on our sensibility.
>
> —George Steiner[1]

> Their memory had now assumed the form of the landscape itself. A metaphor had become a reality; an absence had become a presence.
>
> —Simon Schama[2]

1. Entering the Memory Theater

In an intriguing essay reprinted in *The Fourth Gospel in First-Century Media Culture*, Tom Thatcher suggests an unusual and provocative model with which to conceive of John's Gospel.[3] Thatcher's proposed imagery of a memory theater reflects a hermeneutical approach not normally associated with gospel studies, nor for that matter with biblical interpretation in general. Thatcher, who sketches the essential evolution of classic memory arts through Plato, Aristotle, Cicero, and Quintilian—a craft extended

---

* An earlier draft of this paper was presented in the Johannine Literature Section at the annual meeting of the Society of Biblical Literature in Baltimore, MD, November 25, 2013.

1. George Steiner, *In Bluebeard's Castle: Some Notes towards the Redefinition of Culture* (New Haven: Yale University Press, 1971), 3.

2. Simon Schama, *Landscape and Memory* (New York: Vintage, 1995), 25.

3. Tom Thatcher, "John's Memory Theatre: A Study of Composition in Performance," in *The Fourth Gospel in First-Century Media Culture*, ed. Anthony Le Donne and Tom Thatcher, ESCO, LNTS 426 (London: T&T Clark, 2011), 73–91.

and further developed in the Middle Ages—posits that John fashioned his Gospel by means of established Greco-Roman organizational devices and structures designed to aid the memory, especially that of interior visualization. As Thatcher notes, "Ancient mnemotechnique, and models of composition based on such techniques, were based on strategies for arranging and ordering mental images in ways that would facilitate recall in oral performance."[4] I wish to pursue Thatcher's helpful lead by expanding on and supplementing his highly evocative model as one avenue to better understand John's modus operandi as a master storyteller and scribal purveyor of traditions "new and old" (Matt 13:52).

2. Reenvisioning John's Memorial Project

In a chapter treating the poetics of Johannine memory within a volume that interacts with the scholarship of sociologist and memory theorist Barry Schwartz, I have attempted previously to reconstruct John's complex profile as a skilled and sophisticated collectivist memorian who stood alongside other early Christian memory tradents, including Peter and his reputed function as a memorian underlying Mark's Gospel, and, by extension, the Synoptic tradition.[5] Following in the footsteps of a longstanding, pancultural lineage of scribal authorities—an educationally formative project well documented in David Carr's indispensable study titled *Writing on the Tablet of the Heart: Origins of Scripture and Literature*[6]—John served as an agent of enculturation as he confronted a severe, multifaceted crisis threatening his community, thus crafting and retelling the Jesus story in a particular way and impressing these cherished traditions upon his hearers. One of Carr's central theses is that in antiquity written records served not primarily for textual *storage*, but as a means, typically in the

---

4. Ibid., 79.

5. Jeffrey E. Brickle, "The Memory of the Beloved Disciple: A Poetics of Johannine Memory," in *Memory and Identity in Ancient Judaism and Early Christianity: A Conversation with Barry Schwartz*, ed. Tom Thatcher, SemeiaSt 78 (Atlanta: Society of Biblical Literature, 2014), 187–208.

6. David M. Carr, *Writing on the Tablet of the Heart: Origins of Scripture and Literature* (Oxford: Oxford University Press, 2005). Note also Carr's "Torah on the Heart: Literary Jewish Textuality within Its Ancient Near Eastern Context," *OT* 25 (2010): 17–40; and Jan Assmann, *Cultural Memory and Early Civilization: Writing, Remembrance, and Political Imagination* (Cambridge: Cambridge University Press, 2011).

context of scribal schools, to facilitate the *inscribing* of traditions on the *hearts and minds* of successive generations of scribal custodians.[7]

Viewed from this angle, John's narrative functioned as a vehicle with which to radically shape and reshape the worldview, theology, and ethical constitution of successive generations of Christian communities.[8] A tradent committed to transmitting the scriptural traditions of Israel, the witness of Jesus, and other memories from the life of the early church—and forging them into a coherent, literary text—John conceived of himself "as a living library, one who makes a mental chest of memorized texts and materials, which are then always ready as a reference and meditation tool for … the service of others."[9] John expected that his Gospel, saturated as it is with the living traditions of his own cultural and remembered past, would be encountered in such a way as "to be alive, to speak and converse, to be consumed and digested through the memories of living people."[10] It would be a mistake, of course, to regard John's project as merely a recapitulation of memorized texts and events, for the craft of ancient memory arts promoted fresh and creative syntheses.[11]

---

7. See, for example, Carr's summary in his *Writing on the Tablet*, 4–14. In his fascinating work, *Readers and Reading Culture in the High Roman Empire: A Study of Elite Communities*, CCS (Oxford: Oxford University Press, 2010), 201 (but see also 118–20), William A. Johnson observes that in "the context of the *system*, in which literary texts were at the core of certain elite constructions of identity and community, deep internalization of chosen texts makes sense as an elemental requirement for joining the (exclusive) community" (emphasis original). Note also Paul J. Griffiths, *Religious Reading: The Place of Reading in the Practice of Religion* (Oxford: Oxford University Press, 1999), esp. 22–59; and the chapter titled, "The Psalter as an Anthology to Be Memorized," in Gordon J. Wenham, *Psalms as Torah: Reading Biblical Song Ethically*, STI (Grand Rapids: Baker Academic, 2012), 41–56.

8. For the role in which narratives can shape lives, see also Craig G. Bartholomew and Michael W. Goheen, *The Drama of Scripture: Finding Our Place in the Biblical Story* (Grand Rapids: Baker Academic, 2004), 15–27; Marshall Gregory, *Shaped by Stories: The Ethical Power of Narratives* (Notre Dame: University of Notre Dame Press, 2009).

9. Mary Carruthers, "Mechanisms for the Transmission of Culture: The Role of 'Place' in the Arts of Memory," in *Translatio or the Transmission of Culture in the Middle Ages*, ed. Laura Hollengreen, ASMAR 13 (Turnhout: Brepols, 2008), 1–2.

10. Ibid., 2–3.

11. Mary Carruthers, "*Ars Oblivionalis, Ars Inveniendi*: The Cherub Figure and the Arts of Memory," *Gesta* 48 (2009): 1, affirms that from "antiquity, the arts of memory in Europe were conceived of as investigative tools for recollective reconstruc-

Arguably, John's role as an ancient memorian anticipates or foreshadows later developmental phases of human discourse on memory. As Anne Whitehead has insisted, the notion of memory itself entails a complex phenomenon complete with its own history. It is, in the words of Mieke Bal, whom she quotes, a "traveling concept."[12] In the case of John, we might claim that his ideological relationship to memory, spanning that of a memory artisan to an individual repository of memory to a social or cultural memorian, encompasses what Aleida Assmann describes as the diverging roads of *ars* (the more technical, mechanical art of mnemonic storage, epitomized by the work of the ancient Roman orator Cicero) and *vis* (memory as shaper of identity, exemplified by the modern German philosopher Friedrich Nietzsche).[13]

3. The Art of Memory

In this essay I focus on John as a practitioner of ancient memory arts, though the discussion impinges in important ways on other spheres and aspects of memory. My proposal constitutes a work in progress that admittedly requires additional development and application. Here, I briefly examine and explore some suggestive heuristic devices and paradigms with the goal of better understanding the way John skillfully launches his recollections of the Jesus event across the remembered landscape of Israel's ancestral past. John, of course, does not simply recount reminiscences based on his personal participation,[14] but shapes his narrative

---

tion and selection, serving what we now call creative thinking. The need for structured memory storage was understood as a support for making new thought and composition, not for simply preserving all the past."

12. Anne Whitehead, *Memory*, TNCI (London: Routledge, 2009), 3. Elizabeth Minchin, *Homeric Voices: Discourse, Memory, Gender* (Oxford: Oxford University Press, 2007), 8, likewise cautions: "In everyday contexts we are accustomed to speak of memory as though it were a single entity. This is inaccurate. Memory comprises a range of complementary systems, all of which are capable of storing information." Rafael Rodriguez, *Structuring Early Christian Memory: Jesus in Tradition, Performance, and Text*, ESCO, LNTS 407 (London: T&T Clark, 2010), 81, concurs, noting that "memory is a complex phenomenon (or range of phenomena) rooted in but not limited to psychological processes within an individual."

13. Aleida Assmann, *Cultural Memory and Western Civilization: Functions, Media, Archives* (Cambridge: Cambridge University Press, 2011), 17–18.

14. The identification of this individual with a specific historical figure has long

portrayal of Jesus in relation to an underlying subtext (the Septuagint)[15] deeply seated within the collective memory of Second Temple Judaism. I hope to exploit the phenomenon of "sympathetic resonance," along with other media-oriented models, as metaphors to express and reflect on the rich interplay obtained by John's dynamic superimposition of remembered traditions.

But first, a few words about memory in antiquity are in order. The formal craft of memory, which occupied one of the five canons of rhetoric, was developed originally in classical Greece as a versatile tool to assist orators in recounting speeches in a variety of contexts. The craft was designed to achieve complete mastery of a speech beyond rote memorization alone, facilitating what Mary Carruthers and Jan Ziolkowski term "shuffling"[16]—the flexibility of moving in and out, forward or backward, within that speech's overall structural plan. This crucial capability allowed impromptu detours as needed in the event of distraction, challenge by an opponent, or simply to permit spur-of-the-moment elaboration before returning to the speech's main subject. In her *The Craft of Thought: Meditation, Rhetoric, and the Making of Images, 400–1200*, Carruthers stresses that

> the goal of rhetorical mnemotechnical craft was not to give students a prodigious memory for all the information they might be asked to repeat in an examination, but to give an orator the means and wherewithal to invent his material, both beforehand and—crucially—on the spot. *Memoria* is most usefully thought of as a compositional art. The

---

been debated. For studies equating him with John the apostle, see, for example, Donald A. Carson, *The Gospel according to John*, PNTC (Grand Rapids: Eerdmans, 1991), 68–81; and Craig L. Blomberg, *The Historical Reliability of John's Gospel: Issues and Commentary* (Downers Grove, IL: InterVarsity Press, 2001), 22–41. Alternatively, some scholars propose the author was a distinct John the Elder. See, for example, Martin Hengel, *The Johannine Question*, trans. John Bowden (London: SCM, 1989); and Richard Bauckham, *The Testimony of the Beloved Disciple: Narrative, History, and Theology in the Gospel of John* (Grand Rapids: Baker Academic, 2007), 33–91.

15. One recent attempt to argue for this textual relationship is Bruce G. Schuchard, *Scripture within Scripture: The Interrelationship of Form and Function in the Explicit Old Testaments Citations in the Gospel of John*, SBLDS 133 (Atlanta: Scholars Press, 1992).

16. Mary Carruthers and Jan M. Ziolkowski, eds., *The Medieval Craft of Memory: An Anthology of Texts and Pictures*, MatT (Philadelphia: University of Pennsylvania Press, 2002), 3.

arts of memory are among the arts of thinking, especially involved with fostering the qualities we now revere as "imagination" and "creativity."[17]

Memory is, in Carruthers's words, "an architecture for thinking."[18] It is relevant not only to the compositional strategy of a work but also in facilitating its retention and recall by a lector during recitation or oral performance, as well as reception, recollection, and interpretation by listening audiences.

Lest one be tempted to dismiss such memory arts as antiquated or outmoded, it is helpful to keep in mind (1) the fundamental, intimate connection between storytelling and memory (more on this later); (2) the fact that the craft's essential principles continue to underlie memory-enhancing programs to this day; and (3) the role served by artificial memory in strongly oral cultures seeking to supplement natural memories, a need that ironically grew more urgent as written sources proliferated, necessitating keeping more and more texts straight, organized, and accessible.

As Dale Allison has persuasively argued at the outset of his magisterial *Constructing Jesus: Memory, Imagination, and History*, human recollection is fragile in nature and prone to subjectivity.[19] Allison's overall appraisal is seconded by John Dominic Crossan, who—while his analysis of early Christian tradition and history differs significantly from Allison's—agrees that memory tends to be unreliable.[20] Yosef Yerushalmi concurs, stating that "memory is always problematic, usually deceptive, sometimes treacherous."[21]

---

17. Mary Carruthers, *The Craft of Thought: Meditation, Rhetoric, and the Making of Images, 400–1200*, CSML (Cambridge: Cambridge University Press, 1998), 9. See also Carruthers and Ziolkowski, *Medieval Craft*, 1–4.

18. Carruthers, *Craft of Thought*, 7.

19. Dale C. Allison Jr., *Constructing Jesus: Memory, Imagination, and History* (Grand Rapids: Baker Academic, 2010), esp. 1–17.

20. John Dominic Crossan, *The Birth of Christianity: Discovering What Happened in the Years Immediately after the Execution of Jesus* (San Francisco: HarperSanFrancisco, 1999), 59, suggests that "memory is as much or more creative reconstruction as accurate recollection, and, unfortunately, it is often impossible to tell where one ends and the other begins."

21. Yosef H. Yerushalmi, *Zakhor: Jewish History and Jewish Memory* (Seattle: University of Washington Press, 1982), 5.

I do not wish to enter into a prolonged discussion of memory's trustworthiness here,[22] other than to emphasize that the ancients themselves were certainly well aware of natural memory's shortcomings, and intentionally devised means to compensate. In a culture in which, as Samuel Byrskog points out, "to remember was to live, to forget was to die," too much was at stake to relinquish cherished traditions to the frailties and instability of natural memory alone.[23] Carruthers, in her monograph titled *The Book of Memory*, observes that exceptional memories cannot "be achieved by raw talent alone; indeed natural talent will not produce such facility or accuracy. Memory must be trained, in accordance with certain elementary techniques."[24]

4. Spaces Freighted with Images

The invention of mnemonic arts has often been traced to the famous Greek legend surrounding the lyric poet Simonides of Ceos—the so-called father of memory—who allegedly recalled the order and placement of bodies seated around a table in the aftermath of a collapsed banquet hall. Aristotle in turn introduced an alphabetically oriented sequential or serial system of *topoi* that allowed the user to progress forward and in reverse through a list or series of subjects.[25] The Romans—represented especially by the anonymous author of the *Rhetorica ad Herennium*, Cicero's *De oratore*, and Quintilian's *Institutio oratoria*—developed

---

22. Robert K. McIver's *Memory, Jesus, and the Synoptic Gospels*, SBLRBS 59 (Atlanta: Society of Biblical Literature, 2011), thoroughly treats the reliability of the remembered oral traditions underlying the written gospel accounts. See also the chapter titled "The Gospels' Oral Sources," in Craig S. Keener, *The Historical Jesus of the Gospels* (Grand Rapids: Eerdmans, 2009), 139–61; James D. G. Dunn, *The Oral Gospel Tradition* (Grand Rapids: Eerdmans, 2013); and Eric Eve, *Behind the Gospels: Understanding the Oral Tradition* (London: SPCK, 2013). For a related study employing the lens of social memory theory, see Anthony Le Donne, *The Historiographical Jesus: Memory, Typology, and the Son of David* (Waco, TX: Baylor University Press, 2009).

23. Samuel Byrskog, introduction to *Jesus in Memory: Traditions in Oral and Scribal Perspectives*, ed. Werner H. Kelber and Samuel Byrskog (Waco, TX: Baylor University Press, 2009), 2.

24. Mary Carruthers, *The Book of Memory: A Study of Memory in Medieval Culture*, 2nd ed., CSML (Cambridge: Cambridge University Press, 2008), 8.

25. Jocelyn P. Small, *Wax Tablets of the Mind: Cognitive Studies of Memory and Literacy in Classical Antiquity* (London: Routledge, 1997), 87–94.

a highly effective architectural model or system of *loci* in which imagined locations, such as a temple or palace, were invested in a certain order with strategically placed, symbolically laden images, like an anchor or a sword. When an orator sought to recall information or a speech via this approach, he would revisit and walk through the location in his mind, encountering in order the images—and the elements associated with and evoked by these images—that he had previously deposited.[26]

Memory scholarship has confirmed, in the view of Ruth Van Dyke and Susan Alcock, that "memory is closely integrated with place."[27] If indeed the memory arts, and the spacial-oriented Latin system of *loci* and images in particular, played a role in the composition of ancient literature—and, as William Shiell suggests, in the performance and reception of that literature[28]—then that prospect invites close attention to literary sequence and arrangement, intra- and intertextual spacial relationships, and iconography. Laura Nasrallah has fittingly pointed out that "what is often missing from studies of early Christian literature is ... attention to space, architecture, and art—an understanding of the broader material environment in which this literature was written and the varieties of responses that Christians had to the spaces of empire."[29]

A number of rich and suggestive spacial studies have been carried out in the classical/Hellenistic, biblical, and theological fields, with important applications to and ramifications for the memory arts.[30] In

---

26. Ibid., 95–116; Whitehead, *Memory*, 27–33.

27. Ruth M. Van Dyke and Susan E. Alcock, "Archaeologies of Memory: An Introduction," in *Archaeologies of Memory*, ed. Ruth M. Van Dyke and Susan E. Alcock (Malden, MA: Blackwell, 2003), 5.

28. William D. Shiell, *Delivering from Memory: The Effect of Performance on the Early Christian Audience* (Eugene, OR: Pickwick, 2011), 20–28; Shiell, *Proclaiming the Gospel: First-Century Performance of Mark* (Harrisburg, PA: Trinity Press International, 2003), 103–25. Intriguingly, Rafael Rodriguez, *Oral Tradition and the New Testament: A Guide for the Perplexed* (London: Bloomsbury, 2014), 27–28, explains that one definition of the performance arena is "the 'place' in which readers and/or audiences imagine themselves as they read and/or experience an oral-derived text. An audience experienced with the actual oral tradition of an oral-derived text can summon the memory of the actual space of the performance arena in their reception of the oral-derived text."

29. Laura S. Nasrallah, *Christian Responses to Roman Art and Architecture: The Second-Century Church amid the Spaces of Empire* (Cambridge: Cambridge University Press, 2010), 2.

30. For classical/Hellenistic studies, see, e.g., Michael Paschalis and Stavros Fran-

this regard, Whitney Shiner's pioneering essay in *Performing the Gospel: Orality, Memory, and Mark*, titled "Memory Technology and the Composition of Mark,"[31] entails one of the first studies applying a memory arts-oriented approach to a biblical document. Shiner's fascinating proposal suggests that Mark's organization "facilitate[d] its memorization" and may be accounted for as "the repeated use of a very basic architectural structure that allows for the inclusion of a very limited number of elements."[32] Correspondingly, Shiner submits an imaginative model employing a temple front, similar to that gracing the Parthenon, as a matrix on which the structure of Mark's Gospel could have been strategically plotted on the memory.

5. Mapping John on Ephesus

Following Shiner's lead, and given the Gospel of John's conceivable provenance in Ephesus,[33] any number of well-known public structures located

---

goulidis, *Space in the Ancient Novel*, ANS 1 (Eelde, The Netherlands: Barkhuis, 2002); Alex C. Purves, *Space and Time in Ancient Greek Narrative* (Cambridge: Cambridge University Press, 2010); Irene J. F. de Jong, *Space in Ancient Greek Literature*, SAGN 3, MNS 339 (Leiden: Brill, 2012); Michael Scott, *Space and Society in the Greek and Roman Worlds*, KTAH (Cambridge: Cambridge University Press, 2013). For biblical studies, see, e.g., Elizabeth S. Malbon, *Narrative Space and Mythic Meaning in Mark*, NVBS (San Francisco: Harper & Row, 1986); Walter Brueggemann, *The Land: Place as Gift, Promise, and Challenge in Biblical Faith*, 2nd ed., OBT (Minneapolis: Fortress, 2002); James L. Resseguie, *Spiritual Landscape: Images of the Spiritual Life in the Gospel of Luke* (Peabody, MA: Hendrickson, 2004); Resseguie, *Narrative Criticism of the New Testament: An Introduction* (Grand Rapids: Baker Academic, 2005), 87–120; Mark K. George, *Israel's Tabernacle as Social Space*, AIL 2 (Atlanta: Society of Biblical Literature, 2009); Eric C. Stewart, *Gathered around Jesus: An Alternative Spatial Practice in the Gospel of Mark*, Matrix (Eugene, OR: Cascade, 2009). For theological studies, see, e.g., Craig G. Bartholomew, *Where Mortals Dwell: A Christian View of Place for Today* (Grand Rapids: Baker Academic, 2011); Eric O. Jacobsen, *The Space Between: A Christian Engagement with the Built Environment*, CE (Grand Rapids: Baker Academic, 2012).

31. Whitney T. Shiner, "Memory Technology and the Composition of Mark," in *Performing the Gospel: Orality, Memory, and Mark*, ed. Richard A. Horsley, Jonathan A. Draper, and John M. Foley (Minneapolis: Fortress, 2006), 147–65.

32. Ibid., 156.

33. Paul Trebilco, *The Early Christians in Ephesus from Paul to Ignatius* (Grand Rapids: Eerdmans, 2007), 241–71. Cf., however, J. Ramsey Michaels, *The Gospel of John*, NICNT (Grand Rapids: Eerdmans, 2010), 37–38, who cautions that the evi-

in that ancient metropolis could have served in antiquity as an effective *locus* for arranging and charting this gospel on the imagination—not to mention attempting contemporary mnemonic reconstructions as Shiner has done. Ephesus's rich, varied, and distinctive cityscape would certainly have facilitated such an endeavor. An effective memory scheme could be charted using the layout of any number of Ephesian structures and carefully plotting representative images from the Fourth Gospel's narrative framework upon such sites as the port baths and gymnasium, theater, state agora, and the temple of Artemis.[34]

This particular approach, while having much to commend it, presents some potential drawbacks. First, in my view, it runs the risk of being too static and confining to account for the complexities inherent in John's use of the Old Testament. The social construction of space is an extremely multilayered phenomenon, for as Van Dyke and Alcock critically observe, a "sense of place rests upon, and reconstructs, a history of social engagement with the landscape, and is thus inextricably bound up with remembrance, and with time; its construction is tied into networks of associations."[35] Second, the approach opens itself up to the criticism of imposing an outside or external organization—namely the largely pagan-oriented sphere of Ephesus—which might be better sought within an internal textual matrix comprising the literary canon of Israel and its "sacred" panorama. The nature of John's memorial project in relationship to Jewish Scripture demands a more complex, dynamic, and multidimensional approach, incorporating a memory architecture that takes into account spacial overlaying and interactions.

6. Metaphors for Remembering

At this juncture, I present some heuristic models or paradigms, all interrelated and mutually informing in various ways, for potentially conceiving of

---

dence for Ephesus appears to be "rather thin" and suggests additional locations that the Fourth Gospel may have originated from, including Egypt, Palestine or (more likely in Michaels's judgment) Syria.

34. See Clyde E. Fant and Mitchell G. Reddish, *A Guide to Biblical Sites in Greece and Turkey* (Oxford: Oxford University Press, 2003), 177–207; Jerome Murphy-O'Connor, *St. Paul's Ephesus: Texts and Archaeology* (Collegeville, MN: Liturgical Press, 2008), 186–200.

35. Van Dyke and Alcock, "Archaeologies," 5.

John's mnemonic undertaking vis-à-vis the Old Testament. Since a solitary metaphor cannot adequately capture the complex and dynamic nature of John's project, I propose that the following models be considered in a type of symbiotic relationship. Taken together, therefore, these models suggest a lively avenue through which to conceive of John's complex engagement with Israel's heritage in light of the Jesus event.

6.1. A Theater

As we have already noted, a theater, especially a "memory" theater—including this tradition's evolution into the Middle Ages (well-documented by Frances Yates in her *The Art of Memory*[36])—provides a fitting metaphor. This imaginative venue permitted the dynamic overlaying of and interaction between sometimes contrasting recollections, for the theater "was an important medium for creating new sets of memory that can serve as an alternative to memories that have become collective to a society."[37]

Jo-Ann Brant has exploited the ancient stage to great effect in her *Dialogue and Drama: Elements of Greek Tragedy in the Fourth Gospel*.[38] The concept of a memory theater offers the advantage of combining the sensory apparatuses of sight and sound, both vital aspects of memory. As Jenny Clay has observed in her *Homer's Trojan Theater: Space, Vision, and Memory in the* Iliad, the theater provides a setting by which the audience can become a spectator, intently gazing on the scenario unfolding before it. As Clay aptly suggests, "for the Greek, to see is to know."[39] A theater also captures the dynamic relationship between playwright, text, performance, performer(s), and performative setting. Helpful from the standpoint of mnemonic art, Max Harris has appropriately noted that "what the director does on stage, the reader must do in his imagination."[40] In keeping with John's memorial project, I would suggest that a multistage

---

36. Frances A. Yates, *The Art of Memory* (Chicago: University of Chicago Press, 1966).

37. Doron Mendels, "Societies of Memory in the Graeco-Roman World," in *Memory in the Bible and Antiquity*, ed. Loren T. Stuckenbruck, Stephen C. Barton, and Benjamin G. Wold, WUNT 212 (Mohr Siebeck, 2007), 152.

38. Jo-Ann A. Brant, *Dialogue and Drama: Elements of Greek Tragedy in the Fourth Gospel* (Peabody, MA: Hendrickson, 2004).

39. Jenny Strauss Clay, *Homer's Trojan Theater: Space, Vision, and Memory in the* Iliad (Cambridge: Cambridge University Press, 2011), 2.

40. Max Harris, *Theater and Incarnation* (Grand Rapids: Eerdmans, 1990), 19.

theater *complex*, in which the "theatergoer" moves from performance to performance, helps capture John's intertextual narrative dynamics.

6.2. An Intersection

Barbara Burrell's fascinating analysis of an evolving intersection in ancient Ephesus titled "Reading, Hearing, and Looking at Ephesos"[41] offers another way to conceive of John's multidimensional memory project. Her study investigates the interactive layering of meaning over an extended time as new buildings, gates, and monuments were constructed and bilingual inscriptions engraved at an important crossroads located immediately south of Ephesus's Hellenistic agora, creating "reading experiences"[42] ultimately "emphasiz[ing] and aggrandiz[ing] a burgeoning Helleno-Roman cultural ideal."[43] In Burrell's words, "Buildings attract further building, texts attract texts, whether on those buildings or standing around them, clustered in a new civic nexus which in the process became a focus for speech as well"—a fit model for John's intertextually oriented narrative that constructs new realities over the old.[44]

6.3. A Hypertext

Jay Bolter's study of the relationship of hypertext to rhetoric[45] provides another avenue for conceiving of John's mnemonic design. Hypertext moves beyond "a single, linear presentation" to link or branch out through

---

41. Barbara Burrell, "Reading, Hearing, and Looking at Ephesos," in *Ancient Literacies: The Culture of Reading in Greece and Rome*, ed. William A. Johnson and Holt N. Parker (Oxford: Oxford University Press, 2009), 69–95.

42. Ibid., 89.

43. Ibid., 88.

44. For another example of space exploited for public memory, see Mendels, "Societies of Memory," 156–57. For a discussion and application of the fascinating, allied approach of conceptual blending, see David A. deSilva, "Seeing Things John's Way: Rhetography and Conceptual Blending in Revelation 14:6–13," *BBR* 18 (2008): 271–98. DeSilva explains (276) that the "basic premise is that meaningful communication will often 'blend' together elements of distinct and discrete schemes, scenarios, and experiences to produce new discourse."

45. Jay D. Bolter, "Hypertext and the Rhetorical Canons," in *Rhetorical Memory and Delivery: Classical Concepts for Contemporary Composition and Communication*, ed. John F. Reynolds (Hillsdale, NJ: Erlbaum, 1993), 97–111.

embedded objects to various topics, which can be arranged in a variety of shapes, such as stars or rings.[46] Bolter notes that hypertext transcends the limitations of ancient artificial memory systems, affording nonlinear, network-oriented topical relationships.[47]

Sometimes ancient and medieval books were rendered into a hypertext-like format by notating and (in some cases) decorating their pages with fairly elaborate divisions and figures, transforming "a flat, rectangular surface" into a visually rich network of associations that could "be taken in with a single mental 'look.'"[48] Scribes altered manuscripts in these ways for mnemonic purposes, with the end result that the pages were to be considered "not as flat bits of text but as three dimensional, like boxes (*arcae*) or rooms (*cellae*), packed full of linked matters." Fascinatingly, in the case of one medieval manuscript of the Psalter, "surrounding the main commentaries are margins containing yet more commentary, and in the outermost margins, brackets and abbreviations indicate the sources of the texts."[49]

This type of format may reflect the conceptual network of associations triggered by the various "hyperlinks" embedded in John's narrative,[50] corresponding, for example, to the web of illuminating echoes from the Old Testament evoked by the possible suggestion of a failure of "the Jews" at the wedding celebration in Cana[51] (John 2:1–11) or the tense temple scene that follows[52] (John 2:13–25). These Old Testament references in turn triggered further associations, eliciting reflection on even more related allusions rooted in the Jewish canon.

---

46. Ibid., 97.

47. Ibid., 109.

48. Carruthers, "Mechanisms," 7.

49. Ibid., 9.

50. Brian Capper, as cited by Ronald E. Heine, *Reading the Old Testament with the Ancient Church: Exploring the Formation of Early Christian Thought*, EvangR (Grand Rapids: Baker Academic, 2007), 79, speaks of John's engagement with Israel's heritage as an "intense interweaving of events with symbols drawn from the Old Testament Scriptures."

51. Andreas J. Köstenberger, "John," in *Commentary on the New Testament Use of the Old Testament*, ed. Gregory K. Beale and Donald A. Carson (Grand Rapids: Baker Academic, 2007), 431.

52. Alicia D. Myers, *Characterizing Jesus: A Rhetorical Analysis on the Fourth Gospel's Use of Scripture in Its Presentation of Jesus*, LNTS 458 (London: T&T Clark, 2013), 140–47.

6.4. Sympathetic Resonance

The aural or acoustic model of sympathetic resonance, reflected in this essay's title, suggests that one narrative sets a second in motion—causing the second to "vibrate" in a harmonic relationship to the first and triggering frequencies either in a fundamental register or as overtones. I propose that by keying the Septuagint of Gen 1:1 in the opening phrase of his prologue (ἐν ἀρχῇ, John 1:1), John triggers the entire sweep of the Old Testament narrative soundscape, which flows as an underlying subtext, an undercurrent of vibrating, meaningful sound, beneath John's Gospel. In the manner of Scripture's various new narrative beginnings (e.g., the Noahic [Gen 6], Abrahamic [Gen 12], and exodus [Exod 1] stories), which draw from and recycle creation language, John "layers" his story of new creation over the old, enriching its significance.

6.5. An Image(s)

As noted above, images played a crucial role in the ancient system of memory arts, for images captured, retained, and provided access to the past as a type of shorthand—a virtual snapshot with which to evoke a network of remembered associations.[53] Carruthers points out the "importance of visual images as memorial hooks and cues [as] a basic theme in all memory-training advice and practice from the very earliest Western text we possess, the [pre-Socratic fragment] *Dialexeis*."[54] Imagery, which may be defined as "an analog system for representing and manipulating visual and spacial information,"[55] has the uncanny ability to compress a great

---

53. In trying to uncover the phenomenology of memory, Paul Ricoeur, *Memory, History, Forgetting*, trans. Kathleen Blamey and David Pellauer (Chicago: University of Chicago Press, 2004), 5, affirms that "the presence in which the representation of the past seems to consist does indeed appear to be that of an image."

54. Carruthers, *Book of Memory*, 274. Citing Quintilian, Myers, *Characterizing Jesus*, 49, states that "underpinning [the use of the comparison type *similitudo*] is the virtue of bringing the object before our eyes not only plainly but also concisely and rapidly." Myers later comments (51) that in the case of John, "by incorporating celebrated events and persons from Scripture to contextualize Jesus, the evangelist effectively sets Jesus into a visual context connecting him to Scripture and contributing to his larger characterization."

55. David C. Rubin, *Memory in Oral Traditions: The Cognitive Psychology of Epic, Ballads, and Counting-Out Rhymes* (Oxford: Oxford University Press, 1995), 40.

deal of experience and tradition needing to be recalled into a single, manageable likeness or framework.[56] As Roger Shepard has noted, "Mental imagery is remarkably able to substitute for actual perception.... Possibly, rules governing spatial structures and transformation, having been incorporated into our perceptual machinery by eons of evolution in a three-dimensional world, are now at the service of creative thought."[57]

John's *semeia* ("signs"), discourses, and passion and resurrection scenes conjure up arresting visual images: a wedding banquet with six ritually pure, stone water pots (John 2:1–11); a pool with five porticoes surrounded by the ailing and impotent (John 5:1–3); a vivid discourse on sheep (John 10:1–20); and so forth. Carruthers and Ziolkowski suggest that such "schematic images were often referred to [in medieval accounts] as 'pictures' (*picturae*), and were said to be 'painted' in one's mind as a requirement of composition."[58]

John Harvey's recently published monograph, *The Bible as Visual Culture: When the Text Becomes Image*, investigates the phenomenon that results when the biblical text "is converted into visual culture, and how biblical images act and mediate meaning."[59] Harvey notes that the Scriptures, which were designed "to be read imaginatively," employ

> figurative language and picturesque descriptions of characters, scenes, places, and things on earth and in heaven [that] make the ineffable tangible and the mundane memorable, and also summon vivid mental

---

56. Carol Harrison, *The Art of Listening in the Early Church* (Oxford: Oxford University Press, 2013), 62, draws attention to the fact that the "idea that images were imprinted upon the mind or memory as mental pictures (Greek: *phantasmata, eikon*; Latin: *imago, simulacrum*), in the same way as a seal makes an impression upon wax, was the most common means of describing the way in which the mind either learnt something new or became aware of, and stored within itself, any sensation brought to it by the five senses of the body." Margaret E. Lee and Bernard B. Scott, *Sound Mapping the New Testament* (Salem, OR: Polebridge, 2009), 63, confirm that "treatises on memory in antiquity from Plato and Aristotle through Cicero, *Rhetorica ad Herennium*, and Quintilian universally envision the recording of sensory experience on the mind as the impression a seal makes on wax."
57. Cited by Rubin, *Memory*, 39.
58. Carruthers and Ziolkowski, *Medieval Craft*, 6.
59. John Harvey, *The Bible As Visual Culture: When Text Becomes Image*, BIMW 57 (Sheffield: Sheffield Phoenix, 2013), 7.

images, to which artists and artificers have given fixity and plasticity. In this sense, the Bible is a site of visuality.⁶⁰

Intended for oral reading by a lector,⁶¹ texts such as John were transmuted in the imagination of the first audiences from the medium of sound to internal vision. In this vein, Carruthers suggests that "whatever enters the mind changes into a 'see-able' form for storing in the memory.... Material presented acoustically is turned into visual form so frequently and persistently, even when the subject is sound itself, that the phenomenon amounts to a recognizable trope."⁶² Alan Bruford and Natalya Todd likewise note the "multi-sensory process" resulting from the "co-operation of the 'mind's eye' with the 'mind's ear.'"⁶³

Along these lines, the treatments of such techniques as *ekphrasis* ("vivid description"), *exempla* ("examples"), and *paradeigmata* ("examples" or "paradigms"), found in ancient rhetorical handbooks and *progymnasmata* (school exercises), call for further investigation into how these devices might illuminate John's mnemonic craft. For instance, the sophist Aelius Theon explains that *ekphrasis* involves portraying entities such as "places," "times," and "objects" (*Prog.* 115 [Kennedy]) in such a way as to achieve heightened "clarity and a vivid impression of all-but-seeing what is described" (*Prog.* 119 [Kennedy]).⁶⁴

---

60. Ibid., 1. See also Myers, *Characterizing Jesus*, 94.

61. See William A. Graham, *Beyond the Written Word: Oral Aspects of Scripture in the History of Religion* (Cambridge: Cambridge University Press, 1987); Jeffrey E. Brickle, "Seeing, Hearing, Declaring, Writing: Media Dynamics in the Letters of John," in *The Fourth Gospel in First-Century Media Culture*, ed. Anthony Le Donne and Tom Thatcher, ESCO, LNTS 426 (London: T&T Clark, 2011), 11–28; Brickle, *Aural Design and Coherence in the Prologue of First John* (ESCO; LNTS 465; London: T&T Clark, 2012); Brickle, "Transacting Virtue within a Disrupted Community: The Negotiation of Ethics in the First Epistle of John," in *Rethinking the Ethics of John: "Implicit Ethics" in the Johannine Writings*, ed. Jan G. van Der Watt and Ruben Zimmermann, WUNT 291, KNNE 3 (Tübingen: Mohr Siebeck, 2012), 340–49; and Bruce G. Schuchard, *1–3 John*, ConcC (St. Louis: Concordia, 2012), 23–33.

62. Carruthers, *Book of Memory*, 20. For the relationship between orality, textuality, performance, and memory, see Richard Horsley and Tom Thatcher, *John, Jesus, and the Renewal of Israel* (Grand Rapids: Eerdmans, 2013), 74–95.

63. Alan Bruford and Natalya Todd, "The Eye behind the Mouth: The Contribution of Visual Memory to Oral Storytelling," in *Orality, Literacy, and Modern Media*, ed. Dietrich Scheunemann (Columbia, SC: Camden House, 1996), 7–14.

64. Cicero (*De or.* 3.53.202 [Rackham, LCL]) notes that "a great impression is

While John is certainly capable of employing elements of vivid description to assist the imagination in cases where his audience might be unfamiliar with a particular setting (e.g., Jerusalem's porticoed pool of Bethesda, John 5:1–3), he seems to prefer to leverage memory's potency in accord with Cicero's valuation of "distinct and concise brevity" and the notion that "more is to be understood than you have expressed" (*De or.* 3.53.202 [Rackham, LCL]).[65] John relies on his audience's recall of Old Testament events, often providing just enough detail to jog their memory (e.g., John 4:5–6). The mere imagery of the Logos having "tabernacled" (ἐσκήνωσεν, John 1:14) evokes rich associations, for example, especially since extended depictions of Israel's tabernacle and its functions presumably resided deep within the audience's conceptual storehouse, helping them immediately appreciate such profound, symbolic linkage.

It is also possible to "view" John's account and the grand epic narrative he evokes—the Old Testament—not only as a *series* of images but each as a *single* image captured in essentially a solitary glance. Alex Purves, in her *Space and Time in Ancient Greek Narrative*, notes that George Puttenham described Homer's poetic craft as "the practice of making, marking, planning, and measuring out an object or place"—in short, characterizing the poet as "a perfect surveyor."[66] Purves goes on to affirm Puttenham's perspective because it suggests that the *Iliad*'s reader might envisage its epic drama from the lofty viewpoint of the Muses "as a kind of literary landscape that we might survey in our mind's eye, as if it were a vista"[67] or as a "perfectly shaped and viewable plot."[68] Clay notes that traditional

---

made by dwelling on a single point, and also by clear explanation and almost visual presentation of events *as if practically going on*" (emphasis added). The anonymous author of *Rhet. Her.* (Cicero, *Rhet. Her.* 4.55.68 [Caplan, LCL]) defines the related "Ocular Demonstration" as "when an event is so described in words that the business seems to be enacted and the subject to pass vividly before our eyes." Quintilian (*Inst.* 8.3.61 [Butler, LCL]) likewise cites the power of "vivid illustration, or, as some prefer to call it, representation, [as] something more than mere clearness, since the latter merely lets itself be seen, whereas the former *thrusts itself upon our notice*" (emphasis added).

65. *Rhet. Her.* (Cicero, *Rhet. Her.* 4.54.68 [Caplan, LCL]) adds that "conciseness expresses a multitude of things within the limits of but a few words, and is therefore to be used often, either when the facts do not require a long discourse or when time will not permit dwelling upon them."

66. Purves, *Space and Time*, 1.
67. Ibid.
68. Ibid., 6.

storytellers often characterize the strikingly vivid manner in which they envision their narrative in nearly eidetic terms, as though they viewed the entire story as a complete whole.[69]

We might surmise that John similarly envisioned the span of his literary work from the elevated perspective of the Logos[70] (John 1:1), who came from above (John 8:23) and "is above all" (ἐπάνω πάντων ἐστίν, John 3:31). And, in evoking the transcendent perspective of the original creation account in his prologue (John 1:1), he likewise may have viewed the entire Old Testament landscape more or less as a single cartographic or maplike image.[71] In this regard, it is interesting to consider that each evangelist evidently selected a single image with which to exemplify or embody his version of the gospel account:[72] Matthew (1:1), a "book" (βίβλος); Mark (1:1), a "gospel" (εὐαγγέλιον); and Luke (1:1), a "narrative" (διήγησις) or "account" (λόγος, with Acts 1:1 referring to Luke's previous account; note also the double occurrence of λόγος in Luke 1:2, 4). In framing his account, John seems to have incorporated in various ways the images employed by his predecessors, Matthew (βίβλια, John 21:25) and Luke (λόγος, John 1:1), images which themselves trigger rich Old Testament associations.[73]

---

69. Clay, *Trojan Theater*, 26–27. In terms of how lengthy texts can be shrunk down in the mind to a manageable single image, Carruthers, "Mechanisms," 14, explains that if "the 'places' of memory are thought of as 'little rooms' or 'seats' in a scheme, then the dimensions of each 'place' is a single *conspectus* or inner gaze." The shortness of such a division is tantamount to the "length that 'the mind's eye' can take in during a single glance or gaze of a memory place."

70. Note also the chapter titled, "In the Beginning Were the Words: The Apotheosis and Narrative Displacement of the Logos," in Werner H. Kelber, *Imprints, Voiceprints, and Footprints of Memory: Collected Essays of Werner H. Kelber*, SBLRBS 74 (Atlanta: Society of Biblical Literature, 2013), 75–101.

71. Carruthers, "Mechanisms," 3, points out that "in order to develop the memory into a powerful engine of invention, it was conceived of in spatial and locational terms like a kind of map, with its places and routes plainly marked." This approach to remembering was not uncommon, given that "the rules for making, filing, and organizing such spaces were taught as a basic aspect of the crafting of one's memory in the schools of antiquity and the Middle Ages."

72. That Augustine thought in these terms is noted by Francis Watson, *Gospel Writing: A Canonical Perspective* (Grand Rapids: Eerdmans, 2013), 26, who observes that in "applying the image of the eagle to John rather than to Mark, Augustine has used the traditional symbolism as he says it should be used: to characterize an entire gospel in its differentiation from the others."

73. See also Richard Bauckham, "John for Readers of Mark," in *The Gospels for All*

6.6. A Mnemonic Journey

The recent monograph by Hanne Bewernick, titled *The Storyteller's Memory Palace*,[74] is rich with insights on applying ancient mnemonic theory to narrative texts. Bewernick draws an important connection between storytelling and memory, namely, that both "arrange images in an ordered structure."[75] For Bewernick,

> by visualising the imaginary landscape contained within the words of a text, the reader gains more direct access to the underlying ideas of a story.... The narrative is placed in space and time in some form of architectural framework or landscape, a type of memory palace the author sees in his mind's eye.... The author's memory processes are embedded in the story's structure and in the visual aspects of the language; for example, in the use of location, backgrounds, images and in the sequences of events. By looking out for these building bricks in the text, readers can attempt to rebuild and enter the memory palace which the author has used as his blueprint for the story.[76]

Significantly, Bewernick lays out a helpful approach in which she applies mnemonic arts to medieval and modern literature (though her approach is equally relevant to the analysis of ancient literature) in four steps, beginning with (1) gaining an understanding of the general concept behind the memory arts, (2) determining the particular type of background, (3) noting the structural connection of backgrounds, and (4) identifying the meaning or significance of the images.[77]

Among the various mnemonic methodologies she surveys, ranging from the alphabetic and numeric systems to memory mapping and memory building, the journey method inferred by Quintilian is, in my estimation, very suitable to Jesus's peregrinations in John in relation to John's use of the Old Testament. The metaphor of a mnemonic journey, therefore, which capitalizes on space *and* time, offers another convenient lens for exploring

---

Christians: Rethinking the Gospel Audiences, ed. Richard Bauckham (Grand Rapids: Eerdmans, 1998), 147–71.

74. Hanne Bewernick, *The Storyteller's Memory Palace*, EUS, ASLL 14 (Frankfurt: Lang, 2010).
75. Ibid., 9.
76. Ibid., 10.
77. Ibid., 15, 17–46.

John's appropriation of the Old Testament[78]—and comports with ancient Judaism's pilgrimaging proclivity.[79] As Bewernick notes, the journey method is advantageous in that it is not limited by the confinement associated with the "enclosed space" or "tangible barriers" of memory buildings.[80] Purves characterizes this nonstatic, nonmaplike memory discourse in which the storyteller walks through time, as "countercartographic."[81] We might suggest that John, as Jaś Elsner has argued for Pausanias's literary tour of Greece, "turned the landscape of Greece [or in our case, Palestine] into a rhetorical discourse."[82]

Bewernick observes that in some cases ancient theorists extended the journey method to envision the "entire world."[83] Interestingly, while Jesus transverses the typography of ancient Israel, John seems to decentralize and desacralize traditional sacred space, refocusing and panning from Palestine and its ideological, geopolitical center (the temple at Jerusalem—which Gregory Beale notes was considered "a microcosm of the entire heaven and earth"[84]) to universal and cosmic space in which Jesus embodies God's presence (John 1:14), connects heaven and earth (John 1:51), and the temple is "destroyed" (John 2:19); worship is no longer "confined"

---

78. For a related analysis of Luke, see Charles H. H. Scobie, "A Canonical Approach to Interpreting Luke: The Journey Motif as a Hermeneutical Key," in *Reading Luke: Interpretation, Reflection, Formation*, ed. Craig G. Bartholomew, Joel B. Green, and Anthony C. Thiselton, SHS 3 (Grand Rapids: Zondervan, 2005), 327–49.

79. See the chapter titled, "Sacred Space: The Land and Pilgrimage," in Jacob Neusner, *Judaism When Christianity Began: A Survey of Belief and Practice* (Louisville: Westminster John Knox, 2002), 135–46.

80. Bewernick, *Memory Palace*, 32.

81. Purves, *Space and Time*, 2.

82. Jaś Elsner, "Structuring 'Greece': Pausanias's *Periegesis* As a Literary Construct," in *Pausanias: Travel and Memory in Roman Greece*, ed. Susan E. Alcock, John F. Cherry, and Jaś Elsner (Oxford: Oxford University Press, 2001), 18. For a study treating the application of a "powerful place-oriented rhetoric" to one ancient city, see Christine Shepardson, *Controlling Contested Places: Late Antique Antioch and the Spacial Politics of Religious Controversy* (Berkeley: University of California Press, 2014), 3, who notes that "physically controlling the appearance and use of places and rhetorically shaping perceptions of them were significant, though as yet largely unrecognized, means through which ancient leaders negotiated the complex power struggles of their times."

83. Bewernick, *Memory Palace*, 31.

84. Gregory K. Beale, *The Temple and the Church's Mission: A Biblical Theology of the Dwelling Place of God*, NSBT 17 (Downers Grove, IL: InterVarsity Press, 2004), 31.

to Jerusalem and Gerizim (John 4:20–24); Greeks, presumably from the Diaspora, seek an audience with Jesus (John 12:20); the παράκλητος will dwell within the disciples (John 14:15–17);[85] and the entire world seemingly cannot contain the written remembrances of Jesus's acts (John 21:25).

6.7. A Film or Motion Picture

This final metaphor in many ways brings us back full circle to a memory theater, for as a multimedia phenomenon it capitalizes on the senses of sight and sound. Perhaps the most vivid manifestation of interior visualization is that of a "film" viewed from the perspective of the mind's eye. In this paradigm, John "sees" the events he narrates enfolding before his eyes as a motion picture, and expects that his listening audience will do the same, both in terms of envisioning his own story and in a simultaneous replaying of the Old Testament—perhaps as a type of theatrical trailer—viewed in a memory theater of the mind. Bruford and Todd cite one traditional storyteller who describes his understanding of his craft as visualizing a film, sometimes in color, playing out in his mind, which, "once started, is propelled by its own momentum, [with] one sequence necessarily lead[ing] to another."[86] This phenomenon does not simply reflect a series of bullet points, topics, or literarily oriented structural devices, but may be envisioned as an interior matinee or IMAX theater. More radical still, those who have experienced the graphic realism of holographic projection might compare that state-of-the-art technology to the capacity of the brain to virtually replay reality in a manner that is astoundingly realistic.

7. Signing Off with *Mnemosyne*

In drawing together these various metaphors, I wish to suggest, therefore, that John's Gospel, with its uncluttered yet vivid scenes featuring sparse but striking images and characters, lends itself well to an analysis from the standpoint of the arts of memory. As an artisan skilled in mnemonic craft John arguably employed the Jewish Scriptures as the primary locus,

---

85. Whereas the temple was an inanimate and stationary structure, the disciples were living beings with feet and voices with which to convey Christ's presence and message across the earth.

86. Bruford and Todd, "Eye Behind the Mouth," 9.

backdrop, or frame[87] on which to place the *loci* and images of his mnemonic journey through the events surrounding Jesus's *semeia*, passion, and resurrection.

In his first four chapters alone, for example, John ranges across a remembered Old Testament landscape that is simply staggering in scope. He summons readers steeped in the texts of Judaism to imaginatively revisit the Torah or "the law given through Moses," all the while staging and airing vibrant images and "audio clips" of deeds and speech acts of Jesus—through whom, on the other hand, "grace and truth" came (John 1:17). John calls to mind such conceptual backdrops as the creation of the cosmos (Gen 1:1–2:3; John 1:1–5), the nuptial union of Adam and Eve (Gen 2:21–25; John 2:1–11), and the celebration of the Passover lamb (Exod 12:1–28; John 1:29), along with various patriarchal and wilderness episodes, including Jacob's divine encounter at Bethel (Gen 28:10–22; John 1:51), the bronze serpent incident (Num 21:4–9; John 3:14), and rendezvous at wells leading to betrothal (Gen 24:1–67; 29:1–39; Exod 2:15–21; John 4:6–7). The implications alone of the portrayal of the Logos (John 1:1–14) juxtaposed against the backdrop of ancient Near Eastern cosmology are astounding in their hermeneutical significance.[88]

Journeying through the text in this highly suggestive fashion—paying close attention to the narrative's sequencing of "rooms" or spaces in relationship to the Old Testament's—helps us see how John has conceptually arranged the lower and upper floors (corresponding to the Old Testament and his Gospel, respectively) of his two-level memory "palace." We should thus envision the Gospel of John not merely as a story here and there evoking critical connections to Old Testament texts, but rather as a story embarking on a virtual tour of an all-encompassing, masterfully designed mnemonic edifice. Along with applying Bewernick's methodology to John

---

87. For the use of conceptual frame theory, see Alan Kirk, "Social and Cultural Memory," in *Memory, Tradition, and Text: Uses of the Past in Early Christianity*, ed. Alan Kirk and Tom Thatcher, SemeiaSt 52 (Atlanta: Society of Biblical Literature, 2005), 1–24; and Yoon-Man Park, *Mark's Memory Resources and the Controversy Stories (Mark 2:1–3:6): An Application of the Frame Theory of Cognitive Science to the Markan Oral-Aural Narrative*, LBS 2 (Leiden: Brill, 2010).

88. For relevant research on ancient Near Eastern cosmology, see the illuminating work of John H. Walton, including his *Genesis One as Ancient Cosmology* (Winona Lake, IN: Eisenbrauns, 2011), along with his more popular-level *The Lost World of Genesis One: Ancient Cosmology and the Origins Debate* (Downers Grove, IL: InterVarsity Press, 2009).

in a thoroughgoing way (see above), more work remains to chart the overlaying of John's narrative over the Old Testament and then to explore the full interpretive possibilities resulting from the linear correlations between the texts.

The overall approach to John's Gospel I am advocating here clearly challenges modern print-culture assumptions by paying focused attention to the forms and functions of the tools of ancient media culture—a point well-argued in Werner Kelber's classic work, *The Oral and the Written Gospel: The Hermeneutics of Speaking and Writing in the Synoptic Tradition, Mark, Paul, and Q*,[89] along with a collection of his essays titled *Imprints, Voiceprints, and Footprints of Memory*. In the essay "The Works of Memory: Christian Origins as Mnemohistory," Kelber cautions that "we can no longer ignore oral and memorial culture in favor of textual hermeneutics."[90] Concerning the legend of *Mnemosyne*, Greek goddess of remembrance, he writes: "As mother of the Muses, Mnemosyne was the origin of all artistic and scientific labors and the wellspring of civilization. From the perspective of myth, it was not scribality or literary exegesis, not logic or rhetoric even, that was perceived to be the central, civilizing agency, but memory."[91]

Ultimately, whatever particular memory model(s) we might adopt, modify, or reject as we reflect on the way the ancient mnemonist John relates his account of Jesus via the employment of memory arts, the role *memoria* arguably played invites us to rethink his storytelling mode from the ground up—away from a modern outline-oriented organization to one acclimated to oral performance and interior mnemonic mapping and visualization, and hence significantly more dynamic and multi-

---

89. Werner H. Kelber, *The Oral and the Written Gospel: The Hermeneutics of Speaking and Writing in the Synoptic Tradition, Mark, Paul, and Q* (Philadelphia: Fortress, 1983).

90. Kelber, *Imprints*, 265.

91. Ibid., 267. Regarding the Muses, Rosalind Thomas, *Literacy and Orality in Ancient Greece*, KTAH (Cambridge: Cambridge University Press, 1992), 116, notes that it "is the Muses, as goddesses, who know and are present, while the humans know nothing without their help. They seem to be guardians of the facts, the details difficult to remember. The elaborate invocation at the beginning of this most difficult of lists [in Homer's *Iliad* book 2] suggests strongly that the poet calls on them to help his memory, and invokes them as guardians or guarantors of those details of the past which mere mortals could not know if it were not for memory and poetry. The Muses are often invoked before a particularly difficult passage or catalogue."

dimensional in its engagement with an interwoven tapestry of texts in conversation. John evidently stretched the Roman architectural memory model—at least as we know of it from extant sources—to its limits. While *Mnemosyne* held considerable sway in the Hellenized world, John's own mnemonic skills—with perhaps no little assistance from the παράκλητος (John 16:4; 14:26)—permitted him to set in motion his own sophisticated form of sympathetic resonance.

Conclusion

Bruce G. Schuchard

This collection of essays provides an overview of past and present research on the use of Scripture in the Gospel of John, making it useful for those who have an interest in this kind of study as well as for those whose focus is more generally the use of Scripture in the entire New Testament. It will also be of use to those whose interest is in sociological, rhetorical, and memory theory studies and the New Testament. Though not intended primarily for the latter, this volume has the potential to be used in classes exploring any of these areas of study as well.

Several recent monographs have been published on John's use of Scripture and on areas related to it. More are sure to come. The list of those recently completed includes the revised dissertations of three of the contributing authors to the present volume. Five additional experts in the field have also contributed essays. Their work provides an update on the status of this study, offering a much-needed description and evaluation of approaches past and present that highlights especially the latest developments in the state of the research that still is being done. The combination of this variety of approaches and perspectives into a single volume on John's use of Scripture makes the present volume important both for those acquainted with the field and for those just entering into their own research into these and related matters. An up-to-date summary of the research that predates this book situates the current efforts of those who continue to pursue it in the state of the question. A diversity of contributors gives voice to a variety of present-day approaches within the context of more established perspectives. A mix of methodological approaches makes the present volume significant both for those generally engaged in the study of the use of Scripture in the New Testament and for those whose more specific focus is the Gospel of John. The present volume purposefully highlights particular examples of present approaches that have been and still are on the rise, especially rhetorical theories (both classical and contemporary) and memory and performance theories, and advances several different possible applications for the greater study of the New Testament's use of Scripture.

The persistence of the steady stream of publications on this volume's topic speaks to its continuing importance. And yet, no recent collection of essays on the subject has brought together the work of a variety of scholars so as to exemplify what has been and still is being done. Thus the present volume constitutes a uniquely valuable and hopefully stimulating resource for study, since it brings together a representative mix of perspectives in the context of both past and present research. It deliberately continues the conversation on John's use of Scripture, offering both studies that highlight and perpetuate several of the approaches discussed above as well as others that suggest possibilities yet to be explored. A first chapter situates its reader in the conversation that has gone on and still goes on surrounding John's use of Scripture. Those that follow are grouped into three sections that highlight at least three promising areas for continuing research.

1. The Source(s) and Form of John's References to Scripture

Great variety of scholarly opinion continues to describe the study of the source(s) and form of John's references to Scripture, causing some actually to question the value of the continuing pursuit of such questions. How many sources are there? Is it one? Are there several? Are they Greek or Hebrew sources, or both? Are targumic traditions somehow influential? Do excerpts from the Dead Sea Scrolls shed light in any way? Did any other contemporaneous traditions, some known, some quite possibly not yet known to us, have a part to play? Which, if any, of these proposed influences is dominant? Or is the varied influence of a pluriformity of traditions more likely? That more than one tradition of the Hebrew Bible existed in the Gospel's day for it to recall is now clear. But if a regular hearer of the Gospel's story was in no way likely to have been familiar with the Hebrew texts of Scripture, how likely or helpful would recourse to such texts in the construction of the Gospel's narrative have been? How many knew Aramaic? How dominant was Greek? What are the implications of these and other questions? Which ongoing or perhaps even new research directions does the variety and relatedness of such considerations commend?

Though its results are frequently diverse and too often at odds with each others, the source-, form-, and redaction-critical study of the Gospel continues. While some continue to posit the Gospel's possible use of *testimonia*, others instead see in its references to Scripture evidence for the close and careful crafting of tradition to fit the theological perspective of its author and his community. Where some see prooftexting with little regard for the original context of a citation, others see regular and significant attention being paid to and even a consistent invoking of the greater literary and historical context from which a citation comes. Few agree on the precise definition of a "citation." So little consensus exists regarding the actual number of these to be found in John. Where one finds allusions and/or echoes/intertexts and what one is to make of these continues to be an ongoing source of debate.

Therefore, those engaged in such study of the Gospel dispute still, sometimes rather vociferously, the precise frequency and nature of its references to Scripture, how they are made and incorporated into their eventual and surrounding contexts, as well as and perhaps especially the possible implications of their incorporation. Still, such study remains important and in fact has succeeded in establishing at least a few basic areas of significant agreement. It also continues to suggest areas of ongoing study both old and new where the greatest current potential for important additional discoveries exists, holding out the very real promise of even greater future agreement. For example, most today readily acknowledge that John's references, if not consistently, at least regularly rely on its day's established and available Greek texts of Scripture. Especially John's explicit citations consistently exhibit a traceable reliance on such texts. Generally emphasizing the Fourth Gospel's regular use of the Greek, most likewise typically also cite Jewish interpretive practices as that which first informs the evangelist's own manner of intentionally drawing on and adapting his references to their new literary and theological contexts. Appreciation for the fact that John, like all other ancient texts of its kind, is quite intentionally written in relationship to such previously existing texts and, as such, reverberates with both conscious and unconscious, direct and indirect echoes of the same has encouraged many to explore with renewed interest the relationship between John's references to Scripture and the larger contexts from which they come. Rather than seeing John's manner of employing Scripture as little more than mere prooftexting, more and more find support in the evidence for the Gospel's awareness of the contexts from which its references to Scripture come, suggesting that there is in John considerable additional depth to its incorporation of Israel's sacred story into its own that is yet to be mined for all its worth.

Thus the present-day study of the Fourth Gospel's use of Scripture has exhibited a markedly increasing appreciation for both the final form of the Gospel and the depth of its literary and theological sophistication in making intentional changes to its Scripture references for the purpose of highlighting certain unique and profound aspects of its theology, especially its Christology. The Gospel evinces the understandable influence of traditions that are both Second Temple Jewish (the evangelist was a Jew, and many but not all of the first hearers of the Gospel were Jewish Christians) and Greco-Roman (the evangelist composed the Gospel first for Greek-speaking Christians living in the Greco-Roman world). Therefore, its interpretive techniques and rhetorical strategies are similarly both Jewish and Greco-Roman. At the same time, its decidedly and distinctively Christocentric hermeneutic sets it apart, so that comparisons with, for example, the exegetical techniques in evidence at Qumran are of only limited value.

Steadily rising appreciation for the contribution of the Gospel's discerning and effective citation style to the equally impressive design of its significantly stylized narrative has prompted more than a few to observe that many of John's citations share certain distinguishing features. Some citations are introduced with the same or similar citation formulas. Some come from the same Old Testament book. Some come from the same character(s) in the telling of the Gospel's story. Such commonalities quite possibly suggest that citations sharing them should be interpreted in light of each other and may well form an informing contextual matrix for understanding their roles individually and collectively in the Gospel's greater design. Such possibilities often also promote the suggestion of an alternative understanding of the Gospel's greater form, informed by the conspicuously frequent use of *inclusios* and other related and established literary and rhetorical devices of the period. Such considerations carry possible profound implications for the Gospel's interpretation and have prompted others not only to a reconsideration of the well-worn question of the Gospel's reliability but also to a new understanding of the evangelist and his community's self-understanding in the production and dissemination of the last of the canonical Gospels. The greater the suggestion of the Gospel's preference for references to established texts of Scripture that in its day were available in Greek, the greater is the possible alignment of the evangelist and his community with the earliest church and to its circumstance, including its significant, initial, and fairly long-standing first preference for a Greek form of the Scriptures, both Old and New. Such possibilities also prompt a variety of related considerations, all of them important to an understanding of the identity of the evangelist and his contemporaries, their circumstance, and their self-understanding over against others in response to forces internal and external, positive and negative.

Building on these and related conclusions, interpreters continue to seek to understand especially the unique aspects of the theology of the Gospel, especially its christological emphases, as well as its wider implications. The Gospel evinces a hermeneutic that is unequivocally Christocentric and cruciform. Its Scripture quotations and allusions, its echoes and/or intertexts, therefore consistently appear in support of the Gospel's presentation of not just the person but also the work of Jesus as the Christ, the Son of God (20:30–31), chiefly the work of his suffering for all and for our salvation, with the goal of convincing the hearer to believe and have life in his name.

These and other developments have stimulated the opening of a welcome number of fresh and promising avenues for continued reflection on the nature and significance of the employment of Scripture in John, encouraging investigative and interpretive possibilities that heretofore have remained largely unconsidered and unexplored, and taking seriously the full range of implications that naturally emerge from the vigorous study of the incorporation of Scripture into the narrative of the Gospel. A variety of innovative interpretive approaches have surfaced, particularly those seeking to discover how texts that were intentionally constructed to be spoken out loud were consciously devised in the hope that they would be heard with appreciation and taken to heart by ancient audiences. Increasing interest in what the form of John's references to Scripture can reveal about their Gospel function and continued research into these and other areas are pushing our understanding of John's use of Scripture in new and promising directions, sometimes down avenues rather divergent from those that previously led to certain widely accepted conclusions. Of these, two more recent approaches especially have given rise already to particularly promising results. One has sought an understanding of the function of John's references to Scripture through the application of sociological and/or rhetorical methodologies. Another has done so from the standpoint of memory theory and performance theory.

2. Social and/or Rhetorical Perspectives in the Study of John

While the earlier study of the source(s) and form of John's references to Scripture and their incorporation into the Gospel's narrative previously served well to shed needed light on the Gospel's theological interest in its employment of Scripture, generally such study offered little, if any, insight into the possible literary and/or sociological or rhetorical functions of its references to Scripture. More recently, however, the study of these and other promising ongoing considerations has pursued increasingly and with profit the investigation of a variety of ancient and modern literary, sociological, and rhetorical models and strategies for categories to understand not only John's use of Scripture but also the use of Scripture in the rest of the New Testament writings. The upshot has been an ever-increasing understanding of and appreciation for the deliberate and effective impact of John's artful literary and rhetorical employment of Scripture on the construction and maintenance of the social identity of persons living both inside and outside the communities where the Gospel was revered and passed on. Scripture served for each of these communities as an unquestioned authority, shaping and informing the self-understanding of each in response to forces from within and without. Mindful of this, scholars representing an important mix of methodological pursuits informed by ancient and modern literary, sociological, and rhetorical theory while still paying regular attention to ancient Jewish practices of biblical interpretation have successfully advanced a helpful combination of approaches for understanding John's use of Scripture that, going forward, promises to lead to ever greater and more meaningful discovery.

As an example, insight into ancient and modern strategies for the employment of these and other techniques has contributed importantly to a better understanding of what John's use of Scripture contributes to characterization in John. In order to bolster or perhaps alternatively to undermine a character's credibility in the telling of its story, the Gospel creates through its employment of Scripture a *synkrisis* between a character in John and one from Israel's past who was either famous or infamous. In this way, the fate of one of the Gospel's characters is blended with that of one from Israel's past to advance the suggestion that the person and work of Jesus and those allied with him lie at the center of the sacred history of the Lord's salvific dealings with those whom he counts as his own. As an authority revered and unquestioned, Scripture employed in this way thus works to make both pleasing and compelling the Gospel's deliberately constructed rhetoric for persuading its audience to embrace and never depart from its understanding of Jesus. Bolstering Jesus's credibility and that of those with whom he is most closely allied, such strategies enhance the Gospel's suggestion of the summing significance of John's own story. By means of a variety of such *synkristic* associations John makes credible not only its depiction of Jesus but also its depiction of its narrator, who himself provides through his telling of the Gospel's story and its employment of Scripture the very testimony that must be heard if any are to believe in Jesus and have life in his name.

Employing a lively mix of impressive and distinguishing literary and rhetorical strategies, the Fourth Gospel sets the stage for its audience's desired acceptance of its exceptional claims. Furthering also his own necessarily prominent status at the center of Scripture's sacred story, the evangelist employs a theologically astute combination of literary and rhetorical strategies by which these and their devices (deliberate ambiguity, incongruity, double entendre, misunderstanding, irony, and the like, all these deliberately promoting ever deeper levels of purposeful meaning) effectively serve to invite the Gospel's audience to a first concealed now revealed understanding of Jesus's previously perplexing and seemingly divergent words and deeds. From a postresurrection perspective with full Spirit-wrought appreciation for the sole sufficiency of the words from and about Jesus that must be heard if any are to comprehend him, take him to heart, and believe in him, the Gospel invites its hearers to have life in his name.

The ongoing study of the Gospel coincides with the recent, greater use of literary and rhetorical strategies both ancient and modern to analyze the design of the rest of the New Testament, especially its discourse-like material elsewhere. The frequency and depth of the extended discourses of Jesus in John make the Gospel a natural for the similar and fruitful pursuit of such study. A genuine mix of both ancient Jewish and Greco-Roman ways of thinking and conventionalized strategies for advancing an argument was doubtless present in the Gospel's milieu. Thus the more recent study of the Fourth Gospel holds out great promise for providing ever greater insight into the Gospel's own reasons for its employment of Scripture. All such study continues to provide an abundance of suggestive examples of how one might quote and/or allude effectively to revered traditions in ways that would have been especially memorable so as to pursue the greatest possible potential for persuasion.

3. Memory and Scripture in John

A final area of recent and fruitful research into John's use of Scripture has surfaced with mounting interest in the study of memory and performance theory. Drawing on insights from the field of memory theory and its subdisciplines in an effort to explore how the Gospel's shaping of scriptural subtexts promotes the personal participation of its hearers in the claims of the Gospel, research into John has attempted to improve our understanding of how John uses Israel's Scripture as a principal source from which it constructs its memory images for its anticipated hearers.

In the footsteps of those who previously have argued for the Gospel's careful crafting through the frequent utilization of well-known Greco-Roman mnemotechniques, the more recent study of the Gospel has sought a greater understanding of the evangelist's multifaceted role as ancient social memorian and practitioner of memory arts. Focusing on the way the Gospel impressively superimposes its own remembrance of Jesus on the revered landscape of Israel's ancestral past, the latest study of the Gospel has paid particular attention to John's portrait of Jesus as this relates to the deeply rooted underlying subtext that was Israel's collective memory of itself. Such study of the Gospel has therefore examined with profit the ways John prompts the remembrance of noteworthy figures and defining events from Israel's past. Drawing on social memory theory and social identity theory, it has investigated the Gospel's reconfiguration in its narrative of Israel's own remembrance of such figures and events. Attending to a variety of mnemonic strategies, it has sought a better understanding of how the Gospel's christological conviction and its possible conflict with others influenced the shaping of its references to Scripture as witness to Jesus or as prototype of the communal identity of its hearers. It has helped to identify the Gospel's rhetorical strategies for claiming, establishing, and maintaining the significance of its recollection of Scripture in the self-understanding of its hearers. It has pondered whether or not a better understanding of the Gospel's milieu and its demonstrable preference for orality helps at all to inform the manner with which the Gospel has incorporated the fabled persons and seminal events of Israel's past into John's rhetorical strategy for persuasively advancing its own story of the person and work of Jesus.

Focusing on the experience of "sympathetic resonance" as a helpful way to describe the rich interaction of cherished traditions that the Gospel achieves through its dynamic superimposition of them, the recent study of John's use of Scripture has improved our understanding of the nature of its memorial aims over against Israel's Scripture. The ongoing study of the employment of Scripture in John continues to shed light on John the mnemonist's manner of artfully crafting the telling of his story.

Not surprisingly, such study has posited importantly that the backdrop of Israel's Scripture served as the Gospel's primary locus on which it placed its memory images. Drawing on the insight of theorists pursuing the study of a helpful assortment of related subdisciplines, the ongoing study of the Gospel promises to provide through the coordinated application of a diversity of research methodologies a welcome number of important additional means for improving our understanding of the sophisticated nature and function of John's use of Scripture.

4. The Study of John's Use of Scripture Going Forward

As is the case with so much of the rest of the New Testament, Scripture supplies and informs the very substructure from which John's narrative has been written. And yet, the Gospel has been accused also of being anti-Jewish on account of its manner of characterizing "the Jews." This seemingly contradictory state of affairs presents one who is new to the study of the Gospel with more than a few challenges. In an effort to clarify and to suggest some possible ways forward, the present volume offers both a review of the work that previously has been done in the study of John's use of Scripture and a snapshot of some of the most promising work that is happening now. Its collected essays showcase a number of current approaches to the study of the Gospel that have already produced important insights and are likely to suggest to future researchers additional profitable directions to consider as the work goes on in years to come.

The study of the nature and implications of John's use of Scripture is perhaps as vigorous now as it ever has been. Though the Gospel of John is frequently accused of being anti-Jewish, it is nevertheless also a gospel that celebrates Israel's Scripture as that which foundationally informs a necessary understanding of the person and work of Jesus as the Christ, the Son of God (20:30–31). Affirming just such a foundational and informing role for Scripture in John's Gospel, this volume's essays argue also for the deliberate crafting of the Gospel's frequent and artful references to Scripture in light of its late first-century context. They furthermore speak in favor of the Gospel's likely regular interest in the original greater contexts from which its references to Scripture come, and they explore the extent to which said contexts influence the rhetoric and the theology of the Gospel. They also give expression to an important variety of promising and productive perspectives, including those still investigating the source(s) and form of John's references to Scripture, its literary and rhetorical aims and techniques in its employment of Scripture and its likely sociological impact, and the role of memory and performance in the aesthetically engaging and purposefully persuasive interplay of Israel's story and its story.

In this way, it is hoped that the present collection of essays succeeds in its aim to inform its readers regarding the past and present study of the use of Scripture in the Gospel of John, encouraging others to the ongoing pursuit of these and still other perspectives yet to be identified let alone explored in the continuing study of John's use of Scripture. The evangelist of John's Gospel beloved by readers both ancient and modern claims that he is the last of the eyewitnesses. The church therefore received the testimony of the last of the canonical Gospels as abiding words with an abiding authority, as Scripture founded upon Scripture. If the Gospel's enduring popularity is any indication of the sociological success of the evangelist's literary and rhetorical effort in purposefully producing the most arresting theological engagement of the memory-scape of Scripture that he could, we may say with some confidence that his intention for his Gospel was in the end accomplished.

Bibliography

Abl, Martin C. *"And Scripture Cannot Be Broken": The Form and Function of the Early Christian Testimonia Collections*. NovTSup 96. Leiden: Brill, 1999.

Achtemeier, Elizabeth. *Nahum–Malachi*. IBC. Atlanta: John Knox, 1986.

Achtemeier, Paul J. "*Omne verbum sonat*: The New Testament and the Oral Environment of Late Western Antiquity." *JBL* 109 (1990): 3–27.

Ahn, Sanghee Michael. *The Christological Witness Function of the Old Testament Characters in the Gospel of John*. PBM. Colorado Springs, CO: Paternoster, 2014.

Alkier, Stefan. "Intertextuality and the Semiotics of Biblical Texts." Pages 3–22 in *Reading the Bible Intertextually*. Edited by Richard B. Hays, Stefan Alkier, and Leroy A. Huizenga. Waco, TX: Baylor University Press, 2008.

Allison, Dale C., Jr. *Constructing Jesus: Memory, Imagination, and History*. Grand Rapids: Baker Academic, 2010.

Anderson, Paul. "The Having-Sent-Me Father: Aspects of Agency, Encounter, and Irony in the Johannine Father-Son Relationship." *Semeia* 85 (1999): 33–57.

Anderson, Paul, Felix Just, and Tom Thatcher, eds. *Aspects of Historicity in the Fourth Gospel*. Volume 2 of *John, Jesus, and History*. ECIL 2. Atlanta: Society of Biblical Literature, 2009.

———. *Critical Appraisals of Critical Views*. Volume 1 of *John, Jesus, and History*. SBLSymS 44. Atlanta: Society of Biblical Literature, 2007.

Archer, Gleason L., and Gregory Chirichigno. *Old Testament Quotations in the New Testament*. Eugene, OR: Wipf & Stock, 2005.

Aristotle. *Art of Rhetoric*. Translated by J. H. Freese. LCL. Cambridge: Harvard University Press, 1926.

———. *Problems. Books 1–21*. Translated by W. S. Hett. LCL. Cambridge: Harvard University Press, 1936.

Ashley, Timothy R. *The Book of Numbers*. Grand Rapids: Eerdmans, 1993.

Ashton, John. *The Gospel of John and Christian Origins*. Minneapolis: Fortress, 2014.
Asiedu-Peprah, Martin. *Johannine Sabbath Conflicts as Juridical Controversy*. WUNT 2/132. Tübingen: Mohr Siebeck, 2001.
Assmann, Aleida. *Cultural Memory and Western Civilization: Functions, Media, Archives*. Cambridge: Cambridge University Press, 2011.
Assmann, Jan. "Collective Memory and Cultural Identity." *NGC* 65 (1995): 125-33.
———. *Cultural Memory and Early Civilization: Writing, Remembrance, and Political Imagination*. Cambridge: Cambridge University Press, 2011.
———. *Das kulturelle Gedächtnis: Schrift, Erinnerung und politische Identität in frühen Hochkulturen*. Munich: Beck, 1992.
Attridge, Harold W. "Argumentation in John 5." Pages 188-99 in *Rhetorical Argumentation in Biblical Texts: Essays from the Lund 2000 Conference*. Edited by Anders Eriksson, Thomas H. Olbricht, and Walter Übelacker. ESEC 8. Harrisburg, PA: Trinity Press International, 2002.
———. *Essays on John and Hebrews*. Tübingen: Mohr Siebeck, 2010.
Barmash, Pamela. *Homicide in the Biblical World*. Cambridge: Cambridge University Press, 2005.
Barrett, Charles Kingsley. *The Gospel according to John: An Introduction and Commentary with Notes on the Greek*. 2nd ed. Philadelphia: Westminster, 1978.
Bartholomew, Craig G. *Where Mortals Dwell: A Christian View of Place for Today*. Grand Rapids: Baker Academic, 2011.
Bartholomew, Craig G., and Michael W. Goheen. *The Drama of Scripture: Finding Our Place in the Biblical Story*. Grand Rapids: Baker Academic, 2004.
Bates, Matthew W. *The Hermeneutics of the Apostolic Proclamation: The Center of Paul's Method of Scriptural Interpretation*. Waco, TX: Baylor University Press, 2012.
Bauckham, Richard. "The Audience of the Fourth Gospel." Pages 101-12 in *Jesus in Johannine Tradition*. Edited by Robert T. Fortna and Tom Thatcher. Louisville: Westminster John Knox, 2001.
———. *Jesus and the Eyewitnesses: The Gospels as Eyewitness Testimony*. Grand Rapids: Eerdmans, 2006.
———. "John for Readers of Mark." Pages 147-71 in *The Gospels for All Christians: Rethinking the Gospel Audiences*. Edited by Richard Bauckham. Grand Rapids: Eerdmans, 1998.

———. *The Testimony of the Beloved Disciple: Narrative, History, and Theology in the Gospel of John.* Grand Rapids: Baker Academic, 2007.
Beale, Gregory K. *The Temple and the Church's Mission: A Biblical Theology of the Dwelling Place of God.* NSBT 17. Downers Grove, IL: InterVarsity Press, 2004.
Beale, Gregory. K., and D. A. Carson, eds. *Commentary on the New Testament Use of the Old Testament.* Grand Rapids: Baker Academic, 2007.
Beutler, Johannes. *Studien zu den johanneischen Schriften.* SBAB 25. Stuttgart: Katholisches Bibelwerk, 1998.
Bewernick, Hanne. *The Storyteller's Memory Palace.* EUS. ASLL 14. Frankfurt: Peter Lang, 2010.
Black, Clifton C. "Kennedy and the Gospels: An Ambiguous Legacy, a Promising Bequest." Pages 63-80 in *Words Well Spoken: George Kennedy's Rhetoric of the New Testament.* Edited by Clifton C. Black and Duane F. Watson. SRR 8. Waco, TX: Baylor University Press, 2008.
Blenkinsopp, Joseph. "The Oracle of Judah and the Messianic Entry." *JBL* 80 (1961): 55–64.
Blomberg, Craig L. *The Historical Reliability of John's Gospel: Issues and Commentary.* Downers Grove, IL: InterVarsity Press, 2001.
Boer, Martinus C. de. "The Depiction of 'the Jews' in John's Gospel: Matters of Behavior and Identity." Pages 260-80 in *Anti-Judaism and the Fourth Gospel: Papers of the Leuven Colloquium, 2000.* Edited by Reimund Bierhinger, Didier Pollefeyt, and Frederique Vandercasteele-Vanneuville. Assen: Van Gorcum, 2001.
Boice, James Montgomery. *The Gospel of John.* Grand Rapids: Zondervan, 1985.
Boismard, Marie-Émile, and Arnaud Lamouille. *L'Évangile de Jean.* Vol. 3 of *Synopse des quatre évangiles en français.* New ed. Paris: Cerf, 1987.
Bolter, Jay D. "Hypertext and the Rhetorical Canons." Pages 97–111 in *Rhetorical Memory and Delivery: Classical Concepts for Contemporary Composition and Communication.* Edited by John F. Reynolds. Hillsdale, NJ: Erlbaum, 1993.
Borgen, Peder. *Bread from Heaven: An Exegetical Study of the Concept of Manna in the Gospel of John and the Writings of Philo.* NovTSup 10. Leiden, Brill: 1965.
———. "John 6: Tradition, Interpretation, and Composition." Pages 95–114 in *Critical Readings of John 6.* Edited by R. Alan Culpepper. BIS 22. Leiden: Brill, 1997.

———. "The Scriptures and the Words and Works of Jesus." Pages 39–58 in *What We Have Heard from the Beginning: The Past, Present, and Future of Johannine Studies*. Edited by Tom Thatcher. Waco, TX: Baylor University Press, 2007.

Brant, Jo-Ann A. *Dialogue and Drama: Elements of Greek Tragedy in the Fourth Gospel*. Peabody, MA: Hendrickson, 2004.

———. *John*. PCNT. Grand Rapids: Baker Academic, 2011.

Brawley, Robert L. "An Absent Complement and Intertextuality in John 19:28–29." *JBL* 112 (1993): 427–43.

Brickle, Jeffrey E. *Aural Design and Coherence in the Prologue of First John*. ESCO. LNTS 465. London: T&T Clark, 2012.

———. "The Memory of the Beloved Disciple: A Poetics of Johannine Memory." Pages 185–206 in *Memory and Identity in Ancient Judaism and Early Christianity: A Conversation with Barry Schwartz*. Edited by Tom Thatcher. SBLRBS. Atlanta: Society of Biblical Literature, 2014.

———. "Seeing, Hearing, Declaring, Writing: Media Dynamics in the Letters of John." Pages 11–28 in *The Fourth Gospel in First-Century Media Culture*. Edited by Anthony Le Donne and Tom Thatcher. ESCO. LNTS 426. London: T&T Clark, 2011.

———. "Transacting Virtue within a Disrupted Community: The Negotiation of Ethics in the First Epistle of John." Pages 340–49 in *Rethinking the Ethics of John: "Implicit Ethics" in the Johannine Writings*. Edited by Jan G. van der Watt and Ruben Zimmermann. WUNT 291. Tübingen: Mohr Siebeck, 2012.

Brodie, Thomas L. *The Gospel according to John: A Literary and Theological Commentary*. Oxford: Oxford University Press, 1993.

———. *The Quest for the Origin of John's Gospel*. Oxford: Oxford University Press, 1993.

Brooke, George J. *The Dead Sea Scrolls and the New Testament: Essays in Mutual Illumination*. London: SPCK, 2005.

Brown, David. "John." Pages 1079–153 in *The Classic Bible Commentary*. Edited by Owen Collins. Wheaton, IL: Crossway, 1999.

Brown, Raymond E. *The Community of the Beloved Disciple: The Life, Loves, and Hates of an Individual Church in New Testament Times*. New York: Paulist, 1979.

———. *The Gospel according to John*. 2 vols. AB 29–29A. Garden City, NY: Doubleday, 1966–1970.

———. *The Gospel and Epistles of John: A Concise Commentary*. Collegeville, MN: Liturgical Press, 1988.

Brown, Raymond E. *An Introduction to the Gospel of John*. Edited by Francis J. Moloney. New York: Doubleday, 2003.

Brown, Sherri. "John the Baptist: Witness and Embodiment of the Prologue in the Gospel of John." Pages 147–64 in *Characters and Characterization in the Gospel of John*. Edited by Christopher W. Skinner. LNTS 449. London: T&T Clark, 2013.

Bruce, F. F. *The Gospel of John*. Grand Rapids: Eerdmans, 1983.

Brueggemann, Walter. *The Land: Place as Gift, Promise, and Challenge in Biblical Faith*. 2nd ed. OBT. Minneapolis: Fortress, 2002.

Bruford, Alan, and Natalya Todd. "The Eye behind the Mouth: The Contribution of Visual Memory to Oral Storytelling." Pages 7–14 in *Orality, Literacy, and Modern Media*. Edited by Dietrich Scheunemann. Columbia, SC: Camden House, 1996.

Brunson, Andrew C. *Psalm 118 in the Gospel of John*. WUNT 2/158. Tübingen: Mohr Siebeck, 2003.

Bryan, Steven M. "Consumed by Zeal: John's Use of Psalm 69:9 and the Action in the Temple." *BBR* 21 (2011): 479–94.

Budd, Philip. *Numbers*. WBC 4. Nashville: Nelson, 1984.

Bullock, C. Hassell. "Ezekiel, Bridge between the Testaments." *JETS* 25 (1982): 23–31.

Bultmann, Rudolf. *Das Evangelium des Johannes*. 18th ed. KEK 2. Göttingen: Vandenhoeck & Ruprecht, 1964.

———. *The Gospel of John: A Commentary*. Translated by George R. Beasley-Murray. Philadelphia: Westminster, 1971.

Burge, Gary M. *The Anointed Community: The Holy Spirit in the Johannine Tradition*. Grand Rapids: Eerdmans, 1987.

Burrell, Barbara. "Reading, Hearing, and Looking at Ephesos." Pages 69–95 in *Ancient Literacies: The Culture of Reading in Greece and Rome*. Edited by William A. Johnson and Holt N. Parker. Oxford: Oxford University Press, 2009.

Burridge, Richard A. *What Are the Gospels? A Comparison with Graeco-Roman Biography*. 2nd ed. Grand Rapids: Eerdmans, 2004.

Busse, Ulrich. *Das Johannesevangelium: Bildlichkeit, Diskurs, und Ritual*. BETL 162. Leuven: Leuven University Press, 2002.

Bynum, William Randolph. *The Fourth Gospel and the Scriptures: Illuminating the Form and Meaning of Scriptural Citation in John 19:37*. NovTSup 144. Leiden: Brill, 2012.

Byrskog, Samuel. Introduction to *Jesus in Memory: Traditions in Oral and Scribal Perspectives*. Edited by Werner H. Kelber and Samuel Byrskog. Waco, TX: Baylor University Press, 2009.

———. "A New Quest for the Sitz im Leben: Social Memory, the Jesus Tradition, and the Gospel of Matthew." *NTS* 52 (2006): 319-36.

Campbell, Jonathan G. *The Use of Scripture in the Damascus Document 1-8, 19-20*. Berlin: de Gruyter, 1995.

Carr, David M. "Torah on the Heart: Literary Jewish Textuality within Its Ancient Near Eastern Context." *OT* 25 (2010): 17-40.

———. *Writing on the Tablet of the Heart: Origins of Scripture and Literature*. Oxford: Oxford University Press, 2005.

Carruthers, Mary. "*Ars Oblivionalis, Ars Inveniendi*: The Cherub Figure and the Arts of Memory." *Gesta* 48, no. 2 (2009): 1-19.

———. *The Book of Memory: A Study of Memory in Medieval Culture*. 2nd ed. CSML. Cambridge: Cambridge University Press, 2008.

———. *The Craft of Thought: Meditation, Rhetoric, and the Making of Images, 400-1200*. CSML. Cambridge: Cambridge University Press, 1998.

———. "Mechanisms for the Transmission of Culture: The Role of 'Place' in the Arts of Memory." Pages 1-26 in *Translatio or the Transmission of Culture in the Middle Ages: Modes and Messages*. Edited by Laura Hollengreen. ASMAR 13. Turnhout: Brepols, 2008.

Carruthers, Mary, and Jan M. Ziolkowski, eds. *The Medieval Craft of Memory: An Anthology of Texts and Pictures*. MatT. Philadelphia: University of Pennsylvania Press, 2002.

Carson, Donald A. *The Gospel according to John*. PNTC. Grand Rapids: Eerdmans, 1991.

———. "John and the Johannine Epistles." Pages 245-64 in *It Is Written: Scripture Citing Scripture*. Edited by D. A. Carson and H. G. M. Williamson. Cambridge: Cambridge University Press, 1998.

———. "Syntactical and Text-Critical Observations on John 20.30-31: One More Round on the Purpose of the Fourth Gospel." *JBL* 124 (2005): 693-714.

Carson, Donald A., and Douglas J. Moo. *An Introduction to the New Testament*. 2nd ed. Grand Rapids: Zondervan, 2005.

Carter, Warren. "The Prologue and John's Gospel: Function, Symbol, and the Definitive Word." *JSNT* 39 (1990): 35-58.

Childs, Brevard S. *Introduction to the Old Testament as Scripture*. Philadelphia: Fortress, 1979.

Christensen, Duane L. *Deuteronomy 1:1–21:9*. 2nd ed. WBC. Nashville: Nelson, 2001.

Chrysostom, John. *Discourses against the Judaizing Christians*. Translated by Paul W. Harkins. Washington, DC: Catholic University of America Press, 1979.

Cicero. *On the Orator*. Translated by Harris Rackham and Edward W. Sutton. 2 vols. LCL. Cambridge: Harvard University Press, 1942.

———. *Rhetorica ad Herennium*. Translated by Harry Caplan. LCL. Cambridge: Harvard University Press, 1954.

———. *On Invention, The Best Kind of Orator, Topics*. Translated by H. M. Hubbell. LCL. Cambridge: Harvard University Press, 1949.

Clark-Soles, Jaime. *Scripture Cannot Be Broken: The Social Function of the Use of Scripture in the Fourth Gospel*. Leiden: Brill, 2003.

Clay, Jenny Strauss. *Homer's Trojan Theater: Space, Vision, and Memory in the* Iliad. Cambridge: Cambridge University Press, 2011.

Clifford, Richard J. *Creation Accounts in the Ancient Near East and in the Bible*. CBQMS 26. Washington, DC: Catholic Biblical Association of America, 1994.

Coloe, Mary. "The Structure of the Johannine Prologue and Genesis 1." *ABR* 45 (1997): 40–55.

Craigie, Peter M. *The Book of Deuteronomy*. Grand Rapids: Eerdmans, 1976.

Crossan, John Dominic. *The Birth of Christianity: Discovering What Happened in the Years Immediately after the Execution of Jesus*. San Francisco: HarperSanFrancisco, 1999.

Culpepper, R. Alan. *Anatomy of the Fourth Gospel: A Study in Literary Design*. Philadelphia: Fortress, 1983.

———. "The Pivot of John's Prologue." *NTS* 27 (1981): 1–31.

Dahl, Nils Alstrup. "The Johannine Church and History." Pages 147–67 in *The Interpretation of John*. Edited by John Ashton. 2nd ed. SNTI. Edinburgh: T&T Clark, 1997.

Daise, Michael A. *Feasts in John: Jewish Festivals and Jesus' "Hour" in the Fourth Gospel*. WUNT 2/229. Tübingen: Mohr Siebeck, 2007.

———. "Quotations in John and the Judaean Desert Texts." Paper presented to the Johannine Literature section of the SBL, International Meeting. University of St. Andrews. St. Andrews, Scotland, July 8, 2013.

Daly-Denton, Margaret. *David in the Fourth Gospel: The Johannine Reception of the Psalms*. AGJU 47. Leiden: Brill, 2000.

Daube, David. "Rabbinic Methods of Interpretation and Hellenistic Rhetoric." *HUCA* 22 (1949): 251–59.
Derrett, J. Duncan M. "Zeal of the House and the Cleansing of the Temple." *DRev* 95 (1977): 79–94.
DeSilva, David A. "Seeing Things John's Way: Rhetography and Conceptual Blending in Revelation 14:6–13." *BBR* 18 (2008): 271–98.
Dodd, C. H. *According to the Scriptures: The Substructure of New Testament Theology*. London: Collins, 1952.
———. *The Interpretation of the Fourth Gospel*. Cambridge: Cambridge University Press, 1953.
Draper, Jonathan. "Practicing the Presence of God in John: Ritual Use of Scripture and the *Eidos Theou* in John 5:37." Pages 155–70 in *Orality, Literacy, and Colonialism in Antiquity*. Edited by Jonathan Draper. Atlanta: Society of Biblical Literature, 2004.
Duke, Paul D. *Irony in the Fourth Gospel*. Atlanta: John Knox, 1985.
Dunn, James D. G. *The Oral Gospel Tradition*. Grand Rapids: Eerdmans, 2013.
Ellens, J. Harold. "A Christian Pesher: John 1:51." *Proceedings: Eastern Great Lakes Biblical Society* 25 (2005): 143–55.
Ellis, Peter. *The Genius of John: A Compositional-Critical Commentary on the Fourth Gospel*. Collegeville, MN: Liturgical Press, 1984.
Elowsky, Joel C., ed. *John 11–21*. ACCS NT 14B. Downers Grove, IL: InterVarsity Press, 2007.
Elsner, Jaś. "Structuring 'Greece': Pausanias's *Periegesis* as a Literary Construct." Pages 3–20 in *Pausanias: Travel and Memory in Roman Greece*. Edited by Susan E. Alcock, John F. Cherry, and Jaś Elsner. Oxford: Oxford University Press, 2001.
Esler, Philip F. "Collective Memory and Hebrews 11: Outlining a New Investigative Framework." Pages 151–71 in *Memory, Tradition, and Text: Uses of the Past in Early Christianity*. Edited by Alan Kirk and Tom Thatcher. SemeiaSt 52. Atlanta: Society of Biblical Literature, 2005.
Evans, C. Stephen. "The Historical Reliability of John's Gospel: From What Perspective Should It Be Assessed?" Pages 91–119 in *The Gospel of John and Christian Theology*. Edited by Richard Bauckham and Carl Mosser. Grand Rapids: Eerdmans, 2008.
Evans, Craig A. "Jesus' Action in the Temple: Cleansing or Portent of Destruction?" *CBQ* 51 (1989): 237–70.

———. *Jesus and His Contemporaries: Comparative Studies.* Leiden: Brill, 2001.

———. "Obduracy and the Lord's Servant: Some Observations on the Use of the Old Testament in the Fourth Gospel." Pages 221-36 in *Early Jewish and Christian Exegesis: Studies in Memory of William Hugh Brownlee.* Edited by Craig A. Evans and William F. Stinespring. Atlanta: Scholars Press, 1987.

———. *Word and Glory: On the Exegetical and Theological Background of John's Prologue.* JSNTSup 89. Sheffield: Sheffield Academic, 1993.

Eve, Eric. *Behind the Gospels: Understanding the Oral Tradition.* London: SPCK, 2013.

Falcetta, Alessandro. "The Testimony Research of James Rendel Harris." *NovT* 45 (2003): 280-99.

Fant, Clyde E., and Mitchell G. Reddish. *A Guide to Biblical Sites in Greece and Turkey.* Oxford: Oxford University Press, 2003.

Faure, Alexander. "Die alttestamentlichen Zitate im 4. Evangelium und die Quellenscheidungshypothese." *ZNW* 21 (1922): 99-122.

Faussett, A. R. "Zechariah." Pages 839-69 in *The Classic Bible Commentary.* Edited by Owen Collins. Wheaton, IL: Crossway, 1999.

Fee, Gordon D. "On the Text and Meaning of John 20.30-31." Pages 2193-205 in *The Four Gospels 1992: Festschrift Frans Neirynck.* 3 vols. Edited by F. Van Segbroeck et al. BETL 100. Leuven: Leuven University Press, 1992.

Felsch, Dorit. *Die Feste im Johannesevangelium: Jüdische Tradition und christologische Deutung.* WUNT 2/308. Tübingen: Mohr Siebeck, 2011.

Fentress, James, and Chris Wickham. *Social Memory: New Perspectives on the Past.* Oxford: Blackwell, 1992.

Ferreiro, Alberto, ed. *The Twelve Prophets.* ACCS OT 14. Downers Grove, IL: InterVarsity Press, 2003.

Fishbane, Michael A. *Biblical Interpretation in Ancient Israel.* Oxford: Clarendon, 1985.

Franke, August H. *Das Alte Testament bei Johannes: Ein Beitrag zur Erklärung und Beurtheilung der johanneischen schriften.* Göttingen: Vandenhoeck & Ruprecht, 1885.

Freed, Edwin D. *Old Testament Quotations in the Gospel of John.* NovTSup 11. Leiden: Brill, 1965.

Freedman, David Noel, ed. *Anchor Bible Dictionary.* 6 vols. New York: Doubleday, 1992.

Frey, Jörg. "'Dass sie meine Herrlichkeit schauen' (Joh 17.24): Zu Hintergrund, Sinn, und Funktion der johanneischen Rede von der δόξα Jesu." *NTS* 54 (2008): 375-97.

———. "'Wie Mose die Schlange in der Wüste erhöht hat …' Zur frühjüdischen Deutung der 'ehernen Schlange' und ihrer christologischen Rezeption in Johannes 3,14f." Pages 153-205 in *Schriftauslegung im antiken Judentum und im Urchristentum*. Edited by Martin Hengel and Hermut Löhr. WUNT 73. Tübingen: Mohr Siebeck, 1994.

Gabel, John B., Charles B. Wheeler, and Anthony D. York. *The Bible as Literature, an Introduction*. 3rd ed. Oxford: Oxford University Press, 1996.

Garfinkel, Harold. "Conditions of Successful Degradation Ceremonies." *AJS* 61 (1956): 420-24.

Gaston, Lloyd. *No Stone on Another: Studies in the Significance of the Fall of Jerusalem in the Synoptic Gospels*. NovTSup 23. Leiden: Brill, 1970.

Genette, Gérard. *Narrative Discourse: An Essay in Method*. Translated by Jane E. Lewin. Ithaca, NY: Cornell University Press, 1983.

George, Mark K. *Israel's Tabernacle as Social Space*. AIL 2. Atlanta: Society of Biblical Literature, 2009.

Gleason, Maud W. *Making Men: Sophists and Self-Presentation in Ancient Rome*. Princeton: Princeton University Press, 1995.

Goodwin, Charles. "How Did John Treat His Sources?" *JBL* 73 (1954): 61-75.

Graham, William A. *Beyond the Written Word: Oral Aspects of Scripture in the History of Religion*. Cambridge: Cambridge University Press, 1987.

Gregory, Marshall. *Shaped by Stories: The Ethical Power of Narratives*. Notre Dame: University of Notre Dame Press, 2009.

Griffiths, Paul J. *Religious Reading: The Place of Reading in the Practice of Religion*. Oxford: Oxford University Press, 1999.

Groenewald, Alphonso. "'Indeed—The Zeal for Your House Has Consumed Me!': Possible Historical Background to Psalm 69:10AB." Pages 177-85 in *Stimulation from Leiden: Collected Communications to the XVIIIth Congress of the International Organization for the Study of the Old Testament, Leiden 2004*. Edited by Hermann Michael Niemann and Matthias Augustin. Frankfurt am Main: Lang, 2006.

Halbwachs, Maurice. *Les Cadres sociaux de la mémoire*. Paris: Alcan, 1925.

———. *La Mémoire collective*. Paris: Éditions Albin Michel, 1997.

———. *On Collective Memory*. Edited by Lewis A. Coser. Translated by Lewis A. Coser. Chicago: University of Chicago Press, 1992.

———. *La Topographie légendaire des évangiles en terre sainte: Étude de mémoire collective*. Paris: Presses Universitaires de France, 1941.

Hamid-Khani, Saeed. *Revelation and Concealment of Christ: A Theological Inquiry into the Elusive Language of the Fourth Gospel*. WUNT 2/120. Tübingen: Mohr Siebeck, 2000.

Hanson, Anthony Tyrrell. *The New Testament Interpretation of Scripture*. London: SPCK, 1980.

Harris, J. Rendel. *Testimonies*. 2 vols. Cambridge: Cambridge University Press, 1916–1920.

Harris, Max. *Theater and Incarnation*. Grand Rapids: Eerdmans, 1990.

Harrison, Carol. *The Art of Listening in the Early Church*. Oxford: Oxford University Press, 2013.

Harstine, Stan. *Moses as a Character in the Fourth Gospel: A Study of Ancient Reading Techniques*. JSNTSup 229. Sheffield: Sheffield Academic, 2002.

Harvey, Anthony E. *Jesus on Trial: A Study in the Fourth Gospel*. London: SPCK, 1976.

Harvey, John. *The Bible as Visual Culture: When Text Becomes Image*. BIMW 57. Sheffield: Sheffield Phoenix, 2013.

Hasitschka, Martin. "Die Führer Israels: Mose, Josua, und die Richter." Pages 117-40 in *Alttestamentliche Gestalten im Neuen Testament: Beiträge zur biblischen Theologie*. Edited by Markus Öhler. Darmstadt: Wissenschaftliche Buchgesellschaft, 1999.

Hatina, Thomas R. "Intertextuality and Historical Criticism in New Testament Studies: Is There a Relationship." *BibInt* 7 (1999): 28-43.

Hays, Richard B. *The Conversion of the Imagination: Paul as Interpreter of Israel's Scripture*. Grand Rapids: Eerdmans, 2005.

———. *Echoes of Scripture in the Letters of Paul*. New Haven: Yale University Press, 1989.

———. *Reading Backwards: Figural Christology and the Fourfold Gospel Witness*. Waco, TX: Baylor University Press, 2014.

———. "Reading Scripture in Light of the Resurrection." Pages 216–38 in *The Art of Reading Scripture*. Edited by Ellen F. Davis and Richard B. Hays. Grand Rapids: Eerdmans, 2003.

Hearon, Holly E. "The Construction of Social Memory in Biblical Interpretation." *Enc* 6 (2006): 343-60.

Heine, Ronald E. *Reading the Old Testament with the Ancient Church: Exploring the Formation of Early Christian Thought*. EvangR. Grand Rapids: Baker Academic, 2007.

Hendriksen, William. *Exposition of the Gospel according to John*. NTC. 2 vols. Grand Rapids: Baker, 1953.
Hengel, Martin. *The Johannine Question*. Translated by John Bowdon. London: SCM, 1989.
———. "The Old Testament in the Fourth Gospel." Pages 380–95 in *The Gospels and the Scriptures of Israel*. Edited by Craig A. Evans and W. Richard Stegner. JSNTSup 104. Sheffield: Sheffield Academic, 1994.
———. "The Old Testament in the Fourth Gospel." *HBT* 12 (1990): 19–41.
———. "The Prologue of the Gospel of John as the Gateway to Christological Truth." Pages 265–94 in *The Gospel of John and Christian Theology*. Edited by Richard Bauckham and Carl Mosser. Grand Rapids: Eerdmans, 2008
———. "Die Schriftauslegung des 4. Evangeliums auf dem Hintergrund der urchristlichen Exegese." *JBT* 4 (1989): 249–88.
———. *The Septuagint as Christian Scripture: Its Prehistory and the Problem of Its Canon*. Translated by Mark E. Biddle. Grand Rapids: Baker Academic, 2002.
———. *Die Zeloten: Untersuchungen zur jüdischen Freiheitsbewegung in der Zeit von Herodes I. bis 70 n. Chr.* 3rd ed. Edited by Roland Deines, and Claus-Jürgen Thornton. WUNT 283. Tübingen: Mohr Siebeck, 2011.
Hollander, John. *The Figure of an Echo: A Model of Allusion in Milton and After*. Berkeley: University of California Press, 1981.
Holmes, Michael W. *The Greek New Testament: SBL Edition*. Bellingham, WA: Logos Bible Software, 2010.
Horsley, Richard, and Tom Thatcher. *John, Jesus, and the Renewal of Israel*. Grand Rapids: Eerdmans, 2013.
Hoskyns, Edwyn C. *The Fourth Gospel*. Edited by Francis Noel Davey. 2nd ed. London: Faber & Faber, 1947.
Householder, Fred W., Jr. *Literary Quotation and Allusion in Lucian*. Morningside Heights, NY: King's Crown Press, 1941.
Hübner, Hans. "New Testament Interpretation of the Old Testament." Pages 332–72 in *From the Beginnings to the Middle Ages (Until 1300)*. Volume 1 of *Hebrew Bible/Old Testament: The History of Its Interpretation*. Edited by Magne Saebo. Göttingen: Vandenhoeck & Ruprecht, 1996.
Huizenga, Leroy. *The New Isaac: Tradition and Intertextuality in the Gospel of Matthew*. NovTSup 131. Leiden: Brill, 2009.
Hylen, Susan. *Allusion and Meaning in John 6*. BZNW 137. Berlin: de Gruyter, 2005.

Instone-Brewer, David. "Jesus of Nazareth's Trial in the Uncensored Talmud." *TynBul* 62 (2011): 269–94.

Jacobsen, Eric O. *The Space Between: A Christian Engagement with the Built Environment.* Grand Rapids: Baker Academic, 2012.

Jobes, Karen H., and Moises Silva. *Invitation to the Septuagint.* Grand Rapids: Baker Academic, 2000.

Johnson, Luke Timothy. "Anti-Judaism and the New Testament." Pages 1609–38 in *Handbook for the Study of the Historical Jesus.* Edited by Tom Holmén and Stanley E. Porter. Leiden: Brill, 2011.

Johnson, William A. *Readers and Reading Culture in the High Roman Empire: A Study of Elite Communities.* CCS. Oxford: Oxford University Press, 2010.

Jong, Irene J. F. de. *Space in Ancient Greek Literature.* SAGN 3. MNS 339. Leiden: Brill, 2012.

Juel, Donald H. *Messianic Exegesis: Christological Interpretation of the Old Testament in Early Christianity.* Philadelphia: Fortress, 1988.

Keck, Leander E. "Derivation as Destiny: 'Of-ness' in Johannine Christology, Anthropology, and Soteriology." Pages 274–88 in *Exploring the Gospel of John.* Edited by R. Alan Culpepper and C. Clifton Black. Louisville: Westminster John Knox, 1996.

Keener, Craig S. *The Gospel of John: A Commentary.* 2 vols. Peabody, MA: Hendrickson, 2003.

———. *The Historical Jesus of the Gospels.* Grand Rapids: Eerdmans, 2009.

Keith, Chris. *The Pericopae Adultera, the Gospel of John, and the Literacy of Jesus.* NTTSD 38. Leiden: Brill, 2009.

Kelber, Werner H. *Imprints, Voiceprints, and Footprints of Memory: Collected Essays of Werner H. Kelber.* SBLRBS 74. Atlanta: Society of Biblical Literature, 2013.

———. *The Oral and the Written Gospel: The Hermeneutics of Speaking and Writing in the Synoptic Tradition, Mark, Paul, and Q.* Philadelphia: Fortress, 1983.

———. "The Works of Memory: Christian Origins as Mnemohistory— A Response." Pages 221–48 in *Memory, Tradition, and Text: Uses of the Past in Early Christianity.* Edited by Alan Kirk and Tom Thatcher. SemeiaSt 52. Atlanta: Society of Biblical Literature, 2005.

Kennedy, George A. *New Testament Interpretation through Rhetorical Criticism.* Studies in Religion. Chapel Hill: University of North Carolina Press, 1984.

———, trans. *Progymnasmata: Greek Textbooks of Composition and Rhetoric*. WGRW 10. Atlanta: Society of Biblical Literature, 2003.

Kerr, Alan R. *The Temple of Jesus' Body: The Temple Theme in the Gospel of John*. London: Sheffield Academic, 2002.

Kirk, Alan. "Social and Cultural Memory." Pages 1–24 in *Memory, Tradition, and Text: Uses of the Past in Early Christianity*. Edited by Alan Kirk and Tom Thatcher. SemeiaSt 52. Atlanta: Society of Biblical Literature, 2005.

Kittel, Georg, and Georg Friedrich, eds. *Theological Dictionary of the New Testament*. Translated by Geofrey W. Bromily. 10 vols. Grand Rapids: Eerdmans, 1964–1976.

Klassen, William. "Jesus and Phineas: A Rejected Role Model." Pages 490–500 in *SBL Seminar Papers, 1986*. SBLSP 25. Atlanta: Scholars Press, 1979.

Koester, Craig R. "Jesus' Resurrection, the Signs, and the Dynamics of Faith in the Gospel of John." Pages 47–74 in *The Resurrection of Jesus in the Gospel of John*. Edited by Craig R. Koester and Reimund Bieringer. WUNT 222. Tübingen: Mohr Siebeck, 2008.

Köstenberger, Andreas J. "John." Pages 415–512 in *Commentary on the New Testament Use of the Old Testament*. Edited by G. K. Beale and D. A. Carson. Grand Rapids: Baker Academic, 2007.

———. *John*. BECNT. Grand Rapids: Baker Academic, 2004.

———. *A Theology of John's Gospel and Letters: The Word, the Christ, the Son of God*. BTNT. Grand Rapids: Zondervan, 2009.

Kristeva, Julia. "Word, Dialogue, and Novel." Pages 34–61 in *The Kristeva Reader*. Edited by Toril Moi. New York: Columbia University Press, 1986.

Kubiś, Adam. *The Book of Zechariah in the Gospel of John*. EBib n.s. 64. Paris: Gabalda, 2012.

Labahn, Michael. "Deuteronomy in John's Gospel." Pages 82–98 in *Deuteronomy in the New Testament*. Edited by Maarten J. J. Menken and Steve Moyise. London: T&T Clark, 2007.

Lange, Tineke de. *Abraham in John 8:31–59: His Significance in the Conflict between Johannine Christianity and Its Jewish Environment*. Amsterdam: Amphora, 2008.

Lappenga, Benjamin J. "Misdirected Emulation and Paradoxical Zeal: Paul's Redefinition of 'The Good' as Object of ζῆλος in Gal 4:12–20." *JBL* 131 (2012): 775–96.

Le Donne, Anthony. *The Historiographical Jesus: Memory, Typology, and the Son of David*. Waco, TX: Baylor University Press, 2009.
Lee, Margaret E., and Bernard B. Scott. *Sound Mapping the New Testament*. Salem, OR: Polebridge, 2009.
Levine, Baruch A. *Numbers 21–36*. AB 4A. New York: Doubleday, 2000.
Levinson, Bernard M. *Deuteronomy and the Hermeneutics of Legal Innovation*. Oxford: Oxford University Press, 1997.
Lewis, Scott M. *The Gospel according to John and the Johannine Letters*. NCBC 4. Collegeville, MN: Liturgical Press, 2005.
Liebermann, Saul. *Hellenism in Jewish Palestine: Studies in the Literary Transition, Beliefs, and Manners of Palestine in the I Century B.C.E–IV Century C.E*. TS 18. New York: Jewish Theological Seminary of America, 1962.
Lierman, John. "The Mosaic Pattern of John's Christology." Pages 210-34 in *Challenging Perspectives on the Gospel of John*. Edited by John Lierman. WUNT 2/219. Tübingen: Mohr Siebeck, 2006.
Lieu, Judith M. "Narrative Analysis and Scripture in John." Pages 144-63 in *The Old Testament in the New Testament: Essays in Honor of J. L. North*. Edited by Steve Moyise. JSNTSup 189. Sheffield: Sheffield Academic, 2000.
———. "Temple and Synagogue in John." *NTS* 45 (1999): 51-69.
Lincoln, Andrew T. *The Gospel according to St. John*. BNTC 4. New York: Continuum, 2005.
———. *Truth on Trial: The Lawsuit Motif in the Fourth Gospel*. Peabody, MA: Hendrickson, 2000.
Lindars, Barnabas. *The Gospel of John*. NCB. England: Oliphants, 1972.
———. *New Testament Apologetic: The Doctrinal Significance of the Old Testament Quotations*. London: SCM, 1961.
Loisy, Alfred Firmin. *Le Quatrième Évangile, Les Épitres dites de Jean*. 2nd ed. Paris: Nourry, 1921.
Longenecker, Bruce W. *Rhetoric at the Boundaries: The Art and Theology of New Testament Chain Link Transitions*. Waco, TX: Baylor University Press, 2005.
Longenecker, Richard N. *Biblical Exegesis in the Apostolic Period*. 2nd ed. Grand Rapids: Eerdmans, 1999.
Lust, Johan, Erik Eynikel, and Karin Hauspie, eds. *Greek-English Lexicon of the Septuagint*. Stuttgart: Deutsche Bibelgesellschaft, 2003.
Malbon, Elizabeth S. *Narrative Space and Mythic Meaning in Mark*. NVBS. San Francisco: Harper & Row, 1986.

Malina, Bruce, and Richard Rohrbaugh. *Social Science Commentary on the Gospel of John*. Minneapolis: Fortress, 1998.
Manning, Gary T. *Echoes of a Prophet: The Use of Ezekiel in the Gospel of John and in the Literature of the Second Temple Period*. JSNTSup 270. London: T&T Clark, 2004.
Manns, Frédéric. "Exégèse Rabbanique et Exégèse Johannique." *RB* 92 (1985): 525–38.
———. "Zacharie 12,10 Relu en Jean 19.37." *LASBF* 56 (2006): 301–10.
Marcos, Natalio Fernández. *The Septuagint in Context: Introduction to the Greek Versions of the Bible*. Translated by Wilfred G. E. Watson. Leiden: Brill, 2001.
Marcus, Joel. "No More Zealots in the House of the Lord: A Note on the History of Interpretation of Zechariah 14:21." *NovT* 55 (2013): 22–30.
Marincola, John. "Speeches in Classical Historiography." Pages 118-32 in *Companion to Greek and Roman Historiography*. Edited by John Marincola. 2 vols. BCAW. Malden, MA: Blackwell, 2007.
Martin, Michael W. "Progymnastic Topic Lists: A Compositional Template for Luke and Other Bioi." *NTS* 54 (2008): 18–41.
Martyn, J. Louis. "Listening to John and Paul on the Subject of Gospel and Scripture." *WW* 12 (1992): 68–81.
Mason, Steve. "Jews, Judaeans, Judaizing, Judaism: Problems of the Categorization in Ancient History." *JSJ* 38 (2007): 457–512.
McConnell, James R., Jr. *The Topos of Divine Testimony in Luke-Acts*. Eugene, OR: Pickwick, 2014.
McIver, Robert K. *Memory, Jesus, and the Synoptic Gospels*. SBLRBS 59. Atlanta: Society of Biblical Literature, 2011.
McLay, R. Timothy. "Biblical Texts and the Scriptures for the New Testament Church." Pages 38–58 in *Hearing the Old Testament in the New Testament*. Edited by Stanley E. Porter. Grand Rapids: Eerdmans, 2006.
Meeks, Wayne A. *The Prophet-King: Moses Traditions and the Johannine Christology*. NovTSup 14. Leiden: Brill, 1967.
Mendels, Doron. "Societies of Memory in the Graeco-Roman World." Pages 143–62 in *Memory in the Bible and Antiquity*. Edited by Loren T. Stuckenbruck, Stephen C. Barton, and Benjamin G. Wold. WUNT 212. Tübingen: Mohr Siebeck, 2007.
Menken, Maarten J. J. "The Minor Prophets in John's Gospel." Pages 79-96 in *The Minor Prophets in the New Testament*. Edited by Maarten J. J. Menken and Steve Moyise. LNTS 377. NTSI. London: T&T Clark, 2009.

———. *Old Testament Quotations in the Fourth Gospel: Studies in Textual Form*. CBET 15. Kampen: Kok Pharos, 1996.

———. "The Quotation from Isa 40,3 in John 1,23." *Bib* 66 (1985): 190-205.

———. "The Use of the Septuagint in Three Quotations in John: Jn 10,34; 12,38; 19,24." Pages 367-93 in *The Scriptures in the Gospels*. Edited by Christopher M. Tuckett. Leuven: Leuven University Press, 1997.

Meyers, Carol L. and Eric M. Meyers. *Zechariah 9-14*. AB 25C. New York: Doubleday, 1993.

Metzger, Bruce M. *A Textual Commentary on the Greek New Testament*. 2nd ed. New York: United Bible Societies, 2000.

Michaels, J. Ramsey. *The Gospel of John*. NICNT. Grand Rapids: Eerdmans, 2010.

Milgrom, Jacob. *Numbers*. JPSTC. Philadelphia: Jewish Publication Society, 1990.

Miller, Paul. "'They Saw His Glory and Spoke of Him': The Gospel of John and the Old Testament." Pages 127-51 in *Hearing the Old Testament in the New Testament*. Edited by Stanley E. Porter. Grand Rapids: Eerdmans, 2006.

Minchin, Elizabeth. *Homeric Voices: Discourse, Memory, Gender*. Oxford: Oxford University Press, 2007.

Mitchell, David C. "Messiah bar Ephraim in the Targums." *Aramaic Studies* (2006): 545-53.

Mlakuzhyil, George. *The Christocentric Literary Structure of the Fourth Gospel*. AnBib 117. Rome: Editrice Pontificia Istituto Biblico, 1987.

Moloney, Francis J. "The Gospel of John as Scripture." *CBQ* 67 (2005): 454-68.

———. "The Gospel of John: The 'End' of Scripture." *Int* 63 (2009): 356-66.

———. *John*. SP 4. Collegeville, MN: Liturgical Press, 1998.

———. "Reading John 2:13-22: The Purification of the Temple." *RB* 97 (1990): 432-52.

Morris, Leon. *The Gospel according to John: The English Text with Introduction, Exposition, and Notes*. NICNT. Grand Rapids: Eerdmans, 1971.

Motyer, Stephen. *Your Father the Devil? A New Approach to John and "The Jews."* Carlisle, UK: Paternoster, 1997.

Moyise, Steve. "Intertextuality and the Study of the Old Testament in the New Testament." Pages 14-41 in *The Old Testament in the New Testament: Essays in Honor of J. L. Noth*. Edited by Steve Moiyse. JSNTSup 189. Sheffield: Sheffield Academic, 2000.

———. *Jesus and Scripture: Studying the New Testament Use of the Old Testament*. Grand Rapids: Baker Academic, 2011.

Müller, Mogens. "Schriftbeweis oder Vollendung? Das Johannesevangelium und das Alte Testament." Pages 151-71 in *Bekenntnis und Erinnerung*. Edited by Klaus-Michael Bull and Eckart Reinmuth. Münster: LIT, 2004.

Murphy-O'Connor, Jerome. *St. Paul's Ephesus: Texts and Archaeology*. Collegeville, MN: Liturgical Press, 2008.

Myers, Alicia D. *Characterizing Jesus: A Rhetorical Analysis on the Fourth Gospel's Use of Scripture in Its Presentation of Jesus*. LNTS 458. London: T&T Clark, 2012.

———. "'Jesus Said to Them': The Adaptation of Juridical Rhetoric in John 5:19-47." *JBL* 132 (2013): 421-25.

———. "'The One of Whom Moses Wrote': The Characterization of Jesus through Old Testament Moses Traditions in the Gospel of John." Pages 1-20 in *The Letters and Liturgical Traditions*. Volume 2 of *"What Does the Scripture Say?" Studies in the Function of Scripture in Early Judaism and Christianity*. Edited by Craig A. Evans and H. Daniel Zacharias. LNTS 470. SSEJC 18. London: Bloomsbury, 2012.

Nasrallah, Laura S. *Christian Responses to Roman Art and Architecture: The Second-Century Church amid the Spaces of Empire*. Cambridge: Cambridge University Press, 2010.

Nelson, Richard D. *Deuteronomy*. Louisville: Westminster John Knox, 2001.

Neusner, Jacob. *Judaism When Christianity Began: A Survey of Belief and Practice*. Louisville: Westminster John Knox, 2002.

Neyrey, Jerome. *The Gospel of John in Cultural and Rhetorical Perspective*. Grand Rapids: Eerdmans, 2009.

———. "Jesus the Judge: Forensic Processes in John 8:21-59." *Bib* 68 (1987): 509-42.

Neyrey, Jerome, and Richard L. Rohrbaugh. "'He Must Increase, I Must Decrease' (John 3:30): A Cultural and Social Interpretation." *CBQ* 63 (2001): 464-83.

Noth, Martin. *Numbers*. Translated by James D. Martin. OTL. London: SCM, 1968.

Obermann, Andreas. *Die christologische Erfüllung der Schrift im Johannesevangelium: Eine Untersuchung zur johanneischen Hermeneutik anhand der Schriftzitate*. WUNT 2/83. Tübingen: Mohr Siebeck, 1996.

Öhler, Marcus. "Who Was John the Baptist? From John 1:19–28 to Heracleon." Pages 101–18 in *"For It Is Written": Essays on the Function of Scripture in Early Judaism and Christianity*. Edited by Jan Dochhorn. New York: Peter Lang, 2011.
Olick, Jeffrey K. "Products, Processes, and Practices: A Non-Reificatory Approach to Collective Memory." *BTB* 36 (2006): 5–14.
Olick, Jeffrey K., and Joyce Robbins. "Social Memory Studies: From 'Collective Memory' to the Historical Sociology of Mnemonic Practices." *ARS* 24 (1988): 105–40.
Orchard, Helen C. *Courting Betrayal: Jesus as Victim in the Gospel of John*. Sheffield: Sheffield Academic, 1998.
Østenstad, Gunnar. "The Structure of the Fourth Gospel: Can It Be Defined Objectively." *ST* 45 (1991): 33–55.
Padilla, Osvaldo. "Hellenistic Paideia and Luke's Education: A Critique of Recent Approaches." *NTS* 55 (2009): 416–37.
Pancaro, Severino. *The Law in the Fourth Gospel: The Torah and the Gospel, Moses and Jesus, Judaism and Christianity according to John*. NovTSup 42. Leiden: Brill, 1975.
Park, Yoon-Man. *Mark's Memory Resources and the Controversy Stories (Mark 2:1–3:6): An Application of the Frame Theory of Cognitive Science to the Markan Oral-Aural Narrative*. LBS 2. Leiden: Brill, 2010.
Parsenios, George L. *Rhetoric and Drama in the Johannine Lawsuit Motif*. WUNT 258. Tübingen: Mohr Siebeck, 2010.
Paschalis, Michael, and Stavros Frangoulidis. *Space in the Ancient Novel*. ANS 1. Eelde, The Netherlands: Barkhuis, 2002.
Phillips, Peter M. *The Prologue of the Fourth Gospel: A Sequential Reading*. JSNTSup 294. London: T&T Clark, 2006.
Porter, Stanley E. "The Use of the Old Testament in the New Testament: A Brief Comment on Method and Terminology." Pages 80–88 in *Early Christian Interpretation of the Scriptures of Israel*. Edited by Craig A. Evans and James A. Sanders. JSNTSup 148. Sheffield: Sheffield Academic, 1997.
Pryor, John. *John: Evangelist of the Covenant People*. Downers Grove, IL: InterVarsity Press, 1992.
Purves, Alex C. *Space and Time in Ancient Greek Narrative*. Cambridge: Cambridge University Press, 2010.
Quek, Tze-Ming. "A Text-Critical Study of John 1.34." *NTS* 55 (2009): 22–34.

Quintilian. *Institutio oratoria*. Translated by H. E. Butler. 4 vols. LCL. Cambridge: Harvard University Press, 1920–22.

———. *The Orator's Education*. Edited and translated by Donald. A. Russell. LCL. Cambridge: Harvard University Press, 2001–2002.

Redditt, Paul L. *Zechariah 9-14*. IECOT. Stuttgart: Kohlhammer, 2012.

Reim, Günter. *Jochanan: Erweiterte Studien zum Alttestamentlichen Hintergrund des Johannesevangeliums*. Erlangen: Verlag der Ev.-Luth. Mission, 1995.

———. *Studien zum alttestamentlichen Hintergrund des Johannesevangeliums*. SNTSMS 22. Cambridge: Cambridge University Press, 1974.

Reinhartz, Adele. "'And the Word Was Begotten': Divine Epigenesis in the Gospel of John." *Semeia* 85 (1999): 83–103.

———. *Befriending the Beloved Disciple*. London: Continuum, 2002.

Resseguie, James L. *Narrative Criticism of the New Testament: An Introduction*. Grand Rapids: Baker Academic, 2005.

———. *Spiritual Landscape: Images of the Spiritual Life in the Gospel of Luke*. Peabody, MA: Hendrickson, 2004.

Richter, Georg. "Die alttestamentlichen Zitate in der Rede vom Himmelsbrot Joh 6,26–51a." Pages 199–265 in *Studien zum Johannesevangelium*. Edited by J. Hainz. BU 13. Regensburg: Verlag Friedrich Pustet, 1977.

Ricoeur, Paul. *Memory, History, Forgetting*. Translated by Kathleen Blamey and David Pellauer. Chicago: University of Chicago Press, 2004.

Ridderbos, Herman. *The Gospel according to John: A Theological Commentary*. Translated by John Vriend. Grand Rapids: Eerdmans, 1997.

Rissi, Mathias. "Der Aufbau des vierten Evangeliums." *NTS* 29 (1983): 48–54.

———. "Die Hochzeit in Kana Joh 2,1–11." Pages 76–92 in *Oikonomia: Heilsgeschichte als Thema der Theologie. Oscar Cullmann zum 65. Geburtstag gewidmet*. Edited by Felix Christ. Hamburg: Reick, 1967.

Robertson, A. T. *Word Pictures in the New Testament*. 6 vols. New York: Harper & Brothers, 1932.

Rodriguez, Rafael. *Structuring Early Christian Memory: Jesus in Tradition, Performance, and Text*. ESCO. LNTS 407. London: T&T Clark, 2010.

———. *Oral Tradition and the New Testament: A Guide for the Perplexed*. London: Bloomsbury, 2014.

Rofé, Alexander. *Deuteronomy: Issues and Interpretation*. London: T&T Clark, 2002.

Rubin, David C. *Memory in Oral Traditions: The Cognitive Psychology of Epic, Ballads, and Counting-Out Rhymes*. Oxford: Oxford University Press, 1995.
Sanders, E. P. *Jesus and Judaism*. Philadelphia: Fortress, 1985.
Schafer, Peter. *Jesus in the Talmud*. Princeton: Princeton University Press, 2007.
Schama, Simon. *Landscape and Memory*. New York: Vintage, 1995.
Schapdick, Stefan. "Religious Authority Re-Evaluated: The Character of Moses in the Fourth Gospel." Pages 181-209 in *Moses in Biblical and Extra-Biblical Traditions*. Edited by Axel Graupner and Michael Wolter. BZNW 372. Berlin: de Gruyter, 2007.
Schnackenburg, Rudolf. *The Gospel according to St. John*. Translated by Kevin Smyth et al. 3 vols. Freiburg im Breisgau: Herder, 1965-1975.
Schuchard, Bruce G. *1-3 John*. ConcC. St. Louis: Concordia, 2012.
———. *Scripture within Scripture: The Interrelationship of Form and Function in the Explicit Old Testament Citations in the Gospel of John*. SBLDS 133. Atlanta: Scholars Press, 1992.
———. "The Wedding Feast at Cana and the Christological Monomania of St. John." Pages 101-16 in *All Theology Is Christology: Essays in Honor of David P. Scaer*. Edited by Dean O. Wenthe et al. Fort Wayne, IN: Concordia Theological Seminary Press, 2000.
Schwartz, Barry. *Abraham Lincoln and the Forge of National Memory*. Chicago: University of Chicago Press, 2000.
———. "Frame Image: Towards a Semiotics of Collective Memory." *Semiotica* 121 (1998): 1-38.
———. "Memory as a Cultural System: Abraham Lincoln in World War II." *ASR* 61 (1996): 908-27.
Schwier, Helmut. *Tempel und Tempelzerstörung: Untersuchungen zu den theologischen und ideologischen Faktoren im ersten jüdisch-römischen Krieg (66-74 n. Chr.)*. NTOA 11. Göttingen: Vandenhoeck & Ruprecht, 1989.
Scobie, Charles H. H. "A Canonical Approach to Interpreting Luke: The Journey Motif as a Hermeneutical Key." Pages 327-49 in *Reading Luke: Interpretation, Reflection, Formation*. Edited by Craig G. Bartholomew, Joel B. Green, and Anthony C. Thiselton. SHS 3. Grand Rapids: Zondervan, 2005.
Scott, Michael. *Space and Society in the Greek and Roman Worlds*. KTAH. Cambridge: Cambridge University Press, 2013.

Scrutton, Anastasia. "The Truth Will Set You Free." Pages 359–68 in *The Gospel of John and Christian Theology*. Edited by Richard Bauckham and Carl Mosser. Grand Rapids: Eerdmans, 2008.

Segovia, Fernando. "The Journey(s) of the Word of God: A Reading of the Plot of the Fourth Gospel." *Semeia* 53 (1991): 23–54.

Seim, Turid Karlsen. "Descent and Divine Paternity in the Gospel of John: Does the Mother Matter?" *NTS* 51 (2005): 361–75.

Shepardson, Christine. *Controlling Contested Places: Late Antique Antioch and the Spacial Politics of Religious Controversy*. Berkeley: University of California Press, 2014.

Sheridan, Ruth. *Retelling Scripture: "The Jews" and the Scriptural Citations in John 1:19–12:15*. BIS 110. Leiden: Brill, 2012.

Shiell, William D. *Delivering from Memory: The Effect of Performance on the Early Christian Audience*. Eugene, OR: Pickwick, 2011.

———. *Proclaiming the Gospel: First-Century Performance of Mark*. Harrisburg, PA: Trinity Press International, 2003.

Shiner, Whitney T. "Memory Technology and the Composition of Mark." Pages 147–65 in *Performing the Gospel: Orality, Memory and Mark*. Edited by Richard A. Horsley, Jonathan A. Draper, and John Miles Foley. Minneapolis: Fortress, 2006.

Small, Jocelyn P. *Wax Tablets of the Mind: Cognitive Studies of Memory and Literacy in Classical Antiquity*. London: Routledge, 1997.

Smend, Friedrich. "Die Behandlung alttestamentlicher Zitate als Ausgangspunkt der Quellenscheidung im 4. Evangelium." *ZNW* 24 (1925): 147–50.

Smith, D. Moody. *The Fourth Gospel in Four Dimensions: Judaism and Jesus, the Gospels and Scripture*. Columbia: University of South Carolina Press, 2008.

Spaulding, Mary B. *Commemorative Identities: Jewish Social Memory and the Johannine Feast of Booths*. London: T&T Clark, 2009.

Staley, Jeffrey L. *The Print's First Kiss: A Rhetorical Investigation of the Implied Reader in the Fourth Gospel*. SBLDS 82. Atlanta: Scholars Press, 1988.

———. "The Structure of John's Prologue: Its Implications for the Gospel's Narrative Structure." *CBQ* 48 (1986): 241–64.

Stamps, Dennis L. "Use of the Old Testament in the New Testament as a Rhetorical Device." Pages 9–37 in *Hearing the Old Testament in the New Testament*. Edited by Stanley E. Porter. Grand Rapids: Eerdmans, 2006.

Stanley, Christopher D. "The Rhetoric of Quotations: An Essay on Method." Pages 44-58 in *Early Christian Interpretation of the Scriptures*. Edited by Craig A. Evans and James A. Sanders. JSNTSup 148. Sheffield: Sheffield Academic, 1997.

Stauffer, Ethelbert. "Historische Elemente im vierten Evangelium." Pages 33-51 in *Bekenntnis zur Kirche: Festgabe für Ernst Sommerlath*. Edited by E. H. Amberg and U. Kuhn. Berlin: Evangelische Verlagsanstalt, 1960.

Steiner, George. *In Bluebeard's Castle: Some Notes towards the Redefinition of Culture*. New Haven: Yale University Press, 1971.

Stewart, Eric C. *Gathered around Jesus: An Alternative Spatial Practice in the Gospel of Mark*. Matrix 6. Eugene, OR: Cascade, 2009.

Stibbe, Mark W. G. *John's Gospel*. NTR. London: Routledge, 1994.

Swancutt, Diana M. "Hungers Assuaged by the Bread of Heaven: 'Eating Jesus' as Isaian Call to Belief: The Confluence of Isaiah 55 and Psalm 78(77) in John 6.22-71." Pages 218-51 in *Early Christian Interpretation of the Scriptures of Israel*. Edited by Craig A. Evans and James A. Sanders. JSNTSup 148. SSEJC 5. Sheffield: Sheffield Academic, 1997.

Sweeney, Marvin A. *The Twelve Prophets*. 2 vols. BO. Collegeville, MN: Liturgical Press, 2000.

Swidler, Ann. "Culture in Action: Symbols and Strategies." *ASR* 51 (1986): 273-86.

Tabb, Brian J. "Johannine Fulfillment of Scripture: Continuity and Escalation." *BBR* 21 (2011): 495-505.

Thatcher, Tom. "Cain and Abel in Early Christian Memory: A Case Study in 'The Use of the Old Testament in the New.'" *CBQ* 72 (2010): 732-51.

———. "Cain the Jew the AntiChrist: Collective Memory and the Johannine Ethic of Loving and Hating." Pages 350-73 in *Rethinking the Ethics of John: "Implicit Ethics" in the Johannine Writings*. Contexts and Norms of New Testament Ethics 3. Edited by Jan G. van der Watt and Ruben Zimmermann. WUNT 291. Tübingen: Mohr Siebeck, 2012.

———. "John's Memory Theatre: A Study of Composition in Performance." Pages 73-91 in *The Fourth Gospel in First-Century Media Culture*. Edited by Anthony Le Donne and Tom Thatcher. LNTS 426. London: T&T Clark, 2011.

Theobald, Michael. "Abraham- (Isaak-) Jakob. Israel's Väter im Johannesevangelium." Pages 158-83 in *Israel und seine Heilstraditionen im Johannesevangelium: Festgabe für Johannes Beutler SJ zum 70. Geburt-*

stag. Edited by Michael Labahn et al. Paderborn: Ferdinand Schöningh, 2004.

Thomas, Rosalind. *Literacy and Orality in Ancient Greece*. KTAH. Cambridge: Cambridge University Press, 1992.

Thompson, Marianne Meye. *John*. NTL. Louisville: Westminster John Knox, forthcoming.

———. "'They Bear Witness to Me': The Psalms in the Passion Narrative of the Gospel of John." Pages 267-83 in *The Word Leaps the Gap: Essays on Scripture and Theology in Honor of Richard B. Hays*. Edited by J. Ross Wagner, C. Kavin Rowe, and Katherine Grieb. Grand Rapids: Eerdmans, 2008.

Tigay, Jeffrey H. *Deuteronomy*. JPSTC. Philadelphia: Jewish Publication Society, 1996.

Torrey, Charles Cutler. *Four Gospels: A New Translation*. 2nd ed. New York: Harper & Brothers, 1947.

Trebilco, Paul. *The Early Christians in Ephesus from Paul to Ignatius*. Grand Rapids: Eerdmans, 2007.

Trites, Allison A. *The New Testament Concept of Witness*. SNTSMS 31. Cambridge: Cambridge University Press, 1977.

Ulrich, Eugene. "The Bible in the Making." Pages 51-66 in *The Bible at Qumran: Text, Shape, and Interpretation*. Edited by Peter W. Flint. Grand Rapids: Eerdmans, 2001.

Van Dyke, Ruth M., and Susan E. Alcock. "Archaeologies of Memory: An Introduction." Pages 1-13 in *Archaeologies of Memory*. Edited by Ruth M. Van Dyke and Susan E. Alcock. Malden, MA: Blackwell, 2003.

VanderKam, James C., and Peter Flint. *The Meaning of the Dead Sea Scrolls: Their Significance for Understanding the Bible, Judaism, Jesus, and Christianity*. San Francisco: HarperSanFrancisco, 2002.

Voorwinde, Stephen. *Jesus' Emotions in the Fourth Gospel: Human or Divine?* London: T&T Clark, 2005.

Walton, John H. *Genesis 1 as Ancient Cosmology*. Winona Lake, IN: Eisenbrauns, 2011.

———. *The Lost World of Genesis One: Ancient Cosmology and the Origins Debate*. Downers Grove, IL: InterVarsity Press, 2009.

Watson, Francis. *Gospel Writing: A Canonical Perspective*. Grand Rapids: Eerdmans, 2013.

Webb, Ruth. "The *Progymnasmata* in Practice." Pages 289-316 in *Education in Greek and Roman Antiquity*. Edited by Yun Lee Too. Leiden: Brill, 2001.

Webster, Jane S. *Ingesting Jesus: Eating and Drinking in the Gospel of John.* Atlanta: Society of Biblical Literature, 2003.

Welborn, Laurence L. "By the Mouth of Two or Three Witnesses: Paul's Invocation of a Deuteronomic Statute." *NovT* 52 (2010): 207-20.

Wellhausen, Julius. *Prolegomena zur Geschichte Israels.* 6th ed. Berlin: Neudruck, 1927.

Wenham, Gordon J. *Psalms as Torah: Reading Biblical Song Ethically.* STI. Grand Rapids: Baker Academic, 2012.

Wenzel, Heiko. *Reading Zechariah with Zechariah 1:1-6 as the Introduction to the Entire Book.* Leuven: Peeters, 2011.

Weren, Wim. "Jesus' Entry into Jerusalem: Matthew 21:1-17 in the Light of the Hebrew Bible and the Septuagint." Pages 117-41 in *The Scriptures in the Gospels.* Edited by Christopher M. Tuckett. BETL 131. Leuven: Leuven University Press, 1997.

Westermann, Claus. *The Gospel of John in the Light of the Old Testament.* Translated by Siegfried S. Schatzmann. Peabody, MA: Hendrickson, 1998.

Whitehead, Anne. *Memory.* NCI. London: Routledge, 2009.

Williams, Catrin H. "Abraham as a Figure of Memory in John 8:31-59." Pages 205-22 in *The Fourth Gospel in First-Century Media Culture.* Edited by Anthony Le Donne and Tom Thatcher. LNTS 426. London: T&T Clark, 2011.

———. "John (the Baptist): The Wilderness on the Threshold." Pages 46-60 in *Character Studies in the Fourth Gospel: Narrative Approaches to Seventy Figures.* Edited by Steven A. Hunt, D. Francois Tolmie, and Ruben Zimmermann. WUNT 314. Tübingen: Mohr Siebeck, 2013.

———. "The Testimony of Isaiah and Johannine Christology." Pages 107-24 in *"As Those Who Are Taught": The Interpretation of Isaiah from the LXX to the SBL.* Edited by Claire Matthews McGinnis and Patricia K. Tull. SBLSymS 27. Atlanta: Society of Biblical Literature, 2006.

Wilson, Britanny E. "Pugnacious Precursors and the Bearer of Peace: Jael, Judith, and Mary in Luke 1:42." *CBQ* 68 (2006): 436-56.

Witmer, Stephen E. "Approaches to Scripture in the Fourth Gospel and the Qumran *Pesharim*." *NovT* 48 (2006): 313-28.

Wucherpfennig, Ansgar. *Heracleon Philologus: Gnostische Johannesexegese im zweiten Jahrhundert.* WUNT 142. Tübingen: Mohr Siebeck, 2002.

Wyller, Egil A. "In Solomon's Porch: A Henological Analysis of the Architectonic of the Fourth Gospel." *ST* 42 (1988): 151-67.

Yates, Frances A. *The Art of Memory*. Chicago: University of Chicago Press, 1966.
Yerushalmi, Yosef H. *Zakhor: Jewish History and Jewish Memory*. Seattle: University of Washington Press, 1982.
Zelizer, Barbie. "Reading the Past against the Grain: The Shape of Memory Studies." *CSMC* 12 (1995): 214–39.
Zerubavel, Eviatar. *Ancestors and Relatives: Genealogy, Identity, and Community*. Oxford: Oxford University Press, 2012.
———. "In the Beginning: Notes on the Social Construction of Historical Discontinuity." *SI* 63 (1993): 457–59.
———. *Time Maps: Collective Memory and the Social Shape of the Past*. Chicago: University of Chicago Press, 2003.
Zumstein, Jean. *L'Évangile selon Saint Jean*. 2 vols. CNT 4AB. Geneva: Labor et Fides, 2014.

Contributors

Jeffrey E. Brickle is associate professor of biblical studies at Urshan Graduate School of Theology in Florissant, Missouri. He holds a PhD from Concordia Seminary, St. Louis, and is the author of *Aural Design and Coherence in the Prologue of First John* (2012). His research centers on the confluence of Johannine literature with ancient media culture, with a special focus on how the dynamics of orality, memory, and performance influenced ancient texts, lectors, and audiences.

William Randolph Bynum holds a PhD from the University of Manchester. He is bivocational, teaching Bible part-time at Northwest Nazarene University and pastoring in Nampa, Idaho. He is author of *The Fourth Gospel and the Scriptures* (2012) and "What the Dead Sea Scrolls Can Tell Us about Contemporary Bible Issues" (*The Bible Tells Me So*, 2011). His research focuses on LXX textual history, textual criticism, the Book of the Twelve, the Dead Sea Scrolls, and the Gospel of John.

Jaime Clark-Soles is associate professor of New Testament at Perkins School of Theology, Southern Methodist University in Dallas, Texas. She is the author of *Scripture Cannot Be Broken* (2003), *Death and Afterlife in the New Testament* (2006), and *Engaging the Word* (2010). Her current projects include two books, *Reading for Dear Life: The Gospel of John* and *Women in the Bible*, and current essays exploring disability studies as it relates to Johannine literature and the reception history of the Johannine Epistles.

Michael A. Daise is associate professor of religious studies at the College of William and Mary, where he teaches formative Judaism and the origins of Christianity. He has published a number of articles on the Gospel of John, the Dead Sea Scrolls, the historical Jesus, and the Old Testament Pseudepigrapha. He has coedited (with James H. Charlesworth) *Light in a Spotless Mirror* (2003) and is author of *Feasts in John* (2007).

Benjamin J. Lappenga is assistant professor of theology at Dordt College in Sioux Center, Iowa, earned his PhD from Fuller Theological Seminary, and has had articles published in leading journals in the field of biblical studies, including *Journal of Biblical Literature* and *Catholic Biblical Quarterly*. He is currently revising his doctoral dissertation on Paul's language of ζῆλος for publication as a monograph in 2015.

Alicia D. Myers is assistant professor of New Testament and Greek at Campbell University Divinity School in Buies Creek, North Carolina, and previously assistant professor at United Theological Seminary, Dayton, Ohio. She is the author of *Characterizing Jesus* (2012) as well as several journal articles on the Gospel of John and the use of Scripture in the New Testament. Her current research focuses on expectations surrounding mothers and motherhood in Mediterranean antiquity as a lens for New Testament interpretation.

Bruce G. Schuchard is professor of exegetical theology (New Testament) at Concordia Seminary, St. Louis, Missouri, where he has taught since 1997. Previously he served as a parish pastor at St. James Lutheran Church in Victor, Iowa. He holds a PhD in biblical studies from Union Theological Seminary in Richmond, Virginia. He is author of *Scripture within Scripture* (1992) and *1–3 John* (Concordia Commentary Series, 2012).

Ruth Sheridan is currently a postdoctoral research fellow at the Faculty of Arts, Charles Sturt University (North Parramatta campus), Sydney. She specializes in the rhetorical and narratological dimensions of early Christian anti-Judaism, specifically in the Gospel of John. Her first monograph, *Retelling Scripture* (2012), won the 2013 Manfred Lautenschlaeger Award for Theological Promise. She is currently at work on another monograph (T&T Clark), which analyzes the role of Abraham in John 8.

Catrin H. Williams is senior lecturer in New Testament Studies and currently joint head of the School of Theology, Religious Studies, and Islamic Studies at the University of Wales Trinity Saint David, having previously been senior lecturer at Bangor University and university lecturer and tutorial fellow at the University of Oxford. She is the author of *I Am He* (2000) and has recently coedited two volumes on John's Gospel (*John's Gospel and Intimations of Apocalyptic* with Christopher Rowland, 2013; *Historical Tradition in the Fourth Gospel* with Tom Thatcher, 2013).

Subject Index

Abraham, 20, 188–189, 192, 201–7, 209 n. 53, 210–12, 226. *See also* Genesis
 Apocalypse of Abraham, 203, 205
 Testament of Abraham, 203, 205
Acts, 109 n. 24, 146 n. 17, 158, 230
apostasy (idolatry), 19, 108, 170–72, 175–77, 180–82, 184, 202–3
Augustine of Hippo, 230 n. 72
avenger of blood, 174–75, 178–79, 183–84
Baptist, John the, 19, 36, 37 n. 62, 39, 44–45, 48, 101, 116, 119–39, 150, 165, 207–8
2 Baruch, 195, 206
blindness (and sight), 31–33, 63, 71–74, 103, 105, 108, 113, 130 n. 26, 133 n. 32, 158, 188, 195–96, 205–12, 223
 blind man, 157 n. 40, 199,
Book of the Twelve. *See* Twelve, Book of the
Christology, 7, 9 n. 30, 14–17, 20, 41, 47–49, 51, 53–54, 62, 68, 71–73, 86, 95–96 n. 2, 112 n. 29, 138–39, 180, 188, 205, 207, 240–41, 244–45
 bridegroom (nuptial, marriage), 38 n. 67, 131, 174 n. 41, 234
 christocentric hermeneutic, 2–4, 10, 15, 18, 57, 75–76 n. 4, 208, 240–41
 christocentric literary structure, 35
 creator, 38 n. 67, 88–90, 133, 226, 230, 234
 Logos (Word), 16, 89, 133 n. 32, 137, 193–94, 229–30, 234
 king, 16, 32–33, 38 n. 66, 50–52, 54, 56, 59–63, 73–74, 81–85, 88–90, 156

Chrysostom, John, 146 n. 17, 183–84 n. 65
circumcision, 198–99
cities of refuge, 173–79
classical rhetoric, 12–13, 19–20, 119–39, 213–36, 237–38, 240–43
 ancient authors
  Aelius Theon, 123–24, 126–27, 129 n. 23, 130–31 n. 28, 134 n. 33, 135 n. 35, 228
  Aristotle (Pseudo-Aristotle), 119 n. 1, 121,123 n. 13, 125–28, 129 n. 23, 134 n. 34, 213, 219, 227 n. 56
  Cicero (Pseudo-Cicero), 119 n. 1, 121, 124, 125 nn. 16–17, 126, 127 n. 20, 134 n. 33, 135–37, 213, 216, 219, 227 n. 56, 228–29
  Pseudo-Hermogenes, 135 n. 35
  Quintilian, 119 n. 1, 121, 123 n. 11, 124–27, 129 n. 23, 130, 131 n. 29, 134–37, 213, 219, 226 n. 54, 227 n. 56, 228–29 n. 64, 231
 mimesis (imitation), 12, 122–23, 127 n. 20, 128–29, 138–39
 paideia (education), 122–23 n. 9
 progymnasmata, 12–13, 119 n. 1, 121, 123–24, 126–27, 129, 131, 134–35, 228
 species of rhetoric
  epideictic, 120–21
  juridical (forensic), 6, 119–21, 132–33, 136, 172 n. 38
 techniques
  climax (κλῖμαξ), 129–30, 138

classical rhetoric: techniques (cont.)
  comparison (*synkrisis, similitudo,* παραβολή), 124–27, 134–36, 225 n. 54, 242–43
  example (*exempla*, πράγματα, παραδείγματα), 19, 121, 123 n. 11, 125–27, 134–35, 138–39, 203, 211, 228
  proofs, 126–27, 132, 134–35, 137. *See also* testimony and witness
  speech-in-character (*prosōpopoiia, ēthopoiia*), 127, 133–34, 138
  topoi (topics), 120 n. 6, 123, 130–31 n. 28, 219
1 Clement, 159
consume, 19, 30, 78–80, 88–89 n. 40, 141–59
1–2 Corinthians, 72, 110 n. 26, 158, 164, 176
criticisms
  form criticism, 5, 238–39
  historical criticism, 5, 15 n. 45
  literary criticism, 13, 19, 85, 129 n. 25, 159, 166–67, 169 n. 32
  literary-rhetorical criticism, 115, 120
  memory theory, 20, 187–212, 213–36, 237–38, 241, 243–45, 246
  performance theory, 20, 95, 122, 131, 213–36, 238, 241, 243–44, 246
  reader-response criticism, 159
  redaction criticism, 5–7, 14, 23–45, 47–74, 75–91, 189, 238–39
  rhetorical criticism, 4, 9, 12, 17, 19–20, 26, 41, 52, 55, 57–58, 76 n. 4, 95 n. 2, 97, 100, 106, 115–16, 119–39, 141–59, 161–84
  sociological criticism, 4, 15–16, 19–20, 95–117, 187–212, 213–36, 237, 241–42, 245–46
  source criticism, 4–8, 9, 14, 17–18, 23–45, 47–74, 75–91, 169 n. 32, 238–41
  tradition criticism, 85 n. 34
crucifixion (cross), 3, 18, 37 n. 63, 39 n. 70, 47, 49, 65–66, 69–74, 77, 90 n. 42, 108, 150, 156, 195–96, 209. *See also* passion narrative under John, Gospel (selected portions)
David, 50 n. 20, 143, 156–57
Dead Sea Scrolls, 6–8, 10, 16, 77 n. 7, 97–98, 113, 143, 148, 164, 176, 180, 238, 240.
Deuteronomy, 19, 128, 163–64, 170–84, 192, 195, 197
disciples, 18, 36, 37 n. 64, 38 n. 67, 39, 44–45, 61–62, 65, 69, 77, 78, 80, 82–83, 86–91, 101, 102, 107–15, 131, 141, 149, 151–54, 158, 199–201, 204, 206, 207, 233
  Andrew, 44
  Beloved Disciple, the, 44, 109 n. 23
  Judas, 37, 44, 101, 102, 108, 110, 183
  Nathanael, 44, 130 n. 27, 195
  Peter, 44, 214
  Philip, 38, 44, 195
  Thomas, 37, 44
drama, 48, 223–24, 229–30, 233
echoes (allusions), 1, 2, 5, 9, 13, 17, 47 n. 1–5, 48, 69, 124, 127, 131, 136–38, 157, 166–79, 184, 192, 194, 203, 225, 239, 241
eschatology, 10, 51, 70
Elijah, 128, 133, 143
Ephesians, 109 n. 24
Exodus, 30–31, 37, 42, 45, 71, 77–79, 81 n. 19, 128, 135, 142, 172, 173 n. 39, 194–95, 197, 226, 234
Ezekiel, 142–43
4 Ezra, 195, 205
  foot-washing, 37, 44
formulae, 6, 26, 38–41, 45, 51–54, 65–66, 72, 75–91, 101–3, 207, 240
fulfillment, 39 n. 72, 40–41, 45, 52–54, 65–66, 72, 77, 88, 102–3
Genesis, 33–34, 38 n. 67, 81 n. 19, 83–84, 89–90, 128–29, 174, 179, 198, 203, 205, 226, 234
glory (δόξα/δοξάζω), 38, 51 n. 22, 72, 82, 87, 103, 106, 108, 130, 132–33, 135, 137, 142, 145–46, 153, 188, 193–95, 207–11

SUBJECT INDEX

Greco-Roman rhetoric. *See* classical rhetoric
Greek OT (LXX, Old Greek), 6–8, 17–18, 20, 24, 27–35, 42–43, 45, 50 n. 21, 55–57, 59, 67–69, 76, 78–81, 83–85, 110 121, 143, 149, 154–57, 163, 171–72, 174–78, 181, 183, 196, 207 n. 49, 208–9, 217, 226, 238–40
Hebrew Bible (MT), 7, 24, 27–28, 31–32, 34–35, 56 n. 42, 58–59, 67–69, 76, 77 n. 7, 78 n. 8, 79, 81, 83–85, 143, 155, 174 n. 41, 175–76, 181, 238
Hebrews, 4, 109 n. 24, 164, 176
Hosea, 107 n. 22, 171 n. 37
hour, 36 n. 60, 37–38, 40–41, 44, 111 nn. 27–28, 153
house (household, family, kin, children, sons, daughters), 19, 30, 32, 37 n. 64, 52, 74, 78–80, 84–85, 88–89, 100–101, 105, 107, 111 n. 27, 116, 130, 141–59, 174 n. 41, 179, 183, 201–5, 207
inclusio (frames, framing), 18–19, 36 n. 59, 37, 39, 40 n. 77, 44, 45, 47–48, 65, 69, 71, 73, 86, 89–90, 109, 111 n. 27, 207, 211, 240
intertextuality, 9, 13–15, 17, 34 n. 51, 76 n. 4, 121–28, 139, 164, 166–84, 187, 213–36, 239, 241,
  metaleptic intertextuality, 166–70, 180, 183
introductory formulae. *See* formulae
Isaiah, 20, 121, 131, 136, 188–89, 192, 210–12
  book of Isaiah, 7, 9 n. 30, 14, 19, 23, 28, 29, 31, 33, 39, 40, 42, 43, 45, 47, 52, 55, 59, 77–79, 81 n. 18–19, 88 n. 39, 101–3, 105–8, 110 n. 26, 121, 128, 131–39, 150, 171, 172, 174, 175, 207–10
  Testament of Isaiah, 208
James, 109
Jeremiah, 81 n. 19, 83, 107, 171 n. 37, 175 n. 43
Jerusalem (and Zion), 32, 37 n. 61, 50, 51 n. 22, 52, 54, 59–63, 73, 74, 80, 82, 83–85, 89, 109 n. 25, 131–33, 135, 138, 143, 146 n. 17, 148, 149, 158, 172, 180, 229, 232, 233
Jesus. *See also* Christology
Jesus, characterization of, 17, 226 n. 54, 242–43
Jesus, historical, 8, 95–96 n. 2
Jewish festivals, 1, 38 n. 67, 80, 131, 180
  Passover, 38, 44, 48, 71–72, 83, 86, 89–90, 131, 146–47 n. 17, 148, 234
Jews, the (οἱ Ἰουδαῖοι), 1–3, 7, 9–20, 25, 27–28, 31–32 nn. 40 and 42, 33 n. 49, 35, 53, 57, 63–64, 68–69, 77, 80, 87–88 n. 37, 98 n. 3, 101–2, 107, 128, 130 n. 27, 131, 134, 137, 139. *See also* Dead Sea Scrolls; Pharisees
  anti-Judaism (anti-Semitism), 1, 17, 20, 114–15, 159, 166, 182, 184, 245
  Jews, characterization of, 1, 17, 19, 53, 76 n. 4, 80, 104–6, 110, 132, 141–59, 161–84, 187–212, 213–36, 239–40, 242–46
Johannine community
  historical situation, 15–17, 63–65, 68, 74, 95–117, 158–59, 168, 194 n. 23, 210 n. 56, 214
  perspective as ideal ("insider") audience, 9, 14–20, 48, 53, 57–59, 62–65, 68, 70–74, 76 n. 4, 95–117, 119–39, 141–59, 161–84, 187–212, 213–36, 239–40
1 John, 28 n. 23, 72, 109 n. 24, 129
John, Gospel (selected portions)
  prologue, 1, 20, 37 n. 62, 38 n. 67, 44–45, 74, 89–90, 111 n. 27, 112, 121, 128–34, 136–39, 148–49, 153–54, 183, 193–98, 200–201, 204, 209, 211, 226, 229–30, 232, 234
  Book of Jesus's Hour (John 11–20), 36–41, 44–45
  Book of the Signs (John 1–12), 18–19, 41, 45, 86, 89–90, 111 n. 27
  Book of the Testimony (John 1–10), 36–41, 44–45

SUBJECT INDEX

John, Gospel (selected portions) (cont.)
   triumphal entry, 16, 32–34, 37 n. 63, 38 n. 66–67, 39, 45, 47–74, 75–91, 115–16, 129, 153
   passion narrative (John 13–19), 6, 18, 20, 30 n. 34, 37–38, 44, 47–74, 156–57
   epilogue, 20, 33 n. 48, 36 n. 60, 37 n. 62, 38 n. 66, 44–45, 109 n. 23, 114, 121, 230, 233
Josephus, 143, 144 n. 11, 147 n. 19
   Jewish Antiquities 143, 147 n. 19–20, 148, 203
   Jewish War, 143, 144 n. 11, 147 n. 19
Joshua, 30 n. 32, 171 n. 37, 177 n. 46
Jubilees, book of, 143, 197, 203, 205
Jude, 109 n. 24
judge, judgment, 6, 33 n. 49, 38 n. 66, 50, 70, 97, 116, 119–121, 132–33, 136, 148 n. 21, 161, 164–65, 166, 171–73, 178, 182–84. *See also* trial; testimony and witness
Judges, 171 n. 37
Justin Martyr, 155 n. 36, 181 n. 61
1–2 Kings, 33 n. 47, 142, 143, 171 n. 37, 172, 179
Lamentations, 107 n. 22
Lazarus, 36–37, 64, 105, 147 n. 18
Leviticus, 109–10, 174 n. 41, 175 n. 43, 176
Logos (Word). *See* Christology
1–2 Maccabees, 143, 146 n. 17, 158
3–4 Maccabees, 158
Masoretic Text (MT). *See* Hebrew Bible
meals, 37, 44. *See also* Jewish festivals
memory, 5, 7–8, 20, 24, 25 n. 6, 56, 131 n. 29, 188–89, 213–36, 237–38, 241, 243–46 . *See* criticisms
   remembrance, 3 n. 7, 18, 75–91, 102, 110, 112, 116, 141, 149, 151–54, 158, 192–212, 244
Minor Prophets. *See* Twelve, Book of the
Moses, 27 n. 16, 37 n. 61, 39 n. 68, 108, 110 n. 26, 130 n. 27, 147 n. 20, 165, 181, 188–89, 192–201, 204, 207, 210–12, 234. *See also* Torah (Law)
   prophet-like-Moses, 128, 195
   Testament of Moses, 149
murder, 125 n. 17, 173–80, 182–83, 204
Nehemiah, 81 n. 19, 143, 149, 174 n. 41
Nicodemus, 44, 69, 104 n. 19, 105, 110, 195
Numbers, 19, 72, 77, 79, 81 n. 19, 108, 143, 163, 170, 171 n. 37, 173 n. 39, 174 n. 41, 177–79, 180, 183, 184, 195–97, 199, 234
orality (and aurality), 20, 24 n. 5, 56, 95 n. 2, 187, 228 n. 62, 235, 244
Origen of Alexandria, 87, 155 n. 36
Passover. *See* Jewish festivals
patriarchs, 198, 205, 216, 234, 244. *See also* Abraham
Paul, 4, 72, 106, 109, 110 n. 26, 119, 158, 159 n. 45, 166, 168, 176 n. 44
perjury, 19, 170, 175–77, 180, 182, 183 n. 65, 184
Pharisees, 104, 110, 146, 161, 163, 165–66, 170, 180–82, 199, 210
Philo of Alexandria, 10, 143, 144
   Legatio ad Gaius, 144
   Life of Moses, 147 n. 19
   De specialibus legibus, 146, 148
Pilate, 147, 154, 183
Phinehas, 143, 158
Plato, 123, 213, 227 n. 56,
pneumatology, 3 n. 7, 19, 85, 86–88, 90
   Paraclete, 86, 138
   Holy Spirit, 3 n. 7, 54, 62, 86–91, 107, 129, 134, 137–39, 243
priests (and chief priests, high priests), 89, 128, 144, 146, 171–73, 179, 180
   Caiaphas, 146–47, 152
prophets, 14, 27 n. 16, 39, 40, 51 n. 22, 63, 67, 73, 101, 104, 106–7, 110 n. 26, 121, 128, 131–39, 145, 148, 171, 182, 188, 192, 195, 205, 207–10. *See also* Isaiah
Psalms, 13, 19, 28–31, 33–34, 42–43, 45, 55, 72, 77–85, 88–90, 107, 110, 141–43, 148–51, 153, 154–57, 159, 197, 225 *See also* David
Psalms of Solomon, 143, 149

SUBJECT INDEX

Qumran, *See* Dead Sea Scrolls
rabbis/rabbinic interpretations, 11, 65, 181
  middot, 11–12
  midrash, 10–11, 13
  Mishnah, 69 n. 111, 144, 181 n. 62, 199
  pesher, 10–11, 13
  Talmud, 181
  Targum, 81 n. 19
Revelation, 28 n. 23, 29 n. 27, 47 n. 2, 69, 70, 109, 224 n. 44
Romans, Letter to the, 109 n. 24, 158, 159
Sabbath, 37 n. 63, 89, 113, 146, 198–99
1–2 Samuel, 34, 143, 171 n. 37, 173 n. 39, 179
sect/sectarianism. *See* Dead Sea Scrolls
Septuagint (LXX). *See* Greek OT
servant, 9, 14, 112, 209
signs (σημεῖα), 37 n. 61, 38 n. 67, 41 n. 82, 49, 52–54, 60, 73, 103–4, 137–38, 141, 145, 150, 151, 197, 209, 227
Sirach (Ben Sira, Ecclesiasticus), 81 n. 19, 143, 195, 208 n. 51
sociology. *See* criticisms
symbol (symbolism), 13 n. 41, 49, 60, 73–74, 98–99, 145, 148, 149 n. 22, 179, 190–92, 206, 209–10, 213, 220, 225 n. 50, 229, 230 n. 72
synagogue, 27 nn. 15–16, 38 n. 66, 68, 104, 108, 147, 210
Synoptic Gospels, 7 n. 25, 57, 76, 78–79, 82–83 n. 23, 105–6, 108, 121, 128, 149, 214
temple, 16, 78, 80, 85 n. 34, 87 n. 37, 88–90, 130, 141–59, 162, 165, 171–75, 177–78, 180–82, 209, 219–222, 225, 232–33
testimonia, 5, 9 n. 29, 41 n. 84, 156 n. 38, 239
testimony and witness, 1, 13 n. 41, 16–17, 19–20, 26, 30 n.34, 31, n. 40, 36, 39, 40 n. 79, 44, 48, 56, 58, 60, 71–73, 79 n. 13, 80 n. 38, 99–101, 105, 112, 122, 128–30, 132–39, 149–50, 154 n. 32, 156 n. 38, 157 n. 42, 161–84, 195, 207, 217 n. 14, 246
  of scripture generally, 2, 9 n. 30, 14 n. 43–44, 16, 19, 39, 44, 81 n. 18, 113, 161–84, 170, 175, 181–82, 184, 186, 188, 192–97, 200, 207–12, 215, 243–44
  classical rhetorical techniques, 19, 119, 121, 125–26, 132–34, 136–39
theology, 3, 7, 15, 17, 20, 30 n. 34, 36 n. 59, 38 n. 67, 54 n. 30, 56 n. 43, 70, 72 n. 122, 77, 131 n. 29, 150 n. 23, 167 n. 26, 215, 217 n. 14, 232 n. 84, 240–41, 245
  God as Father, 19, 38 n.66, 60, 72 n. 123, 74, 78, 86, 89, 105, 109, 111 n. 27, 113–14, 130, 133 n. 32, 145–46, 149, 153, 157 n. 41, 158, 161–62, 183–84, 197, 203–5
Thomas, 37, 44
1 Timothy, 164, 176
Titus, 109 n. 24, 158
Torah (Law), 3, 40, 58 n. 52, 63 n. 82, 64 n. 82, 101–2, 108, 110, 113, 130 n.26, 142, 147, 161–66, 170–73, 180 n. 57, 181–84, 188, 193, 195–96, 198–201, 211, 234
trial, 120 n. 3, 133–34, 152 n. 26, 153 n. 27, 165–66, 171–72, 174, 178, 180–84, 210 n. 56. *See also* judge, judgment; classical rhetoric: species of rhetoric: juridical
Twelve, Book of the, 39 n. 71, 47, 58, 68
week(s), 37–40, 44, 49, 89
wisdom, 8 n. 25, 111
  Logos. *See* Christology
witness. *See* testimony and witness
world (κόσμος), 3, 12, 16, 20, 34, 38 n. 66, 48, 58, 72–73, 97–99, 109–14, 119 n. 1, 120, 122, 123 n. 13, 129, 131 n. 29, 134, 139, 141 n. 1, 157 n. 40, 161, 163, 166, 172 n. 38, 191 n. 11, 197–98, 208, 215, 221 n. 3, 223 n. 37, 227, 232–34, 236
zeal (ζῆλος), 19, 30, 78, 89–90, 141–54, 156 n. 36, 156 n. 38, 157–59

zeal (ζῆλος) (cont.)
    Zealots, 142–44, 147 n. 19, 158–59
Zechariah, 8, 18, 31, 32 n. 42–43, 33,
    39, 42, 43, 45, 47–74, 77–79, 81–82,
    84–85, 88–90, 144 n. 11, 153
Zephaniah, 59, 81, 84

Modern Authors Index

Abl, Martin C.   5
Achtemeier, Elizabeth   61, 63
Achtemeier, Paul J.   8
Ahn, Sanghee Michael   188
Alcock, Susan E.   220, 222, 232
Alkier, Stefan   13, 15
Allison Jr., Dale C.   218
Anderson, Paul   161, 183
Archer, Gleason L.   55, 68
Ashley, Timothy R.   179
Ashton, John   196, 198
Asiedu-Peprah, Martin   165
Assmann, Aleida   216
Assmann, Jan   190, 199, 202, 214
Attridge, Harold W.   12, 119, 120, 155
Barmash, Pamela   172, 173, 174, 176
Barrett, C. K.   28, 59, 79, 82, 83, 110, 163, 165, 181, 184
Bartholomew, Craig G.   215, 221
Bates, Matthew W.   155
Bauckham, Richard   26, 64, 217, 230
Beale, Gregory K.   55, 232
Beutler, Johannes   177
Bewernick, Hanne   231, 232
Black, Clifton C.   119
Blenkinsopp, Joseph   81
Blomberg, Craig L.   56, 217
Boer, Martinus C. de.   199
Boice, James Montgomery   60, 66, 70
Boismard, Marie-Émile   81, 89
Bolter, Jay D.   224, 225
Borgen, Peder   10
Brant, Jo-Ann A.   12, 55, 56, 61, 66, 72, 120, 129, 130, 223
Brawley, Robert L.   13

Brickle, Jeffrey E.   20, 24, 214, 228,
Brodie, Thomas L.   48, 60, 64
Brooke, George J.   48, 58
Brown, David   67
Brown, Raymond E.   47, 48, 59, 65, 80–84, 87, 89, 104, 109, 110, 141, 148, 157, 159, 162
Brown, Sherri   136
Bruce, F. F.   59, 60, 72
Brueggemann, Walter   221
Bruford, Alan   228, 233
Brunson, Andrew   13
Bryan, Steven M.   30, 148
Bullock, C. Hassell   143
Bultmann, Rudolf   80, 84, 87, 89, 110, 148, 193
Burge, Gary M.   88
Burrell, Barbara   224
Burridge, Richard A.   120
Busse, Ulrich   157, 158
Bynum, Wm. Randolph   7, 8, 18, 26–28, 30–32, 34, 35, 39, 41, 47, 56, 58, 64, 65, 67, 68,
Byrskog, Samuel   189, 191, 203, 219
Campbell, Jonathan G.   110
Carr, David M.   214, 215
Carruthers, Mary   215, 217–19, 225–28, 230
Carson, Donald A.   2, 26, 36, 52, 55, 61, 62, 64, 217
Carter, Warren   194
Christensen, Duane L.   171–73
Clark-Soles, Jaime   15, 16, 19, 76, 95
Clay, Jenny Strauss   223, 229, 230
Clifford, Richard J.   88

Coloe, Mary	128, 161	Goheen, Michael W.	215
Craigie, Peter M.	171, 172	Goodwin, Charles	5
Crossan, John Dominic	218	Graham, William A.	228
Culpepper, R. Alan	103, 110, 128, 153	Gregory, Marshall.	215
Dahl, Nils Alstrup	208	Griffiths, Paul J.	215
Daise, Michael A.	1, 18, 77	Groenewald, Alphonso	154
Daly-Denton, Margaret	13, 30, 145, 153, 155, 156	Halbwachs, Maurice	189, 190, 202
Daube, David	12	Hamid-Khani, Saeed	16
Derrett, J. Duncan M.	143	Hanson, Anthony Tyrrell	194
deSilva, David A.	224	Harris, J. Rendel	5
Dodd, C. H.	2–5, 8, 9, 110, 148, 156, 162, 167	Harris, Max	223
		Harrison, Carol	227
Draper, Jonathan	95	Harstine, Stan	196
Duke, Paul D.	110	Harvey, Anthony E.	165
Dunn, James D. G.	219	Harvey, John	227
Ellens, J. Harold	10	Hasitschka, Martin	200
Ellis, Peter.	162	Hatina, Thomas R.	169
Elowsky, Joel C.	67, 70	Hauspie, Karin	175
Elsner, Jaś	232	Hays, Richard B.	13, 152, 153, 166–69
Esler, Philip F.	189	Hearon, Holly E.	189
Evans, C. Stephen	56	Heine, Ronald E.	156, 225
Evans, Craig A.	60, 149, 194, 209	Hendriksen, William	51, 66, 67
Eve, Eric	219	Hengel, Martin	10, 27, 32, 38, 40, 41, 54, 64, 89, 90, 144, 155, 196, 217
Eynikel, Erik	175	Hollander, John	166–68
Falcetta, Alessandro	5	Horsley, Richard	228
Fant, Clyde E.	222	Hoskyns, Edwyn C.	82, 110
Faure, Alexander	5, 6, 75	Householder, Jr., Fred W.	123
Faussett, A. R.	61	Huizenga, Leroy	13, 169
Fee, Gordon D.	2	Hylen, Susan	13
Felsch, Dorit	1	Instone-Brewer, David	181
Fentress, James	192	Jacobsen, Eric O.	221
Ferreiro, Alberto	62, 70	Jobes, Karen H.	27, 34
Fishbane, Michael A.	11	Johnson, Luke Timothy	141
Flint, Peter	76	Johnson, William A.	215, 224
Franke, August H.	75, 76, 78, 79, 81	Jong, Irene J. F. de	221
Freed, Edwin D.	5, 6, 7, 33, 35, 75, 77, 80, 81, 155	Juel, Donald H.	3, 10, 12
		Keck, Leander E.	112
Frey, Jörg	196, 209	Keener, Craig S.	162, 219
Gabel, John B.	56, 57, 70	Keith, Chris	181
Garfinkel, Harold	98–100, 106, 114, 150	Kelber, Werner H.	190, 230, 235
Gaston, Lloyd		Kennedy, George A.	12, 119, 123, 228
Genette, Gérard	167	Kerr, Alan R.	147, 154
George, Mark K.	221	Kirk, Alan	192, 196, 234
Gleason, Maud W.	122, 123	Klassen, William	143, 158

Koester, Craig R.	37	Mitchell, David C.	69
Köstenberger, Andreas J.	26, 30–33, 36–38, 55, 64, 65, 70, 225	Mlakuzhyil, George	36
		Moloney, Francis J.	15, 27, 40, 53, 55, 96, 141, 145, 165, 166,
Kristeva, Julia	13		
Kubiś, Adam	39, 76, 77	Moo, Douglas J.	36
Labahn, Michael	163	Morris, Leon	67, 110, 184
Lange, Tineke de	201	Motyer, Stephen	159
Lappenga, Benjamin J.	19, 159	Moyise, Steve	14, 15, 31, 47, 60, 96, 129, 163, 194
Le Donne, Anthony	219		
Lee, Margaret E.	227	Müller, Mogens	164
Levine, Baruch A.	177, 179	Murphy-O'Connor, Jerome	222
Levinson, Bernard M.	172	Myers, Alicia D.	vii, 12, 17, 23, 26, 48, 49, 53, 56, 57, 62, 65, 66, 68, 86, 87, 95, 120, 123, 125, 126, 134, 197, 225, 226, 228
Liebermann, Saul	12		
Lierman, John	192		
Lieu, Judith M.	129, 145, 179, 194, 198		
Lincoln, Andrew T.	119, 120, 152, 153, 165, 194, 198, 200, 210	Nasrallah, Laura S.	220
		Nelson, Richard D.	173, 175
Lindars, Barnabas	3, 4, 8, 10, 110, 162	Neusner, Jacob	232
Loisy, Alfred Firmin	82	Neyrey, Jerome	12, 120, 131, 164
Longenecker, Bruce W.	131	Noth, Martin	179
Longenecker, Richard N.	3, 10	Obermann, Andreas	15, 16, 75–77, 81, 164
Lust, Johan	175		
Malbon, Elizabeth S.	221	Öhler, Marcus	95
Malina, Bruce	162	Olick, Jeffrey K.	190, 206
Manning, Gary T.	13	Orchard, Helen C.	156
Manns, Frédéric	11, 49	Østenstad, Gunnar	36
Marcos, Natalio Fernández	27	Padilla, Osvaldo	121
Marcus, Joel	144	Pancaro, Severino	63
Marincola, John	134	Park, Yoon-Man	234
Martin, Michael W.	121	Parsenios, George L.	12, 119, 120
Martyn, J. Louis	2	Paschalis, Michael	220
Mason, Steve	141	Phillips, Peter M.	129
McConnell, James R.	136	Porter, Stanley E.	15
McIver, Robert K.	219	Pryor, John	61
McLay, R. Timothy	57, 58	Purves, Alex C.	221, 229, 232
Meeks, Wayne A.	15, 110, 192	Quek, Tze-Ming	128
Mendels, Doron	223, 224	Redditt, Paul L.	50, 63
Menken, Maarten J. J.	5–9, 14, 23–26, 28, 29, 31, 33–35, 39, 47, 56, 57, 59, 68, 75–77, 79, 80, 155, 163, 164, 197, 207	Reim, Günter	5–7, 75, 90, 155
		Reinhartz, Adele	133, 153, 161,
		Resseguie, James L.	221
Metzger, Bruce M.	74	Rhoads, David	142
Michaels, J. Ramsey	55, 67, 147, 221, 222	Richter, Georg	81
Milgrom, Jacob	172, 179	Ricoeur, Paul	226
Miller, Paul	52, 53, 54, 67	Ridderbos, Herman	61, 62
Minchin, Elizabeth	216	Rissi, Mathias	35, 36, 37

MODERN AUTHORS INDEX

Robbins, Joyce 190
Robertson, A. T. 55, 67
Rodriguez, Rafael 189, 216, 220
Rofé, Alexander 172
Rohrbaugh, Richard 162
Rubin, David C. 226, 227
Sanders, E. P. 149
Schafer, Peter 181
Schama, Simon 213
Schapdick, Stefan 194, 199
Schnackenburg, Rudolf 55, 67, 68, 70, 71, 83, 84, 87, 89, 110, 145, 148
Schuchard, Bruce G. 7, 8, 18, 26, 28, 33, 34, 36, 40, 41, 48, 52, 56, 57, 68, 75, 79, 80, 82, 155, 164, 207, 217, 228
Schwartz, Barry 190–93, 202, 206, 209, 214
Schwier, Helmut 145
Scobie, Charles H. H. 232
Scott, Bernard B. 227
Scott, Michael 221
Scrutton, Anastasia 72
Segovia, Fernando 36
Seim, Turid Karlsen 133
Shepardson, Christine 232
Sheridan, Ruth 17, 19, 23, 25, 26, 76, 77,
Shiell, William D. 220
Shiner, Whitney T. 221, 222
Small, Jocelyn P. 219
Smend, Friedrich 75
Smith, D. Moody 56, 57, 112
Spaulding, Mary B. 204
Staley, Jeffrey L. 35, 36, 128
Stamps, Dennis L. 12, 57, 64
Stanley, Christopher D. 52, 122, 126
Stauffer, Ethelbart 143
Steiner, George 213
Stewart, Eric C. 221
Stibbe, Mark W. G. 56, 60
Swancutt, Diana M. 13
Sweeney, Marvin A. 63
Swidler, Ann 98
Tabb, Brian J. 39, 41
Thatcher, Tom 8, 188–92, 194, 202, 213, 214, 228
Theobald, Michael 210
Thomas, Rosalind 235
Thompson, Marianne Meye 30, 31, 40, 145, 150, 156, 157,
Tigay, Jeffrey H. 173
Todd, Natalya 228, 233
Torrey, Charles Cutler 81
Trebilco, Paul 221
Trites, Allison A. 88
Ulrich, Eugene 58, 157, 158
Van Dyke, Ruth M. 220, 222
VanderKam, James C. 76
Voorwinde, Stephen 154
Walton, Johon H. 234
Watson, Francis 230
Webb, Ruth 124
Webster, Jane S. 148
Welborn, Laurence L. 176
Wellhausen, Julius 172
Wenham, Gordon J. 215
Wenzel, Heiko 49, 51
Weren, Wim 59
Wheeler, Charles B. 56, 57, 70
Whitehead, Ann 216, 220
Wickham, Chris 192
Williams, Catrin H. 9, 14, 20, 129, 136, 201, 208
Wilson, Brittany E. 169
Witmer, Stephen E. 10
Wucherpfennig, Ansgar 156
Wyller, Egil A. 36
Yates, Frances A. 223
Yerushalmi, Josef H. 218
York, Anthony D. 56, 57, 70
Zelizer, Barbie 205
Zerubavel, Eviatar 191, 203, 212
Ziolkowski, Jan M. 217, 218, 227
Zumstein, Jean 193

www.ingramcontent.com/pod-product-compliance
Lightning Source LLC
Chambersburg PA
CBHW020642300426
44112CB00007B/210